Wellness Counseling

Baker College
of Auburn Hills

Wellness Counseling

Paul F. Granello
The Ohio State University

Baker College
of Auburn Hills

PEARSON

Boston Columbus Indianapolis New York San Francisco Upper Saddle River
Amsterdam Cape Town Dubai London Madrid Milan Munich Paris Montreal Toronto
Delhi Mexico City São Paulo Sydney Hong Kong Seoul Singapore Taipei Tokyo

Vice President and Editorial Director: Jeffery W. Johnston
Senior Acquisitions Editor: Meredith D. Fossel
Vice President, Director of Marketing: Margaret Waples
Senior Marketing Manager: Christopher Barry
Senior Managing Editor: Pamela Bennett
Senior Project Manager: Mary M. Irvin
Production Manager: Susan Hannahs
Senior Art Director: Jayne Conte
Cover Designer: Karen Salzbach
Cover Art: Paul F. Granello
Full-Service Project Manager: Anitha K.R, Element LLC
Composition: Element LLC
Printer/Binder: R. R. Donnelley & Sons Company
Cover Printer: R. R. Donnelley & Sons Company
Text Font: 10/12 Times

Credits and acknowledgments borrowed from other sources and reproduced, with permission, in this textbook appear on the appropriate page within text.

Every effort has been made to provide accurate and current Internet information in this book. However, the Internet and information posted on it are constantly changing, so it is inevitable that some of the Internet addresses listed in this textbook will change.

Copyright © 2013 by **Pearson Education, Inc.** All rights reserved. Printed in the United States of America. This publication is protected by Copyright and permission should be obtained from the publisher prior to any prohibited reproduction, storage in a retrieval system, or transmission in any form or by any means, electronic, mechanical, photocopying, recording, or likewise. To obtain permission(s) to use material from this work, please submit a written request to Pearson Education, Inc., Permissions Department, One Lake Street, Upper Saddle River, New Jersey 07458 or you may fax your request to 201-236-3290.

CIP data not available at time of publication.

10 9 8 7 6 5 4 3 2 1

ISBN 10: 0-13-299657-X
ISBN 13: 978-0-13-299657-0

This book is dedicated to

Dr. J. Melvin Witmer

A wellness pioneer, mentor, and fully actualized human being.

PREFACE

Wellness and prevention are center stage topics in our national healthcare debate. The modern demands being placed on our healthcare system due to 45% of the adults in the United States being afflicted with chronic illnesses, the impacts of the obesity epidemic, and, of course, healthcare economics have made it so. It has been my belief for some time that the future of professional counseling (and all helping professions) is going to be strongly related to prevention and wellness.

The purpose of this book is to provide a usable yet comprehensive textbook for a course on wellness (prevention or lifestyle-habit change). Counselor educators and other educators wishing to prepare their students responsibly for the behavioral healthcare environment of the 21st century will find this book an excellent source of information.

Wellness Counseling is written and edited to provide information on wellness basics such as wellness models and theories of behavior change. The book is also comprehensive in its coverage of many of the wellness domains, including cognitive, social, spiritual, cultural, emotional, physical, and nutritional. No text in the field is as comprehensive.

Further, experts in each area of wellness have contributed to the text. Among them are Dr. Mark Young, who contributed chapters on spirituality and meaning; Dr. Sam Gladding, who contributed the chapter on creativity; and Dr. Brian Focht, who contributed the chapter on physical activity. These scholars are known in the field as experts in their subject areas.

I have been teaching my graduate course on wellness and prevention at The Ohio State University for 15 years now. Over that time, I have learned a great deal on the subject of wellness through both teaching and research. I have had the privilege to study with Dr. J. Melvin Witmer, who is one of the founding pioneers of wellness in counseling. Mel encouraged me to do my dissertation on a wellness topic, and since then I have thought it would be so helpful for others to have a book that would provide much needed practical information on wellness.

The book is laid out in three major parts. Part I: Wellness: A Paradigm for Behavioral Healthcare illustrates why wellness is the behavioral healthcare paradigm for the future. The first chapter strongly makes the case that modern healthcare is mismatched with our needs. Also in this part, a history of wellness is provided that contextualizes the topic for the student. The last chapter in this part provides an overview of wellness models and theory.

Part II: Wellness Counseling in Practice provides a practical example of how to engage with clients from a wellness frame of reference. An extensive chapter also focuses on behavior change models and presents a novel behavior change model related to curative factors in counseling. The last chapter in this part covers complementary and alternative treatments, which are being sought and used by more and more clients in counseling today.

Part III: Dimensions of Wellness, comprises information that focuses on 10 specific dimensions of wellness. These chapters provide a readable but in-depth resource for counseling students and counselors currently in practice of the important research related to each of the specific wellness domains addressed.

It is my hope that educators and students alike will use this book to help provide structure in their studies on wellness and prevention. I firmly believe that counselors can help clients from becoming seriously ill, manage disease states to minimize harm, and encourage and support all people to maximize their individual health and well-being.

ACKNOWLEDGMENTS

I want to acknowledge all of the contributors to this book, to whom I owe a great deal: Maria Elliott, Clinical Counselor; Sam Gladding, Professor, Wake Forest University; Michelle Hunnicutt-Hollenbaugh, doctoral student, The Ohio State University; Brian Focht, Associate Professor, The Ohio State University; Mike Lewis, Director of Counseling, Ohio Dominican University; Anne Ober, Assistant Professor, Walsh University; Leila Roach, Associate Professor, Stetson University; Heather L. Smith, registered dietician and nutritionist, Associate Professor, Vanderbilt University; J. Melvin Witmer, Professor Emeritus, Ohio University; Pei Chen Yeh, counselor, Nation College of Nursing, Taipei, Taiwan; and Mark Young, Professor, Counselor Education, University of Central Florida. They not only gave of their knowledge but also their patience. I also would like to thank my editor at Pearson, Meredith Fossel, without whose patience and support this book would never have been completed. And I would like to express my thanks to Darcy, who encourages me in all my work and makes my life meaningful.

Finally, I would like to thank the following reviewers for their time and input: Bette S. Katsekas, University of Southern Maine; Nathalie Kees, Colorado State University; Michele McGrady, Western Michigan University; and Shawn L. Spurgeon, University of Tennessee, Knoxville.

BRIEF CONTENTS

CONTENTS

PART I

WELLNESS: A PARADIGM FOR BEHAVIORAL HEALTHCARE

The objectives of this first part are:

1. To place emphasis concerning the relevance and importance of a wellness approach on our present day healthcare crisis.
2. To present the construct of individual wellness.
3. To provide a historical context for wellness in behavioral healthcare and counseling.
4. To promote wellness counseling as within the scope of practice of professional counselors.

Chapter One: The Wellness Challenge The current healthcare crisis in the United States is illustrated. Also, the current situation of behavioral healthcare in the United States is discussed, offering wellness as a direction for the future. A challenge is offered to counselors concerning our profession's role in the pursuit of knowledge concerning well-being.

Chapter Two: Evolution of Wellness In this chapter Dr. J. Melvin Witmer provides a historical overview of the development of the concept of individual wellness. Dr. Witmer draws on research and historical information from the fields of religion, medicine, psychology, neurology, and counseling to paint a rich context for the modern developments of the wellness approach to therapy.

Chapter Three: Theoretical Models for Wellness Counseling Dr. Paul Granello and Dr. J. Melvin Witmer outline in this chapter some of the current models to helping clients achieve better health. Wellness counseling is presented as a significantly different approach to helping clients improve their lifestyle. Finally, a case is made for the unique abilities of professional counselors that make them especially suited for wellness-related, health-related care.

1 THE WELLNESS CHALLENGE

Paul F. Granello and J. Melvin Witmer

Health is a state of complete physical, mental and social well-being, and not merely the absence of disease or infirmity.

WORLD HEALTH ORGANIZATION, 1948

Healthcare in the United States is a very, very hot topic. Daily, the news contains information on issues related to the "healthcare crises" in our country. Healthcare issues impact almost all individuals in our society in one way or another because they encompass almost all social spheres: economic (rising costs), legal (medical malpractice lawsuits, privacy in use of electronic medical records), business (managed care, pharmaceutical company profits), scientific (stem cell research), technological (telemedicine, online counseling), religious (abortion, spirituality in counseling), and of course political (equity of access for the uninsured, mental health insurance parity). While it certainly could be argued that all of these issues are significantly important in their own right and deserve attention, this chapter makes the argument that they are just the symptoms of a much more fundamental and entrenched problem with the healthcare system in the United States today.

HEALTHCARE: A FUNDAMENTAL MISMATCH

The problem simply put is that our traditional biomedical paradigm of healthcare is grossly mismatched for our American society's 21st century healthcare needs. It is this basic mismatch between our present day needs and the dominant traditional biomedical paradigm that is either directly causing or significantly contributing to our problems with healthcare in the United States today. To illustrate the mismatch between our modern healthcare needs and our traditional healthcare approach, let us look at how the causes of death have changed from a century ago to the present day (see Table 1.1). In 1900, our traditional biomedical model of healthcare with a focus on finding the underlying pathogens (germs) that cause an infectious disease worked very well. The average lifespan was 49 years and most people died of infectious diseases like influenza and tuberculosis. Treatment was focused on helping sick people manage the symptoms of disease. Today, things are very different with the average lifespan now being 77.7 years. People in the United States

TABLE 1.1 Leading Causes of Death

Causes of Death 1900*	Causes of Death 2007**
Pneumonia (all forms) and influenza	Heart disease
Tuberculosis (all forms)	Cancer
Diarrhea, enteritis, and ulceration of the intestines	Stroke (cerebrovascular diseases)
Diseases of the heart	Chronic lower respiratory diseases
Intracranial lesions of vascular origin	Accidents (unintentional injuries)
Nephritis (all forms)	Diabetes
All accidents	Alzheimer's disease
Cancer and other malignant tumors	Influenza and pneumonia
Senility	Nephritis
Diphtheria	Septicemia

Source: *1900–1940 tables ranked in National Office of Vital Statistics, December 1947.
**CDC/National Center for Health Statistics.

are not dying of infection-related disease but instead of **chronic lifestyle-related diseases.** In our modern society we are dying from cardiovascular diseases, cancer, and diabetes (Kott et al., 2009).

In fact, in 2004, the U.S. Department of Health and Human Services, Centers for Disease Control and Prevention reported that at least half of the premature deaths in the United States are caused by **lifestyle and behavioral factors** (Centers for Disease Control and Prevention [CDC], 2008). The Centers for Disease Control and Prevention also report that smoking, poor nutrition, and lack of physical activity are directly causal of one-third of the deaths in the United States and that nearly two-thirds of Americans are overweight or obese (2009). Examples of conditions influenced by lifestyle and health behaviors are heart disease, cancer, stroke, injuries, diabetes, alcoholism, drug abuse, low birth weight, and diseases preventable by immunization. A report in the *American Medical Association Journal* for the actual causes of death in 2000 noted that obesity would soon surpass smoking as the leading preventable cause of premature death (Mokdad, Marks, Stroup, & Gerberding, 2004). The reality is that most of what Americans are dying from today is either caused directly or exacerbated by our lifestyles. The shame is that many illnesses could be ameliorated if people knew how to live in a healthy way and had help from healthcare providers in achieving their health goals.

Despite the knowledge that what we really need is help with avoiding and managing chronic illnesses, our healthcare system's primary attention is still focused on treatment of "sickness" and "dysfunction." Little attention has been given to prevention of disease through the enhancement of health and well-being. As a society we have committed ourselves and our resources almost exclusively to remediating problems rather than attempting to prevent them from occurring.

In the United States today:

- 45% of Americans suffer from at least one chronic disease higher than in any other country.
- Chronic diseases, such as heart disease, diabetes, pulmonary disease, and cancer, are among the most costly and most preventable diseases in the United States.
- Three out of every four healthcare dollars are spent treating chronic disease and 7 out of 10 deaths are caused by chronic disease (Kott et al., 2009).

Our current philosophy of healthcare in the United States appears to be something like "Let's wait till people get really sick. Then we will treat them with high-tech procedures delivered by highly specialized medical doctors and technicians, and this will definitely cost everyone a lot of money." This philosophy is certainly reflected in the fact that of government funds spent on healthcare, 75% are for chronic disease treatment with a total of only 1% federal and 2% state funds allocated to prevent these diseases (DeVol, et al., 2007).

The noted physician Dr. Andrew Weil summed up the current situation quite well when he stated, "We do not have a healthcare system we have a disease management system." There truly appears to be a very fundamental mismatch between our present day population's needs for prevention of chronic disease and the focus of our traditional healthcare system on treating the already sick.

RESULTS OF THE HEALTHCARE MISMATCH

If there were no problems that resulted from the mismatch between our present day healthcare system and the rest of our social context then perhaps it would be of little consequence. At present, however, our traditional approach to healthcare has produced two very significant problems.

The first problem has to do with **quality.** A basic question that may help us understand about the quality of care problem concerns a central function of any healthcare system, namely "Is the healthcare system effectively reducing human suffering?" Reducing human suffering by keeping people from getting severely sick (prevention) would seem to be a logical primary goal of any healthcare system (Woolf, 2006). Yet healthcare in the United States at present is doing a poor job at reducing suffering through the prevention of illness. A case in point is that in 1996 the five most costly (in terms of expenditures) medical conditions were:

- Heart Disease
- Trauma-Related Disorders
- Cancer
- Asthma
- Mental Disorders

A decade later in 2006 another ranking was done of the five most costly medical conditions and they were exactly the same ones (Soni, 2009)!

Further, there was an increase in the expenditures for each of these conditions and also an increase in the number of people associated with these conditions except trauma-related disorders. In fact, a study in 2008 ranked the United States dead last out of 14 industrialized countries in amendable deaths, which are deaths that could have been prevented with timely and effective care (The Commonwealth Fund Commission on a High Performance Health System, 2008).

Of particular interest to counselors may be the fact that of the five disorders the largest increase in expenditures was for **mental disorders,** which rose from $35.2 billion in 1996 (in 2006 dollars) to $57.5 billion in 2006. Mental disorders did not only have the biggest increase in overall expenditure but also the largest increase in the number of people (19.3 million to 36.2 million) being treated. Finally, of the five conditions, the out-of-pocket payments were highest for those individuals with mental disorders in both 1996 and 2006 (23.1% and 25.0%, respectively).

The increased costs of providing healthcare to people with diagnosed mental disorders could be a good sign. What if we are providing healthcare that is having a positive effect? Are people with mental illness accessing medical care that is improving their physical health? This positive outcome would possibly justify the extra costs. Frighteningly, this is not the case. **Recent data from several states have found that people with serious mental illness served by our public mental health systems die, on average, at least 25 years earlier than the general population** (Parks, Svendsen, Singer, & Foti, 2006).

People with mental health disorders generally receive less preventive healthcare, have more difficulties accessing care, are treated with a reduced quality of care, and have increased morbidity as an outcome of illness when compared to a nondiagnosed population (Druss, Rosenheck, Desai, & Perlin, 2002).

The meaning of these facts would seem to be that our current model or paradigm for delivery of healthcare is not providing the quality that we would like to have in America. However, the definition of what constitutes "quality" healthcare may be different depending on the healthcare paradigm that is being used. In the current biomedical paradigm, quality has evolved to mean that we focus on treating the chronically or severely ill with cutting-edge technologies delivered by specialist doctors at very great expense. The American healthcare system has had many impressive accomplishments using this approach. For example, American survival rates for many diseases such as cancer and heart disease are some of the best in the world. Hospitals in the United States are the best equipped in the world and we have highly trained physicians and nurses. Medical research in the United States is the world leader on development of many wonder drugs and technologies such as imaging and hip replacements (Reid, 2009). Despite all of its problems, the fact is that for a very sick individual with the capacity to pay for care, our healthcare system can truly be life saving.

Given that our healthcare system does provide good care for people who are acutely ill, perhaps the real question concerning quality is not about the provision of medical care to individuals but is instead a broader public health question. What would our healthcare system be like if it were not focused on treating very sick individuals but instead focused on preventing illness in the population as a whole? Such an approach employs a much different paradigm for defining quality of care. Quality of care in this paradigm is not defined as the healthcare outcome of a particular individual but rather as the overall health of the total population. Employing a prevention paradigm for healthcare might actually help to reduce human suffering and realize significant cost savings. For example, recent research indicates that if the United States can make modest improvements in prevention and management of disease by 2023, as many as 40 million cases of chronic disease could be avoided for a potential savings of $218 billion annually in treatment costs. Further, improved productivity due to a decrease in chronic disease could contribute to an increase in the Gross Domestic Product of the United States by $905 billion.

This brings us to the second problem with healthcare in America. The second problem is much less a matter of philosophic approach than an economic reality. It is simply that healthcare has become **prohibitively expensive.** Today, many individuals and employers are — finding it impossible to purchase affordable adequate healthcare insurance. Since 1999, health insurance premiums have increased 119% for employers. Employers, especially small or mid-sized companies, cannot afford to offer healthcare benefits to employees. Further, employees' spending for health insurance coverage (employees' share of family coverage) has increased 117% between 1999 and 2008 ((The Henry J. Kaiser Family Foundation, 2008). As a result of these dramatic increases in cost, more Americans are simply having to do without healthcare insurance. In 2007 nearly 46 million Americans, or 18% of the population under the age of 65, were without health insurance (U.S. Census Bureau, 2009). This is of course not only an economic issue but also a humanitarian issue, as the uninsured receive less preventive care, are diagnosed at more advanced disease stages, and once diagnosed, tend to receive less therapeutic care and have higher mortality rates than insured individuals (National Center for Health Statistics, 2009). Further, millions more Americans, although insured, actually have coverage that will not provide them with sufficient reimbursement to cover the costs of treating a serious illness. This is why the number of bankruptcies due to medical debt in the United States is approximately 700,000 families a year—many of these people had insurance that simply would not adequately cover the costs of required healthcare. At the same time the number of bankruptcies due to medical debt in Great Britain, Germany, the Netherlands, France, Japan, and Canada—zero. (Reid, 2009)!

Overall, healthcare costs have become a significant drain on our economy. Gross domestic product (GDP) is the value of all the goods and services that a country produces. In a review of the nature of our healthcare costs, Myers and Sweeney (2005) observed that the costs of illness have increased from 5% to almost 16% of our gross domestic product in the period from 1960 to 2000. Currently, the health share of GDP is projected to reach 20.3% by 2018. In dollars and cents this means that by 2018 Americans will be spending 20% of our entire economic output or an estimated $4.3 trillion on healthcare. Individually, the more money we have to spend on healthcare the less money we have to spend on anything else we may need, such as food, housing, clothing, or education (Partnership to Fight Chronic Disease, 2009).

Information published by the World Health Organization (WHO) may best sum up both the problems of paradigm and prohibitive cost that currently characterize America's health system. WHO data indicate that the United States spends more money than any other country in the world per capita on healthcare and yet at the same time ranks 37th in the world on healthcare quality. Americans know they are not getting their money's worth from our healthcare system. According to a CBS News Poll, 90% of Americans believe the American healthcare system needs fundamental changes or needs to be completely rebuilt. Two-thirds of Americans believe the federal government should guarantee universal healthcare for all citizens (CBS News, Polls, 2007). At present it is interesting to note that the United States is the only industrialized country in the world that does not provide a universal healthcare program.

Only one conclusion can be drawn from the data. **The United States healthcare system as it is now functioning and the biomedical paradigm upon which it is founded is no longer meeting our 21st century health needs for prevention of chronic illnesses and is no longer economically sustainable.**

Leaders in healthcare, government, business, and academia have known this crisis was coming for a long time. Many leaders knew we needed to make substantial changes in our approach to healthcare and that continuing business as usual in our healthcare system would lead us down a path of poor quality and high cost. In fact, almost two decades ago, the U.S. government established health-promotion and disease-prevention goals. In 1990, Health and Human Services Secretary Dr. Louis Sullivan released the *Healthy People 2000* report, which challenged all Americans to healthier living (U.S. Department of Health and Human Services, 1990). The purpose of the report was to bring us to our full potential by: (1) increasing the span of healthy life for Americans; (2) reducing health disparities among Americans; and (3) achieving access to preventive services for all Americans. Health promotion categories were physical activities and fitness; nutrition; tobacco; alcohol and other drugs; family planning; mental health and mental disorders; violent and abusive behavior; and educational and community-based programs.

These goals, if they had been acted upon, may have taken us on a route that would have prevented a great deal of human suffering and economic burden. Why then did our government and healthcare system fail to embrace prevention and wellness in the 1990s?

There are potentially many reasons that could be given for why our healthcare system has been so slow to change from an illness treatment system to a prevention and health enhancement system. These reasons are political and economic in nature and are deeply tied to the core of how our democratic and capitalistic society functions. Healthcare is of course big business in the United States. Many large companies employing significant numbers of people have interests in the healthcare system remaining at status quo. In 2009 alone the healthcare industry spent almost $280 million lobbying Congress (see Table 1.2). This amount does not include additional direct contributions to congressional campaign funds by healthcare companies, healthcare associations, political action committees, or individuals working for healthcare companies.

The American Medical Association (AMA) has consistently fought the adoption of a universal healthcare system in the United States. The AMA has funded public relations firms to promote the idea that "*socialized medicine*" (a term coined by the AMA) would lead to poor healthcare for Americans. It is interesting to note that American physicians earn two to three times more than their European counterparts. The United States is also the only developed country that relies on private companies to provide health insurance to its citizens. Private insurance companies generally have a 20% margin for administrative costs and profit. These companies generally oppose any government regulation of their businesses. Lastly, American pharmaceutical companies oppose a national healthcare plan, fearing regulation of prices for drugs and a loss of profits. The pharmaceutical industry is the single largest group lobbying Congress and has spent over $1.6 billion since 1998 lobbying Congress.

Incredibly, against this backdrop of enormous sums of money spent to inform Congress of the healthcare industries viewpoints, businesses and institutions sought methods to control

TABLE 1.2 Lobbying for Healthcare in 2009

Industry	Amount Spent
Makers of drugs and health products	$134,458,183
Hospitals and nursing homes	$50,330,605
Doctors and health professionals	$39,408,563
Health services and HMOs	$34,646,637
Miscellaneous health	$4,582,251
Health insurers	$16,315,247
TOTAL	$279,741,486

Source: Center for Responsive Politics

the ever increasing costs of healthcare. In fact, a number of approaches have been implemented with greater or lesser degrees of success to cope with both the quality and cost issues. Chief among these approaches has been the development of managed healthcare. The managed healthcare industry approach to insurance cost containment boomed in the 1990s. Currently, there are approximately 241 million Americans who receive their insurance coverage under the watchful eye of a managed care corporation. Managed care companies hired by employers attempt to hold down costs by negotiating fees with healthcare providers and controlling access to specialized care. The level of success managed care has had in controlling healthcare expenditure can be debated. However, at present the cost savings associated with this approach have probably already been maximized. So, faced with real quality of care issues and the current economic realities the question persists: Where can we go now with our approach to healthcare that will bring about positive changes?

Wellness: Healthcare Paradigm of the Future

> A study by the Trust for America's Health recently projected that an annual investment of $10 per person in evidence-based community prevention programs can yield significant cost savings. In five years, Medicare and Medicaid alone could yield net savings of $7 billion annually, and total U.S. medical spending could be reduced by $16 billion annually. (Levi, Segal, & Juliano, 2008)

Wellness as a term in the English language has its origin in the mid 17th century. The recent development of the wellness concept using the language of "wellness" has been reviewed by Myers and Sweeney (2005). The World Health Organization as early as 1947 defined *health* as being more than the absence of disease, and in 1964 emphasized the well-being aspect with its definition of optimal health as "a state of complete physical, mental, and social well-being and not merely the absence of disease or infirmity" (World Health Organization [WHO], 1964, p. 1).

Wellness, as presented in this book, is a term used to represent an emerging treatment paradigm for both healthcare generally and the mental health field specifically (Granello, 1995). The wellness paradigm represents a reevaluation of the biomedical model of healthcare and the Western philosophical tradition of Cartesian dualism upon which it is based (Gordon, 1981; Gross, 1980). The traditional medical model has a pathogenic, reductionist, and disease focus, while in contrast the wellness model has a salutogenic (health enhancing) focus that is related to constant striving for optimal functioning (Granello, 1995). Please see Figure 1.1.

Wellness and the Counseling Profession

Counseling as a profession is historically rooted in a developmental lifespan approach to understanding human beings which may be uniquely suited to thriving in a wellness-oriented healthcare system (Witmer & Granello, 2005).

Counselors already have the skills needed to help clients with health issues related to both disease management and disease prevention. Although the content may be different, the

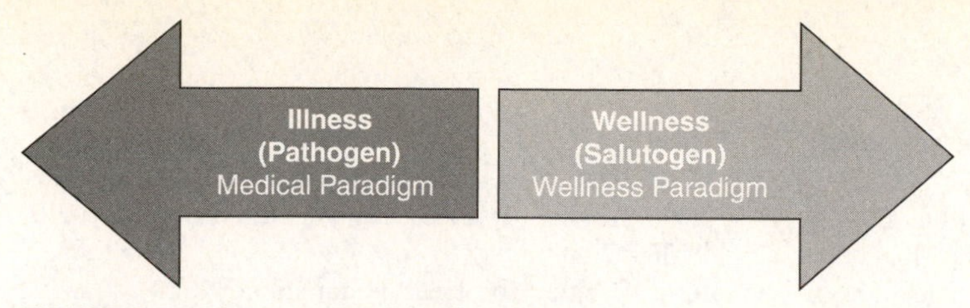

FIGURE 1.1 Divergent Models of Healthcare

processes of treatment (assessing the client, negotiating goals, developing a plan for guiding the therapeutic process, applying interventions, and encouraging and supporting clients in achieving or completing that plan) are all paralleled in wellness work just as they are in traditional therapy for clients with a mental illness. Working with clients on improving their lifestyles and changing their habits for wellness promotion can be a rewarding experience for many mental health professions.

The Wellness Challenge

Counselors in the 21st century are now at a point in time where there will be change in our society's approach to healthcare. What role will counselors take in this new paradigm of wellness-oriented preventive healthcare? Will we embrace our rich history while striving for a greater role in the overall healthcare and well-being of our clients? Will we accept the wellness challenge and focus on maximizing our own and our client's potential?

Counselors individually and as a profession should be asking questions like: What are the outer limits of human possibilities? Of what are human beings capable? What is high level wellness? Human potential refers to the possibilities there are in being human. Our potential is limited to a large extent by our image of what we are and our vision of what we can become. Will we as individuals and the counseling profession as a whole take up the wellness approach and have a seat at the table, providing care that is in tune with the healthcare paradigm of the future?

Until recently, physical and mental health has been defined in terms of the absence of disease and infirmity. Our standard for human development and adjustment has been the norm as a statistical average instead of looking toward what is exceptional. The healthy person has been defined in terms of averages rather than what is genetically possible. The wellness continuum progresses from the treatment of illness to prevention and maintenance to growth, with a major emphasis on the latter—enhancement of life.

The wellness journey is one that never ends. It is not so much a point of destination but the continuous traveling that brings its own satisfaction. Becoming a part of that process is a choice. Lack of knowledge is no longer a reason for not being a part of the journey, whether for one's own well-being or that of persons whom we encounter in our work as healthcare professionals and educators. What greater challenge is there than to take the road that leads us and our clients to the farthest reaches of human nature—happiness, life satisfaction, and fulfillment over the lifespan.

In the next chapter we will take a journey through history to see how the wellness paradigm for healthcare has evolved over time to bring us to our present level of knowledge.

References

CBS News Polls. (2007). http://www.cbsnews.com/htdocs/CBSNews_polls/health_care.pdf

Centers for Disease Control and Prevention. (2008, March). Chronic disease overview [Fact sheet].

Centers for Disease Control and Prevention. (2009, May). Overweight and obesity: Health consequences [Fact sheet].

The Commonwealth Fund Commission on a High Performance Health System. (2008, July). *Why not the best? Results from the national scorecard on U.S. health system performance, 2008*. The Commonwealth Fund.

DeNavas-Walt, Proctor, C. B., & Smith, J. (2008, August). *Income, poverty, and health insurance coverage in the United States: 2007*. U.S. Census Bureau.

DeVol, R. et al. (2007). *An unhealthy America: The economic burden of chronic disease*. Santa Monica, CA: The Milken Institute.

Druss, B. G., Rosenheck R. A., Desai, M. M., & Perlin, J. B. (2002). Quality of preventive medical care for patients with mental disorders. *Medical Care, 4*, 129–36.

Gordon, M. E. (1981). The capacity for experience. *PsycCRITIQUES, 26*(1), 31–32.

Granello, P. F. (1995). Wellness as a Function of Perceived Social Support Network and Ability to Empathize. (Doctoral dissertation, Ohio University, 1995). Dissertation Abstracts.

Gross, S. J. (1980). The holistic health movement. *Personnel & Guidance Journal, 59*(2), 96–100.

The Henry J. Kaiser Family Foundation. (2008, September). *Employee Health Benefits: 2008 Annual Survey*. http://www.kff.org/insurance/7672/index.cfm.

Kott, A., Fruh, D, Cameron, L., Greger, C., Klein, K., Lethert, C., et al. (2009). 2009 almanac of chronic disease: Impact of chronic disease. Partnership to Fight Chronic Disease.

Levi, J., Segal, L. M., Juliano, C. (2008). *Prevention for a healthier America*. Washington, DC: Trust for America's Health.

Myers, J. E., & Sweeney, T. J. (2005). *Counseling for wellness: Theory, research, and practice*. Alexandria, VA: American Counseling Association.

Mokdad, A. H., Marks, J. S., Stroup, D. F., & Gerberding, J. L. (2004). Actual causes of death in the United States, 2000. *Journal of the American Medical Association, 291*, 1238–1245.

National Center for Health Statistics. (2009). *Health, United States, 2007: With chartbook on trends in the health of Americans*. Center for American Progress, The Case for Health Reform.

Parks, S., Svendsen, D., Singer, F., & Foti, M. (2006, October). *Morbidity and mortality in people with serious mental illness*. National Association of State Mental Health Program Directors, Medical Directors Council, report available at: http://www.nasmhpd.org

Partnership to Fight Chronic Disease. (2009). The impact of chronic disease on U. S. health and prosperity: A call to action for **health** reform.

Reid, T. R. (2009). *The healing of america: A global quest for better, cheaper, and fairer health care*. Penguin Press HC.

Soni, Anita. (2009, July). *The Five Most Costly Conditions, 1996 and 2006: Estimates for the U.S. Civilian Noninstitutionalized Population*. Statistical Brief #248. Rockville, MD: Agency for Healthcare Research and Quality. http://www.meps.ahrq.gov/mepsweb/data_files/publications/st248/stat248.pdf

U.S. Census Bureau (2009). National Health Statistics Reports. Number 17, July 1, 2009.

U.S. Department of Health and Human Services (1990). *Healthy People 2000*. National Health Promotion and Disease Prevention Objectives. Washington, D.C.: U.S. Government Printing Office, DHHS Publication No. (PHS) 91-50212, 1990.

Witmer, M J. & Granello, P. F., (2005). Wellness in Counselor Education and Supervision. In J. E. Myers & T. J. Sweeney (Eds.,), *Counseling for Wellness: Theory, Research, and Practice*. Alexandria, VA: American Counseling Association.

Woolf, S. H. (2006, Fall). The big answer: Rediscovering prevention at a time of crisis in healthcare. *Harvard Health Policy Review, 7*(2), 5–20.

2 EVOLUTION OF WELLNESS

J. Melvin Witmer

Human life will never be understood unless its highest aspirations are taken into account. Growth, self-actualization, the striving toward health, the quest for identity and autonomy, the yearning for excellence (and other ways of phrasing the striving "upward") must now be accepted beyond question as a widespread and perhaps universal human tendency.

MASLOW, 1970, XII AND XIII

STRIVING FOR HEALTH AND WELLNESS

We, who are living at the beginning of the 21st century, are the first in human history to know what the characteristics of the well person are. Scientific research over the last 35 years has identified the factors that enhance the quality of our lives and extend longevity. Confirmation of self-defeating beliefs and destructive lifestyle behaviors has enabled us to understand the cause-effect relationships that contribute to disease, dysfunctional living, and premature death. In our knowledge, we have progressed from treatment and prevention of disease to the health and wellness of living. Spiritual, mental, emotional, physical, and social factors that enhance our well-being have been validated. More specifically, a meaningful life, realistic and rational thinking, a positive attitude, regular exercise, nutritional eating, and satisfying work, leisure, and interpersonal relationships are dimensions for improving the quality of living and extending the length of life. The key to adding life to our years and years to our life is self-responsibility, that is, taking responsibility for self-care and lifestyle choices.

The inner desire for a life of health and wholeness is not a late 20th century phenomenon. Our language reveals the presence of a holistic philosophy when Middle English terms were created to describe a state of well-being. As a Middle English word, *health* shares a root meaning with the words *hale, hearty, holy, heal,* and *whole*. Health even then was viewed as more than the absence of disease but rather a soundness of mind, body, and spirit. Although holistic health includes the prevention of illness and the management of disease, its focus is on enhancing one's well-being. Wellness extends this meaning to include a person's physical, mental, and emotional states, social relationships, spiritual growth, and lifestyle.

Our brain operates as a health maintenance organization (Orstein & Sobel, 1990). Each of the three major sections of the brain and its subsystems has as its primary function minding the health of the body. Two of the systems, the brain stem and the limbic, function automatically to manage the safety and maintenance of the body such as breathing, heart rate, body temperature, blood pressure, and blood sugar level. Besides maintaining internal stability of the physiological processes, the limbic system is involved in emotional reactions that have to do with survival and self-protection. The third system, the cortex, is the seat for rational abilities we develop. It is responsible for processing information, making decisions, and carrying out actions while the other two systems function automatically to assist the organism to maintain optimal health.

The above phenomenon was observed by Maslow (1970) from a psychological perspective when he noted that there appears to be a universal human striving toward health. This tendency to actualize the self is driven by an innate process. However, the development of the rational part of the brain, the cortex, introduces a conscious, free-thinking self. The individual can think and act in ways that affect the inner process, either to enhance health and well-being or impede it. Modern research can add knowledge to the collective wisdom of past generations to prevent disease and maximize health.

First this chapter will provide a brief review of history and will provide examples of this human tendency toward wholeness, an innate and inner striving toward what is humanly possible for high-level wellness. Next, we will finish the chapter by noting more recent contributions from academic disciplines and individuals related to the modern American wellness movement.

GREEK HEALTH AND MEDICINE

Hippocrates

Western medicine begins with Hippocrates, a Greek physician in the fourth century BCE. His injunctions, "First do no harm," and "Physician—heal thyself," are well known. Lesser known is his breadth of vision on health and healing. He and his followers developed a scientific approach to medicine by respecting observation and experimentation of natural events and disease. Hippocrates appreciated the social and ecological context in which illness occurs and the way physical manifestations of disease are shaped by psychological and spiritual forces (Gordon, 1996). He also taught that food was useful as medicine. Dreams were believed to have prophetic, diagnostic, and psychologically important messages.

Aristotle

A student of Plato and a Greek philosopher who wrote of the "good life," Aristotle taught long ago that what all people seek is happiness. He believed that those who were happy were people who identified with living well and doing well. One needs to follow the "golden mean," doing all things in moderation and avoiding extremes.

Aristotle distinguished happiness from pleasure. Happiness is not merely a subjective state of pleasure or contentment but the kind of life we would all want to live if we understood our essential nature. When we fulfill the ideal of the virtuous life, we are happy. This view became known as virtue ethics and defines the importance of character development in pursuing the good life (Warburton, 1999). It is only by cultivating the virtues that one can flourish as a human being. According to Aristotle, everyone wants to flourish, which is sometimes translated as "happiness." The original Greek word applies to a whole life, not just to particular states you might find yourself in from day to day. Achieving a true happiness is living your life successfully.

Interestingly, one of the most current, popular courses at Harvard University is Positive Psychology, an emphasis in psychological development pioneered by Martin Seligman, a professor at the University of Pennsylvania (Seligman, 2002). Underlying the academic study of the positive aspects of human development is the theme of happiness and creating a fulfilling and flourishing life. A similar course is being taught in more than 100 campuses around the country.

Asclepius

The Greeks attributed certain ideals and values to their gods and goddesses. The god of healing was Asclepius who had two daughters, each one symbolizing different approaches to health, one being treatment and the other prevention. Panacea was knowledgeable in the use of medication to *treat* diseases, embodying the principles of today's ongoing search for panaceas, drugs, and other treatments to cure disease. Hygieia was the other daughter who was an expert on teaching ways of living in harmony with nature in order to *prevent* disease, today's equivalent of *hygiene* or *health* and the forerunner of *wellness*, a word that has its origin in the mid-17th century.

An Ancient Greek Wellness Center

Epidaurus was an ancient Greek sanctuary for several Greek gods. Asklepius held first place in the religious life of Epidaurus from the fifth century BCE to the fourth century CE. It began as a religious center, then developed into a hospital sanctuary where persons went for the treatment of physical and mental illnesses (Charitonidou, 1978). It also became a social center with a serene and pleasant environment, hot and cold baths, guest houses, gymnasia, stadiums, and an amphitheater for theatrical performances. The spring waters were thought to have special pharmaceutical qualities.

Persons arriving there for healing had an unquestioning faith in its curative powers. Prayers, sacrifices, and purifications were required. Upon arriving they were met by a priest who told them to expect a dream in which a god would appear and assure them of a miracle and the treatment. For example, the god might order the patient to take daily physical exercise under the supervision of a special trainer. Certain foods or drinks might be prescribed. In certain respects, Epidaurus more than 2,000 years ago was even more comprehensive in treating the whole person than our modern day so-called wellness centers and health spas. Even today, the Greeks greet one another with a wellness expression which means, "health to you."

JEWISH AND CHRISTIAN EMPHASES

Hebrew Health and Healing

In the Old Testament God revealed himself as a healer and was sometimes referred to as "The Lord who heals." Throughout the Old Testament, healing prayers were addressed to God. The Lord was also seen as giving prescribed laws of health, which were observed as antidotes to sickness and disease. These laws can be summarized under six main headings: (a) the law of sanitation, (b) the law of cleansing, (c) the law of isolation, (d) the law of dietetics, (e) the law of personal disciplines, and (f) the law of rest (Stanger, 1978). There was growing awareness among the Hebrews that wholeness related to the total person. They believed that such wholeness began by being in harmony with God. *Shalom* in Hebrew is an expression for well-being, wholeness, individual health, and communal harmony.

The Early Christian Church

The notion of caring for the sick has religious roots. Certainly this is true for Christianity. New Testament writers often related the health of the body to the spiritual life of the individual. A wholesome spiritual life was believed to contribute to the health of mind and body. In the first century after the death of Jesus, the Romans and non-Christian groups noted how the Christians cared for one another in their communities. The care was holistic in that they showed concern for their economic, social, and spiritual well-being, including health.

By the fourth century CE, Christians began to build hospitals and healing centers. In 379 CE, St. Basil built a 300 bed hospital in Caesarea, a city in Asia Minor, now Turkey. Similar healing centers were built in the growing cities of the Eastern and Western Christian empires. Religiously affiliated hospitals, foundling homes, and hospices spread with the establishment of cathedrals and monasteries. Although the healing ministry of the church waned for several centuries, each century throughout the Middle Ages had Christian leaders who kept it alive. Priests, monks, and nuns cared for the ill in sanctuaries throughout Western Europe. The ministry of sacramental healing continued in the life of the church until the spirit of secular materialism invaded most of our institutions, even the church, in the 18th century (Kelsey, 1985). Science and medicine began to take over the treatment of disease and restoration to health.

Later Christian Emphases

Religiously affiliated colleges and universities trained large numbers of physicians in the Victorian age. The early 20th century saw dozens of hospitals built throughout the United States by religious groups. Although they may no longer be directly affiliated with a religious organization, many of these institutions still bear a reference to their Baptist, Catholic, Methodist, or Presbyterian roots in name if not in organization.

The rapid growth of medicine and medical research in the early 20th century replaced the traditional dependence upon religion for healing. Although the churches gave less emphasis on individual healing, they aligned themselves with medical science and the creation of institutions to heal the sick. By the 1970s there was a revival of interest on the part of the older, Protestant denominations in the healing ministry. Prayer for individual healing and health continues to be a central part of Christian communities. Churches have also been adding congregational nurses in their total ministry to the congregation with an emphasis on education and prevention along with supportive and supplemental health services. The healing ministry of the Christian church has never been entirely lost in its 2,000 years of its existence. The world's major religions continue with practices for healing the sick. Today nearly two-thirds of America's medical schools teach required or elective courses on the relationship between religion and spirituality and medicine.

NATIVE AMERICAN HEALING

Akin to the Eastern philosophy is a belief of Native Americans in a holistic understanding of disease. They believe that disease is due to disharmony with nature which includes family, friends, and the environment. While healing practices among Native Americans have varied widely, some commonalities are present in philosophy and practice (Krippner, 1995). At the time of the North American conquest, at least 500 tribes lived in the territory that now comprises the United States, thus global statements can be misleading. This review is intended to be more historic than current in its perspective.

As part of the holism that characterizes Native American medicine, the patient's spiritual condition is assessed and considered during diagnosis and treatment. Furthermore, many Native American treatments are considered spiritual in nature. Tribes make no arbitrary division between body and mind. In treatment, however, they may differentiate between those that are "natural disorders" and others that are believed to be "supernatural disorders." The natural disorders may be treated by herbs, diet, massage, and sweat baths and the supernatural by rituals and magic, such as medicine wheels and sand paintings. Upholding the traditions of the family and the culture are important for maintaining health and overcoming disease.

Many Native American treatments were remarkably effective. Practitioners lanced boils, removed tumors, treated fractures and dislocations, and cleaned wounds in ways that were hygienic. Of the herbs used by the Rappachannock tribe, 60% have been found to have unquestionable medicinal value (Krippner, 1995). Any diagnosis and treatment in Native American healing considers patient behavior beyond the reporting of symptoms.

EASTERN AND CHINESE MEDICINE

The Eastern mind has viewed health as an integral part to one's total being with no separation between the mind and body. Lifestyle is always in a dynamic relationship with the well-being of the person. In the Chinese language, mind and body are not separated. One word exists for describing the organism as a whole. They do, however, have many words to describe different types of energy in the body. Similarities exist between the Chinese and Indian view of energy and human life (Chin, 1992). All energy comes from one universal source. The energy that exists within the universe is the same energy that exists within us. Movement of this energy is the basis of all life and must have something or somewhere to move to.

Eastern medicine has viewed the body not according to how each part functions on its own, but rather how it functions in relationship to the whole system (Chin, 1992). By looking at the body/mind in a holistic way, Eastern practitioners discovered a highly organized system of energy channels or pathways in addition to other body systems. It is distinct from the cardiovascular and nervous systems, yet intimately connected. Good health requires a lifestyle and self-responsibility for maintaining balance in this energy system. If illness occurs, the balance in energy needs to be restored, thus calling for holistic methods to redistribute the energy to reach the balance for which it is constantly striving.

As an example of an Eastern discipline for holistic health, yoga combines the spiritual, mental, and physical. Self-effort, self-examination, and self-awareness are integral to disciplining one's mind, developing a philosophy of life, and exercising the body. Yoga practices include breathing properly, eating a balanced and nutritious diet, exercising with yoga postures, and engaging in some form of meditation which stills the mind. Qi gong and t'ai chi are other energy balancing exercises that bring into harmony the flow of energy throughout and within the body and all its organs. The Eastern integrated approach also uses massage, herbal therapy, dietary changes, and acupuncture (Gordon, 1996). The goal of the Chinese model of healing is the dual purpose of relieving and preventing pain and tension, and to promote harmony within the body and between the person and the environment.

MODERN WESTERN MEDICINE

With the rise of the scientific revolution and rationalistic thinking, body and mind were separated. Religion and science were also separated between the 15th and 17th centuries. Conflict highlighted by the Copernicus and church split over a sun-centered universe, was eventually resolved with religion taking the soul and science the mind and body. The dominant view has been that the physical and mental aspects of health are separate and subject to only limited interaction. The traditional model of illness became known as *dualistic* with a newer biopsychosocial model emerging in the latter 20th century known as *holistic* (Bernard & Krupat, 1994). Four characteristics of the traditional model are *dualistic, mechanistic, reductionist,* and *disease oriented.* Health was defined as the absence of disease.

Reductionism in science led to the mind being separated from the body with each being further separated into systems, organs, tissues, and cells. The natural environment was treated as if it consisted of separate parts. Individual, social, and cultural environments were treated separately. The individual and the ecological environment were also treated separately. Lifestyle was separated from health and disease.

Medicine led the way in this dualistic thinking with its preoccupation with disease and treating the symptoms of illness in a mechanistic way. The interrelationships of body, mind, and one's lifestyle were largely ignored as progress was made in treating and curing certain diseases (Shealy & Church, 2006). Research and treatment in much of Western medicine has been based upon studying cadavers, a germ theory of disease, and the pathology of illness. Eastern medicine, on the other hand, has obtained much of its knowledge from the systematic study of living, healthy human beings, and the harmony and balance of life forces sustaining health.

MULTIDISCIPLINARY AND INTERDISCIPLINARY WELLNESS

Historical aspects in the development of healing, health, and wellness have been sketched in the form of concepts and practices. What follows is a summary of selected academic areas that are contributing to the scientific understanding of the "good life" as seen by Aristotle and contemporary efforts to improve the quality of life and longevity. The daughters of Asclepius, Panacea and Hygeia, are the two interacting concepts for wellness research, with the primary emphasis on the latter.

Jung, Adler, and the Drive Toward Wholeness

The mind does not like to be divided. Psychologist C. G. Jung (Storr, 1983) called this a drive toward wholeness and integration, in which all elements of the person come together to form a larger entity, the *Self.* The conscious and unconscious aspects of thoughts, feelings, and experiences strive to make sense to the mind. Major world religions, in a spiritual sense, are the striving of the individual in response to a godlike image that is part of the collective unconscious. The divine nature of the unique human personality combines this uniqueness of *Self* with eternity and the individual with the universe.

Alfred Adler (1927/1954), a psychologist and contemporary of Jung, wrote that the human organism strives to fulfill its purpose. Human behavior can be understood on the basis of what the individual perceives as being meaningful and goal achieving. Inherent in this goal is the desire to protect the self while striving to fulfill one's potential, thereby achieving a sense of wholeness. Any part of the person could be understood by understanding the unified, indivisible whole (Adler, 1927/1954; Sweeney, 1998). With today's knowledge, Adler would be inclined to consider health and wellness as the ultimate goal and striving of humankind (Sweeney & Witmer, 1991).

Humanistic Psychology

Maslow, Rogers, and other humanistic psychologists created a "third force" in the development of psychology. The clinical and behavioral approaches developed in the 1940s and early 1950s focused predominantly on the disease model of human behavior. Psychoanalysis was the dominant clinical theory in the first half of the 20th century. Its focus was primarily on the influence of unconscious forces such as repressed impulses, internal conflicts, and childhood traumas on the mental life and adjustment of the individual. Assessing and treating mental illness was the main menu of empirical research. Maslow (1968, 1971) noted psychology's preoccupation with the unhealthy and average. His research attempted to define human beings in terms of what they can become. In his study of exceptional individuals, the individual's beliefs, emotions, values, healthy characteristics, and possibilities became eminent. Growth, autonomy, and the characteristics of the healthy personality reached fulfillment in what he called self-realization or the fully functioning person.

Rogers (1951, 1961, 1983) pioneered in developing psychological and educational methods that facilitated personal growth. Positive regard, genuineness, and empathy were core conditions that facilitated growth as well as therapeutic change. Rogers's study of therapeutic change and Maslow's study of self-actualizing persons give us a glimpse of the "growing tip" of humankind, a stage of development described as "fully human."

Health and Social Psychology

Health psychology was officially recognized as a new field when the American Psychological Association approved their recognition as Division 38 of APA in 1978 (Stone, Cox, Valdimarsdottir, Jandorf, & Neale, 1987). The discipline recognizes the physical, psychological, and social as three broad categories of factors involved in illness and health (Bernard & Krupat, 1994). While not as much a separate area for professional identity, the academic area of social psychology emerged as the application of social dimensions to how lifestyle events and certain behaviors influence one's health, for example, unsatisfactory social relationships and cardiovascular diseases. Friendship, marriage, divorce, loneliness, volunteer work, and involvement in community groups are legitimate areas for research and clinical applications in exploring their relationship to health and disease.

Behavioral Medicine and Medical Research

At about the same time, another group of psychologists and physicians met to organize the Society of Behavioral Medicine. Behavioral medicine, or mind/body approaches, address not only physical symptoms, but also the framework of attitudes and behavior that surround that condition. It unites modern scientific medicine, psychology, nursing, nutrition, and exercise physiology to enhance the natural healing capacity of the body and mind (Benson & Stuart, 1992).

Publications on wellness, health, and fitness appearing in the early 1990s are indicative of how far medical research had advanced within two decades of the mind/body and wellness movement. The researchers are multidisciplinary with backgrounds in medical, biomedical, psychological, and health specialties. Leading authorities from the nation's top medical centers reported their findings in publications such as *The Wellness Encyclopedia* (University of California, Berkeley, Wellness Letter, 1991); *The Wellness Book* (Benson & Stuart, 1992); *Mind/Body Medicine* (Goleman & Gurin, 1993); and *Fresh Start: The Stanford Medical School Health and Fitness Program* (Stanford Center for Research in Disease Prevention, 1996). Top medical centers represented in these publications are Stanford University, Duke University, University of Pittsburgh, Harvard, Johns Hopkins, Vanderbilt, University of Massachusetts, The Ohio State University, Case Western Reserve University, University of California, Cornell University, University of Michigan, Sloan-Kettering Cancer Center, and the Mayo Clinic.

General topics from the research relating to disease, health, and longevity are mind-body basics; the mind's role in illness; emotions and health; nutrition; exercise; social support from family, friends, and groups; relaxation, stress management, and coping; personal health habits such as sleeping; self-care; and environment and safety (Dossey, 1999).

The above areas derive their knowledge and methodology from psychology and the biomedical sciences in general and have made significant contributions to understanding the optimal factors that reduce the risk of disease. They likewise give greater understanding for physical, mental, and social attributes that contribute to optimal health.

Stress Research

Stress research at first evolved very slowly and almost single-handedly from the pioneer work of Hans Selye (1974), who coined the term *stress*. While the term *stress* has long been associated with medical, psychosomatic, emotional, and interpersonal difficulties, as well as anxiety and burnout, there is no generally agreed upon definition of stress. Considerable evidence regarding the effects of stress suggests that high stress levels, if chronically sustained, may contribute to a lowering of energy levels, ineffective mental functioning, performance failures, difficulty in interpersonal relationships, emotional disturbances, a weakened immune system, and illnesses of various kinds.

Two factors determine whether personal and environmental events might be stressful. First is the *cognitive appraisal* of the stressor. The formulation of this *appraisal* and the resulting *coping response* is best described by Lazarus and Folkman (1984) as "a relationship between the person and the environment that is appraised as taxing or exceeding his or her resources and endangering his or her well-being" (p. 21). The efficacy of the *coping response* is determined by the individual's *coping strategies and techniques*: coping behaviors such as stress monitoring, information seeking, and problem-solving skills; and *coping resources* such as beliefs and values, self-esteem, and emotional-social support.

Stress appraisal and coping are part of a wellness model of health rather than a pathogenic orientation in which disease is the focus. A wellness orientation leads one to think in terms of factors promoting movement toward the healthy end of the disease-health continuum. It is looking at how people stay healthy and what promotes well-being.

Quality of Life and Longevity Research

Quality of life and longevity research go hand in hand. The principles that play the most significant role in quality of life, with a few minor exceptions, are the very same ones for achieving our biological potential (Bortz, 1991; Pelletier, 1981). What contributes to the quality of life tends to extend the longevity of life. Applying the results of these two avenues of research shifts the emphasis from pathology to longevity promotion that sustains an optimal quality of life. Research in this area includes longitudinal study of individuals or groups over years and the cross-sectional study of older persons and their habits and lifestyles; for example, centenarian communities such as the Georgians in the Caucasus Mountains of Georgia, formerly part of the Soviet Union.

Three extensive studies of wellness were conducted in the 1970s. Research by Belloc (1973) and Belloc and Breslow (1972) focused on the positive health behaviors of over 7,000 adults who were studied over a period of five and one-half years. Seven factors were significantly related to life expectancy and health: (a) three meals a day and no snacking; (b) breakfast every day; (c) moderate exercise two or three times a day; (d) adequate sleep (seven or eight hours a night); (e) no smoking; (f) moderate weight; and (g) no alcohol or only in moderation.

Flanagan (1978), operating out of the American Institute for Research (Palo Alto, CA), found that 15 needs areas were significantly related to the quality of life. Major areas were physical health; economic status; relationships with family, friends, and community; helping others; intellectual development; work role; and leisure and recreational activities.

Another research effort to assess well-being in America was conducted by Angus Campbell (1981) and the staff at the Institute for Social Research, the University of Michigan. Personal, social, educational, occupational, and environmental factors made up 12 domains of life that were correlated as to their influence on the satisfaction of life in general. Findings from the above studies and those listed below characterize the quality of life indicators that also contribute to longevity.

Genetic, lifestyle, and environmental factors all play a part in longevity. Among the common denominators of longevity in individuals and cultures throughout the world are (a) heredity or genetic influences; (b) dietary and nutritional factors; (c) being physically and mentally active throughout life; (d) abstinence or moderate consumption of alcohol; (e) continued productive involvement in family and community affairs; (f) positive philosophical or religious attitudes (e.g., optimistic); (g) work satisfaction; and (h) an enduring sense of the meaning and purpose in life (Bortz, 1991; Pelletier, 1981; Peterson & Bossio, 1991; Santrock & Bartlett, 1986). Additional predictors are having parents or grandparents living past the age of 80, living in a rural area, being married, having at least two close friends, having high socioeconomic status, sleeping six to eight hours every night, and nonsmoking.

The environment, healthcare (especially of the young and old), and safe working conditions are other factors that interact with the above ones. While no single choice, habit, or condition may make a huge difference (except smoking and substance abuse), they add up when put together, having a significant impact on the quality of life and longevity. This additive and interactive effect makes it difficult to explain differences between individuals, cultures, and nations on characteristics of wellness.

Positive Psychology

The theme for the convention of the American Psychological Association in 1998 was prevention. Certain psychologists recognized that the disease model prevalent for 50 years did not move psychology closer to prevention of serious personal and relationship problems. Two years later the *American Psychologist* (2000) published a special issue on happiness, excellence, and optimal human functioning.

Researchers were learning that there are human strengths that act as buffers against mental illness: courage, future mindedness, optimism, interpersonal skill, faith, work ethic, hope, honesty, perseverance, and the capacity for flow and insight. Martin Seligman, widely regarded as the father of positive psychology, wrote: The challenge for the new century "will be to create a science of human strength whose mission is to foster these virtues in young people" (Seligman & Csikszentmihalyi, 2000, p. 7).

This new emphasis became known as positive psychology, which has become the scientific study of the strengths and the virtues that enable individuals and communities to thrive. It has three central concerns: positive emotions, positive individual traits, and positive institutions (D. Myers, 2000; Peterson, 2006; Seligman, 2002). Understanding positive emotion entails the study of contentment with the past, happiness in the present, and hope for the future. Understanding

The World's Longest-Lived People: The Okinawa Lifestyle

What we eat, do, think, and believe largely determine our health and longevity.

Okinawa is a string of islands southwest of Japan in the East China Sea. It was an independent kingdom until the Japanese took possession in 1879. It is the home of the longest-lived people in the world. Coronary heart disease, stroke, and cancer occur in Okinawa with the lowest frequency in the world. More than 400 centenarians live in a population of 1.3 million, many of them still healthy, active, and living independently. More important than their *life expectancy* is their *health expectancy*, the number of years they expect to live in good health. The Okinawa lifestyle is a unique approach to health and life based upon centuries of Eastern tradition and wisdom. *The Okinawa Program* is a report by a team of internationally known experts who have scientifically documented the Okinawa Centenarian Study over a 25-year period (Wilcox, Wilcox, & Suzuki, 2001). Their findings reveal the diet, exercise, and lifestyle practices that make the Okinawans the healthiest and longest-lived population in the world. The authors envision the Okinawa Program as a wellness model for the world.

Key Findings of the Okinawa Centenarian Study

After examining over 600 Okinawan centenarians and numerous "youngsters" in their seventies, eighties, and nineties, the researchers saw certain patterns emerge:

Eating Habits A low-calorie, plant-based diet high in unrefined carbohydrates. The elders eat an average of seven servings of vegetables and fruits a day, seven servings of grains a day, two servings of flavonoid-rich soy products per day; omega-3 rich fish several times a week; and minimal dairy products and meat. The average body mass index for the elders ranges from 18–22.

Physical Activity Exercise through the martial arts, traditional dance, gardening, and walking. Tai chi is also popular. They believe that health and longevity can be obtained by nurturing your *chi* or "life energy," and living a balanced lifestyle that is in tune with nature's way.

Psychospiritual Outlook and Practices Their philosophy affirms a faith in humanity, a sincere belief that all people are good, and it emphasizes both personal and group responsibilities. The elders retain remarkable mental clarity, even over the age of 100, partially due to diet. In personality testing, centenarians were low when it came to feelings of "time urgency" and "tension," and high in "self-confidence." Interviews revealed optimistic attitudes, adaptability, and an easy-going approach to life. Moderation was found to be a key cultural value. Health and longevity are celebrated, and health is a theme of most prayers. Low levels of negative emotions and depression are present.

Personal Care They have integrated healthcare with the ancient Eastern and modern Western healing traditions. It focuses not just on the absence of disease but also on optimum health, both physical and psychospiritual. Moderate use of alcohol is the norm.

Social Integration Residents have high levels of social contact. Cultural attitudes place the elderly in an exalted and respected position. Strong social networks and family ties exist, yet a fair amount of independence is retained. They believe in neighbor-sharing practices where villagers cooperate to help one another in work and life tasks.

Source: Wilcox, B. J., Wilcox, D. C., & Suzuki, M. (2001). *The Okinawa Program.* New York: Three Rivers Press. Summary by Mel Witmer, April 5, 2009.

positive individual traits consists of the study of strengths and virtues, such as the capacity for love and work, courage, compassion, resilience, creativity, integrity, self-knowledge, moderation, self-control, and wisdom. The 24 character traits that contribute to optimal functioning are described in *Character Strengths and Virtues* (Peterson & Seligman, 2004). Understanding positive institutions entails the study of meaning and purpose as well as strengths that foster better communities, such as justice, responsibility, civility, parenting, nurturance, work ethic, leadership, teamwork, purpose, and tolerance. Positive psychology proposed to correct this imbalance by focusing on strengths as well as weaknesses, on developing the best things in life as well as repairing the worst.

Faith and Religious Practices

In a review of the accumulated literature on religion and health, Benson (1996) concluded that regardless of how traditional one's practice of religious beliefs, whenever faith is present, remembered wellness is triggered and health can be improved. Religion usually promotes healthy lifestyles. Religious commitment is consistently associated with better health. Benson summarizes the research: "The greater a person's commitment, the fewer his or her psychological symptoms, the better his or her general health, the lower the blood pressure, and the longer the survival" (p. 174). Regardless of age, ethnicity, religion, and patients of very different diseases and conditions, religious commitment brings with it a lifetime of benefits.

More recently Harold Koenig at Duke University and his professional associates have reviewed the relationship between religious beliefs and lifestyle for their influence on physical and mental health (Koenig, 1999; Koenig & Lawson, 2004). The benefits cover illness prevention, illness recovery, and an overall sense of well-being. In their review of several hundred scientific studies comparing religious with non-religious (or less religious) persons, the religious persons: have lower diastolic blood pressure, are hospitalized less often, are less likely to suffer from depression, have healthier lifestyles, have a stronger sense of well-being and life satisfaction (especially older persons), have better health outcomes when suffering from a physical illness, have stronger immune systems, and live longer.

In reviewing the faith and mental health research, he found that "religious beliefs and practices are usually associated with greater well-being, hope, and optimism; more purpose and meaning in life; greater quality of life; and more prosocial traits in terms of forgiveness, sociability, and altruism" (Koenig, 2005, p. 51). Also, religious involvement is consistently related to both a higher level and a higher quality of social support. Even in areas of the world where religion plays a less significant role than in the United States, religious activity still correlates with greater well-being.

In summary, a positive relationship exists between religious faith and health benefits. This effect appears to hold up in different cultures and across various faiths in the United States and other major religions of the world.

Energy Psychology and Medicine

Energy psychology is the integration of quantum physics, psychology, and Eastern medicine (Feinstein, Eden, & Craig, 2005). The body is seen as an energy system that strives to maintain harmony and balance in governing our every movement, feeling, and thought. Growing understanding about the relationship between electromagnetic energy and the molecules that carry information is causing conventional medicine and psychotherapy to update their understanding of healing and health. Tapping into disturbing electrochemical patterns can bring about changes in a wide range of physical and psychological disorders. Energy psychology focuses on the energy disturbance as well as the memory. Stimulating specific electromagnetically sensitive points on the skin while imaging and bringing to mind a disturbing event can change the chemistry in certain areas of the brain.

Changing the internal wiring in relation to a clear-cut problem or symptom can be learned. One method for intervening in a disturbing flow of energy is to stimulate an acupuncture point in the body. This can change brain wave activity, deactivate an area of the brain associated with an undesirable condition, and in some locations cause secretion of serotonin. More intrusive means such as the insertion of needles, electrical stimulation, or the application of heat can be applied. The accupoints are called "windows" into the body's energy system. The body's energy system can be affected by rubbing, tapping, stretching, holding, or tracing specific points or areas on the surface of the skin. Tapping is a common procedure that is being used in clinical treatment and research.

The promise of energy psychology presents powerful tools for personal development, too. Combined with conventional techniques such as affirmations, visualizations, and positive thoughts, the use of energy interventions can improve self-image, evoke potentials, and enhance performance. It is safe and noninvasive, as effective as or more effective than other available therapies for a number of mental health conditions, and also an effective tool in the self-management of thoughts, emotions, and behavior for personal development (Feinstein et al., 2005).

A broader application of the human energy field findings is described by Valerie Hunt in *Infinite Mind: The Science of Human Vibration* (1995). She demonstrates how electromagnetic radiation changes during human interaction and with environmental conditions. Through field research and extensive clinical studies, she provides insight into mind-body interaction, the emotions and creativity, extrasensory human capacities in higher consciousness, and the mystical connections of spirit.

OTHER DISCIPLINES

Additional and interrelated disciplines have made contributions to understanding illness and factors that contribute to health and wellness. Research on burnout and occupational stress has provided strategies for reducing physical and mental distress and introducing health-promotion programs in the work settings. Biofeedback, as a means of monitoring physiological states such as skin temperature, muscle tension, and brain waves, provides visual and auditory information to alter mind-body connections to increase self-awareness and self-control. Its main focus is relaxation of mind and body systems that are aroused by the sympathetic nervous system. Biofeedback has been used in treating a variety of stress related conditions such as headaches, muscle tension related to low back pain, and general anxiety.

Psychoneuroimmunology, the integration of three fields of research, has contributed to some major breakthroughs in our understanding of how thoughts can influence the functioning of the immune system. This new science is charting a labyrinth of mind-body connections, chemical messengers, emotions, and immune cells. Negative thinking can adversely affect moods as well as depress the immune system, therefore making us more vulnerable to an array of illnesses.

Research in the areas of nutrition and exercise has generated extensive scientific data that improve the quality and longevity of life. We now understand how dietary excesses contribute to major health problems in our society. Exercise can assist in healing, add to prevention, and enhance the functioning of the body and the mind. Regular exercise and a nutritional diet are two of the greatest contributors to our overall well-being. Sports psychology has demonstrated performance enhancement by combining such techniques as a positive attitude, relaxation, mental rehearsal, breath control, and physical fitness.

PERSISTENCE OF THE PLACEBO

The placebo effect is probably as old as humankind. Belief-inspired healing has been a part of the healing process practiced by healers and physicians in every culture and time one might study. Benson (1996) has studied the presence of the placebo in the history of healing and notes that "In large measure, the history of medicine is the history of the placebo effect" (p. 109). Even though a substance or procedure may in and of itself have no medical value, the *belief* that it will help has a therapeutic value. Believing that the treatment will remediate a condition seems to activate a natural response within the individual's own health maintenance system. Benson prefers to call the intense desire for health and wholeness "remembered wellness," because it more accurately describes the mental process involved in caring for oneself.

Up until about a hundred years ago, remembered wellness was the treatment of choice. Benson believes that the scientific community is wrong in its dismissal of this phenomenon in its pejorative usage of "just the placebo effect." The facts are that the patient, caregiver, or both of them believing in the treatment conditions contribute to better outcomes. Andrew Weil (1995) observes that the placebo, far from being a nuisance, is potentially the greatest ally doctors can find in their efforts to mitigate disease. He has written extensively on how to discover and enhance the body's natural ability to maintain and heal itself.

Today "the placebo effect" is the benchmark for new drugs and techniques. If a new drug or procedure is no better than a placebo, the new treatment is considered a failure. Studies of the placebo effect over the last half century confirm that they are 30% to 70% effective, depending upon the nature of the illness and compliance. In every incident of remembered wellness, the catalyst is belief. The placebo has three components: the beliefs of the person, the beliefs of the health practitioner, and the relationship between the person and the practitioner. When these are positive, a placebo has a 37% chance of working as well as an active medicine (Benson & Stuart, 1992). History and scientific research confirm the universal presence of the mind-body effect on our health.

WELLNESS IN COUNSELING AND HUMAN DEVELOPMENT

Guidance from the early 1900s was conceived as a part of education but not synonymous with it (Parsons, 1909). Movements within education as well as those in the larger society impacted the philosophical and institutional views of educating the "whole child." Philosopher John Dewey's influence known as "progressive education" gave legitimacy to guidance and counseling as part of creating a learning environment that respects the unique qualities of children while preparing them for the real world in which they find themselves

The nature and scope of guidance was evaluated by Rachel Dunaway Cox in 1945 and reviewed by Hutson (1968). A study of 100 selected counselors in secondary schools revealed that 93% gave a substantial portion of their time to educational-vocational guidance. However, the need for more than counseling for educational-vocational planning and adjustment was reported. A significant amount of time was devoted to emotional and social adjustment. Ninety-five percent considered helping students with conflicts with family, friends, and other human relationships as one of their more important duties.

The philosophical and psychological bases of personnel services (guidance) in education were summarized by Gilbert Wrenn in a 1959 publication by the National Society for the Study of Education (Wrenn, 1959). Above all else, personnel service in education is predicated upon: seeing the learner totally; the right to self-fulfillment; planning for the future as well as optimal living in the present; advocating individual differences; using a varied methodology including counseling and group work; the quality of the relationship being an important element in all services; and personnel services remaining in the central stream of educational effort.

Until the early 1970s, counselor education programs were limited to the preparation of elementary and secondary school counselors. Preparation of secondary school guidance counselors and later elementary school counselors was the basis for the new academic discipline of counselor education. Some programs included preparation for student personnel workers and counselors for the college level. However, regardless of the level or student population, the emphasis was on the developmental aspects of education and human potential.

At the elementary school level, guidance and counseling from its beginning in the 1950s emphasized the personal, educational, and social development of the child. Guidance services included individual counseling, group work, appraisal, educational and vocational placement, and consultation with teachers and parents regarding the total development of the student.

Gilbert Wrenn in a widely influential book, *The Counselor in a Changing World* (1962), set the tone for the 1960s decade with the emphasis on working with others to fulfill developmental needs (Gladding, 1988). Also, the work of Carl Rogers and other humanistic psychologists was having its impact on counselor education as it was in psychology. The earlier emphasis on guidance shifted to counseling as a developmental profession. Counseling took on a more personal growth emphasis with the person taking more responsibility for the counseling process. With the counselor providing the conditions for change through genuineness, empathy, and positive regard, the inner direction of the person moves toward self-actualization (Rogers, 1957). Rogers viewed human nature as essentially good. Humans are characteristically positive, forward-moving, constructive, realistic, and trustworthy (Rogers, 1951, 1961). The role of the counselor is a holistic one in which the client is free to explore all aspects of self. Self-actualization is the strongest motivating drive of existence and encompasses actions that influence the total person.

Community counseling and mental health counseling evolved in the middle 1970s to become a major area of concentration for counselor education. While retaining certain developmental concepts and principles of school counseling, mental health counseling emphasized remediation and promotion of the mental and emotional health of clients served in various community agencies.

Historically, a philosophical and psychological linkage exists between guidance and counseling in its first 75 years and the current multidisciplinary wellness movement. This connection exists through an interdisciplinary approach to wellness that incorporates the mental, physical, social, emotional, vocational, and spiritual dimensions of a fully functioning person. Counseling as it has evolved within and from education has always been a developmentally oriented profession.

EARLY CONTEMPORARY WELLNESS EFFORTS

Wellness as a term in the English language has its origin in the mid-17th century. The recent development of the wellness concept using the language of "wellness" has been reviewed by J. E. Myers and Sweeney (2005a, 2005b). The World Health Organization as early as 1947 defined health as being more than the absence of disease and in 1964 emphasized the well-being aspect with its definition of optimal health as "a state of complete physical, mental, and social well-being and not merely the absence of disease or infirmity" (World Health Organization [WHO], 1968, p. 1).

Perhaps the oldest wellness operation promoting health-conscious behavior in the United States is the YMCA (www.ymca.net, 2008). The organization almost from its inception in the United States in 1851 began to emphasize the physical, mental, social, and spiritual aspects of a healthy lifestyle. As the organization evolved, various sports, bodybuilding, swimming, and aquatic activities were implemented. By 1979, the YMCA began doing fitness evaluations and offering exercise and fitness activities. Educational, social, and spiritual opportunities are still part of their core offerings with character development and physical activities being highlighted. Today more than 2,600 centers offer health-promoting activities for all persons without discrimination as to gender, age, race, ethnic background, or religion.

Halbert Dunn, a physician and professor, is widely credited with being the founding father of the modern wellness movement. His wellness philosophy and principles were presented in a series of short talks published in a book called *High Level Wellness* (Dunn, 1961). The ethic of self-responsibility and the integration of body, mind, and spirit were at the foundation of fulfilling one's potential. Dunn's holistic view is inherent in his definition of wellness as "an integrated method of functioning which is oriented to maximizing the potential of which an individual is capable, within the environment where he is functioning."

Another person whose work gave further impetus to the early wellness movement was Don Ardell, a medical researcher, professor, and health planner. He gives credit to Drs. Halbert Dunn and John Travis for their professional influence on his own work. Ardell's 1977 and 1979 (revised) books, each titled *High Level Wellness,* depict a model conceptualized as a circle with self-responsibility in the center. Four characteristics surrounding the circle and contributing to high level wellness are nutritional awareness, stress management, physical fitness, and environmental sensitivity. A most recent revision is more comprehensive by redefining the wellness circle with three parts: the physical domain, mental domain, and meaning and purpose, each with multiple subcomponents ranging from nutrition to emotional intelligence to relationships. His emphasis has been on the practical use of the model rather than studies to provide empirical support for the hypothesized components and their relationships. Ardell's book is a valuable resource for early references to persons and publications from a variety of disciplines during the 1960s and 1970s.

A third comprehensive approach to assessing wellness as a lifestyle was developed in the latter 1970s by Travis and Ryan (1977, 1981, 1988). Ardell (1979) describes a wellness center developed by Travis and Ryan at Mill Valley, California, as the most thorough portrait of what a health promotion center would be during this period of time. Travis and Ryan published the *Wellness Workbook* that contained a model of wellness. The model includes a *Wellness Index* that has 12 components. These components are illustrated in a Wellness Wheel and include: Self-Responsibility and Love; Breathing; Sensing; Eating; Moving; Feeling; Thinking; Playing/Working; Communicating; Sex; Finding Meaning; and Transcending. Further this model is illustrated by an Illness/Wellness Continuum that shows premature death at the left end and high-level wellness at the right end. The center is the neutral point with no discernable illness. To the left are disabilities, symptoms, and signs of illness; to the right increasing levels of health and well-being. Wellness is viewed within this model as a process and never a static state.

The *Wellness Workbook* by Travis and Ryan also includes a chapter on each of these wellness components with explanations, information, and exercises for one's personal wellness development. The *Wellness Inventory*, an abridged version of the *Wellness Index*, was also made available as was a later publication called *Wellness.* It describes a step by step process covering areas from nutrition to exercise to preventive healthcare to self-awareness (Ryan & Travis, 1991).

The National Wellness Institute founded by Bill Hettler and his colleagues in the 1970s in Stevens Point, Wisconsin, was one of the early wellness centers to establish a comprehensive assessment of health and wellness (Hettler, 1984). The National Wellness Institute continues to host a national wellness conference in Stevens Point annually.

A significant milestone for wellness, related to counseling in particular, was the 1985 publication of Dr. Mel Witmer's book entitled, *Pathways to Personal Growth: Developing a Sense of Worth and Competence*, in which he discusses wellness as a "way of life" and high-level health strategies. Also, during the late 1980s and early 1990s, we saw the development of wellness counseling models (J. E. Myers, Sweeney, & Witmer, 2000; Witmer & Sweeney, 1992). These models will be discussed in some detail in the next chapter.

In the 1990s, mainstream medicine also began to acknowledge the importance of the wellness movement as evidenced by the National Institutes of Health opening its Office of Alternative Medicine (OAM) in 1991 (this office was been renamed the National Center for Complementary and Alternative Medicine in 1998). Also, throughout the 1990s, more mental health practitioners and physicians were learning about and adopting primary prevention and holistic medicine approaches as part of their practices (Pert, 1997).

In the last decade, we have seen a significant growth in the wellness healthcare paradigm. This has been the case in part due to economic reasons as wellness is now seen as a potentially viable means of cost containment but also due to an increase in the public's desire for wellness and alternative healthcare services (Eisenberg et al., 1993). Finally, there has also been a growth in empirical research concerning wellness as an approach to healthcare (J. E. Myers & Sweeney, 2008). The National Center for Complementary and Alternative Medicine has funded much of this research along with private foundations and other government agencies. In the next chapter we will examine first some underlying theory concerning wellness counseling and several wellness counseling models.

References

Adler, A. (1927/1954). *Understanding human nature* (W.B. Wolf, Trans.). Fawcett Premier. (Original work published 1927)

Ardell, D. (1977; 1979). *High level wellness: An alternative to doctors, drugs, and disease* (rev.). Emmaus, PA: Rodale Press.

Belloc, N. B. (1973). Relationship of health practices and mortality. *Preventive Medicine, 2,* 67–81.

Belloc, N. B., & Breslow, L. (1972). Relationship of physical health status and health practices. *Preventive Medicine, 1,* 409–421.

Benson, H. (1996). *Timeless healing: The power of biology and belief.* New York: Scribner.

Benson, H., & Stuart, E. M. (1992). *The wellness book: The comprehensive guide to maintaining health and treating stress-related illness.* New York: Fireside, Simon & Schuster.

Bernard, L. C., & Krupat, E. (1994). *Health psychology: Biopsychosocial factors in health and illness.* New York: Harcourt Brace.

Bortz, W. M. (1991). *We live too short and die too long.* New York: Bantam.

Campbell, A. (1981). *The sense of well-being in America: Recent patterns and trends.* New York: McGraw-Hill.

Charitonidou, A. (1978). *Epidaurus: The sanctuary of Asclepios and the museum.* Epidaurus, Greece: Clio Editions.

Chin, R. M. (1992). *The energy within: The science behind every Oriental therapy from acupuncture to yoga.* New York: Paragon House.

Dossey, L. (1999). *Reinventing medicine: Beyond the mind-body to a new era of healing.* San Francisco: Harper.

Dunn, H. L. (1961). *High-level wellness.* Arlington, VA: R. W. Beatty.

Eisenberg, D. M., Kessler, R. C., Foster, C., Norlock, F. E., Calkins, D. R., & Delbanko, T. L. K. (1993). Unconventional medicine in the United States: Prevalence, costs, and patterns of use. *New England Journal of Medicine, 328,* 246–252.

Feinstein, D., Eden, D., & Craig, G. (2005). *The promise of energy psychology.* New York: Tarcher/Penguin.

Flanagan, J. (1978). A research approach to improving our quality of life. *American Psychologist, 33,* 138–147.

Gladding, S. F. (1988). *Counseling: A comprehensive profession.* Columbus, OH: Merrill.

Goleman, D., & Gurin, J. (Eds.). (1993). *Mind/body medicine: How to use your mind for better health.* Yonkers, NY: Consumer Reports Books.

Gordon, J. S. (1996). *Manifesto for a new medicine.* Reading, MA: Addison-Wesley.

Hettler, W. (1984). Wellness: Encouraging a lifetime pursuit of excellence. *Health Values: Achieving High Level Wellness, 8,* 13–17.

Hunt, V. H. (1995). *Infinite mind: The science of human vibrations.* Malibu, CA: Malibu Publishing.

Hutson, P. W. (1968). *The guidance function in education.* New York: Appleton-Century-Crofts.

Kelsey, M. (1985). Foreword. In K. L. Bakken, *The call to wholeness* (p. viii). New York: Crossroad.

Koenig, H. G., (1999). *The healing power of faith: Science explores medicine's last frontier.* New York: Simon & Schuster.

Koenig, H. G. (2005). *Faith & mental health.* Philadelphia: Templeton Foundation Press.

Koenig, H. G., & Lawson, D. M. (2004). *Faith in the future: Healthcare, aging, and the role of religion.* Philadelphia: Templeton Foundation Press.

Krippner, S. (1995). Cross-cultural comparison of four healing models. *Alternative Therapies in Health and Medicine, 1*(1), 21–29.

Lazarus, R. S., & Folkman, S. (1984). *Stress, appraisal, and coping.* New York: Springer.

Maslow, A. H. (1968). *Toward a psychology of being* (2nd ed.). New York: D. van Nostrand.

Maslow, A. H. (1970). *Motivation and personality* (2nd ed.). New York: Harper & Row.

Maslow, A. H. (1971). *The farther reaches of human nature.* New York: Viking Press.

Myers, D. (2000). *The American paradox.* New Haven: Yale.

Myers, J. E., & Sweeney, T. J. (2005a). *Counseling for wellness: Theory, research, and practice.* Alexandria, VA: American Counseling Association.

Myers, J. E., & Sweeney, T. J. (2005b). The indivisible self: An evidence-based model of wellness. In J. E. Myers & T. J. Sweeney (Eds.), *Counseling for wellness: Theory, research, and practice* (pp. 29–37). Alexandria, VA: American Counseling Association.

Myers, J. E., & Sweeney, T. J. (2008). Wellness counseling: The evidence base for practice. *Journal of Counseling & Development, 86,* 482–493.

Myers, J. E., Sweeney, T. J., & Witmer, J. M. (2000). The Wheel of Wellness for counseling: A holistic model for treatment planning. *Journal of Counseling & Development, 78,* 251–266.

Ornstein, R., & Sobel, D. S. (1990). The brain as a health maintenance organization. In R. Orstein & C. Swencionis (Eds.), *The healing brain: A scientific reader*, (pp. 10–21). New York: Guilford Press.

Parsons, F. (1909). *Choosing a vocation.* Boston: Houghton Mifflin.

Pelletier, K. R. (1981). *Longevity: Fulfilling our biological potential.* New York: Delacorte Press/Seymour Lawrence.

Peterson, C. (2006). *Primer in positive psychology.* New York: Oxford University Press.

Peterson, C., & Bossio, L. M. (1991). *Health and optimism.* New York: Free Press.

Peterson, C., & Seligman, M. E. P. (Eds.). (2004). *Character strengths and virtues: A handbook and classification.* Washington, DC: American Counseling Association.

Rogers, C. R. (1951). *Client-centered therapy.* Boston: Houghton Mifflin.

Rogers, C. R. (1957). The necessary and sufficient conditions of therapeutic personality change. *Journal of Consulting Psychology, 21,* 95–103.

Rogers, C. R. (1961). *On becoming a person.* Boston: Houghton Mifflin.

Rogers, C. R. (1983). *Freedom to learn for the 80s.* Columbus, OH: Charles E. Merrill.

Ryan, R. S., & Travis, J. W. (1991). *Wellness: Small changes you can use to make a big difference.* Berkeley, CA: Ten Speed Press.

Santrock, J. W., & Bartlett, J. C. (1986). *Developmental psychology: A life cycle perspective.* Dubuque, IA: Wm. C. Brown.

Seligman, M. E. P. (2002). *Authentic happiness: Using the new positive psychology to realize your potential for lasting fulfillment.* New York: Free Press/Simon & Schuster.

Seligman, M. E. P., & Csikszentmihalyi, M. (2000). Positive psychology: An introduction. *American Psychology, 55,* 5–14.

Selye, H. (1974). *Stress without distress.* New York: Lippincott.

Shealy, C. N., & Church, D. (2006). *Soul medicine: Awakening your inner blueprint for abundant health and energy.* Santa Rosa, CA: Elite Books.

Stanford Center for Research in Disease Prevention. (1996). *Fresh start: The Stanford Medical School health and fitness program.* San Francisco: KQED Books.

Stanger, F. B. (1978). *God's healing community.* Nashville: Abingdon.

Stone, A. A., Cox, D. S., Valdimarsdottir, A., Jandorf, L., & Neale, J. M. (1987). Evidence that IgA antibody is associated with daily mood. *Journal of Personality and Social Psychology, 52,* 988–993.

Storr, A. (1983). *The essential Jung.* Princeton: Princeton University Press.

Sweeney, T. J. (1998). *Adlerian counseling: A practitioner's approach* (4th ed.). Philadelphia: Taylor & Francis.

Sweeney, T. J., & Witmer, J. M. (1991). Beyond social interest: Striving toward optimal health and wellness. *Individual Psychology, 47,* 527–540.

Travis, J. W. (1977). *Wellness workbook: A guide to attaining high level wellness.* Mill Valley, CA: Wellness Resource Center.

Travis, J. W., & Ryan, R. S. (1981; 1988). *Wellness workbook* (2nd ed.). Berkeley, CA: Ten Speed Press.

University of California, Berkeley, Wellness Letter. (Eds.). (1991). *The wellness encyclopedia.* Boston: Houghton Mifflin.

Warburton, N. (1999). *Philosophy: The basics* (3rd ed.). New York: Routledge.

Weil. A. (1995). *Spontaneous healing.* New York: Alfred A. Knopf.

Witmer, J. M. (1985). *Pathways to personal growth.* Muncie, IN: Accelerated Development.

Witmer, J. M., & Sweeney, T. J. (1992). A holistic model for wellness and prevention over the life span. *Journal of Counseling & Development, 71,* 140–148.

World Health Organization. (1968). *Constitution of the World Health Organization.* Geneva, Switzerland: Author.

Wrenn, C. G. (1959). Philosophical and psychological bases of personnel services in education. In N. B. Henry (Ed.), *Personnel services in education: The fifty-eighth yearbook of the National Society for the Study of Education* (pp. 41–81). Chicago: University of Chicago Press.

Wrenn, C. G. (1962). *The counselor in a changing world.* Washington, DC: American Personnel and Guidance Association.

3 THEORETICAL MODELS FOR WELLNESS COUNSELING

Paul F. Granello and J. Melvin Witmer

Life is not merely being alive, but being well.

MARCUS AURELIUS (ROMAN EMPEROR, BEST KNOWN FOR HIS *MEDITATIONS ON STOIC PHILOSOPHY*, AD 121–180)

A wellness approach to counseling can be defined as a holistic approach that strives for the **responsible integration** of effective counseling approaches with a variety of complimentary health practices. Responsible integration means utilizing practices that have been established through research as efficacious. Wellness counselors do not endorse using therapy techniques that have not been supported through verifiable research, out of compliance with the professions ethical guidelines, or those lying outside of a counselor's scope of practice.

Wellness counseling is an approach to helping based upon a belief in human potential and client strengths. Wellness counselors practice with the belief that a client's lifestyle is a major determinant of well-being. The counselor's commitment is to nurture and enhance human abilities and functioning rather than solely focus on the treatment of pathologies. The wellness counselor assists the client in striving for his or her highest level of functioning across all of the dimensions of human life.

WELLNESS COUNSELING THEMES

The ten themes illustrated below are descriptive of a wellness counseling approach and the principles that govern its application to therapy. The themes are consistent with the overarching wellness counseling goal of helping clients to develop and function to their highest potential.

STRIVING FOR WELLNESS AND WELL-BEING The central goal of wellness counseling is to promote the overall health and well-being of the client. Wellness counselors seek to prevent illness, minimize disease, improve the overall quality of life, and increase the longevity of the client. Wellness counselors focus on challenging clients to continually strive for the highest level of multisystem health possible (not simply the remission of a particular set of presenting symptoms in one domain of functioning). Wellness counselors may work with clients at all levels of health. Since disease despite our best efforts may be an inevitable part of the lifespan, wellness counselors can help clients strive to maintain a sense of well-being through coping with an affliction in a proactive healthy way.

UNITY OF ALL DIMENSIONS OF HUMAN EXISTENCE Wellness counselors believe that the well-being of the person is interwoven between all the dimensions of human experience. The individual exists on many different levels or domains, (e.g., the cognitive, affective, behavioral, social, spiritual, and physical). All the components are interrelated and interdependent. The level of function (or dysfunction) of one affects the functioning of the others. A person is more than one's body. Every human being is a holistic being, comprised of interdependent relationships of body, mind, emotions, and spirit. The goals for therapy in wellness counseling encompass the whole person in all spheres of human existence including the physical, cognitive, emotional, social, cultural, vocational, and spiritual aspects of life.

CONCERN FOR BOTH QUALITY AND LONGEVITY OF LIFE Three real questions for wellness living are: *How long* will I live? *How healthy and vigorous* will my life be while living it? And a third existential question, *How* do I want to live? With medical science and lifestyle changes extending the longevity of life, many times the quality of life suffers. Conversely, by seeking to help clients improve the quality of their life wellness counselors believe that there will be an increase the length of life. The wellness counseling model values *adding more life to living* as much as extending the life that one lives.

PERSON ORIENTED RATHER THAN DISEASE ORIENTED Each person must be seen as a unique individual and treated in a way appropriate to that person. Positive regard, understanding of the total person, and genuineness in the relationship are essential ingredients in any health or healing endeavors. The disorder or dysfunction is never the sole focus of the services a wellness counselor provides. Wellness counselors are democratic and tolerant rather than authoritarian understanding that the quality of the relationship between the client and the counselor exerts a powerful influence on the health of the client.

DEVELOPMENTALLY ALL INCLUSIVE Wellness counselors work with clients at all stages of life. They believe that all clients can adapt, change, and practice lifestyle habits to increase their well-being. No individual is too old or too young to learn new ideas or behaviors and in doing so improve some aspect of their lives. However, sound health practices cannot begin in adult life, since by this time much damage may have already been done. The traits of wellness naturally unfold early in life and continue throughout the lifespan when they are nurtured. Characteristics such as a sense of humor, an optimistic trusting attitude, physical activity, and living in the present moment are all characteristics of healthy children and can contribute to our well-being until the end of life.

CROSS-CULTURAL UNIVERSAL QUALITIES Wellness counselors believe that the dimensions of wellness apply universally to all humankind. The opportunity to pursue high level wellness is a fundamental right of all human beings, not just those from select or privileged groups.

SENSITIVITY TO CONTEXT Contextual variables impact the health of the individual through local, institutional, environmental, and global events. We are not immune or isolated from such influences. Events in the environment, often beyond our control, impact our daily lives and the quality of living. Wars, poverty, natural disasters, crime, violence, disease, environmental pollution, economic exploitation, unemployment, and competition for limited resources are all stressors. A holistic approach to wellness counseling requires that the individual be understood in the context of political, social, economic, and environmental factors that affect every one of us day in and day out. Wellness counselors contextualize their interventions with clients so that they are culturally relevant, sensitive, and realistic.

INTEGRATED MULTIDISCIPLINARY APPROACHES AND METHODS Wellness counselors are holistic healthcare providers, drawing on perspectives and practices from Eastern, Western, and indigenous cultures. Wellness counselors believe that clients can benefit from breaking down the silos of subspecialization that dehumanize the present day medical system. Modern medical technology and perennial wisdom are both given an honorable place. Knowledge and practices are accepted from multiple professional disciplines. Current medical science and practices are also respected. Cultural wisdom and religious practices (e.g., meditation, yoga) may also be seen as sources of knowledge for creating healthier persons. The holistic approach is pragmatic in its criterion of using "what works" and does not require the process be fully understood, although processes that have supportive research are highly desirable. Wellness counselors are open to coordinating care and consulting with professionals from many different healthcare and social institutions. These professionals may include those in medicine, education, religious, government and public service, recreation or physical development, allied health, business, and many others. Whatever methods are used should contribute to the well-being of the individual and his or her becoming a more fully functioning person.

PERSONAL RESPONSIBILITY AND SELF-CARE Primary care is self-care. Wellness requires that individuals take responsibility for their own health over the lifespan. It teaches us to mobilize our power to heal ourselves and enhance our well-being. Personal control, empowerment, and self-efficacy may be the ultimate determinants in human health and aging. We are to make full use of the extraordinary capacity of our minds to influence the body. Although we still have much to learn about just how we can improve the quality and length of life, our current knowledge far exceeds our commitment to live a "healthy lifestyle." Wellness counselors believe that by applying what is known today clients can improve the quality of life significantly. Our understanding of health is shifting from dependence upon a "healer" to taking full responsibility for good health attitudes and practices. We are the writer, producer, director, and actor in fulfilling our own biological potential, social contribution, and spiritual destiny.

PROACTIVE RATHER THAN REACTIVE Organizations must take the initiative and responsibility for healthcare systems that emphasize primary prevention rather than crisis intervention. Parental, school, community, and religious teachings should encourage healthy lifestyle behaviors. Wellness counselors encourage the client to be an active participant in a collaborative process in their healthcare and not just a passive recipient of care. Although the individual has the responsibility for choosing a healthy lifestyle, professionals in the healthcare business must also see their role as part of a holistic view of the person's well-being. Wellness counselors proactively advocate on behalf of their clients and the overall community to encourage organizational systems to promote a wellness approach to health.

SOCIAL CONNECTIVITY Wellness counselors value the health effects of positive social support systems. A sense of belonging and connection to other people is a basic human need. Altruism, "the helping gene," provides health benefits for those who give and help others. Wellness counseling approaches encourage social connections and the great untapped power that ordinary people have to understand and help one another through the family, neighborhood, small support groups, civic organizations, churches, schools, and the workplace.

In summary the basic themes outlined above reflect a philosophy that asserts a positive view of humanity. Humans are viewed as holistic beings operating across many interrelated dimensions of life and having the ability to strive to achieve enhanced levels of health and well-being. Humans can learn, adapt, change, and create. This philosophy serves as the core of a wellness approach to counseling.

COUNSELING MODELS OF WELLNESS

Just as it is important to have a theoretical orientation in all mental health interventions (Young, 2008), so too it is important to have a theoretical road map when working with clients from a wellness approach. Wellness models that indicate specific psychological and sociological variables can be used as the basis for structuring wellness work with clients.

Several authors have suggested models with specific psychological and sociological variables that contribute to an individual's wellness.

Zimpher Wellness Model

Zimpher (1992) proposed a wellness model based upon his treatment of clients with cancer. The model includes eight areas of treatment important for client wellness: medical health, immune function, lifestyle management, spiritual beliefs and attitudes, psychodynamics, energy forces, and interpersonal relations. Specific techniques are related to each category. An example under the interpersonal area would be the encouragement of a client to meditate with a partner, thereby assisting the client to maintain a social support network (Zimpher, 1992). The Zimpher model may be best suited to working with clients who are already diagnosed with a serious illness and who are looking to receive therapy as an adjunct to their medical care.

Hettler Hexogonal Model of Wellness

A second wellness model developed by Hettler attempts to provide specific factors that comprise wellness (Opatz, 1986). This model has a broader focus than the Zimpfer model and was developed and implemented for a college campus environment (Hettler, 1980). The six dimensions of wellness that are specifically defined in this model are: intellectual, emotional, physical, social, occupational, and spiritual wellness. Further, each of the categories is divided into subtasks; for example, under the category of social wellness, behavior of an individual that involves actively seeking interdependent relationships is viewed as contributing to wellness. This model has been used in a variety of industrial and college settings (Mareno, 2010) and is used by the National Wellness Institute at Stevens Point, Wisconsin (Granello, 2000; Hettler, 1980).

The Lifespan Model of Wellness

The Lifespan Model of wellness is much more comprehensive than either of the two models illustrated above. The Adlerian concepts of social interest and striving for mastery are used as the theoretical basis of this model and are used to provide a rationale to explain why individuals wish to achieve a wellness lifestyle (Sweeney & Witmer, 1991).

The model, developed by Witmer and Sweeney (1991), uses five "life task" categories that are viewed as necessary to wellness. These life task categories are: spirituality, self-direction, work and leisure, friendship, and love. Each of the life tasks is further separated into a total of 15 subscales (spirituality, sense of worth sense of control, realistic beliefs, emotional responsiveness, intellectual stimulation, sense of humor, exercise, nutrition, self-care, gender identity, cultural identity, stress management, work, leisure, friendship, and love). For example, the life task of friendship is separated into two components: social interest and connectedness, and social support, interpersonal relations, and health. The authors provide cited research to support the logic of including each of the 15 subcomponents in the overall wellness model (Witmer & Sweeney, 1991). This model is well grounded in research and may be the most useful for practitioners wishing to do wellness counseling with the general public (Myers, Sweeney, & Witmer, 2000). See Figure 3.1.

The Indivisible Self-Wellness Model (5-F WEL)

After 10 years of research involving four separate and increasingly more useful versions of the Wellness Evaluation of Lifestyle (WEL), 17 discrete factors of wellness were identified. The lack of factor-analytic studies with the original WEL limits its usefulness for research but still

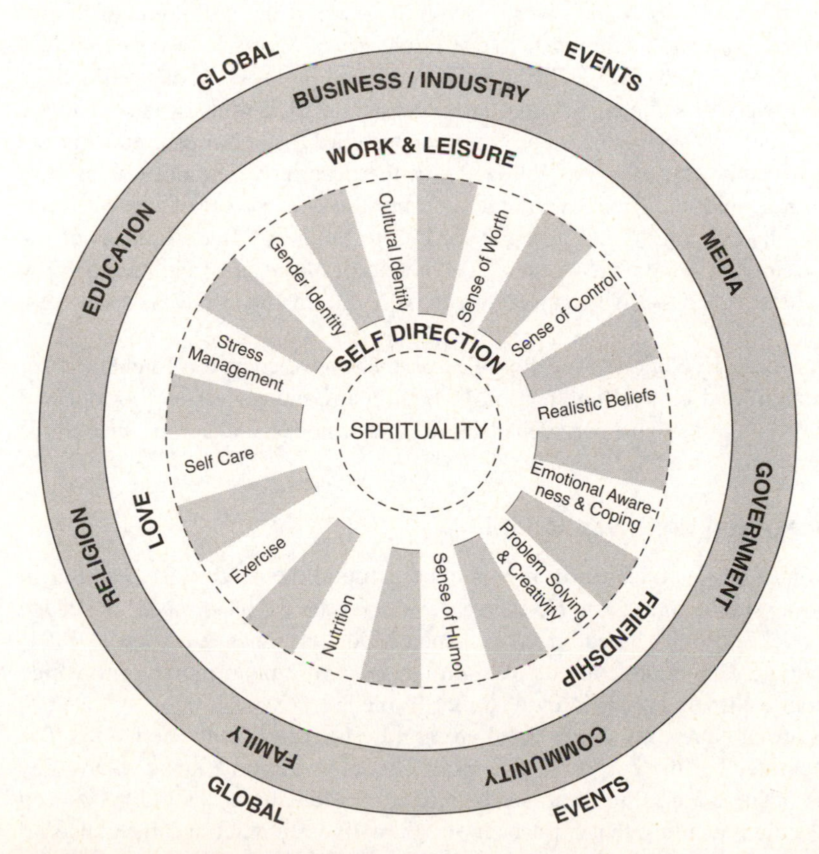

FIGURE 3.1 The Wheel of Wellness.
Source: "The Wheel of Wellness," Witmer & Sweeny, 1991

TABLE 3.1 Indivisible Self Model (Five Factor Wellness Model)

Five Factors	Wellness Evaluation of Lifestyle Subscales
Creative Self	Problem Solving and Creativity, Sense of Control, Emotional Awareness and Coping, Sense of Humor, Work
Coping Self	Leisure, Stress Management, Sense of Worth, Realistic Beliefs
Social Self	Friendship, Love
Essential Self	Essence of Spirituality, Self-Care, Gender Identity, Cultural Identity
Physical Self	Nutrition, Exercise

has usefulness for educational and workshop purposes. Its successor, the 5-F WEL, grew out of the factor analytic studies of the original WEL database. The lead researchers, Myers and Sweeney, describe the five factors of wellness assessment in their publication *Counseling for Wellness* (Myers, 2005).

The Five Factor Wellness Inventory (5-F WEL) is a paper-and-pencil instrument that includes 73 items measuring a single order factor, total wellness, and five second order factors. Reliability data along with convergent and divergent validity support the usefulness of the instrument for research purposes and its implications for clinical use (Myers & Sweeney, 2005). The 37 studies using the WEL and the 5-F WEL are summarized in Table 3.1 that reflects its wide application to a variety of settings, different ages, gender, marital status, socioeconomic status, and cultural diversity (Myers, 2005). The five second order factors to emerge from the exploratory and confirmatory studies are as follows with the descriptive dimensions used in the original WEL to indicate the content of the factor. The initial 17 scales of the WEL did emerge as independent factors but did not group according to the initial five life tasks of the hypothesized wheel. Using the Adlerian (Sweeney, 2009) concept of the unity and indivisibility of the self, the researchers named the five factors that emerged empirically as facets of wellness, as shown in Table 3.1.

The clinical and research editions of wellness assessment have created a foundation for theoretical, measurement, and clinical application to healthcare and understanding optimal wellness. Currently it is one of the most comprehensive wellness models and assessments in the field of counseling and holistic health (Myers, 2005, 2008).

Clinical and Educational Wellness Model

Applying wellness counseling with clients in my practice, I found the need to have a clinical wellness model that was simple to explain. So I have developed the wellness model portrayed in Figure 3.2. The model is heavily based on the Lifespan Model (Witmer & Sweeney, 1991) with my own adaptations. The model consists of eight domains of human functioning which contribute to the overall well-being of the individual. See Table 3.2.

These domains are of course not discrete and are highly interactive with each other. The domains are only separated for the purposes of helping clients to examine areas where they might have strengths or have a need to improve their functioning. Clients should be viewed holistically, with the understanding that all aspects of their lives interact and influence all others. The third section of this book is comprised of chapters that examine each of the wellness domains in some detail.

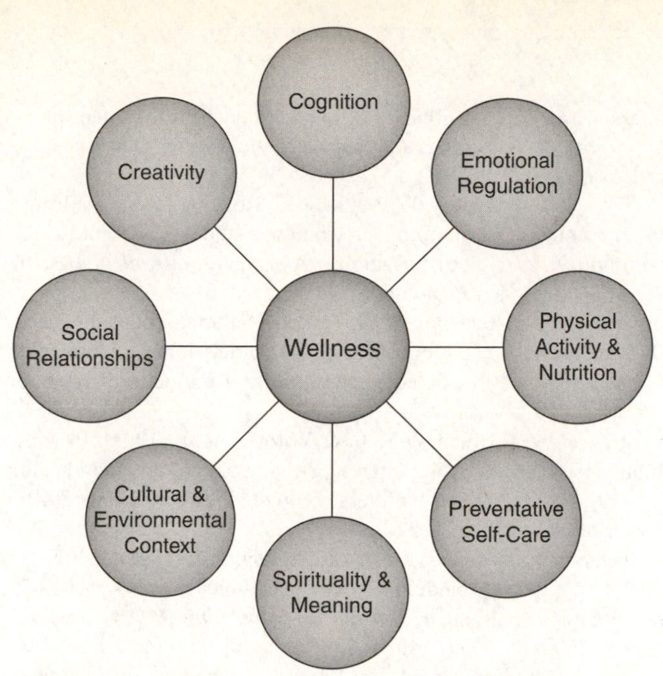

FIGURE 3.2 Clinical and Educational Model of Wellness

TABLE 3.2 Eight Domains of the Clinical and Educational Wellness Model

Cognition	Encompasses all of the mental activities of the individuals' brain that create consciousness. Perception, memory, attribution, appraisal are all examples. Example: ability to purposefully appraise potential stressors.
Emotional Regulation	The ability of individuals to monitor and modify their emotions for the purpose of controlling their level of arousal. Example: managing arousal from negative emotions by engaging in an activity such as yoga or through breathing exercises.
Physical Activity and Nutrition	The positive use of exercise and diet to achieve and maintain healthy body and mind. Example: eating a well balanced diet.
Preventative Self-Care	Engaging in health and safety habits that promote mental and physical health. Examples include: yearly physical examinations, wearing seat belts, brushing your teeth.
Spirituality and Meaning	An individual's system of beliefs or values that provide a sense of purpose in life. Example: the belief in an organizing principle or creator for the universe.
Cultural and Environmental Context	The impacts that the setting in time and place in which individuals exist have upon their health. For example: access to healthcare, safe drinking water, beliefs about women's rights.
Social Relationships	The influences of interactions with others on the health of the individual. Example: The ability to draw on and provide tangible or emotional support with others.
Creativity	Process of novel problem solving, cognitive flexibility, creation of purposeful new ways of relating, understanding, and interpreting.

References

Granello, P. (2000). Integrating wellness work into mental health private practice. *Journal of Psychotherapy in Independent Practice, 1*(1), 3–16.

Hettler, B. (1980). Wellness promotion on a university campus. Family and Community. *Health, 3*(1), 77–95.

Hettler, B. (1986). Strategies for wellness and recreation program development. In F. Leafgren (Ed.), *Developing campus recreation and wellness programs*. San Francisco: Jossey-Bass.

Mareno, N. (2010). Wellness characteristics and health risk behaviors of young adult university students. Abstract.

Myers, J. E. (2005). Counseling for wellness: Theory, research, and practice. American Counseling Assn.

Myers, J. E. (2008). Wellness counseling: The evidence base for practice *Journal of Counseling & Development*, 86, 482–493.

Myers, J. E., & Sweeney, T. J. (2005). The indivisible self: An evidence-based model of wellness (reprint). *Journal of Individual Psychology, 61*(3), 269–279.

Myers, J. E., Sweeney, T. J., & Witmer, J. M. (2000). The wheel of wellness counseling for wellness: A holistic model for treatment planning. *Journal of Counseling & Development, 78*(3), 251–266.

Opatz, J. P. (1986). Stevens Point: A long-standing program for students at a midwestern university. *American Journal of Health Promotion.*

Sweeney, T. J. (2009). Adlerian counseling and psychotherapy: A practitioner's approach (5th ed.). New York: Routledge, Taylor & Francis Group.

Sweeney, T. J., & Witmer, M. J. (1991). Beyond social interest: Striving toward optimum health and wellness. *Individual Psychology, 47*(40), 527–540.

Witmer, M. J., & Sweeney, T. J. (1991). A holistic model for wellness and prevention over the life span. *Journal of Counseling & Development, 71,* 140–148.

Young, M. E. (2008). Learning the art of helping: Building blocks and techniques (4th ed.). Upper Saddle River, NJ: Prentice Hall.

Zimpfer, D. G. (1992). Psychosocial treatment of life-threatening disease: A wellness model. *Journal of Counseling & Development, 71,* 203–209.

WELLNESS COUNSELING IN PRACTICE

The objectives for this part are:

1. To provide information about models and methods for helping clients make positive behavioral changes.
2. To provide information and resources related to complementary and alternative treatments.
3. To introduce a model for behavior change that incorporates a curative factors approach to counseling.
4. To provide an illustration through case example of how a counselor can approach helping a client achieve increased individual wellness.

Chapter Four: Change Science: Models and Methods In this chapter the concept of "client change" in therapy is discussed and several models for behavioral change are presented. Dr. Granello introduces a hybrid model of behavior change that contextualizes a behavior change model within a counseling therapy relationship.

Chapter Five: Complementary and Alternative Treatments Americans are using complementary and alternative (CAM) treatments in increasing numbers. This chapter outlines the major classifications of these treatments according to the National Center for Complementary and Alternative Medicine based at the National Institutes of Health. The relationship of wellness counseling to these types of treatments is also presented.

Chapter Six: Incorporating Wellness Counseling into Clinical Practice: A Case Example A case example is provided that illustrates how a counselor operating from a wellness orientation can assess and collaboratively assist a client wishing to enhance his or her overall wellness.

4 CHANGE SCIENCE: MODELS AND METHODS

Paul F. Granello

Everyone thinks of changing the world, but no one thinks of changing himself.

LEO TOLSTOY

Achieving significant "change" is a central goal of all counseling. One way of thinking about the behavioral change process is that it is the actual means, method, or steps by which a new behavior is adopted. Yet it has not been until relatively recently that the "change process" has been studied independently. Traditionally, most counselors and mental health professionals learn that there has been an evolution in counseling theory, with a wide variety of counseling theories being proposed over time. Each of these approaches to counseling developed as an explanation of mental function and also as a set of methods for treating pathological dysfunction. Additionally, we are taught that through outcome research and meta-analytical studies, generally psychotherapy has been shown to be an effective intervention. These developments have led to the current state of therapy research which is seeking to answer more specifically what types of therapy work best for what specific diagnoses, and for what types of clients.

What if, however, the factors that were most important to helping clients make substantial changes were not related to a single counseling theory but rather common among many theories? Given that there are many different counseling approaches that may be effective in helping a client to make a change, could there be some universal underlying change process that is common among the wide diversity of counseling approaches? Further, what if the actual process of client change is completely independent of any specific theory? As a result of these questions and others like them researchers began to study the change process as a topic independent of specific counseling theories. Additionally, many change models have been derived not from the mental health professions but from other professional disciplines that are concerned with understanding how to help people change their behavior. Disciplines such as public health, exercise science, medicine, and nutrition have contributed greatly to the understanding of the change process.

BUT JUST EXACTLY HOW DO CLIENTS MAKE CHANGES? Like so many questions in social sciences the answer to "How do people change?" is a very complex one. People are of course complicated, having not only past experiences but also expectations about the future that influence their behavior. Further, humans are social creatures continuously influencing others and being influenced by the social context in which they live. Attempting to "sum up" in any one model an aspect of human behavior as complicated as change is not only bound to be challenging but also to produce a model with limitations. Despite this challenging task, however, a number of useful models for understanding the change process have been proposed. It is important to learn about change models because when they are understood and applied by wellness counselors they can assist as therapy modalities for facilitating client change. Much of your work in wellness counseling will involve encouraging clients to make and maintain positive lifestyle changes. Therefore, it is important for you to develop a better understanding of the conceptual models of change. The purpose of the rest of this chapter is to illustrate several models that have been developed to help explain the process of change.

MODELS OF THE CHANGE PROCESS

Models for understanding the change process have both similarities and differences. One significant difference between current change models can be the primary focus of the model. Some change models focus almost exclusively on behaviors and how to modify them, while others include cognitive elements like beliefs or attitudes, and still others stress the importance of social learning such as observations of others, or even environmental factors like access and availability to healthcare (Shumaker, Ockene, & Riekert, 2009). Similarities also exist between many models. The list below outlines some basic components of behavior change that many models include:

Self-direction: The person must take responsibility for making changes in his or her behavior.

Self-monitoring: The process of becoming aware of one's own cognition, emotion, and behavior. Often self-monitoring involves tracking or charting to establish a baseline for a given targeted behavior to change.

Goal specification: The process of developing and committing to a set of goals and objectives that is specific, measurable, and realistically achievable.

Stimulus control: The process of learning which cues can help to promote a desired behavior or learning which cues can trigger an unwanted behavior.

Self-reinforcement: Encouraging your own success by providing yourself with meaningful rewards for achieving goals.

Social support: Identifying others and soliciting the help of others to make a change, and expressing a public commitment to making a change

Behavioral rehearsal: Make the new behavior change a habit by practicing it. Anticipate potential situations where there may be obstacles to the desired behavior and practice solutions.

BEHAVIORAL LEARNING MODEL

Understanding how people can learn new positive behaviors or unlearn and extinguish maladaptive behaviors is a central focus of the Behavioral Learning Model (BLM). For example, two methods that are based upon the BLM that can help a person perform a new behavior are using a **behavioral chain** and/or utilizing a **behavioral contract**.

BEHAVIORAL CHAIN The sequence of behavioral stimuli that either enhance or detract from the performance of a behavior and its consequences is a behavioral chain. In employing this method, first the wellness counselor would work with the client to analyze the sequence of events (antecedents)

that lead up to the time when the desired behavior is to be performed. We know that certain stimuli (behavioral cues) can either increase or decrease the likelihood of a behavior. Also, it is important to discuss what the results are (consequences) of doing or not doing the desired behavior. Reinforcements that are valued by a client for a behavior can increase its likelihood of being performed. The behavior chain can be fully explored with the client. The manipulation of the antecedents to a behavior (stimulus control) or the manipulation of the consequences to a behavior (reinforcement control) or both can help increase the ability of the client to perform the desired behavior. The example in Figure 4.1 first shows a maladaptive behavior chain for studying (desired behavior) and then shows how the stimuli and reinforcements can be changed to help promote studying.

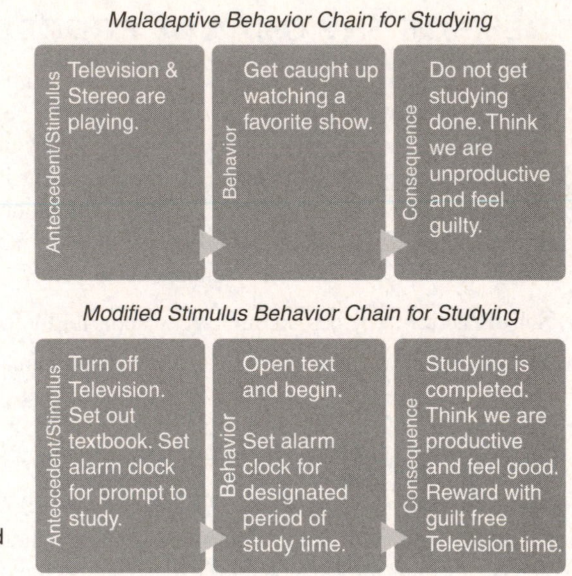

FIGURE 4.1 Maladaptive and Modified Stimulus Behavior Chain for Studying

BEHAVIORAL CONTRACTS Behavioral contracts are statements of commitment to the performance of a behavior with specific consequences (reinforcements) contingent upon the behavior. Behavioral contract goals can be stated using an *If . . . then . . .* format. (See Figure 4.2.)

The BLM has extensive research to back it up and is the basis for many types of behavioral interventions.

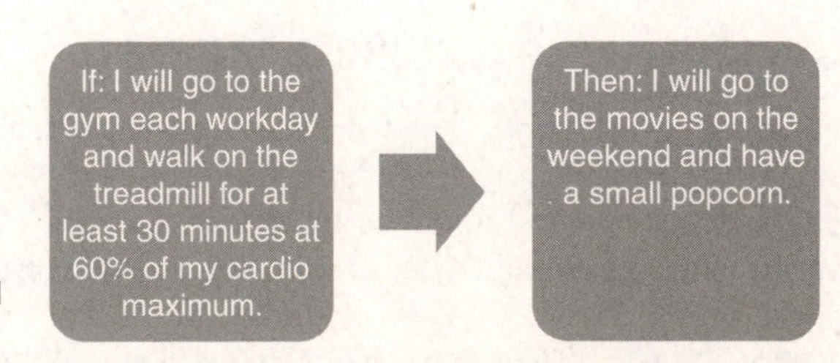

FIGURE 4.2 Example of a Behavioral Contract Goal

HEALTH BELIEF MODEL

The Health Belief Model (HBM) was developed in the 1950s by the U.S. Public Health Service. One of the first health change models developed, the HBM originally resulted from a need to understand why people were not getting screened for tuberculosis, when treatments for the disease had been developed. As a result of their studies in this area the public health researchers developed five basic principles that they thought were essential to understanding why individuals would or would not make behavior changes.

The five principles include:

1. **Perceived severity:** The belief that a health problem is real and potentially serious. The individual must have some knowledge about the condition and that it can have significant harmful effects.
2. **Perceived threat:** The belief that one is susceptible to the problem. The individual must think that he or she is personally at risk due to the health problem.
3. **Perceived benefit:** The belief that changing one's behavior will reduce the threat. The individual must believe that the intervention is valid and that there will be benefits resulting from changing his or her behavior.
4. **Perceived barriers:** A perception of the obstacles to changing one's behavior. The individual must have easy access to an intervention for the health problem and believe that there are no insurmountable barriers for implementing that intervention.
5. **Self-efficacy:** The belief that one has the ability to control and change one's behavior. The more individuals believe they can control their own behavior, the more likely they are to make a change.

Today, the HBM has been used to help plan behavior change interventions in diverse populations. For instance, researchers have applied the HBM to studies that attempt to explain and predict individual participation a wide variety of interventions for influenza, high blood pressure, smoking cessation, exercise, nutrition, and diabetes self-care.

The HBM has been criticized as having two significant limitations. First, the HBM is purely a psychological model, and it does not take into account cultural, environmental, or economic variables that may influence health behaviors. Second, the model does not address the impacts of social norms and peer influences on people's decisions regarding their health behaviors.

THEORY OF REASONED ACTION AND THEORY OF PLANNED BEHAVIOR

In the 1970s two social psychologists, Ajzen and Fishbein, proposed the Theory of Reasoned Action (TRA) (Shumaker et al., 2009). This model of behavior change has as its central premises:

- All of our behavior is under our control.
- Individuals act in their own best self-interest.
- A behavior is performed based on the individual's ***intention*** to perform or not perform the behavior.

Intention is the key component of this model. A person's intention to make a behavior change is based on a number of elements:

Behavioral intention: The individual's willingness to do or not to do a specific behavior.

Attitude toward a behavior: The individual's appraisal of the behavior as a good thing to do or a bad thing to do.

Belief about the behavior: The individual's evaluation as to whether the behavior will help him or her reach a goal.

Evaluation of consequences: The attempt to anticipate if the consequences of performing the behavior will be desirable.

Subjective norm: The consideration that the behavior is good or bad in the eyes or others.

Normative belief: What is the individual's estimation of what others may think about the behavior?

Motivation or intention to comply: How important is it for me to do what others think I should do?

The Theory of Planned Behavior (TPB) is an extension of TRA, which adds the element of **perceived control**. It is essentially whether the person thinks that taking up the new behavior will be easy or hard to achieve. Perceived Control is on a continuum from no control to complete control. The TPB asserts that attitude, subjective norm, and perceived control are all factors that combine to determine the level of effort (or motivation) that one has for accomplishing a goal. For example, Bob wanted to run in a marathon. To achieve this goal according to TPB, he would first need to evaluate the behavior of training as a positive one (attitude). Next, he would need to believe that training behavior was seen by others as an important or acceptable (social norm), and that it was within his control to engage in a training regimen (perceived control).

TRANSTHEORETICAL MODEL

Prochaska and DiClemente developed the Transtheoretical Model (TM) of behavior change in the late 1970s and early 1980s as a model of intentional behavior change (Prochaska, Norcross, & DiClemente, 1994). Originally used to define changes in addictive behavior, particularly smoking cessation, it has been applied to the adoption of positive health behaviors (Prochaska et al., 1994). The TM is sometimes referred to as the *Stages of Change* model, because it has established five distinct stages in the change process: precontemplation, contemplation, preparation, action, and maintenance. These stages roughly represent the "readiness" of an individual to make a change.

Transtheoretical Stages of Change

- **Precontemplation** represents a stage at which the client is not aware of the need or has no significant intention to make a behavioral change.
  - Client: I know smoking is supposed to be bad for you but I feel great.
- **Contemplation** represents the point at which a client is seriously considering making a change but as of yet has not committed to action.
  - Client: I know I should quit smoking—it is really bad for me, but I am not sure how to do it. I hear it is pretty tough to stop.
- **Preparation** represents a stage where the client may make small behavioral attempts to change a behavior.
  - Client: I know I need to quit. I will call and find out if I am eligible for a smoking cessation class.
- **Action stage** is when clients actually engage in a specific behavior to produce a desired lifestyle outcome.

  - Client: I went to the smoking cessation class and I feel pretty good about it.
- **Maintenance** is the last stage and is characterized by efforts of the client to avoid relapse.
  - I have stopped smoking for two weeks now but I still want a cigarette when I get stressed. I need to do my meditation when I first start to feel stressed out.

In addition to dividing the change process into stages, the Transtheoretical Model also goes one step further by also providing suggestions for specific interventions paired with each stage of change. The effectiveness of the approach is not only on assessing the clients' readiness to change with regard to a specific health behavior but also in pairing the therapeutic intervention to fit each client's stage of readiness. For example, a person at the action stage for cholesterol management who is trying to eat foods lower in fat might utilize a "stimulus control intervention" by removing high fat snack foods (cues) from the home so he or she is less tempted to eat them (Prochaska, DiClemente, & Norcross, 1992). One of the strengths of the Transtheoretical Model is that it acknowledges that not everyone is equally ready to change behavior. By developing an understanding of what stage a client may be in terms of readiness to change, a clinician can tailor appropriate interventions to help the client move to the next stage in the change process. It is easy to see then how this model would be useful in designing health programs targeted at particular stages of change or for employing interventions to assist individuals in moving successfully through the different stages.

SOCIAL COGNITIVE THEORY

The Social Cognitive Theory (Bandura, 1977) proposes that behavior change is influenced by a dynamic mutually influencing relationship between the environment, personal factors, and aspects of the behavior itself. The theory explains the change process through a number of "constructs." Those constructs which have applications in the change process are:

1. **Reinforcement:** Reinforcements are either positive or negative consequences of a behavior.
2. **Behavior capability:** For a change to take place, the individual must learn what is required in order to perform the change and how to do it. A person must have the correct skill set to make a behavioral change.
3. **Expectancies:** The value one places on the expected result. If the result is important to the person, the behavior change that will yield the result is more likely to happen.
4. **Self-efficacy:** Belief in one's ability to successfully change one's own behavior. Self-efficacy is connected with another construct called "outcome expectations." These are the benefits one expects to receive by changing one's behavior.
5. **Reciprocal determinism:** The dynamic relationship between the individual and the environment. The actions of the individual may change the environment, and the environment influences the actions of the individual.

Social Cognitive Theory helps explain the complex relationships between the individual and his or her environment, how actions and conditions reinforce or discourage change, and the importance of believing in and knowing how to change. One technique that a wellness counselor may apply in working with a client that is based in social learning theory is called self-efficacy enhancement. **Self-efficacy enhancement** can be defined as the strengthening an individual's confidence in his or her ability to perform a health behavior. For example: A client, Susan, states that her family doctor is concerned about her health. She knows that the most significant thing she can do to impact her health issues is lose 50 pounds of weight that she has put on over the past two years. Susan also goes on to say exactly how she would go about losing the weight and details a very realistic program of nutrition and exercise. Finally, she states that despite knowing what to do, she will fail because losing weight in the past has "never just worked out." This client has all of the intellectual knowledge she needs but is being held back by her belief that she is incapable (low self-efficacy).

The counselor and client decide that helping the client enhance her self-efficacy is an important goal of therapy. The counselor may employ a number of techniques to help the client such as helping to set very small achievable goals, providing a similar successful model, and being verbally persuasive.

The counselor asked Susan to attend a weekly weight loss support group. The counselor is hoping that by observing others like her accomplishing reasonable goals, she will come to believe that she can also achieve. In fact, with a little encouragement from the group, Susan decided to give her nutrition and exercise program a two-week trial.

A client's perceived self-efficacy is often related to their evaluations of past performances of a behavior. If a client has failed in achieving a behavioral goal, he or she will evaluate their competency as low. The counselor can help the client to set small, more reasonably achievable goals at first, so that the client may experience success. The client's self-efficacy will increase as he or she has successive positive experiences in relation to the behavior. Rather than setting the bar so high (I must lose 50 pounds), the counselor helps Susan to break down the long-term goal into a smaller, more manageable one, that of losing 2 pounds a week. Interestingly, Susan is able to lose 2.5 pounds in two weeks. She tells the counselor that she feels encouraged. Early successes help the client experience positive reinforcement, which will help increase her self-efficacy.

The counselor and the support group make a point of regularly providing Susan with persuasive and encouraging messages. The counselor states, "Way to go, see, you can do it! Keep up the good work." Such messages, especially given by those to whom a client attributes expert power and holds in positive regard, can be powerfully reinforcing.

ADHERENCE

The change models that have been illustrated in this chapter show that it can take a considerable amount of effort, strategy, planning, and commitment for a person to make a successful healthy behavior change. Making that healthy change last over a substantial period of time seems to be even harder for many people. Each year, for example, the same pattern repeats itself in gyms and work-out facilities all over the country. In January many people make resolutions to "get into the gym and exercise." In fact, January is the month when many gyms sell the most memberships. People start off well intentioned and begin to go and exercise; they actually make a positive behavior change. Unfortunately, by March or April most of the exercisers are no longer exercising at the gym—the behavior change did not last. Understanding what is behind this phenomenon is a major focus of research in the area of prevention and public health. The question of "How do we get people to adhere to a healthy behavior change over time?" has become a critical one.

COUNSELING MODEL FOR POSITIVE BEHAVIORAL CHANGE

This section of this chapter presents a practical model for behavior change developed for counselors. The model is intended as a guide for counselors to structure a helping intervention for clients wishing to make positive behavior changes. The model is a hybridized model for behavioral change and draws on a wide variety of my own learning over 20 years of providing therapy, supervising, and teaching counseling. The model is eclectic and incorporates many approaches to working with clients.

Background

Two main sources are strongly credited as influential to my thinking about the model. The first main source is a model for behavioral adjustment presented by Creer in his book entitled *Psychology of Adjustment: An Applied Approach* (1996). In his book, Thomas Creer lays out a six-step model for behavior change which includes: goal selection, information collection, information processing and evaluation, decision-making, action, and self-reaction (Creer, 1996). Creer's model emphasizes the use self-monitoring behavioral therapy techniques provide for achieving change.

The **Counseling Model for Positive Behavioral Change (CM-PBC)** is similar to Creer's model in that it is a stage model that lays out a structured process for working with a client to achieve a desired change. Also, as Creer's model does, the CM-PBC places emphasis on the need to assess a baseline for a behavior to be able to measure positive progress in making changes in the behavior. CM-PBC, however, significantly modifies the stages in the Creer model in several ways to reflect the nature of a counselor-client therapy relationship as opposed to a self-management process. Further, the stages are expanded to include a wider consideration of counseling therapy approaches.

One of these therapy approaches is the second main source for the CM-PBC model. It is the REPLAN common (sometimes called curative) factors based therapy model outlined by Mark Young in his book, *Learning the Art of Helping: Building Blocks and Techniques* (2008). REPLAN is an acronym for the essential factors that are believed to be necessary in therapy in order to promote positive outcomes (Young, 2008). These common factors are presented briefly below with a short description of the counselor's role with regard to each therapy.

REPLAN Curative Factors

RELATIONSHIP The counseling relationship has been researched and found to be a critical component of successful therapy (Young, 2008). A well-managed relationship between the counselor and client strongly influences the likelihood of a desired outcome in therapy. The counselor must continuously attend to the dynamics of the therapeutic alliance. Therapy, one of my mentors once told me, is a process of hugging (supporting the client) and kicking (challenging the client to work on goals). Counselors want to monitor support and challenge so that they are providing a safe and helpful therapy experience for clients. Using active empathic listening skills and providing accurate genuine feedback are two ways to help build the therapy relationship.

EFFICACY AND SELF-ESTEEM Self-esteem or having a generally positive regard for oneself is an important aspect of good mental health. Self-efficacy is a more focused term than self-esteem and may be defined as the client's beliefs concerning his or her competency to perform a behavior. When attempting to engage a client in the change process it is important for the client to believe that he or she is competent and capable of making a desired change. The counselor works with the client to increase his or her sense of self-efficacy by using a number of techniques: setting the client up for success by creating achievable goals, having the client acknowledge successes, teaching the client to make positive self-affirmations, having the client identify related or transferable skills, and teaching the client how to refute negative self-attributions.

PRACTICE NEW BEHAVIORS Clients must practice and rehearse new behaviors to make them habitual. Counselors can provide exercises and opportunities for clients to practice and receive feedback about their performance of a desired behavior. Adopting a new behavior can be accomplished in a graded method moving from imaginal rehearsal to role-playing to actual in vivo practice. Counseling groups are excellent places to practice new behaviors. Group members can model behaviors for the client, and provide encouragement and supportive feedback.

LOWER AND RAISE EMOTIONAL AROUSAL Optimal learning of a new behavior may be interfered with when a client is too anxious or depressed. It is simply hard learning new information when you have trouble focusing your attention or are preoccupied with your own feelings. Helping clients learn to modulate their levels of emotional arousal may be necessary to improve the ability of the client to adopt a new behavior. There are many techniques that can help a client lower emotional arousal, such as relaxation imagery, progressive muscle relaxation, mediation, and breath training. Conversely, techniques such as use of the creative arts, confrontation, humor, and role-plays can help promote emotional arousal, interest, and motivation by clients.

ACTIVATE EXPECTATIONS AND MOTIVATION Expectancy beliefs that a client holds concerning the outcome or benefit of engaging in a new behavior have been shown to be powerful predictors of both the initial adoption and the adherence to a behavior change. The counselor works with the client to amplify his or her positive expectations and ameliorate pessimism. One way that counselors can help is to provide consistent encouragement for client effort. Encouragement is more than just providing praise or positive reinforcement for a client. It involves helping the client to develop an internal self-image that is independent, positive, and competent.

NEW LEARNING EXPERIENCES AND CHANGING PERCEPTIONS Clients frequently need to learn a new way of "doing" or different ways of "thinking about" a behavior or themselves before making a substantial change. Clients may simply not have the skills, insight, or knowledge to successfully navigate the change process. The counselor can help the client overcome deficits by providing information, instruction, training, and consultation. Therapists have many tools at their disposal to help clients learn new skills. Among these are providing pamphlets, brochures, reports, or articles, bibliotherapy, assigning research homework (in the library or on the Internet), direct instruction, and modeling. Just as skill deficits may hold a client back from making a positive change so can cognitive processes such as self-defeating thoughts, faulty assumptions, and inaccurate perceptions. Helping clients to alter cognitive processes that interfere with achieving a desired behavior change can pave the way to success for clients. There are many therapy techniques that can be used by a counselor to help a client look at things in a new way: providing interpretations; teaching meta-models (ways of thinking); using humor, metaphors, and reframing; and refuting negative or illogical thoughts.

The task for the counselor when using the REPLAN model is to provide therapy that enhances the presence and effectiveness of the common factors. The REPLAN model can be called systematically eclectic and transtheoretical, in that while it provides a rationale for the selection of techniques that a counselor may use (i.e., the promotion of a specific common factor), the counselor is free to draw on techniques from a wide variety of counseling therapeutic approaches to assist in accomplishing this task.

Description of CM-PBC

The **Counseling Model for Positive Behavioral Change** is different from most health change models in that it is specifically for use by trained mental health counselors. Counselors will need to have achieved some level of expertise and be well versed in a variety of theoretical approaches and corresponding techniques to apply the CM-PBC. The model uses REPLAN, a systematic eclectic therapy approach developed by Young as the context for delivery of a behavior change process. CM-PBC can be thought of as a subprocess of the REPLAN common factors approach to therapy. It is a behavior change model intended to be delivered within the context of a common factors approach to therapy. The REPLAN common factors are used to provide a guide to the counselor for the focus and qualities of therapy for facilitating a specific behavior change process. Unlike many of the behavior change models illustrated in this chapter that were developed in a medical or public healthcare context, CM-PBC is specifically intended for use by trained counselors.

The Counseling Model for Positive Behavioral Change consists of six stages and outlines several tasks for the counselor and client to implement at each stage. The stages of the model are Determine Readiness, Develop Goals, Monitor Initial Performance, Refine Goals and Commit, Performance, and Persistence (see Figure 4.3). Each stage has one or more corresponding common factors to which the counselor may attend while helping the client navigate the change

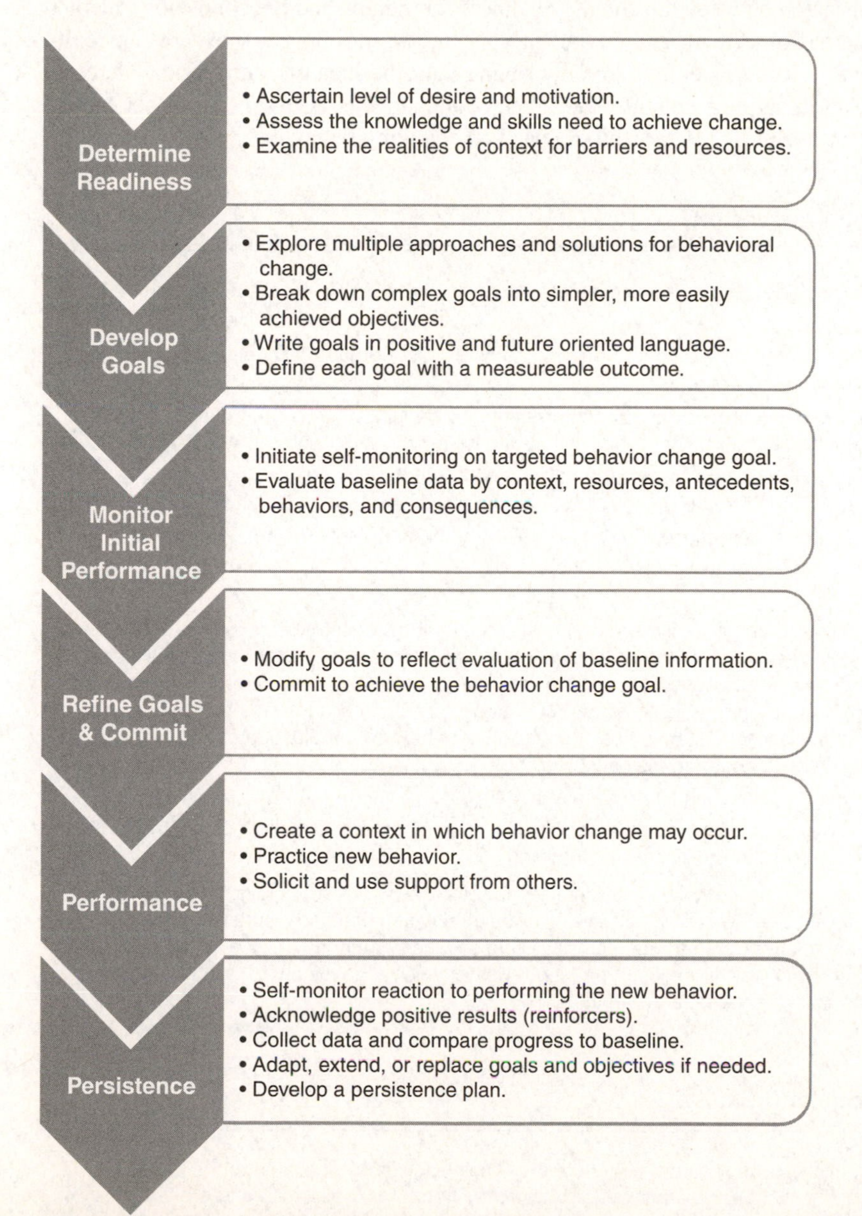

FIGURE 4.3 Counseling Model for Positive Behavior Change

process. Each of these stages and subtasks is discussed in more detail below. A table is provided for each subtask that suggests the purpose for the task, related common factors for the therapist to monitor, and ideas for possible approaches to use when working with a client. Finally, each table contains an "Important Question" for the counselor to consider for each task and an example of why the task may be important to consider when working with a client.

STAGE 1: DETERMINE READINESS It is a fact that many clients drop out of counseling after just one session. There are many possible reasons for this phenomenon but one of them may be that there exists a mismatch between the client's readiness for therapy and the counselor's method of engaging the client. Sometimes clients are only "window shopping"; they are not really invested in being our customers yet and are only toying with the idea of counseling. Therefore one of the critical tasks in helping a client make a behavior change is assessing his or her current ability to engage in a counseling relationship focused on changing behavior.

Ascertain Level of Desire and Motivation.

Purpose	Assess if client is able to engage in a counseling relationship with a likelihood of successful outcome.
Common Factors	**Relationship:** Relate to the client using active listening skills in order to engage the client in the counseling process. **Efficacy and Self-Esteem:** Build client self-esteem by communicating to him or her that it takes initiative and effort to consider making a behavior change. **Activate Expectations and Motivation:** Communicate to the client that many people are successful at making behavior changes when they engage in a counseling relationship. **Lower and Raise Emotional Arousal:** Monitor to see if client is able to participate in counseling. If client is severely anxious or depressed the initial focus may be on helping stabilize mood.
Approach	• Counselors may use the Transtheoretical Stages of Change Model to assess a client's readiness to engage in a behavior change. Staging will allow the counselor to intervene at a level that is appropriate for the client's ability to engage in behavior change. • Approach is based on the client's stage. For example: one approach to helping a client who is at the contemplation stage might be to engage him or her in a reevaluation of why he or she first thought about adopting the new behavior.
Important Questions	Why is the client seeking help now? Is she or he under some sort of duress (medical, legal, relational)? What factors have come together to influence the client to make a change now? Is the client ready and able to engage in counseling?
Example	Counselors sometimes are willing to try interventions for the purpose of helping a client engage in the therapy process because we believe it will be of benefit. These interventions will be more successful if they are tailored to the clients ability to engage in counseling. Vic was a young man in his early 20s who was having heart problems. He was referred to me by his family doctor to discuss his smoking, exercise, and eating behavior.

Assess the Client's Knowledge and Skills.

Purpose	Gather information about clients' current level of knowledge and skill related to the behavior change. It is important not to "put the cart before the horse" or to set goals that a client does not have the skill set to achieve.

Common Factors	**Relationship:** Build rapport with client by using active listening, showing respect, and being genuine. **New Learning:** Counselors may need to educate the client about the necessary skills or steps needed to achieve a goal.
Approach	• Assessment: Many types of assessment may be used from interviews with open ended questions, reviewing past records, formal tests, or direct observations.
Important Questions	What skills, strengths, or assets does the client bring to counseling? What are the deficits with which the client will need help?
Example	A number of clients that I have worked with come to counseling with unrealistic goals because they do not know the steps entailed in achieving them. For example, clients have told me that they want to go to college and have professional careers when they do not yet have a high school diploma. The goal of going to college is not a bad one, only that in order to achieve it the client may want to first set the goal of getting a General Equivalency Diploma (GED).

Examine the Realities of Environmental Context for Barriers and Resources.

Purpose	Develop understanding of the context in which the client lives, including the potential resources and the barriers. Context includes examining the client's social relationships, institutions, culture, and socioeconomic status.
Common Factors	Relationship: Build relationship by listening to clients, being respectful of their living situation, cultural background, and socioeconomic status. New Learning: Provide information to clients on how barriers may have prevented them from achieving change or how resources may be utilized to their benefit.
Approach	• Counselors can help clients to set appropriate goals by realistically aiding them in appraising environmental barriers and resources. • Help clients identify resources in their environment.
Important Questions	What are the resource limitations or barriers that the client may have to overcome in order to achieve the change?
Example	It is easy for a counselor to say to a client: "You should do this or that." But only the client really understands his or her life situation. It is not realistic to tell clients to get a personal trainer or go to a gym if they do not have the resources such as time, transportation, access, and money to do so. It is also important to assess the relationships of the client. I had a married female client tell me that she could not go to the gym and exercise because her husband would become jealous and accuse her of cheating on him.

STAGE 2: DEVELOP GOALS Helping clients to establish realistic and achievable goals that will build self-efficacy is an important skill of wellness counseling.

Explore Multiple Approaches and Solutions for Behavioral Change.

Purpose	Counselors can help by assisting clients to identify transferrable past methods for achieving success or generating new methods for achieving their goals.
Common Factors	**Relationship:** Adopt a nonjudgmental stance. Allow clients to express all their ideas without evaluation. **New Learning:** Provide information on a number of ways a change can be achieved.

Efficacy and Self-Esteem: Build efficacy and self-esteem by showing clients they are capable of generating creative ideas.

Activate Expectations and Motivation: Increase client expectations of success by showing them that they have not exhausted all the possibilities for achieving their goal. Give examples of clients or others who have achieved similar goals in the past.

Approach

- Use Brief Therapy questions to focus the client on developing a positive solution to making the behavior change.
- Encourage creative approaches or solutions to making a change.
- Ask clients how they have been successful in the past.
- Creative arts such as drawing or painting can help clients generate novel ideas.

Important Questions What has been tried in the past? What has worked in the past?

Example Clients have coped with many situations in their lives. What healthy strategies have they employed that are already part of their skill set? Sometimes clients have the right ideas but just need support in implementing a plan. A female client who was the mother of three children and also working full time as a nurse came to counseling because she was stressed and wanted to implement some healthy eating and exercise behavior changes. She knew what she needed to do and was perfectly able to state her goals in very reasonable terms, yet she had not had success in implementing her plan. The client stated that she was discouraged because given her parental responsibilities and work schedule it was "impossible" to get to the gym and exercise. Together we brainstormed about the idea of exercise and fitness and after some time decided that it did not necessarily have to take place at a gym. Once freed from the constraints of place she was able to come up with several ways she could exercise at home with her children.

Break Down Complex Goals Into Simpler, More Easily Achieved Objectives.

Purpose Create a success experience early on for clients. The counselor wants to build the clients' sense of self-efficacy so that they adhere to the change process.

Common Factors

Relationship: Build a collaborative relationship with the client by negotiating goals with the client.

Efficacy and Self-Esteem: Build self-efficacy by making sure that goals are achievable and appropriate for clients' skill level.

Activate Expectations and Motivation: Monitor client's belief that he or she will achieve the goal.

New Learning: Explain the process of goal setting and engage the client in the process. Make sure that the client understands the goals and how to perform his or her target behaviors.

Approach

- Provide positive encouragement.
- Reinforce thoughts of competence and refute thoughts of incompetence.
- Assure the client that achieving the behavior change will be more likely with a well thought out plan.

Important Questions What are the resource limitations or barriers that the client may have to overcome to achieve the change?

Example Clients are more likely to "stick with it" if they believe they are making progress. Sometimes when a client is depressed I suggest we make a goal that he or she start walking outside for a period of time each day. Some clients will say that they do not have the energy to walk, and others will set high goals saying that they intend to start walking for hours each day. I tell the client that perhaps it would be better for them to start out with a reduced amount of walking time at first—5 minutes out and 5 minutes back. The objective is to make the goal almost ridiculously achievable so that the client will actually do it and can get credit for being successful. Often the client will report that once they got outside and started walking they walked for longer than the10 minutes. We can always increase the duration of the walking goal once we have the client successfully engaging in the behavior.

Write Goals in Positive and Future-oriented Language.

Purpose

Place emphasis on learning and performing a positive behavior, not eliminating a negative one.

Common Factors

Relationship: Encourage and support client to engage in positive view of change.

Efficacy and Self-Esteem: Increase the client's sense of self-efficacy by allowing him or her to generate positive solutions to problem statements.

Activate Expectations and Motivation: Create hope by focusing the client on future achievement and not dwelling on past failures.

Approach

- Help clients reframe problems into goals that focus on future solutions.
- Focus on what the client will do, not what he or she will not do.
- Amplify the positive behavior changes by drawing attention to them.
- Encourage positive self-talk.

Important Questions

What will the client be doing when he or she is performing the positive change?

Example

When working with a client to develop goals we state the goals using positive and committed language such as "Client will..." as opposed to "Client will not." The emphasis for goals is placed on what the client can do. Instead of saying: "The client will stop staying up all night" a better goal would be to say: "The client will increase sleep time by going to bed at 11:00 p.m. on work nights."

Define Each Goal with a Measurable Outcome.

Purpose

To monitor and assess client progress on achieving a goal. To provide tangible evidence to the client of his or her progress.

Common Factors

Efficacy and Self-Esteem: Show the client evidence of his or her success in the form of a graph or chart.

Activate Expectations and Motivation: Share with the client that measuring his or her progress will increase the chances of achieving his or her goal.

Approach

- Data for measuring progress can be derived from many different sources, including client self-rating or report, formal instruments, observations, counselor ratings. Make progress on the goal observable on a chart or graph.
- Build the client's investment in the behavior change by helping him or her see even small amounts of progress made.

Important Questions

How will we know if we are moving in the right direction?

Example

Imagine that a client has a goal of becoming more self-confident with performing a new behavior. The counselor can simply ask the client to rate on a scale of 1 to 10 how confident he or she feels about engaging in the behavior change each session (1 being "not confident at all" and 10 being "very confident"). In conjunction with the client's self-ratings the counselor can administer the General Self-Efficacy Scale (GSE) (Schwarzer and Jerusalem, 1995), a 10 item instrument for measuring self-efficacy, at the end of each session. Graph the client's self-ratings and instrument results over the course of counseling to get a reading on the client's level of self-efficacy (http://userpage.fu-berlin.de/~health/selfscal.htm).

STAGE 3: MONITOR INITIAL PERFORMANCE

Begin Initial Performance.

Purpose

To experiment with doing the new behavior.

Common Factors

Relationship: Build trust with the client by not giving him or her an assignment or homework that you do not think the client will achieve. The counselor may wish to express empathy for the client concerning the difficulty with learning and implementing a new behavior. Self-disclosure by the counselor concerning a time when the counselor had to work to learn a new skill will build relationship by humanizing the counselor.

Efficacy and Self-Esteem: Increase the client's sense of self-efficacy by rewarding the client for attempts made to act on the behavior.

New Learning: The counselor may want to model the behavior or role play with the client to make sure he or she has a clear understanding of what to do.

Lower and Raise Emotional Arousal: Lower client's initial anxiety about performing at a high level of skill.

Approach

- Use imagery to have the client form a conceptualization of what he or she will look like when performing the behavior.
- Propose to the client that you would like him or her to experiment with you by "trying on" the new behavior, or "acting as if", he or she has already mastered his or her goal.
- Make sure to check that the client understands what is being asked of him or her. Clients who understand our communications are more apt to comply with them.

Important Question

Can the client mentally form an image of himself or herself performing the behavior? Can the client perform the behavior?

Example

It is one thing to "talk about" performing a new behavior and another to actually "do it." One example is to lower the anxiety of the client's need to "be instantly good" at a new behavior by proposing an experiment or trial period in which it is not expected that he or she will perform at a high level. Another example is to have clients mentally prepare for the behavior by using imagery. I frequently ask clients to imagine themselves in a situation that will allow them to act. The counselor can process and develop solutions with the client for any environmental aspects and internal feelings that are barriers to the behavior.

Initiate Monitoring on Targeted Behavior Change Goal.

Purpose

Establish a baseline for the client's ability to perform the behavior.

Common Factors

New Learning: Teach the client how to gather data on his or her goals between counseling sessions.

Approach

- Many methods can be used to gather data about client's performance. These may include formal assessment instruments, self-reports or ratings, and even direct observations.
- Be creative and flexible with how to gather the information you need to see how the client is performing.

Important Question

Where we starting from or what are the baseline of the behaviors? Are we collecting data in a way that is simple and logical to the client?

Example

The counselor can help the client by supplying a log or form for recording goal data. Simple calendar pages or having the client make notations in their daybook may suffice. *The important thing is to get the data.* Counselors need to be flexible in how to get this information. For example: Bill was a busy executive who simply would forget to keep a log of his goal activity. He simply was not accustomed to writing down things. However, he was constantly on his cell phone. I asked him to call his data into my voicemail which he subsequently did with perfect compliance.

Evaluate Baseline Data by Context, Antecedents, and Consequences.

Purpose	Determine what is helping or hurting the client in performing the behavior.
Common Factors	**New Learning:** Assist the client by having him or her identify the specific circumstances in which he or she is being successful with the behavior.
Approach	• Help the client identify antecedents (prompts, stimulus) and consequences (positive rewards) that promote the successful performance of the behavior. These may be external environmental context in nature or internal thoughts or emotional states of the client. • Get down to the details: Where, when, and with what results did the client perform?
Important Question	To what extent are we hitting our target? What internal or external conditions need to be modified to help increase the likelihood of compliance? Does the client need some resource or skill to help him or her perform the behavior?
Example	Balance in Life is a six-week course I teach to help community members improve their wellness. At the end of each week's lesson the participants and I learn a new relaxation skill starting with Breathing Techniques. I used to just assign the homework of practicing breathing (deep, even, and slow) for three minutes each day until the next class. Almost no one was compliant with this task and the baseline performance was zero. Everyone said that they would have done the breathing but they just did not think about it during their busy workday. It seemed that some sort of antecedent stimulus was needed to help them to remember to practice. I asked the class to come up with some ideas on how they could be prompted to remember to practice for the next week. Many ideas were generated from receiving a reminder e-mail, to linking breathing to a time of day, or a regular work habit like going to the photocopier. The next week in class 100% of the class reported that they had practiced their relaxation breathing. Now when I assign the breathing homework a sticky red dot is given to each student. The students then place the dots on their watches or cell phones. Each time the students see the dot they are reminded about practicing their breathing. Providing an antecedent stimulus to practice has significantly increased the practice by the students. Although many behaviors are much more complicated than breathing practice, it is important to take the time to help the client identify what comes before and after performing the target behavior. Manipulating these variables can help the client increase his or her compliance.

STAGE 4: REFINE GOALS AND COMMIT Once knowledge of the client's ability to engage in the behavior change has been determined, then it is important to refine the goals to accurately represent the next step for the change process. It is also important to engage the client to make a commitment to achieve them.

Modify Goals to Reflect Evaluation of Baseline Information.

Purpose	Use data about initial performance to change, target a more specific outcome, or modify goals to increase client's ability to achieve.
Common Factors	**Relationship:** Build relationship by empathetically and respectfully supporting the client's attempts to try the new change. **New Learning:** Illuminate the process and purpose of modifying or developing new goals and objectives to the client. Involve the client in generating solutions to increase compliance.
Approach	• Counselors need to be flexible and modify goals if they are not helping the client to achieve. • If the intervention is not working try something different—if it is working do more of it.
Important Question	Do we need to modify our goals, interventions, or expectations to help the client achieve? What can we do to promote increased successful performance of the behavior?

Example

Once a client demonstrates that he or she can perform a goal behavior, the client may still need to have goals adjusted to increase the likelihood of further performance, improve the quality of performance, or assist in generalization. For example, initially I was working with a client on a goal of becoming more expressive and assertive with her needs and wants to others. In sessions we began by learning about how to be consistently assertive without becoming aggressive and also practicing through some role play activities. A few weeks later the client indicated to me that she was able to be appropriately assertive with her coworkers. She was very happy about this but was still upset that she was "completely passive" when responding to the demands of her parents and sisters. When I asked her what made it more difficult to be assertive with her family she stated, "Well I love them and do not want them to be mad with me and besides I am just the baby of the family." As a result the client and I changed the goal; the focus was changed from practicing assertion (a skill she already had achieved) to examining her pattern of thoughts about how being assertive with her family would lead to family conflict or her being dismissed or discounted. It turned out that these thoughts actually led her to experience a fair amount of anxiety and were holding her back from her goal. It was helpful to "step back" and explore the cognitive messages the client was giving herself and work on reframing them rather than just insist that she be more assertive with her family. The emotional ties to her family did make performing the behavior with them more challenging. It is important for the therapist to be able to be flexible. Too often, counselors blame clients for not performing when often I believe we have not adapted our methods (goals or interventions) to provide what the client needs to succeed.

Commit to Achieve the Behavior Change Goal.

Purpose

Counseling will be more successful when clients believe that they are acting in their own positive self-interest.

Common Factors

Activate Expectations and Motivation: Tell the client that he or she is increasing the likelihood of his or her success by making a public commitment to achieve his or her goals.

Approach

- Help by having clients tell you again in their own words why the behavior change is important to them and how they will benefit from achieving it.
- Use a behavioral contract to put in writing the clients' commitment to change.
- Encourage the clients to make public their intentions to make the change.

Important Question

Is the client committed? What is interfering with the client's ability to commit to the goal?

Example

Nichol was a client that was full of good intentions but low on follow through. She would tell me that she was going to enroll in the one course she needed to finish her master's degree, but several semesters passed and she never acted. One day I asked her about her level of commitment to the goal and if it was still important to her. She stated: "I really do want and need to enroll because getting my master's will give me an instant raise at work but I get busy at work and home and just put it off. I really am letting myself down and feel bad about it but at least I am not disappointing anyone." I confronted Nichol and told her that perhaps she was disappointing someone, herself. I also asked Nichol if she was ready and willing to make a public commitment to her goal of enrolling in the course for the next semester. She stated that she was willing to do so. Together we wrote an e-mail to her grandmother, parents, housemates, myself, and her pastor about her goal and the reasons she needed to achieve it and asking for their support. The purpose of this e-mail was two-fold. First, it raised the stakes for Nichol for not acting on the goal by making her intentions public. Everyone would know if she did or did not pursue the goal, and not disappointing others was important to her. Second, the e-mails allowed Nichol to engage social support from significant others. Two weeks later Nichol called and told me that she had arranged her schedule and enrolled in the course. She said she just had to get going on enrolling because everyone was asking her if she had enrolled and was offering their help and encouragement. Nichol stated a significant insight that she had during the week: "as it turns out I was disappointing my family and friends by not finishing my degree and that no matter what, I am worth doing it for myself."

STAGE 5: PERFORMANCE At some point the client must actually attempt the behavior change. Talking about a behavior change and planning for one is not the same as performing the behavior.

Create a Context in Which Behavior Change May Occur.

Purpose

Ensure that the environment is as conducive as possible for the behavior to be performed.

Common Factors

New Learning: Clients may need to learn how to structure their environment to help them make a behavior change. Time management, goal setting, problem solving, or other skills may be needed.

Approach

- Counselors need to help clients learn to surround themselves with people, places, and things that are supportive of the goals they are trying to achieve.
- Help the clients identify ways that they can physically modify their environment by removing distractions and adding prompts or reinforcements.
- Make sure the clients are allowing time in their schedule to engage in the new behavior.
- Counselors may have to advocate for opportunities or access for their clients with government agencies or other institutions.

Important Question

What environmental factors (people, places, things, time) will support the clients in engaging in the behavior?

Example

Alan was a severely obese man in his mid 40s. He was referred by his primary care doctor who was concerned about Alan's hypertension and diabetes. In our first session he stated that he wanted help on how to improve his self-image, and on how to lose weight. I told Alan that I would not specifically work with him on "losing weight" but that I would work with him on learning new behaviors that he could incorporate into his lifestyle that would help him be more active and eat healthier. After working with Alan for a while, he let me know that he was bullied as a child for being "uncoordinated" and this was one of the reasons he did not like to go exercise "in public" despite the fact he was already paying for a gym membership.

I called Mike, a personal trainer at the gym, and asked if he would be willing to work with Alan when the gym was least crowded. I went with Alan to the gym to meet Mike, which helped Alan to feel more comfortable. Mike was very helpful setting up a very gradual and manageable exercise program for Alan at times when the gym was not crowded or even after closing time. I also had Alan get a consult with a nutritionist concerning a diet that would not just limit calories but also took his diabetes into account and perhaps most importantly that he would actually cook and eat. Of course Alan and I explored a lot of issues that related to his self-image in our counseling sessions. Over the course of the next year Alan felt better, learned to eat better, exercised, and was able to have his hypertension and diabetes under control. Alan needed a special adaptation in the environment to get him going on his exercise behavior. I suppose we could have addressed the social embarrassment issues first and then encouraged exercise but this way he started realizing health benefits sooner rather than later.

Practice New Behavior.

Purpose

The more a behavior is performed the more likely it will become a habit for the client.

Common Factors

Relationship: Monitor clients' needs for support. Counselors may take on a teaching role to help clients engage and perfect their skill with the behavior.

Practice New Behavior: Create meaningful opportunities for clients to engage in the behavior with useful feedback.

Lower and Raise Emotional Arousal: Monitor clients' level of anxiety or other negative emotions that may impede their performance. Normalize clients' uncomfortable feelings.

Efficacy and Self-Esteem: Provide encouragement and recognize clients' progress (point out their successes). Build client confidence by having them demonstrate their ability.

Approach
- Help by providing opportunities in therapy to practice the behavior. Imaginal rehearsal, role-playing, and meaningful homework assignments can be used.
- Providing modeling, genuine feedback, and constructive assistance, can help clients shape their performance.
- Continue to collect data and monitor client progress. Share the data with clients.

Important Question Is the behavior becoming easier for the client to perform? Is the client performing the behavior enough for it to become a habit? What is the quality or skill level of the performance?

Example I am learning Tai Chi, a type of martial art that involves moving in a choreographed manner. My instructor "Benny" is very good and I am learning the moves pretty well. I thought about this and upon reflection realized that one of the reasons is that Benny gives us a lot of opportunity to practice each week. First he has us go through all of the moves we know from the past class three times. Then when he teaches us a new move he demonstrates it at least three times for us and then has us do the new move at least three times. Finally, Benny has us do all the moves we know including the new one three times before we end class. Whew! Practice does make it easier. Modeling new behavior for clients and letting them practice through multiple modalities also allows us to provide feedback to the clients concerning the quality of their performance.

Solicit and Use Support from Others.

Purpose Gain support from a social network for engaging in the behavior.

Common Factors

Efficacy and Self-Esteem: Clients may feel awkward or that they do not know how to ask others for help.

New Learning: Clients may need social skills training or just simply information on where to find support groups.

Activate Expectations and Motivation: Communicate to clients that they will be even more successful with supportive others pulling for them.

Approach
- Help clients to identify others who are actually and actively able to provide assistance, validation, and encouragement.
- Help clients to overcome issues that may impede their ability to take advantage of social supports.

Important Question How can others provide support and encouragement to the client?

Example Many of the men I work with are very reluctant to reach out and engage with others about mental or emotional issues. Perhaps this has to do with American social values about individual independence and the idea that masculinity is linked to emotional "toughness." Yet social support is definitely a factor for increasing the likelihood of achieving goals.

Counselors should always evaluate the social resources of the client. David was a 31-year-old man who also happened to be a police officer. He was experiencing significant depression and had recently increased his intake of alcohol. He told me that he knew that drinking was not the way to deal with life's problems and that is why he came to see me. One of the things that stood out for me about David was that other than his wife and one friend at work, he was very socially isolated. As part of his treatment I encouraged him to pursue ways to connect with other people. After a great deal of discussion and support, he joined a church softball team and made some friends. I was encouraged when I asked him how things were going and he stated that "I guess you are right. Having some buddies in my life really does help." "How?" I asked. He was able to tell me how having nonwork friends allowed him to help with his stress and see that he was not alone with his troubles. I told him that his insight was right on and that I hoped he would not allow himself to become isolated in the future. Helping clients to recruit supportive others or to engage with positive social networks can be a powerful aide for promoting behavior change. Sometimes marshaling the troops is a very good idea.

Self-monitor Reactions to Performing the New Behavior and Acknowledge Positive Results.

Purpose

Client gains awareness and ownership of the feelings and benefits associated with the behavior by keeping track of his or her own reactions.

Common Factors

Relationship: Listen to client and allow him or her to express emotions and thoughts concerning performing the behavior. Acknowledge the client's thoughts and feelings. Provide feedback on positive benefits of the behavior for the client, and do not allow him or her to minimize or dismiss the benefits.

Efficacy and Self-Esteem: Be aware that the client may feel awkward, angry, or embarrassed at not being perfect with his or her performance of the new behavior. Recognize that the client may need encouragement to continue to engage with the change.

Activate Expectations and Motivation: Communicate to the client that he or she can expect to become more comfortable the more he or she practices the behavior.

New Learning: Client may need information on how to cope with uncomfortable emotions when starting to engage in a significant change.

Approach

- Allow clients to express positive and negative thoughts and feelings concerning the new behavior.
- Help clients by making them aware of the success that they have achieved.
- Do not allow clients to minimize or dismiss achievements.

Important Question

Can the client recognize and internalize the benefits of engaging in the behavior?

Example

I often ask clients to track how they are feeling as a result of making a lifestyle change. Bonnie was in her late 70s, lived alone and had few friends. Related to one of her goals in counseling she decided to take a college course on creative writing at a local community college. I asked Bonnie to keep a journal of her thoughts and feelings concerning her experience with attending the course. After the first night of the course I had a session with Bonnie and asked how it went. She said that perhaps she was wrong about wanting to take the course and was thinking about dropping out. She told me that while she had expected to be the oldest person in the class; she had not expected to feel so awkward and "out of the loop" compared to the other students. In our session we explored the reasons that Bonnie had originally had for attending the class and these were still valid. We discussed that it was normal to feel awkward when engaging in new behavior and that there were valid reason she may feel that way. Finally, we discussed if she was willing to give up on her goal or did she want to continue and see if the feelings would change. She agreed to go back to the next class. Bonnie came to our next session beaming and handed me a brief essay paper with an "A" on it. The professor of the course had written a comment that it was obvious from her writing that Bonnie "had a lifetime of experience from upon which to draw for her creative writing." I said, "Wow! an 'A' and a great comment" and teased her by saying "do you plan to set the bar this high for the other students each week?" She stated that now she felt that maybe she had something unique to offer in the class and that made her feel happier. I told her that she had been brave to pursue her goal even despite her initial negative feelings. I also told her that I hoped in future she would not let first impressions or initial negative feelings dissuade her from her pursuits. Remember to encourage, support, and amplify the positives that the client can identify as resulting from the behavior change.

STAGE 6: PERSISTENCE Once the client is actually engaging in the behavior change on a consistent basis with a good level of skill the question becomes, "How do we help them to keep up the good work over a significant period of time so that they can reap the benefits?"

Develop a Persistence Plan.

Purpose

Prepare the client to continue the behavior when no longer in counseling.

Common Factors

Efficacy and Self-Esteem: Remind the client of his or her ability to make positive changes and provide encouragement to continue.

Practice New Behavior: Provide opportunity to anticipate barriers and practice coping skills.

New Learning: Teach client any skills he or she may need to increase likelihood of persistence.

Activate Expectations and Motivation: Communicate to client that you believe he or she is capable of persisting in the behavior. Elicit from client statements regarding all the benefits of persistence.

Approach

- Help clients develop a Persistence Plan.*
- Identify potential situations, conflicts, or circumstances that would interfere with sustaining the behavior. Generate ideas for coping with these barriers.
- Practice the skills for coping with potential barriers.

Important Question

What can I do to help the client persist with his or her new positive behavior?

Example

Many clients can make behavioral changes and execute them when they are getting assistance and support from a counselor. The real trick is for the client to keep up the positive behavior on an ongoing basis even when not in counseling. Nick came to see me after having an intense anxiety attach that he thought was a heart attack. He was a very successful business owner and worked very hard. Over the course of counseling he had made great strides with learning to lower his level of emotional stress. He had begun to meditate, exercise, and even was able to take a day off, trusting his employees to handle some responsibilities at his business. When it was time for treatment to draw to a close I asked Nick how he planned to sustain his new behaviors. He said, "I do not know. I really have not put much thought into it." I encouraged Nick to think about a "Persistence Plan" with contingencies should he begin to slip back into his old high-stress lifestyle. For example: What if things got busy at the office and demanded his attention? Would he skip his meditation, his physical exercise? If so, what would he do to get back on track and within what time period? I think working with clients on a plan of this nature is very important to their long-term success in sustaining a behavior. They need to know that it is just as much effort to keep up a positive behavior change as it is to adopt the change in the first place. Helping clients to anticipate barriers and how they will cope with them is a key strategy for promoting long-term change.

* A Persistence Plan is another name for a relapse prevention plan. The counselor helps the client put in writing goals and strategies for maintaining his or her positive behavior.

Summary

Behavioral change is very complex, with biological, psychological, and social variables that impact the likelihood of success. Counselors working with clients who are attempting to make significant behavioral changes need to be supportive and empathic regarding the level of difficulty that may be present for the client. Currently there is no one model that can capture all of the aspects of the change process. The models shared in this chapter are just examples of the attempts researchers are purposing to help explain the change process. Knowing about such models and using them in our work helps us to facilitate therapy that will assist clients succeed in their behavior change goals. In addition, counselors need to be aware of factors that can impede or facilitate long lasting adherence to a behavior change. In the next chapter we will see how to apply your new knowledge about behavior change models to help a client develop a plan for improving his or her lifestyle and wellness.

References

Bandura, A., & Adams, N. E. (1977). Analysis of self-efficacy theory of behavioral change. *Cognitive Therapy and Research, 1*(4), 287–310.

Creer, T. L. (1996). *Psychology of adjustment: An applied approach.* Upper Saddle River, NJ: Prentice Hall.

Prochaska, J. O., Norcross, J. C., & DiClemente, C. C. (1994). *Changing for good: The revolutionary program that explains the six stages of change and teaches you how to free yourself from bad habits* (1st ed.). New York: W. Morrow.

Prochaska, J. O., DiClemente, C. C., & Norcross, J. C. (1992). In search of how people change: Applications to addictive behaviors. *American Psychologist, 47*(9), 1102–1114.

Prochaska, J. O., Velicer, W. F., Rossi, J. S., Goldstein, M. G., Marcus, B. H., Rokowski, C. F. et al. (1994). Stages of change and decisional balance for 12 problem behaviors. *Health Psychology, 13*(1), 39–46.

Shumaker, S. A., Ockene, J. K., & Kristin A. Riekert. (2009). *The handbook of health behavior change.* New York: Springer.

Schwarzer, R., & Jerusalem, M. (1995). Generalized Self-Efficacy scale. In J. Weinman, S. Wright, & M. Johnston, *Measures in health psychology: A user's portfolio. Causal and control beliefs* (pp. 35–37). Windsor, UK: NFER-Nelson.

Young, M. E. (2008). *Learning the art of helping: Building blocks and techniques* (4th ed.). Upper Saddle River, NJ: Prentice Hall.

5 COMPLEMENTARY AND ALTERNATIVE TREATMENTS

Paul F. Granello

There are more things in heaven and earth, Horatio, than are dreamt of in your philosophy.

WILLIAM SHAKESPEARE, *HAMLET* ACT 1, SCENE 5, 159–167

According to a survey conducted more than 18 years ago by Dr. David Eisenberg and his associates (1993), 34% of the people surveyed had used at least one unconventional therapy in the past year. Most of the visits were for chronic conditions such as back pain, insomnia, and headaches. The number of visits by Americans to alternative health practitioners exceeded the number of visits to primary care physicians in 1990. Interestingly, most of these health expenditures were "out-of-pocket" as insurance companies did not reimburse for these services. In a 1991 *Time/CNN* poll, 62% of Americans who had never sought alternative therapy said they would do so if conventional medicine failed. Although the above data represent an early trend, this shift toward the use of alternative and complementary treatment methods is common practice today.

Americans are increasingly seeking alternatives to the traditional medical system (Micozzi, 2005). Complementary and alternative medicine (CAM) treatments are now being used by approximately 38.3% of adults and 11.8% of children (Barnes, Bloom, & Nahin, 2008). In response to this trend the federal government has established the **National Center for Complementary and Alternative Medicine (NCCAM)** as part of the National Institutes of Health. (See Figure 5.1 and Figure 5.2.)

A significant part of NCCAM's mission is to organize and define the world of CAM so that research may be conducted as to the efficacy of these approaches. Along those lines NCCAM has developed some useful basic standard definitions for CAM:

- **Complementary medicine** is used **together with** conventional medicine. An example of a complementary therapy is using aromatherapy, a therapy in which the scent of essential oils from flowers, herbs, and trees is inhaled to promote health and well-being to help lessen a patient's discomfort following surgery.
- **Alternative medicine** is used **in place of** conventional medicine. An example of an alternative therapy is using a special diet to treat cancer instead of undergoing surgery, radiation, or chemotherapy that has been recommended by a conventional doctor.

FIGURE 5.1 CAM Use by Race/Ethnicity among Adults (2007) *Source:* Barnes, Bloom, & Nahin, 2008

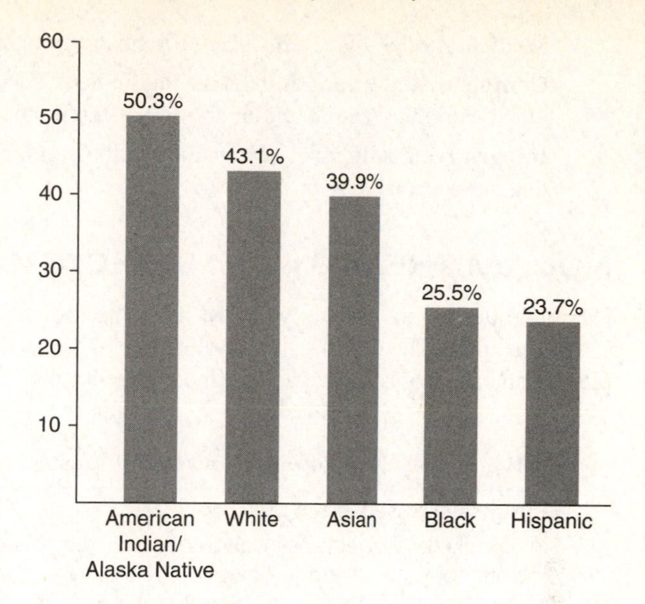

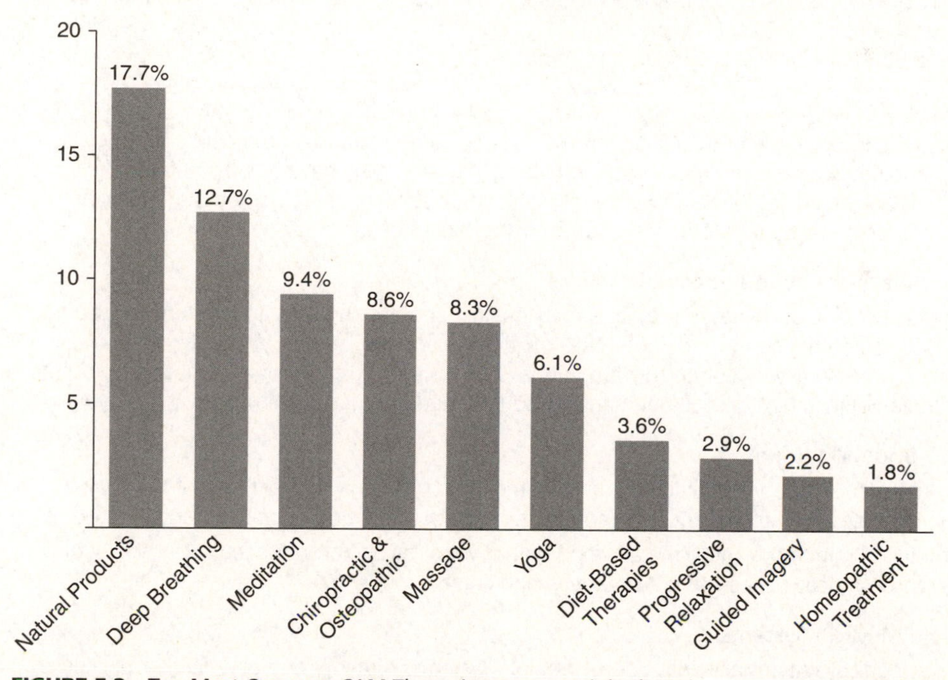

FIGURE 5.2 Ten Most Common CAM Therapies among Adults (2007) *Source:* Barnes, Bloom, & Nahin, 2008

Definitions for Approaches to Healthcare

Conventional medical model—may only deal with the body as a biochemical machine

Wellness counseling—may deal with all of the body, including the brain, consciousness, and essential personhood

Medical model—Western "scientific method" applied to healthcare

Complementary and alternative medicine (CAM)—often derived from indigenous cultures; examples: acupuncture, aboriginal ceremonies, "grandma's remedies"

Integrative healthcare—extensions of the combination of the medical model and CAM that are acceptable to both

NCCAM THERAPY CLASSIFICATIONS

Using the definitions above, NCCAM has gone further and created a classification system for CAM therapies. The classification system has five major categories for organizing CAM therapies. Each category is named and defined in the Table 5.1.

TABLE 5.1 CAM Categories and Definitions According to NCCAM

Biologically Based Practices

Biologically based practices involve adding dietary supplements, functional foods, and other products found in nature to one's diet. A dietary supplement is a product that contains vitamins, minerals, herbs or botanicals, amino acids, enzymes, probiotics, or other ingredients that supplement the diet. Examples of dietary supplements include vitamin B-12, St. John's wort (a botanical), and acidophilus (a probiotic).

Energy Medicine

Energy medicine uses energy fields with the intent to affect health. Some fields, such as magnetic fields, have been measured. Others, such as biofields, have not. Therapies involving biofields are based on the idea that people have a subtle form of energy; energy medicine practitioners believe that illness results from disturbances of these subtle energies.

Manipulative and Body-Based Practices

Manipulative and body-based practices focus mainly on the structures and systems of the body, including the bones and joints, the soft tissues, and the circulatory and lymphatic systems. Some practices come from traditional systems of medicine, such as those from China and India, while others, like spinal manipulation, were developed within the last 150 years.

Mind-Body Medicine

Mind-body medicine, which focuses on how the mind and body interact, uses a variety of techniques designed to enhance the mind's capacity to affect bodily function and symptoms. Examples of mind-body medicine are meditation, yoga, tai chi (pronounced "tie-chee"), qi gong (pronounced "chee-gung"), imagery, and creative outlets.

Whole Medical Systems

Whole medical systems are built upon complete systems of theory and practice. Often, these systems have evolved apart from, and earlier than, the standard medical approach used in the United States. Examples of whole medical systems that have developed in non-Western cultures include traditional Chinese medicine and Ayurvedic medicine. Examples of systems that have developed in Western cultures include homeopathic medicine and naturopathic medicine.

Source: Barnes P. M., Bloom B., & Nahin R. Complementary and alternative medicine use among adults and children: United States, 2007, December 2008, *CDC National Health Statistics Report #12*.

Each of the five broad area definitions can then be used to help classify the diverse world of CAM therapies. Table 5.2 takes each of the five CAM areas and provides some examples of CAM therapies that could be categorized under each area. However, the number and types of CAM therapies available is vast and increasing and a complete review is beyond

TABLE 5.2 Examples of CAM Therapies by CAM Category

CAM Category	Examples of CAM Therapies
Whole Medical Systems	• Ayurveda (Ancient "life-science" of India based on body types) • Traditional Chinese Medicine (TCM) • Homeopathy • Naturopathy • Traditional Indigenous Healers: Native American Shaman

Manipulative and Body-Based Practices	• Chelation Therapy (removal of toxins from the body by use of an attracting substance)
	• Diet-based Therapies
	  • Ornish (strict diet shown to improve cardiac health)
	  • Vegetarian (plant based diet with many positive health effects including longevity)
	• Dietary Supplements
	  • Megavitamin therapy
	  • Nonvitamin, nonmineral, natural products (e.g., herbs)
	• Folk Remedies (traditional culturally based remedies such as chicken soup for a cold)
	• Chiropractic Manipulation
	• Massage
	• Movement Therapies
	  • Alexander technique
	  • Dance Therapy
	  • Pilates
	  • Tai chi
	  • Yoga

Energy Medicine	• Bioelectromagnetic-based Therapies
	  • "Light" therapies
	  • Magnets (external biofield)
	• Biofield Therapies
	  • Qi Gong
	  • Reiki
	  • Therapeutic Touch

Mind-Body Medicine	• Art & Music Therapy • Biofeedback & Neurofeedback • Guided & Non-Directive Imagery • Hypnosis • Meditation

the scope of this chapter. For details concerning specific therapies visit the NCCAM Web site at http://nccam.nih.gov/ and also to read an excellent resource on the topic by Jodi Carlson entitled: *Complementary Therapies and Wellness: Practice Essentials for Holistic Health Care* (Prentice Hall, 2003).

If you are like most counselors you will not be familiar with many of the CAM therapies listed in Table 5.2. The next section provides brief definitions for many of these therapies. It should be noted that many of these therapies have not been validated as effective using rigorous scientific research studies. Visit the NCCAM Web site to get the latest information on the quality of research related to each therapy.

DEFINITIONS OF CAM THERAPIES

ACUPUNCTURE Acupuncture describes a family of procedures involving stimulation of anatomical points on the body by a variety of techniques. American practices of acupuncture incorporate medical traditions from China, Japan, Korea, and other countries. The acupuncture technique that has been most studied scientifically involves penetrating the skin with thin, solid, metallic needles that are manipulated by the hands or by electrical stimulation.

ALEXANDER TECHNIQUE Alexander technique is a movement therapy that uses guidance and education on ways to improve posture and movement. The intent is to teach a person how to use muscles more efficiently to improve the overall functioning of the body. Examples of the Alexander technique as CAM are using it to treat low-back pain and the symptoms of Parkinson's disease.

AYURVEDA Ayurveda is a system of medicine that originated in India several thousand years ago. In the United States, Ayurveda is considered a type of CAM and a whole medical system. As with other such systems, it is based on theories of health and illness and on ways to prevent, manage, or treat health problems. Ayurveda aims to integrate and balance the body, mind, and spirit (thus, some view it as "holistic"). This balance is believed to lead to contentment and health and to help prevent illness. However, Ayurveda also proposes treatments for specific health problems, whether they are physical or mental. A chief aim of Ayurvedic practices is to cleanse the body of substances that can cause disease, and this is believed to help re-establish harmony and balance.

BIOFEEDBACK Biofeedback uses simple electronic devices to teach clients how to consciously regulate bodily functions, such as breathing, heart rate, and blood pressure, to improve overall health. Biofeedback is used to reduce stress, eliminate headaches, recondition injured muscles, control asthmatic attacks, and relieve pain.

CHELATION THERAPY Chelation therapy is a chemical process in which a substance is used to bind molecules, such as metals or minerals, and hold them tightly so that they can be removed from a system, such as the body. In medicine, chelation has been scientifically proven to rid the body of excess or toxic metals. For example, a person who has lead poisoning may be given chelation therapy to bind and remove excess lead from the body before it can cause damage.

CHIROPRACTIC CARE This care involves the adjustment of the spine and joints to influence the body's nervous system and natural defense mechanisms to alleviate pain and improve general health. It is primarily used to treat back problems, headaches, nerve inflammation, muscle spasms, and other injuries and traumas.

CHIROPRACTIC MANIPULATION Chiropractic manipulation is a form of healthcare that focuses on the relationship between the body's structure, primarily of the spine, and function. Doctors of Chiropractic, who are also called Chiropractors or Chiropractic physicians, use a type of hands-on therapy called manipulation (or adjustment) as their core clinical procedure.

DEEP BREATHING Deep breathing involves slow and deep inhalation through the nose, usually to a count of 10, followed by slow and complete exhalation for a similar count. The process may be repeated 5 to 10 times, several times a day.

ENERGY HEALING THERAPY Energy healing therapy involves the channeling of healing energy through the hands of a practitioner into the client's body to restore a normal energy balance and, therefore, health. Energy healing therapy has been used to treat a wide variety of ailments and health problems, and is often used in conjunction with other alternative and conventional medical treatments.

FELDENKREIS Feldenkreis is a movement therapy that uses a method of education in physical coordination and movement. Practitioners use verbal guidance and light touch to teach the method through one-on-one lessons and group classes. The intent is to help the person become more aware of how the body moves through space and to improve physical functioning.

GUIDED IMAGERY Guided imagery involves a series of relaxation techniques followed by the visualization of detailed images, usually calm and peaceful in nature. If used for treatment, the individual will visualize his or her body free of the specific problem or condition. Sessions are typically 20 to 30 minutes in length, and may be practiced several times a week.

HOMEOPATHY Homeopathy is a system of medical practices based on the theory that any substance that can produce symptoms of disease or illness in a healthy person can cure those symptoms in a sick person. For example, someone suffering from insomnia may be given a homeopathic dose of coffee. Administered in diluted form, homeopathic remedies are derived from many natural sources, including plants, metals, and minerals.

HYPNOSIS Hypnosis is an altered state of consciousness characterized by increased responsiveness to suggestion. The hypnotic state is attained by first relaxing the body, then shifting attention toward a narrow range of objects or ideas as suggested by the hypnotist or hypnotherapist. The procedure is used to effect positive changes and to treat numerous health conditions including ulcers, chronic pain, respiratory ailments, stress, and headaches.

MASSAGE Massage therapists manipulate muscle and connective tissue to enhance function of those tissues and promote relaxation and well-being.

MEDITATION Meditation refers to a group of techniques, most of which started in Eastern religious or spiritual traditions. In meditation, a person learns to focus his attention and suspend the stream of thoughts that normally occupy the mind. This practice is believed to result in a state of greater physical relaxation, mental calmness, and psychological balance. Practicing meditation can change how a person relates to the flow of emotions and thoughts in the mind.

NATUROPATHY Naturopathy is an alternative medical system. Naturopathic medicine proposes that there is a healing power in the body that establishes, maintains, and restores health. Practitioners work with the patient with a goal of supporting this power through treatments such as nutrition and lifestyle counseling, dietary supplements, medicinal plants, exercise, homeopathy, and treatments from traditional Chinese medicine. Nonvitamin, nonmineral, natural products are taken by mouth and contain a dietary ingredient intended to supplement the diet other than vitamins and minerals. Examples include herbs or herbal medicine (as single herbs or mixtures), other botanical products such as soy or flax products, and dietary substances such as enzymes and glandulars. Among the most popular are echinacea, ginkgo biloba, ginseng, feverfew, garlic, kava kava, and saw palmetto. Garlic, for example, has been used to treat fevers, sore throats, digestive ailments, hardening of the arteries, and other health problems and conditions.

OSTEOPATHIC MANIPULATION Osteopathic manipulation is a full-body system of hands-on techniques to alleviate pain, restore function, and promote health and well-being.

PILATES Pilates is a movement therapy that uses a method of physical exercise to strengthen and build control of muscles, especially those used for posture. Awareness of breathing and precise control of movements are integral components of Pilates. Special equipment, if available, is often used.

PROGRESSIVE RELAXATION Progressive relaxation is used to relieve tension and stress by systematically tensing and relaxing successive muscle groups.

QI GONG Qi gong is an ancient Chinese discipline combining the use of gentle physical movements, mental focus, and deep breathing directed toward specific parts of the body. Performed in repetitions, the exercises are normally performed two or more times a week for 30 minutes at a time.

REIKI Reiki is an energy medicine practice that originated in Japan. In Reiki, the practitioner places his hands on or near the person receiving treatment, with the intent to transmit ki, believed to be life-force energy.

TAI CHI Tai Chi is a mind-body practice that originated in China as a martial art. A person doing Tai Chi moves his body slowly and gently, while breathing deeply and meditating (Tai Chi is sometimes called "moving meditation"). Many practitioners believe that Tai Chi helps the flow throughout the body of a proposed vital energy called "qi." A person practicing Tai Chi moves her body in a slow, relaxed, and graceful series of movements. One can practice on one's own or in a group. The movements make up what are called forms (or routines).

TRAGER PSYCHOPHYSICAL INTEGRATION Trager Psychophysical Integration is a movement therapy in which practitioners apply a series of gentle, rhythmic rocking movements to the joints. They also teach physical and mental self-care exercises to reinforce the proper movement of the body. The intent is to release physical tension and increase the body's range of motion. An example of Trager Psychophysical Integration as CAM is using it to treat chronic headaches.

YOGA Yoga combines breathing exercises, physical postures, and meditation to calm the nervous system and balance body, mind, and spirit. Usually performed in classes, sessions are conducted once a week or more and roughly last 45 minutes.

Is Chinese Medicine a Conventional Medicine?

SPECIAL FOCUS: CHINESE MEDICINE

In recent years, two main streams in Chinese medicine have developed: traditional Chinese medicine and modern Chinese medicine. Traditional Chinese medicine is usually practiced by self-employed laborers and passed on by one-to-one mentoring. But modern Chinese medicine is derived from an educational system, such as college, graduate school, and the University of Chinese medicine in Taiwan, China, and Honk Kong. Modern Chinese medicine practitioners not only study classical textbooks of traditional Chinese medicine, but also employ scientific methods (for example, studies acupuncture point by GSR technique or extracting effective ingredients from Chinese herbal medicine to make a new medicine). According to NCCAM's definition, CAM is not generally considered part of conventional medicine (practiced by holders of medical doctor degrees). Traditional Chinese medicine is a kind of CAM, but modern Chinese medicine approaches conventional medicine much more than the traditional Chinese medicine of the past.

The theoretical framework of traditional Chinese medicine has several core concepts:

- **Qi and meridians:** Qi is a kind of in vivo energy or force, and meridians are pathways that allow qi to flow through the body. In this system health maintenance is an ongoing process of maintaining fluency and harmony in the circulation of qi.
- **Yin/yang theory:** The concept of two forces that oppose but also complement each other. The classical figure of yin/yang is the Tai Chi figure: a circle of black and white (see Figure 5.3), black represents yin, and white represents yang. Practioners of traditional Chinese medicine believe that it is necessary to have both components of Chi. One would be unable to perceive white if there is no black, and vice versa. Further, there is no complete or pure force of white or black, there is always some black in white or white in black (hence the "dots" of opposing color or force in each section of Figure 5.3. According to yin/yang theory, health is determined by the relative balance between opposing forces rather than an absolute status.
- **The five elements:** Fire, earth, metal, water, and wood do not refer to five substances but five attributes of health. These elements are thought to correspond to five main systems in the body—fire to heart, earth to spleen, metal to lung, water to kidney, and wood to liver. They are in mutual generation and restriction, Chinese medicine studies the relationships between each system, and proposes that health is promoted by keeping the balance of these systems.

Diagnoses in traditional Chinese medicine includes information collection and "whole judgments." Chinese medicine uses four methods to collect information and evaluate a patient's condition which can be summarized in the acronym **OLAP**:

Observation: Observing the patient's physical situation, like color of patient's face or skin tone

Listen (or smell): Listening to the patient's coughing, breathing, or whole body

Asking: Interviewing the patient concerning symptoms and medical history

Pulse or Palpation: Taking the patient's pulse, blood pressure, and/or tapping on specific places on the body

FIGURE 5.3 Tai Chi figure

There are eight principles to make inductive analysis of information gathered from the OLAP process, including yin/yang, exterior/interior, insufficiency/excessiveness, and heat/cold. Chinese medicine uses OLAP and the eight principles to find out the overall characteristics of the current disease, and make the "whole judgment" or diagnosis.

Chinese medicine emphasizes individualized treatment, because the OLAP of each patient is different, the treatment must be customized. Practitioners use a wide variety of treatments to promote health and treat disease, such as Chinese herbal medicine, acupuncture, Chinese massage, qi gong (a system of deep breathing exercises, be designed to increase the fluency and harmony of qi), dietary therapy, cupping (applying a cup on skin to create a suction by heating or deflation, for the purpose of disrupting stagnation of blood in order to assist recovery), and so forth. In general, a complete prescription of Chinese medicine is comprised of advising of emotional regulation, dietetic restraint (e.g., no iced drinks or ice cream), suggestions of exercises (such as qi gong), Chinese herbal medicine, and acupuncture or Chinese massage. Chinese medicine treats the whole person, and the final goal is to maintain the healthy flow of qi and promote body-mind wellness.

A WELLNESS COUNSELOR'S PHILOSOPHY CONCERNING CAM

Wellness counselors are open to working collaboratively with many different kinds of healthcare providers. Since wellness counselors believe that achieving high level wellness is to a great extent a personal responsibility they encourage clients to be proactive in their healthcare. This means helping clients to take advantage of all traditional medicine has to offer by being a well-informed consumer of services, asking questions of their doctor, and advocating for preventative or restorative services such as physical therapy. Further, wellness counselors are open to clients finding complementary or alternative treatments that may offer curative effects for their health and well-being. For example, if a client wishes to pursue acupuncture in addition to traditional psychotherapy for an addiction this would be acceptable.

The openness by wellness counselors to clients' use of complementary or alternative treatments does not mean that they endorse methods that do not have a basis in research or that have not been demonstrated to have curative effects for clients. For example the herb, ginko biloba, has been discredited in the research literature as having beneficial effects for memory enhancement in Alzheimer's patients. Therefore a wellness counselor who had a client who was choosing to engage in taking ginko biloba for memory enhancement would inform the client of the research and recommend that the client consider a different approach that has shown efficacy in the research literature. In summary, therefore, the philosophy of the wellness counselor in regard to CAM can be described as one of "cautious openness." While being accepting of many different approaches to achieving well-being, the wellness counselor is not tolerant of quack cures, dangerous procedures, fallacious claims, or those treatments that could have harmful effects for a client.

PROVIDING OR RECOMMENDING A CAM SERVICE

Wellness counselors may also deliver CAM services within their scope of practice and frequently recommend such services to their clients. Counselors wishing to deliver CAM services as part of their practice should first check with their state counselor licensure board and make sure that providing a CAM service is not out of their scope of practice in their state or in conflict with their professional organizations code of ethics. Next, the counselor should pursue the necessary training, qualifications, and/or credentialing to be a provider of a specific CAM service. Many states now require licensure, or board certification of CAM providers.

While some counselors may wish to develop a CAM service as an adjunct to their counseling practices, it may be more likely that the majority of wellness counselors will recommend a CAM provider or service to a client. The wellness counselor should keep in mind several factors when recommending a CAM service provider:

1. **Counselor familiarity with CAM**
   Do your homework and learn about the CAM therapies and their potential benefits and risks for your clients. Specifically, learn about the providers and therapies provided in your community. Make inquiries into their reputations and credentials and reputation for quality of service. Do not suggest therapies with which you have no information, education, or experience.

2. **Client's orientation toward using CAM**
   Remember to check things out with your client's frame of reference and level of comfort with a specific CAM therapy. For example, significant caution should be used before suggesting that a client use "massage" for stress management if that client has treatment concerns that would be potentially exacerbated by being touched by another person. Another issue to discuss with a client concerns their religious or spiritual values in relation to CAM use. Clients may see a conflict between their religious convictions and participation in certain CAM approaches such as Yoga, which has a strong spiritual component in its practice. As with any counseling intervention, make sure that CAM therapies are understood and voluntarily entered into by the client.

3. **Advise clients on means to pursue CAM use**
   - Suggest NCCAM or other Web sites or sources you identify to increase the client's understanding of the CAM therapy.
   - Suggest means to research practitioner credentials. Teach the client how to check if a provider is licensed by the state in which they are practicing or otherwise credentialed by a legitimate accreditation body.
   - Suggest a "Healthcare Team" approach in which you can suggest providers and monitor their work with the client. Make sure that the client signs appropriate releases of information so that you can communicate with the CAM provider about the case.

4. **Advise clients to clearly understand contraindications**
   As with all medical, psychotherapeutic, counseling, and even educational intervention and therapies there may be potential risks for the client. Make sure the client understands these potential risks before they engage in any CAM practices. Examples of contraindications might include:
   - Body maladies that would be masked by CAM (e.g., hypnosis stopping headache from undiagnosed brain tumor)
   - Client cultural orientation, anxiety, phobia regarding CAM
   - Injuries potentially affected by body based practices
   - Allergic reactions to biologically based practices

Summary

CAM therapies are growing in popularity among Americans. Wellness counselors need to familiarize themselves with a wide range of these therapies and the science that either supports or refutes their usefulness in relation to mental and emotional disorders. Armed with this knowledge, wellness counselors can serve as valuable consultants to clients seeking to augment their counseling with CAM therapies.

References

Barnes, P. M., Bloom, B., & Nahin, R. (2008). *CDC National Health Statistics Report #12*. Complementary and alternative medicine use among adults and children: United States, 2007.

Carlson. J. (2003). *Complementary therapies and wellness,* Upper Saddle River, NJ: Prentice Hall.

Eisenberg, D. M., Kessler, R. C., Foster, C., Norlock, F. E., et al. (1993). Unconventional medicine in the united states: Prevalence, costs, and patterns of use. *The New England Journal of Medicine, 328*(4), 246–252.

Micozzi, M. (2005). *Fundamentals of complementary and alternative medicine*. Philadelphia, PA: Saunders.

National Center for Complementary and Alternative Medicine (part of the National Institutes of Health) (2011). http://nccam.nih.gov/

NCCAM Report. (2007). *Complementary and alternative medicine use among adults and children: United States, 2007.* http://nccam.nih.gov/news/2008/nhsr12.pdf

6 INCORPORATING WELLNESS COUNSELING INTO CLINICAL PRACTICE: A CASE EXAMPLE

Paul F. Granello

Nothing so needs reforming as other people's habits.

MARK TWAIN

The purpose of this chapter is to illustrate how a counselor might work with a client from a wellness counseling perspective. The basic method for working with a client from a wellness counseling approach is very similar to that of working with a client with a diagnosable mental illness. The steps of interview and assessment, goal setting and treatment planning, and therapeutic intervention and support all still apply. Let us now look at how each of these steps might be just a bit different in focus within the context of a wellness counseling approach.

PSYCHOSOCIAL INTERVIEW

A wellness counselor may or may not be working with a client who has a diagnosable mental and emotional disorder. The client may have a physical condition that their doctor believes will benefit from wellness counseling. Or the client may simply have a lot of stress and is seeking to improve their coping skills. So while the focus of the psychosocial interview may be identification of client issues for treatment, it may not be for the purpose of arriving at a DSM-IV diagnosis.

In addition to the areas that are frequently covered within a psychosocial interview such as mental and physical health history, family history, military history, sexual history, substance use, and so forth, a wellness counselor may also like to talk with the client about other areas. Examples of these areas may be:

- **Lifestyle History:** What have been the client's patterns of health and wellness over his or her life so far? Was there a time in his or her life that he or she felt more or less healthy? If so what was he or she doing at these times?
- **Social Support and Involvement:** This category involves not just listing people who the client states are supportive but conducting a more in-depth exploration of the nature of the client's social support system, including structural and functional aspects. It may also involve asking the client about his or her current level of social engagement.

- **Spiritual Practice:** Like the last category, this category goes further than just a question about church attendance but rather involves a discussion about what gives the client meaning and purpose in his or her life, and also inquiring about any regular spiritual practices.
- **CAM Practices:** Ask the client if he or she currently uses any complementary or alternative practices. Does he or she use any supplements of any kind? Has the client ever benefited from a CAM provider's services?
- **Stress and Coping Skills:** How has the client learned to manage stress in his or her life? Does he or she manifest stress somatically? What habits, good or bad, does the client engage in to manage stress?
- **Skills and Strengths:** Wellness counselors always ask about client skills and strengths. What abilities does the client have that can be leveraged to help with the current goals of treatment?

The interview session is also a good time to get the client to sign the appropriate releases and records requests that may be useful and informative. I always ask clients for a release for their primary care physician so that I may call and speak to their doctor if necessary.

WELLNESS ASSESSMENT

In addition to interviewing the client a wellness counselor will also employ the use of formal assessments. A wellness counselor working with a client on wellness issues should assess multiple domains of functioning (social, cognitive, emotional, spiritual, and physical health habits) (P. Granello, 2000). The physical health habits such as diet and exercise have been studied more than the psychological and social mediators of individual wellness, and there are many useful health assessment questionnaires in the literature for measuring exercise and nutrition habits (Abood & Conway, 1992; Belloc & Breslow, 1972; Dana & Hoffman, 1987; Larson, 1997; Shephard, 1989).

Often a small battery of assessment instruments may be necessary including a stress inventory, an exercise and diet survey, a social support inventory, spiritual questionnaire, and an overall measure of lifestyle and wellness.

The use of an assessment that was specifically designed to assess individual wellness is a good starting point when working with clients who wish to make healthier lifestyle choices (Palombi, 1992). It is often helpful and also potentially therapeutic for a client to see his or her current wellness compared to a normative sample. Two examples of instruments that can be used to assess a client's level of wellness from a multidimensional perspective are the Lifestyle Assessment Questionnaire (LAQ), and the Wellness Evaluation of Lifestyle (WEL) inventory. Wellness counselors may find these instruments useful as the results can be reviewed with the client in the context of the wellness model upon which each is based (P. Granello, 2000).

LIFESTYLE ASSESSMENT QUESTIONNAIRE (LAQ) A product of the National Wellness Institute (NWI), the LAQ is a self-scoring wellness instrument, and is based on the Hettler wellness model (Hettler, 1986). The instrument consists of 11 subscales (exercise, nutrition, self-care, vehicle safety, drug usage, environment, awareness, emotional management, intellectual, occupational, and spiritual) that are related to the six dimensions of wellness indicated in the Hettler model (Cooper, 1990). Significant relationships between physiological measures (e.g., blood pressure, body composition) and LAQ scores have been demonstrated, indicating the instruments validity as a global measure of wellness (DeStefano & Richardson, 1992). The emotional subscales of the LAQ have been validated with college students (Freeman, & Ginter, 1989).

THE WELLNESS EVALUATION OF LIFESTYLE (WEL INVENTORY) The Wellness Evaluation of Lifestyle (WEL) inventory was developed to measure individual wellness based on the Lifespan Model described previously (Witmer & Sweeney, 1992). The WEL has 114 items that are organized into five life task categories (Spirituality, Self-Regulation, Work-Leisure, Friendship, and Love). The Self-Regulation life task is further divided into 12 subscales (Sense of Worth, Sense of Control, Realistic Beliefs, Emotional Management, Emotional Response, Intellectual Stimulation, and Creativity). Scores from each subscale are summed to derive a Total Wellness Score for the inventory. Wellness counselors can utilize the results from these assessments to provide an informational basis for assisting clients with developing goals for improving their wellness (P. F. Granello, 1995).

TEACH A WELLNESS MODEL

One thing that a wellness counselor might do that a counselor working with a mentally ill client may not do is teach the client about a specific wellness model. Educating clients about a specific model for wellness has several benefits. These include keeping therapy focused on areas the client is interested in changing, helping the wellness counselor choose interventions related to the client's readiness in specific change area, and enhancing the ability of the client to see the relationship between different but interrelated aspects of his lifestyle. Further, the specific variables of a wellness model (e.g., Lifetasks, Domains) can be used as the organizing axis around which counseling goals can be developed.

DEVELOPING PERSONAL WELLNESS PLANS WITH CLIENTS

After assessing a client through interview and instrument, the information gathered can be used to help develop an individualized wellness plan. Just as a clinician develops a treatment plan with goals and objectives when treating a client with a mental illness, so too should a personalized wellness plan be developed when working with a client from a wellness perspective. The development of a personal wellness plan helps a client stay on track and provides a foundation upon which the wellness counselor can provide consultation and encouragement (P. Granello, 2000). The assistance with the development of an organized wellness plan with specific goals and interventions may be one of the most beneficial services that a wellness counselor can provide a client.

GOAL DEVELOPMENT

Many clients fail to make important lifestyle changes not because they lack the ability to do so but rather because they become discouraged along the way due to poor goals development. First, clients may not know where to begin or be overwhelmed with the potential choices when working on making healthy lifestyle changes. Second, they may set themselves up for failure by unrealistically large goals. Assisting the client in defining measurable, realistic, and achievable goals can be an invaluable service provided by a wellness counselor. Wellness counselors can help clients plan and monitor goals so that they will feel encouraged about their progress in making efforts to improve their wellness. Below there are five parameters to keep in mind for helping a client to set quality goals.

Characteristics of Quality Goals

1. *Desirable*: The goal must be something that the client wants to work on for himself or herself. Goals that are based on what others want for the client or even internalized messages about what the client "should" want are less likely to be achieved. For example, college students who come to the college career counseling service feeling anxiety because they are pursuing the careers their parents want them to pursue rather than making their own choices. Clients are often more motivated to work on a goal if they believe that they have chosen their goals for themselves.
2. *Imaginable*: The clients should be able to get a good visualization of completing the goal, or what their life will be like when they have made significant progress on the goal. Clients who cannot imagine what success will be like have a more difficult time achieving the goal. For example, an adolescent I was working with at a poverty stricken urban high school was unable to envision what his life could be like in college. So he was going to have a much harder time, not knowing what he was working toward, a goal of attending college. He did not have an idea of what the objective of his efforts would be like. The first step here was to arrange for this young man to make several campus visits to local colleges and to meet with others like himself who are attending these schools. Once that was accomplished the young man was able to envision himself also attending college.
3. *Achievable*: The goal should be realistic. The wellness counselor can help the client by breaking down large goals into smaller more manageable steps. Clients will have increased self-efficacy if they can take credit for achieving small goals, making it more likely that they will stick with it to achieve the larger goal. Further, the client may first have to learn new skills or gather resources to help him or her achieve a larger goal; and the wellness counselor can help clients plan how to progress. It is a myth that individuals can achieve anything they desire. For example, everyone cannot be an NBA pro basketball player. I am 5'9" tall and uncoordinated. Although, it might be somehow possible for me to play professional basketball, it is certainly not probable. Wellness counselors need to help clients make goals that are realistic and reasonably achievable.
4. *Measurable*: Goals that have a quantifiable means of measuring progress will be more likely to be achieved. Clients need feedback about their performance and efforts; by setting up a measure for a goal, clients can see their progress. For example, a goal such as "I will lose weight this summer" is more like a good intention than a real goal. A better goal would be more measurable such as "I will go to the gym on Monday, Wednesday, and Fridays, and will do 45 minutes of cardio exercise and then lift weights for 30 minutes." The second goal is much more monitorable and will likely lead to more compliance.
5. *Controllable*: The more achieving a goal is within a client's ability to achieve without the aid of others, the more likely the goal will be achieved. For example, a goal of attending support group meetings is more likely to be achieved if the client does not have to depend on others for transportation. Goals have to realistically take into account the resources the client has available.

Goal Interconnectedness

Wellness plans should focus on one or two areas for the client to work on but emphasize the interconnectedness of the effects of working on one area of well-being will have on other areas of functioning. For example, a client who works on establishing or maintaining an exercise regime may see related improvements in mood and self-efficacy (Calfas, Sallis, Oldenburg, & French, 1997). Conversely, clients who work on self-esteem and affirmation may be more successful in maintaining an exercise program (Dishman, 1982). Clinically, I have seen many clients who improved their diets gain the energy to exercise or those who exercised begin to make healthier food choices.

COUNSELING INTERVENTIONS

Wellness counselors assist clients to achieve the goals on the wellness plan by providing therapeutic interventions. Wellness counselors can bring to bear on wellness goals all of the theoretical knowledge and technical skills that they use with clients working on mental illness issues.

For example, a wellness counselor who is working with a client on developing a wellness promoting lifestyle could use guided imagery to assist the client in controlling stress. Or perhaps the counselor would use brief solution focused therapy interventions and questioning, for example, asking a client "What keeps you from relaxing now?" or "How will you know when things have changed?"

The interventions selected can be from a wide range of theoretical paradigms, diverse fields of knowledge, belief systems, and behavior change models, as long as they are within the counselor's scope of practice and relevant to the client's goals.

A CASE STUDY USING A WELLNESS APPROACH

A clinical example of how stage of change and the use of a wellness model may be used in conjunction might be with a 45-year-old male client named Mike who comes to wellness counseling. Mike is significantly overweight and has been referred from his primary care physician due to high LDL cholesterol and triglycerides. The physician has prescribed a statin drug to help Mike with his high cholesterol but also believes that he would benefit from wellness counseling. Mike is a very successful salesman for a large corporation. He is frequently on the road for his work and states that "I eat whatever I happen to find." Further he stated, "I enjoy the pressure of my job but sometimes it does get to me, and forget about exercise I am embarrassed to go to the gym."

The wellness counselor conducts a psychosocial interview with a mental status exam with the client and determines that there is no clinical diagnosis present (e.g., the client is not clinically depressed) that could be leading to the symptoms for which the client is seeking assistance. Information about the duration, pattern, and previous strategies used by the client toward solving the presenting wellness problem (high stress employment, poor exercise, and high fat diet leading to high cholesterol) is gathered during this interview. Additionally, during the interview the client is asked to respond to five yes/no questions about his readiness to change the specific behaviors of managing stress, eating a lower fat diet, and engaging in more physical activity (e.g., Have you exercised regularly in the past for at least three months?). The client's responses to these questions are used to determine his "readiness to change" in relation to each behavior as specified by the stages of change model discussed previously. Finding out about the client's motivation or readiness to change in relation to specific areas that might be targeted for goals is very useful to the counselor. The counselor can use this information to help the client explore his or her priorities for change and select goals that the client is motivated to work on as a place to start.In the case of our current client, Mike, the wellness counselor decides to assess him using the WEL inventory. The client is given the WEL inventory to complete at home and fax the forms to the clinician prior to the next session (the WEL may also be taken online for a small fee). The wellness counselor scores the WEL for the client and compares the client's results to the appropriate normative group.

Mike has anticipated low scores on the nutrition, and exercise, WEL subscales. Additionally, the wellness counselor notes that the client has a profile that includes unrealistic beliefs associated with perfectionism. Strengths of the client are assessed from the results of the WEL inventory to include strong spiritual beliefs, high intellectual stimulation, and strong social supports. Mike's readiness to change concerning diet and exercise is assessed using the "stages of change" model, and it also becomes apparent the client is in a "contemplation" stage concerning diet and exercise, not presently taking action to modify his eating or exercise habits. For a client at this stage in the change process the transtheoretical model suggests using interventions that increase the client's knowledge about the issues, "consciousness raising," and also the client's personal evaluation of himself related to the problem through "self-reevaluation" (P. Granello, 2000).

The wellness counselor can share the results of the assessments with Mike in the context of the Lifespan Model's Wheel of Wellness (upon which the WEL inventory is based). Mike could then be educated as to the interrelationship of the different variables of the model to his overall wellness.

The wellness counselor, based on the results of the psychosocial interview and assessment instruments, can now begin to develop an individualized wellness plan with Mike. For example, in this case the wellness counselor may help the client to reevaluate by developing quality goals which target the "negative cognitions" that are undermining the client's self-esteem and self-efficacy, and provide encouragement for making progress in this area. One area to explore with Mike might be his beliefs that unless he can be "perfect," for example, at an exercise program, he should not engage in any physical activity. Further, the client's strengths of intellectual stimulation and social support may be utilized. Bibliotherapy, as a form of consciousness raising, goals concerning reading information on healthier diets or exercise plans could be developed and implemented; this further acquisition of information and wellness counselor encouragement can help the client to move from a contemplation to an action stage with regard to diet and exercise.

Clients having being educated in a wellness model may begin to make connections for themselves between aspects of their lifestyle choices and behaviors that they previously viewed as separate. For example, Mike came to understand that the cognitive messages that contributed to his stress also led to overeating as a coping behavior. The client can be empowered, now aware of his pattern of behavior, to begin to choose healthy problem-focused means of coping.

The wellness counselor can also help the client by coordinating other treatment services that may be helpful to this client, such as a nutritional consult and the monitoring of cholesterol by the physician. In the case of Mike, the counselor called a local gym and spoke with a personal trainer that he knew. The counselor had the personal trainer develop a physical activity program for Mike that was appropriate for his level of condition. Also, the personal trainer worked with Mike during off hours when the gym was much less crowded; this helped Mike feel less awkward about exercising in public.

Further, the wellness counselor recommended a CAM provider for Mike, a massage therapist, to help him relax and cope with stress. Wellness counselors may facilitate or refer the client to wellness or disease management support groups, where other clients can help provide support and encouragement for achieving the goals specified on the individual wellness plan.

WELLNESS COUNSELING PRACTICE ISSUES

There are several important practice issues for the mental health practitioner to consider when incorporating wellness counseling into their practice. These include the development of a broad range of expertise, providing high levels of client support, scope of practice issues, working with groups, and fiscal concerns.

DEVELOPMENT OF A WIDE RANGE OF KNOWLEDGE Practitioners must be well read in many different areas when working with clients on wellness issues. Wellness work is eclectic in nature and can combine skills from various parts of the wellness counselor's repertoire of skills. These skills include cognitive therapy, education, social skills training, relaxation and stress management training, behavioral change techniques, and self-care health habits. In addition to keeping up with large amounts of reading, the task of moving from global models of wellness to specific behavioral goals may seem like an overwhelming task for some therapists.

Clients engaged in wellness work often require significant levels of support when changing habits and may require more than a weekly contact. Working with clients on wellness issues means frequently having to adapt the structure and scheduling of client contact as well as the content of the therapy sessions. These increased contacts may include e-mails, list servers, blogs, phone contacts, newsletters, and other means of enriching the frequency of contacts between wellness counselor and client.

Wellness service delivery is often heavily weighted toward psychoeducational and group formats, and practitioners not comfortable with organizing and presenting information to groups may not find this type of work rewarding. For wellness counselors just beginning their wellness work, it may be helpful to create a homogeneous group of clients with similar issues, such as a diabetes management group or an office stress management group. The ability to apply the broad array of topics encompassed under wellness to a specific set of client issues helps to focus the group.

SCOPE OF PRACTICE ISSUES Practitioners also should attend to the scope of their practice. Mental health professionals must be careful about giving exercise prescriptions for clients who have not been medically cleared by a physician for participation in an exercise program, or provide information on diet or nutrition if they are not qualified to do so. For example, without training as a nutritionist, it would be inappropriate to endorse or recommend diets or supplements for clients. It may be appropriate to refer clients for nutritional evaluations and to resources for their own personal reading on the use of supplements.

REIMBURSEMENT FOR WELLNESS COUNSELING Receiving insurance reimbursement for preventative work through most managed care companies can still be difficult. However, this is a limitation that may be surmounted.

First, when a client is referred by a primary care physician, ask the doctor to write a prescription for the client for specific services. For example, I ask doctors to write a prescription for a client who is suffering from chronic pain for relaxation training. Second, there are now preventative Medicare CPT codes that can be billed for working with clients on health-related issues. The wellness counselor needs to be familiar with these codes and use them when appropriate.

One last way to overcome insurance company biases against preventative and wellness counseling services is to work directly with other providers and employers, forming market alliances. Many research studies have now demonstrated the value and cost effectiveness of providing wellness counseling services to employees at their worksite (e.g., Donaldson & Blanchard, 1995; Erfurt, Foote, & Heirch, 1992). Examples of market alliances that have funded wellness groups include corporate human resource departments, retirement and pension plan managers, and others who view delivery of wellness services as good public relations.

Summary

In spite of these limitations, mental health professionals may be uniquely suited to assisting clients with the psychological and social mediators that effect many health and wellness behaviors. The skills required for working with clients on wellness issues are already those most competent counselors possess. A wellness approach includes taking a broader, more holistic, approach with clients who are experiencing a diagnosed illness; it also means working with clients who are mentally healthy and interested in preventive health enhancement.

References

Abood, D. A., & Conway, T. L. (1992). Health value and self esteem as predictors of wellness behavior. *Health Values, 16*(3), 20–26.

Belloc, N. B., & Breslow, L. (1972). Relationship of physical health status and health practices. *Preventive Medicine*, (1), 409–421.

Calfas, K. J., Sallis, J. F., Oldenburg, B., & French, M. (1997). Mediators of change in physical activity following an intervention in primary care. *Preventive Medicine, 26,* 297–304.

Cooper, S. E. (1990). Investigation of the Lifestyle Assessment Questionnaire. *Measurement and Evaluation in Counseling Development, 23,* 83–87

Dana, R. H., & Hoffman, T. A. (1987). Health assessment domains: Reliability and legitimization. *Clinical Psychology Review, 7,* 539–555.

DeStefano, T. J., & Richardson, P. (1992). The relationship of paper and pencil wellness measures to objective physiological indexes. *Journal of Counseling & Development, 71*(2) 226–230.

Dishman, R. K. (1982). Compliance/adherence in health-related exercise. *Health Psychology, 1,* 237–267.

Donaldson, S. I., & Blanchard, A. L. (1995). The seven health practices, well-being, and performance at work: Evidence for the value of reaching small and underserved worksites. *Preventive Medicine, 24*(3), 270–277.

Erfurt, J. C., Foote, A., & Heirich, M. A. (1992). The cost effectiveness of worksite wellness programs for hypertension control, weight-loss, smoking cessation, and exercise. *Personnel Psychology, 45*(1), 5–27.

Freeman, S. T., & Ginter, G. G. (1989). Validation of the lifestyle assessment questionnaire: Targeting students with mental health problems. *College Student Journal, 23*(3), 272–279.

Granello, P. (2000). Integrating wellness work into mental health private practice. *Journal of Psychotherapy in Independent Practice, 1*(1), 3–16.

Granello, P. F. (1995). Wellness as a function of perceived social support network and ability to empathize. *Dissertation Abstracts International.*

Hettler, B. (1980). Wellness promotion on a university campus. *Family and Community Health, 3,* 77–95.

Hettler, B. (1986). Strategies for wellness and recreation program development. In F. Leafgren (Ed.), *Developing campus recreation and wellness programs*. San Francisco: Jossey-Bass.

Larson, J. S. (1997). The Mos 36 item short form health survey: A conceptual analysis. *Evaluation & the Health Professions, 20*(1), 14–27.

Palombi, B. J. (1992). Psychometric properties of wellness instruments. *Journal of Counseling & Development, 71*(2), 221–225.

Shephard, R. J. (1989). Exercise and employee wellness initiatives. *Health Education Research, 4*(2), 233–243.

Witmer, M. J., & Sweeney, T. J. (1992). A holistic model for wellness and prevention over the life span. *Journal of Counseling & Development, 71*, 140–148.

DIMENSIONS OF WELLNESS

The objectives of this section are to provide:

1. Information about specific domains of wellness and their impacts on the individual.
2. A research based examinations of specific wellness dimensions.
3. Examples of how individual wellness dimensions are related to the practice of counseling.

Chapters Seven Through Fourteen The chapters comprising the rest of this book have been contributed by expert authors and wellness counselors. Each of these chapters introduces and covers a dimension of wellness. It is hoped that through reading each chapter the reader will emerge with a better sense of the complexity and breadth of knowledge that encompasses wellness counseling. The presentation of each dimension of wellness in separate chapters is of course a convenience employed for the purposes of study and learning. In the lived complexity of human experience, all of these dimensions interact and influence each other in real time.

7 COGNITION: RULES FOR REALITY

Paul F. Granello

What we think, we become.

BUDDHA, HINDU PRINCE GAUTAMA SIDDHARTA, THE FOUNDER OF BUDDHISM, 563–483 B.C.

Cognition can be defined to encompass all those brain activities that comprise an individual's ability to process information from and act in the environment (Waldstein & Elias, 2003). The word *cognition* is often used as an umbrella term for all of the processes the brain performs (including attention, perception, memory, association, and language skills).

Each cognitive process or "module" has evolved to perform a specific task, like facial recognition or the perception of emotions in others. When these cognitive modules work in conjunction with other cognitive modules we can accurately perceive and function in our environment. Almost all of these cognitive processes work without our awareness of them and in fact work so well together the seamless experience we call the "mind" or "consciousness" is created. Perhaps it is because our lived experience is of one unified mind, that we forget there are really many modules making up a mind. In fact we have over 100 billion neurons in our brains that are organized into sophisticated networks (cognitive modules), each charged with performing a cognitive process we need to survive.

The idea that "mind" (cognitive function) and body are somehow separate is fundamentally biologically inaccurate. The activities of the brain directly affect the body and conversely the systemic health of the body impacts the functioning of the brain (Day, McGuire, & Anderson, 2009). Research has demonstrated that individuals with a cognitive impairment, such as dementia, suffer from over double the number of chronic health conditions that same aged individuals without dementia suffer (Day et al., 2009). For some time now healthcare providers have readily acknowledged that systemic diseases (cancer, cardiovascular, pulmonary, renal, hepatic) can cause physiological damage to the brain and have dramatic effects on cognitive function (Waldstein & Elias, 2003). These alterations have negative impacts on cognition, perception of well-being, mood, and even on the performance of the basic activities of everyday life.

The majority of people today would accept that those individuals afflicted with chronic illnesses may experience significant psychological impacts. For example, we would think it strange if someone who was recently diagnosed with cancer did not experience some anxiety, anger, sadness, or depression. Yet historically healthcare providers have had more difficulty in accepting that the cognitive activities of the brain can directly impact our physical health. Perhaps this was because until recently it was very difficult to observe or measure brain activity. Perhaps this made the workings of the brain seem somehow unrelated, special, or different from other biological processes we could more readily observe.

At present, however, with the advent of new brain scanning technologies such as FMRI (functional magnetic resonance imagery) and PET (positron emission tomography), it has become much easier to observe the brain at work (Raichle, 1998). Brain imaging technologies have now made it possible to directly link brain activity to physiological changes in the body such as secretion of stress response hormones (cortisol), immune cell mobilization, blood pressure, skin conductance, oxytocin production, and many more.

In addition to our knowledge gained through brain imaging technologies, better longitudinal health research is uncovering the long-term effects of our cognitive functioning on our longevity and quality of life (Waldstein & Elias, 2003). Research has supported that certain stable patterns of cognition used by individuals have significant impacts on individual health. Hostility, optimism (Alloy, Abramson, & Chiara, 2000), and realistic thinking styles, have all been shown to relate to health status (Dickerhoof, 2007; Zautra, Davis, & Smith, 2004).

At present, therefore, a rapidly growing body of research exists that has demonstrated significant links between our cognitive activities and our wellness (Brosschot, Gerin, & Thayer, 2006; Cordova, Cunningham, Carlson, & Andrykowski, 2001; Crosby, 1996; Dickerhoof, 2007; Hevey, 2005; Juster, McEwen, & Lupien, 2009; Marcus, Gurley, Marchi, & Bauer, 2007; Nachev, 2006). In this chapter we will look first at the biological underpinnings of our cognitive functioning. Next, we will look at the significant impacts on our cognition made by the social nature of our lives. Lastly, we will share some examples of how a wellness counselor would help a client to be healthier through cognitive interventions.

COGNITION AND WELLNESS: BIOLOGICAL UNDERPINNINGS

Genetic Parameters

All of us are born with a defined genetic inheritance from our parents. Just as our predisposition for many diseases such as cancer, heart disease, and schizophrenia are genetically based, so too our genetics also significantly impact our cognitive abilities. After all, it is our DNA that contains the sequences of genes responsible for organizing the cells that constitute our brains. In fact, it is currently thought that almost two-thirds of the genes in the human genome are related to guiding brain function (Petrella, Mattay, & Doraiswamy, 2008).

The basic cognitive (the term here used to include everything the brain does including thoughts and emotions) foundations of our personalities are set by our genetic inheritance. Genes are thought to establish "set-points" for many of our personality traits. A set-point is the stable point around which a trait varies over an extended period of time (Carr, 2004). Monozygotic twin studies have shown that there is up to a 50% genetic contribution to individuals' sense of well-being, life satisfaction, and happiness. Our genes then establish the baseline biological parameters of our cognitive capacities and our stable cognitive patterns (personality traits) (Carr, 2004). Generally, it can be said, therefore, that some of us are born to be more "cognitively well" than others. Another way of saying this is that some of us are born with a genetic inheritance that predisposes us to think and feel in ways that will contribute to improved health outcomes. So in a very fundamental way our genes influence our health from the very start of our lives.

Biogenic Principles of Cognition

Cognition, like any other biological function, has evolved through natural selection in such a way as to enhance the survival of the individual and ultimately the reproduction of the species. In this light, healthy cognition can be viewed as enhancing our well-being by helping us to accurately perceive, construct, process, interpret, and behave in advantageous ways. Conversely, when our cognitive processes are compromised (such as when an individual has dementia or a psychotic disorder) we may experience problems relating to the world around us and ultimately suffer harmful impacts on our well-being.

One way to organize our thinking about the advantageous contributions of cognitive processes to our wellness is to employ a set of biogenic principles. Biogenic simply means biologically derived. Biogenic principles are broad rules that illustrate how cognitive processes help us to meet a biological need. Used here, they are simply rules for simplifying and illustrating the very complex relationship between our cognitive processes and our well-being.

Four biogenic principles about cognition are illustrated below. Each principle is briefly explained and then examples of how cognitive processes might relate to that principle are given. It is hoped that the reader will understand that human cognition has evolved to help us navigate our world in ways that can preserve and enhance our health.

Biogenic Principle 1: Control

Cognition directly or indirectly modulates the physio-chemical-electrical processes that constitute an organism.

Explanation

Presently we understand that the brain communicates with the major organs of the body in three ways. First is through nerve impulses sent down the spinal cord out to our peripheral nervous system. Similarly, a stimulus (light, sound, temperature, etc.) from the environment is converted into nerve impulses and is sent to the brain. The second channel of brain and body communication is chemical, through hormones released into the bloodstream by the pituitary gland (sometimes called the master gland) which is located on the underside of the brain. Pituitary hormones, such as cortisol, act on the organs of the body regulating their activities. The third way the brain communicates with the body is through the production of small proteins, called neuropeptides, also distributed via the bloodstream (Pert, 1998). Through these channels of communication the brain controls all bodily functions from voluntary muscles to organ function and even perhaps regulation of specific cells.

Example

The "stress response," or as it is sometimes called our "fight or flight" response, is our mind/body adaptation to perceived dangers (stressors) in the environment. The stress response produces significant biochemical changes in all bodily systems, allowing us to either fight off a potential threat or to flee to some safe location. The chemical state with our bodies created by chronic stress has been documented to relate to the acquisition of many diseases (Brosschot et al., 2006; Juster et al., 2009). Richard Lazarus, in his book *Emotion & Adaptation* (Lazarus, 1994), proposes two critical cognitive processes for regulating the stress response, which are called "appraisals." The first of these or the primary appraisal takes place when the organism (in this case us) perceives some event in the environment. The individual must decide if the event is a threat that requires a response. This first cognitive appraisal activates the stress response system. The second cognitive appraisal takes place once a potential threat has been perceived and involves the individual determining if he or she "can cope" with the threat. If due to specific skills, prior experience, or other factors, the threat can be successfully coped with by the individual—then the severity of the stress response is reduced. The cognitive processes of primary and secondary appraisal are key components of the stress response which directly modifies our body's biochemistry. It would seem that our "thoughts" do affect our bodies!

Biogenic Principle 2: Valance

Relative to the organism's needs and/or experience, different properties of the environment will be invested with different degrees of significance, both positive and negative.

Explanation

We learn to discriminate those properties (people, things, situations) in the environment that are positively reinforcing, neutral, or punishing. We develop "beliefs" (schemas, frames, constructs), which are stable ways of interpreting information from the world concerning ourselves, others, and the environment. A belief can be defined as representing a specific "state of things" or interpretation of reality on which the individual bases action, that is, a belief is considered to have predictive reliability for planning and performing further actions (Paglieri, 2003). We therefore can use our stored beliefs about the reality of the world to inform ourselves of how to behave in similar circumstances.

Example

One example of how our exposure to different learning experiences could affect our wellness might be the way our parents taught us about the importance of health. If, for example, we were strongly encouraged to "be healthy" by our parents as children and received positive reinforcement for those behaviors considered healthy, it is then likely we will develop a set of stable beliefs that it is important to eat our vegetables, have a regular bedtime, brush our teeth regularly, and generally avoid unhealthy behaviors.

In relation to wellness, the health beliefs of individuals have been widely studied. Health beliefs are thought to be very important for influencing behavior concerning preventative healthcare, perception of health risks, and help seeking (Hevey, 2005; Lawton, Conner, & Parker, 2007; Patterson, 2001; Shumaker, Ockene, & Riekert, et al., 2009).

Biogenic Principle 3: Judgment

Cognition relates to the (more or less) continuous assessment of system needs relative to prevailing circumstances, the potential for interaction, and whether the current interaction is working or not.

Explanation

To survive and thrive we are constantly monitoring our own needs (food, belonging, security, etc.) and evaluating our ability to meet those needs in the environment (physical and social). Humans therefore have evolved "executive" cognitive modules that help organize and evaluate how well other cognitive modules are performing. This ability to think about our own thinking is defined as **metacognition.**

Metacognitive modules monitor how well we are doing in achieving our goals. A goal may be defined as an anticipatory representation of reality that has the power of driving an individual's behavior (i.e., the person is willing to behave in such a way to act to modify the state of his or her beliefs or the world accordingly to his or her anticipatory representation). It is important to note that both beliefs and goals may vary in importance: namely, strength for beliefs and value for goals. In general we would

(Continued)

expect rational people to act in relation to their goals, on the basis of their beliefs (Paglieri, 2003). It seems matter of fact therefore to state that people are likely to act on beliefs they hold strongly in relation to goals they value greatly.

Example

Attribution is a cognitive process that assigns causality to events. Attribution theory (Weiner, 1980) emphasizes the idea that individuals are strongly motivated by the pleasant outcome of being able to feel good about themselves. It emphasizes that the individuals' current self-perceptions will strongly influence interpretation of the success or failure of current efforts and hence their future tendency to perform these same behaviors.

According to attribution theory, the "explanatory styles" that people tend to make to justify successes or failures can be analyzed in terms of three sets of characteristics:

- First, the cause of the success or failure may be *internal* or *external*. Individuals may believe that the factors producing success or failure have their origins within themselves or they may believe that factors originate outside themselves in the environment.
- Second, the cause of the success or failure may be either *stable* or *unstable*. If individuals attribute a cause as stable, then the outcome is likely to be the same on a later occasion. If the cause for success or failure is unstable, then outcome is likely to be different on a later occasion.
- Third, the factors related to success or failure can either be global or specific. Global attributions indicate that the individual believes the same results will occur across a wide variety of circumstances. Specific attribution indicates that a factor will only apply to a circumstance with very similar characteristics.

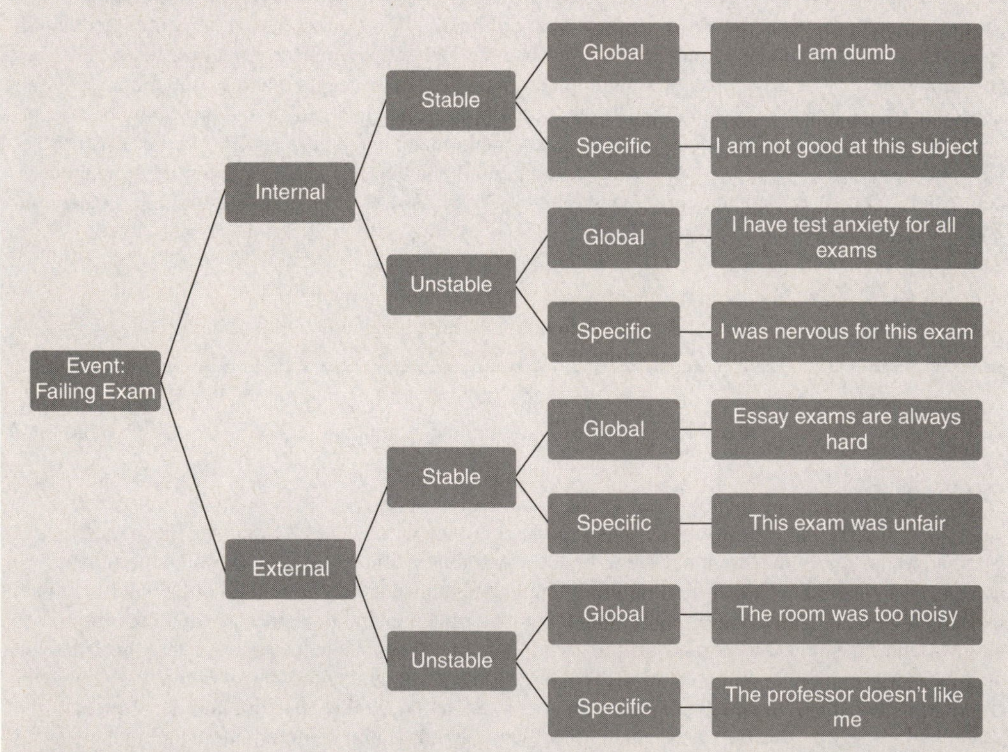

FIGURE 7.1 Explanatory Style: Example failure of an exam *Source:* From ABNORMALITY by Martin E.P. Seligman and David Rosenhan. Copyright © 1998, 1995, 1989, 1984 by W.W. Norton & Co. Used by Permission of W.W. Norton and Company, INC

An important assumption of attribution theory is that people will interpret their environment in such a way as to maintain a positive self-image. That is, they will *attribute* their successes or failures to factors that will enable them to feel as good as possible about themselves. In general, this means that when individuals succeed at a task, they are likely to want to attribute this success to their own efforts or abilities (internal); but when they fail, they will want to attribute their failure to factors over which they have no control, such as bad teaching or bad luck (external).

Explanatory style (Figure 7.1) shows us that two people can experience the same event and have significantly different interpretations of it based on their style of cognitive processing about that event. Further, explanatory styles have been linked to perceptions of well-being, productivity, job turnover, and self-esteem (Proudfoot, Corr, Guest, & Dunn, 2009).

Biogenic Principle 4: Randomness reduction

Cognition is an important mechanism by which biological systems reduce and modulate the influence of random perturbations on their functioning and are, thereby, robust to perturbation.

Explanation

Cognitive processes for succeeding in the environment become ingrained in us. The term **schema** is often used to define a series of cognitive processes that have been grouped together to form a unit. Schemas are employed to help us quickly assess and cope with the environment. Further, they do not immediately change or become discarded when a new problem presents itself. For example, when a schema for perceiving an individual is formed many times it is generalized to all individuals who might share some characteristic with the original individual; this is how stereotypes arise. Also, a problem solving strategy is learned in one context, and many times the same strategy schema that is useful in one setting may be generalized or "tried out" in other contexts. It may be more efficient to draw upon our already learned cognitive processes and behavioral repertoire than to continuously create new strategies for each experience we encounter.

However, sometimes people can be very stubborn about their opinions (beliefs, schemas) despite significant evidence that those opinions are wrong or inaccurate. **Cognitive dissonance** is a term that is often used to describe a confused or anxious state in which a schema is being challenged by new information. If the cognitive dissonance becomes great enough such that the individual can no longer rely on the accuracy of the schema (its predictive utility to assist in coping with reality), then one option is for the individual to modify his or her way of thinking about a specific situation. Of course, another option is for the person to try to modify or control his or her environment (other people, things) in such a way as to fit into his or her schema.

It is of course probably good that our cognitive patterns (values, beliefs, and worldview) are relatively stable or else we would all be constantly changing our personalities with every new situation. Such a state of affairs would be very confusing, making it very hard for individuals to relate to each other in any kind of predictable or consistent manner.

Example

The stability of our cognitive processes may actually be a disadvantage to our wellness. A significant amount of research, public health programming, and money has been put into figuring out how to get people to change their beliefs (cognitive schema) concerning health behaviors. Examples of these efforts include trying to get people to stop smoking, wear seat belts, drink responsibly, get mammograms and prostate exams, and more recently eat nutritionally balanced diets and engage in physical activity.

Perhaps, as a testimony to the tenacious stability of our cognitive processes in the face of dissonant information, these efforts aimed at altering health beliefs of the populace often take many years of public education, social marketing campaigns, product control (restricting advertising), and creating environmental disincentives (like raising taxes on cigarettes or heavy fines for driving under the influence) to produce noticeable effects.

COGNITION AND WELLNESS: SOCIAL AND CULTURAL IMPACTS

So far in this chapter we have been learning about the biological basis and influences on our cognition and ultimately on our wellness and health. Now we will alter our viewpoint and see that even though there are basic biological parameters placed on our cognitive abilities, our patterns of thinking are very much shaped by our learning from the experiences we have in the environment. There are two major ways in which our cognition has been affected by our environment. First, in childhood our neural networks are in fact significantly altered by our environment. Human infants are born with approximately twice the number of neurons as we have as adults. Depending on our exposure to experiences in our environment, certain neural networks are reinforced and maintained, while others not used are weaned and eventually die off. Perhaps that is why children can learn music, languages, and other processes easily; they have a built-in ability to simply absorb information. So in a very real way the environment (our social, cultural, familial, and community) shapes our brains' cognitive processes and the neural networks that function to produce them.

Second, drawing on dominant theory from evolutionary psychology it appears that the modules of cognition in the human brain have evolved to help us live in close social groups. One of the unique things about primates and particularly human beings (*Homo sapiens sapiens*) is that we like to live in groups. Living in groups has survival advantages for us. There are more eyes and ears for

SPECIAL FOCUS

Intellectual Stimulation: Does It Help Us Maintain Our Cognitive Capacity into Old Age?

The median age of the American population is aging and our average lifespan for both men and women is now in the 80s. As a result, the rates of medical diseases that affect cognitive function in old age are rising at a rapid rate. Dementia and Alzheimer's disease are two such illnesses. Currently, 1 in 10 people age 65 and older are afflicted with Alzheimer's disease, which is characterized by many cognitive deficits including memory loss, confusion, and disorientation (Cook, McGuire, & Miranda, 2007; Wilson et al., 2010). These factors and others have raised the interest among the general public and researchers concerning the discovery of interventions that will contribute to healthy cognitive functioning into old age (Granello & Fleming, 2008; Laditka, Beard, & Bryant, 2009).

Several strategies have been identified for promoting cognitive health as we age: prevention and management of chronic conditions (especially those related to blood flow to the brain), nutrition, physical activity, intellectual stimulation, and social engagement (Fillit et al., 2002; Masley, Weaver, Peri, & Phillips, 2008; Yevchak, Loeb, & Fick, 2008).

The cognitive intervention of intellectual stimulation or "brain exercises" has been shown to improve cognitive functioning (Cook, 2007; Edwards et al., 2005). Intellectual stimulation involves keeping the brain active not only in old age but throughout the lifespan. Intellectual stimulation training programs which have focused on memory activities have been shown to produce positive gains on the specific areas related to the training at follow-up after five years (Willis et al., 2006).

However, a recent longitudinal study conducted over a 12-year period produced some disappointing findings concerning the efficacy of intellectual stimulation as an intervention (Wilson et al., 2010). The results of the study indicated that although intellectual stimulation forestalled the development of dementia initially those subjects with high intellectual stimulation as a regular part of their lifestyles actually had significantly accelerated deterioration once developing the cognitive impairments (Wilson et al., 2010).

Therefore, although promising, it appears that the research is currently mixed on the beneficial effects of intellectual stimulation for warding off cognitive diseases like dementia or Alzheimer's.

detecting predators, and there are much better chances of a group of us fending off a lion than one of us. So those individuals that were able to live productively with others in groups had an evolutionary advantage over those who could not. However, living with others in a group (especially groups the size of those in which humans live) requires some special cognitive modules (processes). First, we need to keep track of who is in our group, so we need cognitive modules for facial recognition, and we need a lot of memory ability to store that information. Also, it would be useful to track who we do things for (altruism) and who owes us, so memory is again important as well as a sense of fairness. Finally, it would be really great to communicate with others in our group, so cognitive modules for producing and decoding language would certainly come in handy. According to evolutionary psychologists, many of our cognitive abilities have evolved to aid us with the tasks of living successfully with others. Our minds are naturally attuned to others, having evolved in a social context. Perhaps that is why we experience powerful negative emotions like loneliness when we feel isolated socially (Cacioppo & Patrick, 2008). Conversely, it has been demonstrated that social engagement and activity helps maintain our cognitive abilities (Smith & Christakis, 2008). Although subsequent chapters in this book examine social and cultural impacts on our wellness, it is important to note here that we are cognitively evolved to live in connection with others.

WELLNESS COUNSELING AND COGNITIVE FUNCTIONING

As amazing as our brains are in helping us to navigate the environment, we can still make many cognitive errors. We can inaccurately perceive the environment, or distort and/or deny the information we perceive through our own belief system. We can also be blinded by our drive to achieve our goals and fail to attend to the realities of the world around us. I often think of a man I knew who so adamantly pursued his goal of romancing the girl of his dreams that he could not see that his efforts were actually alienating her. Human cognition is far from infallible and faulty processing of information can lead to complex problems, emotional upset, and the need for change.

Change of any type can be difficult for people; cognitive change is no exception. It takes self-awareness (metacognition) and lots of new learning experiences (practice) to modify long established and ingrained beliefs about "reality." As with any task it may be useful to bring in a professional, in this case a wellness counselor, who has specialized knowledge and skills to assist the client.

Below are four examples of how a wellness counselor might help clients to increase their wellness through cognitive interventions. This list is far from exhaustive but should serve as a means to illustrate the usefulness of helping clients with their cognition concerning health and wellness.

1. *Assisting the client in developing flexible realistic beliefs and goals.* Clients' beliefs and goals need to be "permeable" and open for discussion and change. The more rigidly and demandingly the clients hold onto faulty or unrealistic beliefs and goals, the less well they will be able to respond to changes in their environments. Cognitive behavioral therapy in its many forms is all about helping clients be more adaptive in their thinking. Wellness counselors can help clients identify, refute, and substitute more realistic beliefs and goals for faulty ones. Emmons (1986a) found that having goals, making progress toward goals, and having goals that did not conflict with each other were all predictors of subjective well-being and happiness.
2. *Affirmation of identified and adapted beliefs and goals to improve wellness.* Wellness counselors should not only help the client identify and refute unrealistic beliefs and goals but also provide encouragement and affirmation for adaptive cognitive changes, flexibility, creative problem solving, and problem focused coping.

3. *Help with developing metacognition regarding self-generated stress-inducing demands.* Self-monitoring is a technique that many cognitive approaches promote. Clients are simply encouraged to track their cognitions and behaviors sometimes with journals, diaries, or other methods for collecting data. There is a twofold benefit: first, clients' awareness (metacognition) is raised regarding the beliefs or behaviors, and second, baseline data are collected that can be used to help set goals for change. A research study that involved having adults self-monitor their health cognitions and behaviors revealed significant improvements in health locus of control, health value, personal control over and self-regulation of development-related cognitions, well-being, as well as reductions in psychosomatic complaints, and hopelessness (Krampen, 1996). Teach and help the client to rehearse cognitive stress-reducing self-care skills. Cognitive self-care skills are powerful stress-reducing resources that can prevent psychological stress and that can promote a sense of wellness (Lyon, 2002). One example of a cognitive self-care skill is Mindfulness Meditation. In this type of meditation the goal is to change one's relationship to thoughts instead of changing the content of thoughts themselves (Teasdale, 1995).

Summary

There are of course many reasons that individuals may achieve high level health or succumb to disease. Some of these reasons include health habits, environmental conditions, genetic allocation, access to healthcare, and social supports. This chapter has focused on one of these reasons: cognitive function.

In this chapter we have reviewed aspects of our cognitive functioning's contribution to our health from both a biological and environmental perspective. The information shared here is just the beginning for developing a deeper understanding of how our cognitive abilities relate to our health. The human brain is a very powerful evolutionary development and to date we are only beginning to understand its full abilities and potential. In the future it is hoped that wellness counselors will use and demonstrate the efficacy of cognitive interventions with clients to improve their quality of life, perceptions of wellness, coping abilities, and lower their risk for disease.

References

Alloy, L. B., Abramson, L. Y., & Chiara, A. (2000). *On the mechanisms by which optimism promotes positive mental and physical health: A commentary on Aspinwall and Brunhart.* West Conshohocken, PA: Templeton Foundation Press.

Brosschot, J., Gerin, W., & Thayer, J. (2006). The perseverative cognition hypothesis: A review of worry, prolonged stress-related physiological activation, and health. *Journal of Psychosomatic Research, 60*(2), 113–124.

Cacioppo, J. T., & Patrick, W. (2008). *Loneliness : Human nature and the need for social connection.* New York: W.W. Norton.

Carr, A. (2004). *Positive psychology: The science of happiness and human strengths* (illustrated ed.). New York: Routledge.

Cook, B. L., McGuire, T., & Miranda, J. (2007). Measuring trends in mental health care disparities, 2000–2004. *Psychiatric Services, 58*(12), 1533–1540.

Cordova, M. J., Cunningham, L. L. C., Carlson, C. R., & Andrykowski, M. A. (2001). Social constraints, cognitive processing, and adjustment to breast cancer. *Journal of Consulting and Clinical Psychology, 69*(4), 706–711.

Crosby, R. A. (1996). Cognitive processing and the prevention of HIV transmission: A synthesis of theory into a ten. *Journal of Wellness Perspectives, 12*(3), 140.

Day, K. L., McGuire, L. C., & Anderson, L. A. (2009). The CDC healthy brain initiative: Public health and cognitive impairment. *Generations, 33*(1), 11–17.

Dickerhoof, R. M. (2007). *Expressing optimism and gratitude: A longitudinal investigation of cognitive strategies to increase well-being.* ProQuest Information & Learning. *Dissertation Abstracts International: Section B: The Sciences and Engineering, 68*(6), Dec. 2007.

Emmons, R. A., & Diener, E. (1986a). Influence of impulsivity and sociability on subjective well-being. *Journal of Personality and Social Psychology, 50*(6), 1211–1215.

Edwards, J. D., Wadley, V. G., Vance, D. E., Wood, K., Roenker, D. L., & Ball, K. K. (2005). The impact of speed of processing training on cognitive and everyday performance. *Aging & Mental Health, 9*(3), 262–271.

Fillit, H. M., Butler, R. N., O'Connell, A. W., Albert, M. S., Birren, J. E., Cotman, C. W., . . . Tully, T. (2002). Achieving and maintaining cognitive vitality with aging *Mayo Clinic Proceedings, 77*(7), 681–696.

Granello, P. F., & Fleming, M. S. (2008). Providing counseling for individuals with Alzheimer's disease and their caregivers. *Adultspan Journal 7.1* (Spring 2008).

Hevey, D. (2005). Contextual, cognitive and emotional influences on risk perception for illness. *Irish Journal of Psychology, 26*(1–2), 39–51.

Juster, R. P., McEwen, B. S., & Lupien, S. J. (2009). Allostatic load biomarkers of chronic stress and impact on health and cognition. *Neuroscience and Biobehavioral Reviews.*

Krampen, G. (1996). The program for systematic self-monitoring and reflection of health behavior and health attitudes (SySeRe): Conception and empirical evaluation of a group program on health promotion. *Swiss Journal of Psychology/Schweizerische Zeitschrift Fur Psychologie/ Revue Suisse De Psychologie, 55*(4), 227–240.

Laditka, J. N., Beard, R. L., & Bryant, L. L. (2009). Promoting cognitive health: A formative research collaboration of the healthy aging research network. *The Gerontologist, 49*(S1), S12–S17.

Lawton, R., Conner, M., & Parker, D. (2007). Beyond cognition: Predicting health risk behaviors from instrumental and affective beliefs. *Health Psychology, 26*(3), 259–267.

Lazarus, R. (1994). *Emotion & adaptation.* New York: Oxford University Press.

Lyon, B. L. (2002). Cognitive self-care skills: A model for managing stressful lifestyles. *The Nursing Clinics of North America, 37*(2), 285–294.

Marcus, D. K., Gurley, J. R., Marchi, M. M., & Bauer, C. (2007). Cognitive and perceptual variables in hypochondriasis and health anxiety: A systematic review. *Clinical Psychology Review, 27*(2), 127–139.

Masley, S. C., Weaver, W., Peri, G., & Phillips, S. E. (2008). Efficacy of lifestyle changes in modifying practical markers of wellness and aging. *Alternative Therapies in Health and Medicine, 14*(2), 24–29.

Nachev, P. (2006). Cognition and medial frontal cortex in health and disease. *Current Opinion in Neurology, 19*(6), 586–592.

Paglieri, F. (2003). *Belief revision: Cognitive constraints for modeling more realistic agents.* Working paper, ILLC Amsterdam, December 2003.

Patterson, R. (2001). *Changing patient behavior: Improving outcomes in health and disease management.* San Francisco: Jossey-Bass.

Pert, C. B. (1998). *Molecules of emotion.* New York: Scribner.

Petrella, J. R., Mattay, V. S., & Doraiswamy, P. M. (2008). Imaging genetics of brain longevity and mental wellness: The next frontier? *Radiology, 246*(1), 20–32.

Proudfoot, J. G., Corr, P. J., Guest, D. E., & Dunn, G. (2009). Cognitive-behavioural training to change attributional style improves employee well-being, job satisfaction, productivity, and turnover. *Personality and Individual Differences, 46*(2), 147–153.

Raichle, M. E. (1998). Colloquium Paper: Behind the scenes of functional brain imaging: A historical and physiological perspective. *PNAS 95, 765–772.*

Shumaker, S. A., Ockene, J. K., & Kristin A. Riekert. (2009). *The handbook of health behavior change.* New York: Springer.

Smith, K. P., & Christakis, N. A. (2008). Social networks and health. *Annual Review of Sociology, 34*(1), 405–429.

Teasdale, J. (1995). How does cognitive therapy prevent depressive relapse and why should attentional control (mindfulness) training help? Behaviour Research and Therapy *Behaviour Research and Therapy, 33*(1), 25–39.

Waldstein, S. R., & Elias, M. F. (2003). Introduction to the special section on health and cognitive function. *Health Psychology, 22,* 555–558.

Weiner, B. (1980). The role of affect in rational (attributional) approaches to human motivation. *Educational Researcher, 9*(7), 4–11.

Willis, S. L., Tennstedt, S. L., Marsiske, M., Ball, K., Elias, J., Koepke, K. M., . . . Active Study Group. (2006). Long-term effects of cognitive training on everyday functional outcomes in older adults. *Journal of the American Medical Association, 296*(23), 2805–2814.

Wilson, R. S., Barnes, L. L., Aggarwal, N. T., Boyle, P. A., Hebert, L. E., Evans, D. A. et al. (2010). Cognitive activity and the cognitive morbidity of Alzheimer's disease. *Neurology. 75*(11): 990–996.

Yevchak, A. M., Loeb, S. J., & Fick, D. M. (2008). Promoting cognitive health and vitality: A review of clinical implications. *Geriatric Nursing, 29*(5), 302–310.

Zautra, A. J., Davis, M. C., & Smith, B. W. (Eds.). (2004). Emotions, personality, and health *Journal of Personality, 41,* 1002–1012.

8 EMOTIONAL REGULATION: STONES AND WATER

Karen Michelle Hunnicutt-Hollenbaugh

The strangest and most fantastic fact about negative emotions is that people actually worship them.

P. D. Ouspensky (Russian philosopher)

Wellness Connection

Emotional regulation is a core component of wellness. The plight of children with hyperactivity or individuals with bipolar disorder who are in a manic phase is one of not being able to lower emotional arousal to attend to that which is most important. Similarly, if our emotional arousal is too low, our ability to function and learn is compromised. Individuals with complicated grief or significant depression often have significant difficulty with adapting to their environment and may become compromised in their health.

For most of us, it is not a great tragedy that undermines our health but rather how we handle the much more frequent daily stresses and hassles of life. So like a rock in a stream, if we do not cope well with daily life our health is slowly worn away until it is time for a significant health effect such as a heart attack. In this chapter Michelle Hunnicutt-Hollenbaugh communicates to us the importance of teaching clients how to regulate their emotional arousal as a core component of helping them to achieve wellness.

While many people would regard emotions as a component of our mental health, rarely do we think about the processes we engage in to regulate our emotions, and the effect this may have on our health and well-being. In this chapter, we seek to illuminate the importance of emotions and emotion regulation on wellness. In addition, we discuss the interventions that can be used with clients as well as in our own lives to increase our ability effectively manage emotions. While emotion regulation can be reviewed in the context of regulating others' emotions as well as our own, here emotion regulation will only be explored regarding the regulation of one's own emotions.

EMOTIONS

At its most basic characterization, Merriam Webster (2008) defines emotion as: "a: the affective aspect of consciousness : **feeling** b: a state of feeling c: a conscious mental reaction (as anger or fear) subjectively experienced as strong feeling usually directed toward a specific object and typically accompanied by physiological and behavioral changes in the body."

This definition gives us a starting place, but we can go further. Biologically, emotions begin in the brain, though exactly how emotions work continues to be researched and is mired with uncertainty. It is widely believed that emotions are based in the limbic system, though some current theories suggest the involvement of many different systems (Le Doux, 2000). It is posited that emotions are not something we can control but instead are a phenomenon that happens to us, and we often react to them before we realize it. Most research supports the involvement of the amygdala, a small, almond-shaped brain structure, which studies show has a significant relationship with emotional meaning and memory. Clearly, we have conscious reactions to emotions (for example, making the decision to spend less time with one's mother-in-law as she often elicits feelings of irritation and anger). However, the brain works rapidly to send important information through the thalamus (a part of the brain that is considered to be a relay point and translator of information) to the amygdala (which remembers key factors regarding situations and emotions). Before the message actually reaches the neocortex, (the conscious part of our brain where we normally intervene with our response to the emotion), this information has already been sent to different parts of the brain: for example, the hypothalamus, which releases hormones such as adrenalin. Why? Biologically, humans often need to elicit a rapid behavioral response before making a connection between a stimulus and an emotional response. The amygdala is also thought to be a major component in classical conditioning, as it sends messages to the prefrontal cortex regarding the association between the conditioned and unconditioned stimulus before the individual has conscious realization of this association (Le Doux, 1996).

These biological processes have significant implications for wellness and emotion regulation. Our emotion systems were created at the very beginning of our biological evolution to manage emotions and increase rates of survival in very basic ways (i.e., the prominent "fight or flight" response). Today, however, these emotions can frequently lead to dysfunctional ways of thinking and behaving (Baumeister, DeWall, & Zhang, 2007). We must condition ourselves to regulate our emotions in a healthy manner, or fall victim to methods of regulating emotion that can decrease wellness and spin out of control. Take, for example, the fear of heights (acrophobia). Someone afflicted with acrophobia may have once faced a traumatic experience related to heights, and may have been in danger of falling and being injured. The amygdala then sent messages to the hypothalamus to release adrenal steroids, which increased arousal enough to elicit an immediate response—presumably stopping all physical movement, or moving toward safety (McEwen & Sapolsky, 1995). While this may be helpful during situations of actual danger, the amygdala keeps the memory of this highly stressful emotional response and will initiate the same reaction to similar situations regardless of actual danger (e.g., elevators or planes). This highly emotional reaction can also make it difficult to think clearly, and as result, the individual may develop unhealthy coping responses, such as avoiding all situations involved with height to regulate his or her emotions (LeDoux, 1996).

EMOTION REGULATION

Everyone regulates emotions differently. In conjunction with the biological processes of emotions themselves, regulation of these emotions also takes place in the limbic system, and involves communication between the amygdala, hippocampus, and neocortex (Beer & Lombardo, 2007; Davidson, Fox, & Kalin, 2007). As aforementioned, emotion regulation can be unconscious and automatic (i.e., looking away from the couple kissing in the library because it makes us uncomfortable), but can also be very conscious and deliberate (i.e., suppressing unhappiness with receiving Aunt May's unlikable fruitcake as a gift once again (Gross & Thompson, 2007). These automatic and conscious processes also differ by culture: for example, North American culture holds the belief that it is weak for a man to cry, while individuals in other societies believe showing emotions is seen as a strength (Mauss & Robinson, 2009). Emotion regulation also varies based on the individual; and is at least in part related to how we were raised to act (which behaviors were reinforced and which were not) and our biological level of emotions, as some of us experience higher levels of emotions than others (Mikolajczak, Nelis, Hansenne, & Quoidbach, 2008; Mauss, Cook, Cheng, & Gross, 2007; Linehan, 1993a).

There is also significant research that suggests men and women may differ in their skill level and approach to regulating emotions. In a recent study of the United States, men exhibited less brain activity while using emotion regulation techniques than woman, suggesting men may either be more biologically apt to regulate emotions than women, or (the more likely hypothesis), men were taught culturally to regulate emotions more than women (McRae, Ochsner, Mauss, Gabrieli, & Gross, 2008). This finding coincides with other research that has found that women are more expressive with emotions than men (Kring & Gordon, 1998). This information can have significant implications for our lives and for our clients, as it suggests that men and women choose different emotion regulation techniques, and these different approaches to emotions can have an effect on how people communicate and function in daily life.

There are five basic categories of emotion regulation. Some of these groups are cognitive and others are behavioral. The first, situation selection, refers to the act of looking ahead to choose situations based on our past experiences and the effect these situations may have on our emotions—for example, making the decision to view a comedy as opposed to a horror movie (Gross & Thompson, 2007). This method of regulating emotion can be difficult to use successfully, as we often misjudge how we might react emotionally to any given situation (Lowenstein, 2007). The next group of processes, situation modification, is the act of changing the current situation to manage emotions—for example, instead of leaving when feeling irritated with one's mother-in-law, one might instead change the topic of discussion. However, it should be noted that the differences between situation selection and situation modification are often blurred, as modifying the situation could be considered selecting a new situation. The third category, attention deployment (attention control), encompasses the use of distraction as well as concentration. When unable to change the current situation, we instead redirect our attention to manage emotions. As with all methods of regulating emotions, this can have positive or negative results (i.e., concentrating on things that make you happy or ruminating on an event that elicits sadness). Fourth, cognitive change involves reappraisal—the act of changing the way we think about something in order to regulate how we feel about it (e.g., the sayings "every cloud has a silver lining," and "making lemonade of lemons.") Reappraisal has been widely studied, and will be discussed later in this chapter as a healthier approach to regulating emotions (Nezleck & Kuppens, 2008). Lastly, response modulation encompasses any method of altering our responses to our emotions. This includes taking medication but also how we express our emotions (for example, finding a healthier way to manage anger than yelling or throwing things).

Gross (1998) identifies these categories based on a continuum of when they appear along a timeline. It begins with the situations we choose (situation selection and modification), then where we focus our attention once we are in that situation (attention deployment), how we appraise or evaluate the situation (cognitive change), and then our response to the elicited emotions (response modulation). Although he uses a linear model to demonstrate the processes, he also postulates that this process is not linear but a recurring cycle, as our emotions themselves are cyclical. Emotions can be activated and reactivated based on our cognitive and behavioral response to these emotions. In addition, many of these regulation processes can occur in the brain simultaneously (i.e., feeling sad about my poor performance on the test, but blaming the professor for unfair questions to regulate my sadness, then feeling angry, and at the same time feeling envious of a fellow student that performed better, and feeling guilty for feeling that way). Again, how we modulate our response to emotions can be considered adaptive or maladaptive: varying based on one's age, situation, and culture (Gross & Thompson, 2007). Our ability to regulate our emotions has a direct relationship with every portion of the Wheel of Wellness (Witmer & Sweeney, 1992). This includes our spirituality, relationships, family, mental health, physical well-being, and career. Thus, effective strategies to regulate emotion can improve every aspect of our wellness, whereas negative strategies can be unhealthy and detrimental to wellness.

MENTAL HEALTH

Emotion regulation has a strong connection to mental health. Individuals who are unable to use emotion regulation skills to accept emotional distress have higher levels of anxious arousal and worry (Kashdan, Zvolensky, & McLeish, 2008). Emotion regulation affects mental health, and conversely, mental illness can negatively affect emotion regulation skills (this is cyclical—each impacts the other). Further, a study of emotion regulation skills in children diagnosed with bipolar disorder showed distinct biological differences in their ability to regulate emotions than children that have not been diagnosed with a mental illness (Dickstein & Leibenluft, 2006). In an interview of adolescent girls diagnosed with conduct disorder, it was found that the subjects had few if any methods of regulating emotions that actually achieved relief from negative emotions, suggesting an important relationship between emotion dysregulation and the etiology of conduct disorder, which may also limit healthy social and behavioral growth during this crucial period of human development (Kostiuk & Fouts, 2002).

Relationships

Interpersonal relationships are a major facet of our overall wellness, and when we cannot control our emotions effectively, relationships may be the first aspect of our lives to suffer the consequences. Research has shown that emotion regulation plays a significant role in social difficulties of young boys with developmental delays. Those who showed less ability to tolerate frustration, for example, struggled more in interactions with peers and adults (Wilson, Fernandes-Richards, Aarskog, Osborn, & Capetillo, 2007). Men who used emotion regulation in childhood exhibited higher social functioning in adulthood than those who did not, and conversely, individuals who have been unable to manage and reduce social anxiety have been found to experience low levels of positive emotions (Kashdan & Breen, 2008; Pulkkinen, Nygren, & Kokko, 2002). Indeed, in the DSM-IV, many psychological disorders, including personality disorders, include criteria related to the individual's inability to manage emotions in context of relationships (Gross & Munoz, 1995). For example, individuals with borderline personality disorder are often plagued with real or imagined fear of abandonment, a fear that they are often unable to control, with deleterious results. The individual may push loved ones away completely, or become so completely attached that loved ones feel that they have no choice but to pull away (American Psychiatric Association, 2000).

In the discussion of social relationships, we must also consider romantic partners, as our ability (or inability) to regulate these emotions can have a direct impact on the health of intimate relationships. Specifically, the use of suppression (the act of ignoring or pushing away emotions) can be found to reduce the strength of relationships and limit intimacy (Butler et al., 2007; Gross & John, 2003). Suppressing emotions while discussing relationship conflicts has been found to decrease memory of what was said, and instead increase the memory for the emotions experienced. On the other hand, reappraisal (changing our beliefs about a situation) was shown to increase memory of what was said (Richards, Butler, & Gross, 2003). The point is, if we use suppression as a major method of regulation, we may find ourselves feeling more angry or upset after an argument with our partner, while forgetting things that were said, thus possibly damaging the relationship further. Research also suggests that the ability to regulate anger and sadness may reduce the likelihood of domestic violence in newlywed couples, important information to consider for ourselves, and for our clients (McNulty & Hellmuth, 2008).

Family

The negative consequences associated with our inability to manage our emotions in relationships affect family relationships as well. That being said, there is also evidence that we learn how to regulate our emotions from our nuclear family. For example, individuals who are more emotionally expressive also report higher levels of emotional expression in their families than other respondents (Kring & Gordon, 1998). Conversely, if our family of origin engaged in unhealthy methods of emotion regulation, such as suppression, overeating, or drug and alcohol use, we may learn these behaviors as well. The implications are clear: regulating our own emotions can not only affect our wellness, but the wellness of those around us, especially our children (Morris, Silk, Steinberg, Myers, & Robinson, 2007).

Spirituality

Spiritual beliefs can have profound affects on our ability to regulate emotions, and as a result affects our wellness. For example, higher levels of spirituality are related to a higher ability to cope with stress, as well as reduced symptoms of distress in cancer patients (Laubmeier, Zakowski, & Bair, 2004). The most obvious method of spiritual emotion regulation—prayer—as well as other religious coping methods, (such as forgiveness), were found to have positive associations with higher well-being in patients with chronic pain (Moreira-Almeida & Koenig, 2008). Further, in families who engage in religious and spiritual emotion regulation activities (such as prayer and meditation) the children's mental and physical health was higher, as was academic success and healthy social interactions (Schottenbauer, Spernak, & Hellstrom, 2007).

Nutrition

It has been found that individuals will engage in impulsive behaviors if they believe it will improve their mood—for example, eating less desirable foods (Tice, Bratslavsky, & Baumeister, 2001). Research also shows a significant relationship between negative moods and binge eating behaviors in college students (Lynch et al., 2009). While eating and procrastination may boost positive emotions in the short term, using these behaviors can be detrimental when considering long-term consequences. Consistent use of eating to manage emotions can develop into eating disorders and poor physical health, and the stress that results from repeated procrastination can also have negative effects on health.

Compulsive and Addictive Behaviors

Many addictive behaviors are directly related to dysfunctional methods of regulating emotions, and the consequences can be great. A review of research on tobacco and nicotine addiction shows that many individuals use smoking as an affect regulation strategy, making it more difficult for them to quit and maintain cessation, especially when experiencing anxiety and depression. Precipitating further damage to wellness, many turn to alcohol and other drugs to regulate emotions, and there is a higher relapse rate for those with a comorbid mental illness (Khantzian, 1990; Kushner et al., 2005). A study of college students found that men that struggled with the ability to effectively regulate their emotions also had higher levels of alcohol use than those who reported being able to effectively manage emotions (Fischer, Forthun, Pidcock, & Dowd, 2007). However, studies have shown alcohol to be related to short- and long-term increases in emotion dysregulation, in addition to the other innumerable negative consequences regular alcohol use has on wellness (Sher & Grekin, 2007).

Career

The way we regulate our emotions can also have consequences for our work and career. Invariably, to attain and maintain employment we must be able to effectively manage our emotions. This comprises the knowledge of which emotions to express (happiness and excitement over a promotion or reaching departmental goals), and which to reappraise and regulate (disappointment at not receiving a requested raise) (Gross & Munoz, 1995). Further, being unable to regulate emotions in a healthy manner may have implications for work performance and satisfaction. Here again, suppression rears its ugly head—research shows a significant relationship between emotion suppression at work, unhappiness with the job, and intentions to quit (Cote & Morgan, 2002). In a related study, individuals who reported suppressing anger and depression were more likely to report occupational problems than those who did not. These individuals also reported more anxiety and more interpersonal problems, troubles that are often consequences of poor emotion regulation skills (Hutri & Lindeman, 2002) Finally, it is thought that higher levels of emotional intelligence (a concept that will be discussed later in the chapter) may lead to improved career decision-making and heightened satisfaction with that decision (Emmerling & Cherniss, 2003).

PHYSICAL HEALTH

There is a significant amount of research that indicates a relationship between physical health and regulating emotions, especially negative emotions. Research shows that anger, aggression, and hostility can be considered risk factors for coronary heart disease (Smith, Glazer, Ruiz, & Gallo, 2004). Further, studies show that optimism about life and the future results in fewer problems with physical health symptoms (Scheier & Carver, 1985). Research also supports that optimists are more likely to engage in healthy behaviors than those that are not (Scheier & Carver, 1992). In the company of optimism and positive emotion regulation comes the feeling of hope. Individuals who report more feelings of hope had less likelihood of physical health problems or illnesses over the course of several years (Richman et al., 2005). High levels of negative emotions have a significant relationship with less physical activity, and those that report negative emotions also engage in higher rates of alcohol consumption and saturated fat consumption (Anton & Miller, 2005). These results are not restricted solely to adults—a longitudinal study of emotions in children found that young girls that reported experiencing higher levels of mood swings and anger also reported higher levels of pain and fatigue later in life (Kokkonen, Pulkkinen, & Kinnunen, 2001). In a systematic review of available studies, it was found that one of the highest causes of heart disease was chronic exposure to stress. As reviewed in the section on emotion regulation, situation selection can be a form of emotion regulation, and removing ourselves from consistently stressful situations can not only help regulate our emotions but increase our wellness (French, Senior, Weinman, & Marteau, 2001). The conclusions we wish to draw from this section are that not only is there a connection between poorly regulated negative emotions and poor health, but that regulating our emotions will help us feel better, therefore making us more likely to engage in health-related behaviors, thus increasing our physical health and wellness.

RUMINATION, SUPPRESSION, AND LOCUS OF CONTROL

It benefits our wellness not just in regulating our emotions, but how we do so. While studies show that people may believe that worrying and ruminating about something may be helpful for them emotionally, the results are quite the opposite—the more time subjects spent ruminating on negative events, the longer they experienced depressed and negative feelings, and in a similar but separate study, subjects were found to feel more depressed when ruminating on the negative feelings, whereas those that engaged in distraction reported experiencing significantly less depression (Campbell-Sills, Barlow, Brown, & Hoffman, 2006; Nolen-Hoeksema & Morrow, 1993; Nolen-Hoeksema, Morrow, & Fredrickson, 1993).

There also seems to be a relationship between whether we believe we can control our emotions and our overall wellness. In a study of incoming college freshmen over the course of their first year at college, students that reported less belief that they could control their emotions also reported higher levels of negative emotions, less social adaptation and support, less satisfaction and less well-being than those that felt they could manage their emotions (Tamir, John, Srivastava, & Gross, 2007). In addition, students that felt they could control their emotions reported using reappraisal more than other types of emotion regulation.

As previously mentioned, suppressing our emotions has been found to be detrimental to wellness in a variety of ways. One study demonstrated that reappraisal as a method of regulating emotions was found to increase aspects of wellness for participants in comparison to the act of suppressing emotions, which created the opposite effect (Nezleck & Kuppens, 2008). Suppressing emotions can also lead to increases in bodily stress, and increases in blood pressure (Butler et al., 2007). In addition, suppressing emotions puts more stress on many systems in the body, including the cardiovascular system, which could lead to significant health problems in the future (Mauss & Gross, 2004). As mentioned in the earlier discussion of relationships and emotion regulation, studies have also shown that suppressing emotions significantly reduces our memories regarding the events that took place, and this is not just true for social situations but when viewing something that might be upsetting or elicit emotional expression (Richards & Gross, 2006).

As if these studies were not evidence enough that suppression is damaging to our wellness, in a comparison of suppression and reappraisal as venues to regulate our emotions, research supports that participants who used suppression reported higher levels of depression, less satisfaction with life, lower self-esteem, and less optimism than those that utilized reappraisal (Gross & John, 2003). On the other hand, participants that used reappraisal responded higher on all the aforementioned aspects, in addition to higher responses on personal growth, self-acceptance, and having a clear purpose in life.

INTERVENTIONS

The relationship between emotion regulation and wellness is clear. The next step is to focus on ways we can improve emotion regulation processes, in our lives and the lives of our clients.

Because of the reciprocal nature of emotions and wellness, improvements in any one area will affect the other. For example, increases in physical health activities can help us feel better, and can improve and maintain our employment situation. Abstaining from addictive substances and attending to our relationships in all areas of our lives can also help us to experience more positive emotions. On the contrary, learning to regulate our emotions can improve our physical energy and enhance our relationships.

SPIRITUALITY AND MEDITATION

Spirituality can provide meaning and purpose during stressful and harrowing times, helping to regulate emotions and increasing coping skills in the face of hardship. Many religions include practices such as prayer and meditation. Prayer, in many ways, can be considered reframing, as the individual engaged in prayer also engages in identification of events that he or she cannot control, which then may help him or her to accept the things that may be causing intense and interfering emotions.

Meditation, often considered a spiritual practice, incorporates controlling one's thoughts and behaviors to regulate and control impulsive and unwanted thoughts often related to emotions, and can have important implications for emotion regulation (Watts, 2007). Studies show that individuals who use meditation regularly experience less anxiety and lower heart rates when using meditation skills in the face of a stressful situation than those who do not (Goleman & Schwartz, 1976).

MINDFULNESS AND DIALECTICAL BEHAVIOR THERAPY

Mindfulness, the act of controlling one's attention and thoughts to become more aware of current thoughts and feelings, has been shown repeatedly to be associated with an increased ability to manage negative emotions, decreased physical symptoms, and increased coping skills and well-being (Carmody & Baer, 2008; Carmody, Reed, Kristeller, & Merriam, 2008; Coffey & Hartman, 2008). Mindfulness can be considered the basis for regulating emotions, supplemented by other valuable skills (Linehan, Bohus, & Lynch, 2007). Invariably, emotion regulation is a major module included in Dialectical Behavior Therapy. While this therapy is directed towards patients with borderline personality disorder, these abilities can be helpful for anyone working to improve the regulation of their emotions. The techniques are directed towards several points in the emotion and response continuum—commencing with reducing vulnerability to negative emotions by increasing wellness in other areas (e.g., engaging in physical health activities, engaging in activities that increase feelings of competence), and increasing positive emotions on a daily basis. The skills are then directed toward understanding the emotions that are experienced, using mindfulness to tolerate them, and managing painful emotions effectively by acting opposite to the current emotion—for example, watching a comedy when feeling sad (Linehan, 1993b). Other skills employed in Dialectical Behavior Therapy can contribute significantly in attempts regulate emotions as well, including interpersonal effectiveness and distress tolerance skills (Linehan et al., 2007). Using emotion regulation skills in cognitive behaviorally based treatment interventions has shown to be beneficial not only by increasing mental health outcomes but also by increasing applicability of skills learned (Berking et al., 2008).

COGNITIVE BEHAVIORAL INTERVENTIONS

In a study of the relationship between social anxiety and methods of emotion regulation, it has been found that it was not merely lower levels of anxiety that showed an increase in positive emotions, but also the act of openly expressing emotions as opposed to suppressing them that augments emotions (Kashdan & Breen, 2008). While both techniques proved to be effective emotion regulation techniques, cognitive behavioral techniques have shown to be more effective than mindfulness to increase subjects' ability to cope with pain and stress (Zautra et al., 2008). Emotions and our reactions to those emotions are based on our appraisal of any given situation (Siemer, Mauss, & Gross, 2007). In addition, people that engage in reappraisal have been found to not only experience fewer and less extreme negative emotions (i.e., anger and sadness) but experienced more positive emotions in the face of frustrating or irritating tasks (Mauss et al., 2007).

EMOTIONAL INTELLIGENCE

Emotional intelligence (EI) is another method of helping clients to increase their ability to regulate their thoughts and emotions. EI began with Gardner's *Frames of Mind* (1983), when he postulated that there were several types of intelligence. From this point, EI grew into many forms and resulted in a significant amount of research. One of the most popular models is conceptualized by Salovey and Mayer (1990). They define EI as "the ability to monitor one's own and others' feelings and emotions, to discriminate among them and to use this information to guide one's thinking and actions" (p. 5). They go further to divide EI into four branches—perception of emotion, using emotion to facilitate thought, understanding emotion, and managing emotions. There are many ways to increase one's emotional intelligence based on Salovey and Mayer's model, including increasing skills such as self-awareness, emotion regulation, empathy, and managing relationships (Goleman, 1995). For example, it has been found that participants with higher levels of emotional intelligence were more likely to use adaptive strategies to decrease a variety of negative emotions as well as increase and maintain positive emotions (Mikolajczak et al., 2008).

Indeed, while the importance of emotion regulation as an intervention in our counseling cannot be argued, emotion regulation skills can and should be implemented as a preventive measure as well, at the very base of wellness prevention models. Higher levels of effective emotion regulation equate to less emotion dysregulation, fewer occurrences of severe negative emotions that spin out of control, and thus less depression, anxiety, impulse control, and fewer addiction disorders (Gross & Munoz, 1995).

Summary

Though emotion regulation may not receive as much scrutiny as other aspects of wellness, it is connected to nearly all facets of our health. We have discussed that while there are many things we can control, our emotions are not one of those things. We can, however, regulate them—and our ability to regulate our emotions can limit or enhance our physical health, career, relationships, and decision-making on several levels. The complexities continue; not only is it regulating these emotions but how we regulate them. We have shown that while suppression is often used it can decrease wellness, while reappraisal can increase wellness in every area of our lives. There are many ways to increase our wellness through emotion regulation, including increasing our emotional intelligence and engaging in meditation and cognitive strategies. What is most important is not only that we use this information for ourselves but for our clients, in facilitating their ability to manage their own emotions and thoughts for happiness in every facet of their lives.

References

American Psychiatric Association. (2000). *Diagnostic and statistical manual of mental disorders* (4th ed.). Washington, DC: Author.

Anton, S. D., & Miller, P. M. (2005). Do negative emotions predict alcohol consumption, saturated fat intake, and physical activity in older adults? *Behavior Modification, 29*(4), 677–688.

Baumeister, R. F., DeWall, D. N., & Zhang, L. (2007). Do emotions improve or hinder the decision making process? In K. D. Vohs, R. F. Baumeister, & G. Loewenstein (Eds.), *Do emotions help or hurt decision making?* New York: Russell Sage Foundation.

Beer, J. S., & Lombardo, M. V. (2007). Insights into emotion regulation from neuropsychology. In J. J. Gross (Ed.), *Handbook of emotion regulation.* New York: Guilford Press.

Berking, M., Wupperman, P., Reichardt, A., Pejic, T., Dippel, A., & Znoj, H. (2008). Emotion-regulation skills as a treatment target in psychotherapy. *Behaviour Research & Therapy, 46*(11), 1230–1237.

Butler, E. A., Egloff, B., Wilhelm, F. H., Smith, N. C., Campbell-Sills, L., & Barlow, D. H. (2007). Incorporating emotion regulation into conceptualizations and treatments of anxiety and mood disorders. In J. J. Gross (Ed.), *Handbook of emotion regulation.* New York: Guilford Press.

Campbell-Sills, L., Barlow, D. H., Brown, T. A., & Hofmann, S. G. (2006). Acceptability and suppression of negative emotion in anxiety and mood disorders. *Emotion, 6*(4), 587–595.

Carmody, J., & Baer, R. A. (2008). Relationships between mindfulness practice and levels of mindfulness, medical and psychological symptoms and well-being in a mindfulness-based stress reduction program. *Journal of Behavioral Medicine, 31*(1), 23–33.

Carmody, J., Reed, G., Kristeller, J., & Merriam, P. (2008). Mindfulness, spirituality, and health-related symptoms. *Journal of Psychosomatic Research, 64*(4), 393–403.

Cote, S., & Morgan, L. M. (2002). A longitudinal analysis of the association between emotion regulation, job satisfaction, and intentions to quit. *Journal of Organizational Behavior, 23*(8), 947–962.

Davidson, R. J., Fox, A., & Kalin, N. H. (2007). Neural bases of emotion regulation in nonhuman primates and humans. In J. J. Gross (Ed.), *Handbook of emotion regulation.* New York: Guilford Press.

Dickstein, D. P., & Leibenluft, E. (2006). Emotion regulation in children and adolescents: Boundaries between normalcy and bipolar disorder. *Development and Psychopathology, 18*(4), 1105–1131.

Emmerling, R. J., & Cherniss, G. (2003). Emotional intelligence and the career choice process. *Journal of Career Assessment, 11*(2), 153–167.

Fischer, J. L., Forthun, L. F., Pidcock, B. W., & Dowd, D.A. (2007). Parent relationships, emotion regulation, psychosocial maturity, and college student alcohol use problems. *Journal of Youth and Adolescence, 36,* 912–926.

French, D. P., Senior, V., Weinman, J., & Marteau, T. M. (2001). Causal attributions for heart disease: A systematic review. *Psychology & Health, 16*(1), 77–98.

Gardner, H. (1983). *Frames of mind.* New York: Basic Books.

Goleman, D. (1995). *Emotional intelligence: Why it can matter more than IQ.* New York: Bantam Books.

Goleman, D. J., & Schwartz, G. E. (1976). Meditation as an intervention in stress reactivity. *Journal of Consulting and Clinical Psychology, 44*(3), 456–466.

Gross, J. J. (1998). The emerging field of emotion regulation: An integrative review. *Review of General Psychology, 2*(3), 271–299.

Gross, J. J., & John, O. P. (2003). Individual differences in two emotion regulation processes: Implications for affect, relationships, and well-being. *Journal of Personality and Social Psychology, 85*(2), 348–362.

Gross, J. J., & Munoz, R. F. (1995). Emotion regulation and mental health. *Clinical Psychology: Science and Practice, 2*(2), 151–164.

Gross, J. J., & Thompson, R. A. (2007) Emotion regulation: Conceptual foundations. In J. J. Gross (Ed.), *Handbook of emotion regulation.* New York: Guilford Press.

Hutri, M., & Lindeman, M. (2002). The role of stress and negative emotions in an occupational crisis. *Journal of Career Development, 29*(1), 19–36.

Kashdan, T.B., & Breen, W. E. (2008). Social anxiety and positive emotions: A prospective examination of a self-regulatory model with tendencies to suppress or express emotions as a moderating variable. *Behavior Therapy, 39,* 1–12.

Kashdan, T. B., Zvolensky, M. J., & McLeish, A.C. (2008). Anxiety sensitivity and affect regulatory strategies: Individual and interactive risk factors for anxiety-related symptoms. *Journal of Anxiety Disorders, 22,* 429-440.

Khantzian, E. J. (1990). Self-regulation and self-medication factors in alcoholism and the addictions: similarities and differences. In M. Galanter (Ed.), *Recent developments in alcoholism.* New York: Plenum Press.

Kokkonen, M., Pulkkinen, L., & Kinnunen, T. (2001). Low self-control of emotions as an antecedent of self-reported physical symptoms: A longitudinal perspective. *European Psychologist, 6*(1), 26–35.

Kostiuk, L. M., & Fouts, G. T. (2002). Understanding of emotions and the emotion regulation in adolescent females with conduct problems: A qualitative analysis. *The Qualitative Report, 7*(1). Retrieved August 21, 2008, from http://www.nova.edu/ssss/QR/QR7-1/kostiuk.html

Kring, A. M., & Gordon, A. H. (1998). Sex differences in emotion: Expression, experience, and physiology. *Journal of Personality and Social Psychology, 74*(3), 686–703.

Kushner, M. G., Abrams, K., Thuras, P., Hanson, K. L., Brekke, M., & Sletten, S. (2005). Follow-up study of anxiety disorder and alcohol dependence in comorbid alcoholism treatment patients. *Alcoholism: Clinical and Experimental Research, 29*(8), 1432–1443.

Laubmeier, K. K., Zakowski, S. G., & Bair, J. P. (2004). The role of spirituality in the psychological adjustment to cancer: A test of the transactional model of stress and coping. *International Journal of Behavioral Medicine, 11*(1), 48–55.

Le Doux, J. E. (2000). Emotion circuits in the brain. *Annual Review of Neuroscience, 23*, 155–184.

Le Doux, J. E. (1996). *The emotional brain: The mysterious underpinnings of emotional life.* New York: Simon & Schuster.

Linehan, M. (1993a). *Cognitive-behavioral treatment of borderline personality disorder.* New York: Guilford Press.

Linehan, M. (1993b). *Skills training manual for treating borderline personality disorder.* New York: Guilford Press.

Linehan, M., Bohus, M., & Lynch, T. (2007) Dialectical behavior therapy for pervasive emotion dysregulation: Theoretical and practical underpinnings. In J. J. Gross (Ed.), *Handbook of emotion regulation.* New York: Guilford Press.

Lowenstein, G. (2007) Affect regulation and affective forecasting. In J. J. Gross (Ed.), *Handbook of emotion regulation.* New York: Guilford Press.

Lynch, W. C., Everingham, A., Dubitzky, J., Hartman, M., Mauss, I. B., & Bunge, S. A. et al. (2009). Culture and automatic emotion regulation. In S. Ismer, S. Jung, S. Kronast, C. van Scheve, & M. Vanderkerckhove (Eds.), *Regulating emotions: Culture, social necessity and biological inheritance.* London: Blackwell.

Mauss, I. B., Cook, C. L., Cheng, J. Y. J., & Gross, J. J. (2007). Individual differences in cognitive reappraisal: Experiential and physiological responses to an anger provocation. *International Journal of Psychophysiology.*

Mauss, I. B., & Gross J. J. (2004). Emotion suppression and cardiovascular disease: Is hiding feelings bad for your heart? In I. Nyklicek, L. Temoshok, & A. Vingerhoets (Eds.), *Emotional expression and health: Advances in theory, assessment, and clinical applications.* New York: Brunner-Routledge.

Mauss, I. B., & Robinson, M. D. (2009). Measures of emotion: A review. *Cognition and Emotion, 23*(2), 209–237.

McEwen, B., & Sapolsky, R. (1995). Stress and cognitive functioning. *Current Opinion in Neurobiology, 5*, 205–216.

McNulty, J. K., & Hellmuth, J. C. (2008). Emotion regulation and intimate partner violence in newlyweds. *Journal of Family Psychology, 22*(5), 794–797.

McRae, K., Ochsner, K. N., Mauss, I. B., Gabrieli, J. J. D., & Gross, J. J. (2008). *Gender difference in emotion regulation: An fMRI study of cognitive reappraisal.* [Manuscript submitted for publication]

Merriam Webster's Online Dictionary. (2008). Retrieved October 2, 2008, from http://aolsvc.merriam-webster.aol.com/dictionary/emotion

Mikolajczak, M., Nelis, D., Hansenne, M., & Quoidbach, J. (2008). If you can regulate sadness, you can probably regulate shame: Associations between trait emotional intelligence, emotion regulation, and coping efficiency across emotions. *Personality and Individual Differences, 44*, 1356–1368.

Moreira-Almeia, A., & Koenig, H. G. (2008). Religiousness and spirituality in fibromyalgia and chronic pain patients. *Current Pain and Headache Reports, 12*(5), 327–332.

Morris, A., Silk, J., Steinberg, L., Myers, S., & Robinson, L. (2007). The role of the family context in the development of emotion regulation. *Social Development, 16*(2), 361–388.

Nezleck, J. B., & Kuppens, P. (2008). Regulating positive and negative emotions in daily life. *Journal of Personality, 76*(3), 561–580.

Nolen-Hoeksema, S., & Morrow, J. (1993). Effects of rumination and distraction on naturally occurring depressed mood. *Cognition & Emotion, 7*(6), 561–570.

Nolen-Hoeksema, S., Morrow, J., & Fredrickson, B. L. (1993). Response styles and the duration of episodes of depressed mood. *Journal of Abnormal Psychology, 102*(1), 20–28

Pulkkinen, L., Nygren, H., & Kokko, K. (2002). Successful development: Childhood antecedents of adaptive psychosocial functioning in adulthood. *Journal of Adult Development, 9*(4), 251–265.

Richards, J. M., Butler, E. A., & Gross, J. J. (2003). Emotion regulation in romantic relationships: The cognitive consequences of concealing feelings. *Journal of Social and Personal Relationships, 20*(5), 599–620.

Richards, J. M., & Gross, J. J. (2006). Personality and emotional memory: How regulating emotion impairs memory for emotional events. *Journal of Research in Personality, 40*(5), 631–651.

Richman, L. S., Kubzansky, L., Maselko, J., Kawachi, I., Choo, P., & Bauer, M. (2005). Positive emotion and health: Going beyond the negative. *Health Psychology, 24*(4), 422–429.

Salovey, P., & Mayer, J. D. (1990). Emotional intelligence. *Imagination, Cognition, and Personality, 9*, 185–211.

Scheier, M. F., & Carver, C. S. (1985). Optimism, coping, and health: Assessment and implications of generalized outcome expectancies. *Health Psychology, 4*(3), 219–247.

Scheier, M. F., & Carver, C. S. (1992). Effects of optimism on psychological and physical well-being: Theoretical overview and empirical update. *Cognitive Therapy and Research, 16*(2), 201–228.

Schottenbauer, M. A., Spernak, S. M., & Hellstrom, I. (2007). Relationship between religious behaviors and child well-being among third-grade children. *Mental Health, Religion, & Culture, 10*(2), 191–198.

Sher, K. J., & Grekin, E. R. (2007). In J. J., Gross (Ed.), *Handbook of emotion regulation.* New York: Guilford Press.

Siemer, M., Mauss, I., & Gross, J. J. (2007). Same situation—different emotions: How appraisals shape our emotions. *Emotion, 7*(3), 592–600.

Smith, T. W., Glazer, K., Ruiz, J. M., & Gallo, L. C. (2004). Hostility, anger, aggressiveness, and coronary heart disease: An interpersonal perspective on personality, emotion, and health. *Journal of Personality, 72*(6), 1217–1270.

Tamir, M., John, O., Srivastava, S., & Gross, J. J. (2007). Implicit theories of emotion: Affective and social outcomes across a major life transition. *Journal of Personality and Social Psychology, 92*(4), 731–744.

Tice, D. M., Bratslavsky, E., & Baumeister, R. F. (2001). Emotional distress regulation takes precedence over impulse control: If you feel bad, do it! *Journal of Personality and Social Psychology, 80*(1), 53–67.

Watts, F. (2007). Emotion regulation and religion. In J. J., Gross (Ed.), *Handbook of emotion regulation.* New York: Guilford Press.

Wilson, B.J., Fernandes-Richards, S., Aarskog, C., Osborn, T., & Capetillo, D. (2007). The role of emotion regulation in the social problems of boys with developmental delays. *Early Education and Development, 18*(2), 201–222.

Witmer, J. M., & Sweeney, T. J. (1992). A holistic model for wellness and prevention over the life span. *Journal of Counseling & Development, 71*, 140–148.

Zautra, A. J., Davis, M. C., Reich, J. W., Tennen, H., Nicassio, P., & Finan, P. et al. (2008) Comparison of cognitive behavioral and mindfulness meditation interventions on adaptation to rheumatoid arthritis for patients with and without history of recurrent depression. *Journal of Consulting and Clinical Psychology, 76*(3), 408–421.

9 PHYSICAL ACTIVITY AND PSYCHOLOGICAL WELL-BEING

Brian C. Focht and Michael Lewis

Everyone knows the effects of physical exercise on the mood: how much more cheerful and courageous one feels when the body has been toned up. . . . Our moods are determined by the feelings that come up from our body. Those feelings are sometimes of worry, breathlessness, anxiety; sometimes peace and repose. It is certain that exercise will tend to train the body toward the latter feelings. The latter feelings are certainly an essential ingredient of all perfect human character.

WILLIAM JAMES (1899, PP. 220–221)

Wellness Connection

A significant body of research exists documenting the mental health benefits of exercise. Dr. Brian Focht, exercise physiologist, and Mike Lewis, clinical counselor, highlight some of these research findings and suggest approaches a counselor might use to help clients begin regular physical activity.

Stress, anxiety, and depression have become increasingly prevalent in contemporary society. Recent estimates suggest that over 40 million adults in the United States suffer from clinically meaningful elevations in depressive and anxiety symptoms (Kessler et al., 1994). Emotional disturbance has adverse effects upon health and well-being and represents one of the leading causes of disability-adjusted life years (i.e., years of life lived with meaningfully compromised function and well-being). Taken collectively, the deleterious effects of mood disturbance have serious social, economic, and public health implications. Although effective for many individuals, traditional medical and counseling approaches used in the treatment of mood disturbance are also time-consuming, expensive, and have been associated with potentially adverse side effects. Consequently, there is considerable interest in identifying safe, effective, inexpensive behavioral interventions that can be implemented as either alternative or adjuvant approaches to the prevention and treatment of mood disorders.

The physical health benefits of physical activity are well-established. Regular physical activity and exercise participation is linked with prevention of all-cause mortality and reductions in risk of a variety of chronic diseases including coronary heart disease, cancer, and diabetes (Blair, LaMonte, & Nichaman, 2004). Exercise therapy is advocated for inclusion in the treatment of many chronic diseases including heart disease, arthritis, and diabetes. Furthermore, physical activity is an integral component of weight management strategies and is widely considered an important part of countering the rising obesity epidemic and the mortality risk accompanying being overweight or obese (Bouchard, 2001; Focht, Rejeski, & Rejeski, 2005; Wing, 1999).

In addition to producing improvements in these valuable physical health outcomes, there is now mounting evidence that physical activity is also associated with significant improvements in psychological well-being. Accordingly, scientific and practical interest in determining the value of applying physical activity as an independent treatment, or integrating physical activity in conjunction with traditional mental health treatment approaches, has increased dramatically during the past 30 years. The primary purpose of the present chapter is to provide an overview of the relationship between exercise and psychological well-being. The specific objectives of this review include: (a) summarizing the extant literature addressing the effects of exercise on select psychological well-being outcomes, (b) providing an overview of the mechanisms proposed to explain the psychological benefits of exercise, and (c) addressing the role of psychological responses to exercise in promoting the adoption and maintenance of regular physical activity participation.

PHYSICAL ACTIVITY, EXERCISE, AND PSYCHOLOGICAL WELL-BEING: KEY DEFINITIONS AND DISTINCTIONS

As scientific and applied interest in the psychological benefits of a physically active lifestyle has developed, the importance of appropriately defining both the key aspects of physical activity behavior as well as the relevant psychological outcomes it influences has received increased attention. Accordingly, definitions of physical activity, exercise, and select psychological outcomes that have been investigated in conjunction with physical activity participation are provided in the following sections.

Physical Activity and Exercise

Physical activity is defined as any bodily movement involving the skeletal muscles that results in an appreciable increase in energy expenditure (Blair et al., 2004; Caspersen, 1989). Consistent with this definition, physical activity is now recognized as an umbrella concept that comprises a wide variety of movement-related forms of activities including, but not limited to, exercise, occupational activity, purposeful activity, sports participation, and other physically active leisure time pursuits. By contrast, *exercise* is a subtype of physical activity that is defined as planned, repetitive involvement in various forms of structured physical activity (such as walking, running, cycling, group fitness, strength training, and yoga) for the purpose of attaining desired fitness outcomes such as improvements in cardiovascular endurance, muscular strength, muscle tone, flexibility, body composition, and weight management.

Defining Psychological Well-Being: Distinguishing Key Outcomes

There is evidence that exercise results in beneficial changes in a wide variety of psychological outcomes. Exercise has been linked with improvements in affect, mood, self-esteem, self-efficacy, depression, anxiety, and quality of life (Berger & Tobar, 2007; Dishman & Buckworth 2002;

Ekkekakis & Acevedo, 2007; Lox, Martin Ginis, & Petruzzello, 2006; McAuley & Blissmer, 2000; Rejeski & Mihalko, 2001). As the empirical evidence addressing the mental health benefits of exercise has grown, considerable debate regarding the definition and appropriate measurement of many of these outcomes has emerged in the contemporary exercise psychology literature (Ekkekakis, 2008; Ekkekakis & Petruzzello, 2001; Gauvin & Rejeski, 2001). It has been contended that some researchers in the exercise psychology literature have frequently used terms such as *affect, mood*, and *emotion* synonymously when they actually represent unique psychological constructs with distinct, identifiable characteristics. A consensus regarding the most appropriate definition or measurement approach for each of the psychological constructs that are favorably influenced by exercise has yet to be reached. A comprehensive summary of the definition and measurement debate is beyond the scope of the present chapter. However, for the purposes of this chapter, *psychological well-being* is defined as an individual's perceptions and evaluation of his or her own life that reflects a general state of favorable mental functioning and well-being. Psychological well-being is characterized by the experience of greater positive affect, relative absence of negative affect, successful cognitive function, fulfilling relationships with others, and the ability to effectively cope with stress and adversity.

Psychological well-being encompasses a wide range of psychological outcomes including ratings of basic pleasure and activation (affect), mood, and distinct emotions (i.e., anxiety, depression, and anger). The idea that people feel better following exercise has become very well established. However, there are many different terms used to describe the psychological responses to exercise (Dishman & Buckworth, 2002; Lox et al., 2006). Recently, some researchers in the exercise psychology literature have placed considerable emphasis on resolving what they contend to be confusion, and potential misuse, of the terminology commonly used to describe the psychological outcomes most frequently assessed in conjunction with exercise participation (Ekkekakis, 2008; Ekkekakis & Acevedo, 2007; Ekkekakis & Petruzzello, 2001; Lox et al., 2006).

Although some debate regarding the definition of key psychological constructs persists, there is sufficient consensus to operationally define many of these important outcomes. Thus, distinguishing key terms that are used to describe psychological responses to exercise is an important consideration in the exercise psychology literature. *Feelings* are subjective experiences that reflect bodily sensations, cognitive appraisals, or some combination of these responses (Dishman & Buckworth, 2002; Lox et al., 2006). *Emotions* (i.e., anxiety, depression, anger, fear, and pride) are immediate responses that involve cognitive appraisal of an eliciting stimulus whereby a person, situation, or event is perceived as having a potential impact upon one's well-being. Similarly, *moods* are subjective states that also involve cognitive appraisal. However, moods are considered to be less intense and of longer duration than emotions. Additionally, moods can be experienced temporally more distant or removed from the eliciting stimulus relative to emotions. Conversely, *affect* is considered a more general valenced state involving basic ratings of pleasure and activation. Any valenced state is considered an affective response. Therefore, mood and emotions are often subsumed under the general rubric of affective responses. Irrespective of differences in terminology applied, there is sufficient evidence to contend that exercise produces meaningful improvements in each of these psychological outcomes.

Systematic study of the effects of exercise has been conducted on a variety of psychological outcomes including affect (Ekkekakis & Petruzzello, 1999), mood (Berger & Motl, 2000), self-esteem (Lox et al., 2006), cognitive functioning (Netz, 2007), and quality of life (Berger & Tobar, 2007; Rejeski & Mihalko, 2001). The majority of recent research addressing the relationship between exercise and psychological well-being has focused upon the effects of *exercise participation* on changes in self-reported indices of *affect*, *depression*, and *anxiety*.

EXERCISE AND DEPRESSION

Depression is a stress-related emotion characterized by feelings of sadness, despair, and discouragement (Dishman & Buckworth, 2002; Landers & Arent, 2007). Depressive symptoms are often linked with low self-esteem, withdrawal from interpersonal contact, and disturbances in sleep and eating behaviors. Depression is one of the most prevalent mental health issues in the United States, with estimates that over 19 million Americans experience significant depressive symptoms each year (Kessler et al., 1994).

There is considerable evidence linking physical activity participation with reduced risk of depression. Epidemiological findings demonstrate a significant inverse relationship between physical activity and depressive symptoms with higher levels of activity being associated with lower levels of self-reported depressive symptoms and reduced risk of being diagnosed with depression (Dishman, Washburn, & Heath, 2004; Mutrie, 2000). Findings from the Harvard Alumni study also revealed that men who expended > 2,500 kcal per week through physical activity had a 28% decrease in the risk of developing depression (Paffenbarger, Lee, & Leung, 1994). Taken collectively, inactivity is now acknowledged as being an independent risk factor for developing depressive symptoms and depressive disorders (Lox et al., 2006).

Whereas overall physical activity participation is strongly linked with reduced risk of developing depression, exercise participation has also been consistently shown to produce meaningful reductions in depressive symptoms. Findings from meta-analytic reviews reveal that exercise resulted in significantly greater reduction in depressive symptoms (effect sizes ranging from −.53 to −1.01) when compared to comparison or control treatments (Craft & Landers, 1998; Lawlor & Hopker, 2001; North, McCullagh, & Tran, 1990). The meta-analytic findings indicate that comparable antidepressant benefits are observed for both aerobic exercise and resistance exercise. Additionally, no consistent differences emerged as a function of individual characteristics such as age, gender, ethnicity, or fitness level. However, the observation of higher effect sizes accompanying exercise in individuals with diagnosed depressive disorders (Craft & Landers, 1998) suggests that those exhibiting the highest baseline depressive symptoms may experience the most pronounced reductions in depression following exercise participation. No systematic differences in reductions in depressive symptoms were documented as a function of exercise program characteristics such as intensity, duration, frequency, or mode (Craft & Landers, 1998; Lawlor & Hopker, 2001; North et al., 1990).

Given the beneficial effects accompanying exercise, there has been interest in directly comparing the effects of exercise with those of common treatments for depression such as psychotherapeutic counseling interventions and antidepressant medications. Results from a limited number of studies also demonstrate that exercise is comparable to psychotherapy (Freemont & Craighead, 1987; Greist et al., 1979) and antidepressant medication (Blumenthal et al., 1999). In this regard, there are several findings of interest that warrant additional explanation. For example, it is interesting to note that while exercise has been shown to be similarly effective as traditional cognitive therapy, there does not appear to be any added antidepressant benefit when the treatments are combined (Freemont & Craighead, 1987).

Recent studies directly comparing the effects of exercise to antidepressant medications have yielded similar findings (Babyak et al., 2000; Blumenthal et al., 1999; Brenes et al., 2007). However, while findings of a recent study examining the effects of exercise alone, medication alone, and a combination of exercise and medication resulted in comparable antidepressant effects, there were unique trajectories in the time course of change in depressive symptoms and maintenance of the observed treatment effects between the interventions (Blumenthal et al.,

1999). Notably, whereas antidepressant medication alone intervention elicited the most rapid initial treatment response (Blumenthal et al., 1999), participants receiving exercise alone were less likely to have relapsed six months following the cessation of treatment (Babyak et al., 2000). Therefore, whereas exercise and medication produced comparable reductions in depressive symptoms, the combination of exercise and medication did not operate in a synergistic fashion to yield additional benefit over the implementation of either treatment alone. More importantly, the antidepressant effect persisted longer following exercise, and patients receiving exercise were less likely to experience a recurrence of depression when compared to those that received medication only. Although the mechanisms responsible for the superior maintenance of the treatment effect following exercise presently remain unclear, it is possible that features of the treatments such as the ability to self-administer exercise and the potential development of tolerance to antidepressant medications may contribute to the observed differences.

In contrast to meta-analytic findings (Craft & Landers, 1998; Lawlor & Hopker, 2001; North et al., 1990), there is emerging evidence suggesting that there may be a dose-response effect of exercise on depressive symptoms. Dunn and colleagues (Dunn, Trivedi, Kampert, Clark, & Chambliss, 2005) reported an exercise program in which participants achieved a weekly caloric expenditure consistent with public health recommendations (expenditure of 17.5 kcal/kg of body weight) resulted in more favorable reductions in self-rated depressive symptoms relative to an exercise program that prescribed a lower dose of exercise (expenditure of 7 kcal/kg of body weight). Therefore, achieving public health recommendations for energy expenditure through physical activity is associated with a superior antidepressant effect than an exercise program that required lower energy expenditure.

Parenthetically, in addressing dose-response effects of exercise on depression, it should be acknowledged that short periods of significantly increased exercise participation performed at or near maximal capacity, referred to as overtraining, have been linked with increases in mood disturbance and depressive symptoms (O'Connor, 1997). Staleness, which has been proposed to reflect an exercise-induced form of depression, is believed to be elicited by periods of exercise overtraining and is characterized by increases in overall mood disturbance, depression, anxiety, and fatigue as well as concomitant reductions in energy and overall physical performance. It should be recognized that overtraining and staleness have been observed only among individuals that consistently participate in strenuous exercise training programs (i.e., competitive athletes). The volume and intensity adopted in such rigorous exercise training programs considerably exceeds the amount of physical activity advocated for the derivation of health and well-being benefits. The doses of activity associated with overtraining and the onset of staleness also considerably exceed the typical amount of physical activity performed by the average adult. Consequently, given that rates of sedentary behavior remain alarmingly high among U.S. adults, the risk of experiencing increased mood disturbance accompanying exercise overtraining and staleness is unlikely to be a concern for the majority of Americans, many of whom fail to achieve the minimum amount of moderate intensity physical activity necessary to obtain health benefits.

In summary, epidemiological findings demonstrate that physical activity is associated with reduced risk of developing depression. Additionally, exercise participation is reliably associated with meaningful reductions in depressive symptoms that are comparable to benefits accompanying common treatments such as medication, psychotherapy, and counseling interventions. The antidepressant benefits of exercise are observed independent of differences in individual demographic factors or program characteristics. Thus, it appears that multiple types of exercise prescriptions can yield clinically meaningful antidepressant effects for a wide variety of people. Taken collectively, exercise represents a promising adjuvant behavioral intervention to aid in alleviating depressive symptoms.

The Anxiolytic Effects of Exercise

Anxiety is an unpleasant emotion involving the appraisal of real or imagined threat to self. Anxiety is characterized by feelings of apprehension, self-doubt, and tension as well as physiological symptoms such as increased heart rate, sweating, and breathlessness. Overall, the various anxiety disorders represent the most common forms of mood disturbance in the United States, affecting over 20 million adults.

Over the past 30 years, reductions in anxiety have become one of the most frequently studied psychological effects of exercise participation. However, investigation of the anxiolytic effects of exercise and integration of exercise into treatment approaches designed to alleviate anxiety symptoms had been impeded for some time by erroneous beliefs about the potentially anxiety-precipitating effects accompanying exercise and lactate accumulation among patients with anxiety disorders. Specifically, it was widely believed that the lactate accumulation accompanying exercise participation increases anxiety symptoms and precipitates panic attacks in patients with, or at risk for, anxiety disorders (Pitts & McClure, 1969). However, the Pitts-McClure hypothesis of the exercise-anxiety relationship has been ably refuted by over 30 years of research with virtually no documented incidence of exercise-induced panic attacks (O'Connor, Raglin, & Martinsen, 2000; O'Connor, Smith, & Morgan, 2000) as well as the consistent finding that exercise alleviates anxiety and stress symptoms (Raglin, 1997).

The anxiolytic effects of exercise have been widely investigated. Decreases in state anxiety (i.e., immediate, transient feelings of apprehension in response to perceived threat) following participation in single or acute episodes of aerobic exercise are one of the most frequently documented findings in the contemporary exercise psychology literature (Petruzzello, Landers, Hatfield, Kubitz, & Salazar, 1991; Raglin, 1997). Although studied far less frequently than the effects of acute exercise on state anxiety, exercise training interventions have also reliably yielded clinically meaningful reductions in trait anxiety (i.e., one's general disposition to appraising situations as threatening).

Results of meta-analytic (Petruzzello et al., 1991) and comprehensive narrative reviews (Landers & Arent, 2007; Raglin, 1997) suggest that acute bouts of aerobic exercise produce reductions in state anxiety (effect size = −.25 to −.50) that emerge almost immediately following the cessation of activity and persist for up to six hours postexercise. More recently, findings from a series of investigations also provides support for the anxioltyic benefits of acute bouts of resistance exercise (Arent, Landers, Matt, & Etnier, 2005; Bartholomew & Linder, 1998; Focht, 2002; Focht & Arent, 2008; Focht & Koltyn, 1999; Focht, Koltyn, & Bouchard, 2000). The results of these studies suggest that the most favorable reductions in state anxiety were observed following moderate intensity resistance exercise and the greatest benefits were obtained by those reporting the highest levels of pre-exercise anxiety levels (Focht, 2002; Focht & Arent, 2008). Together, these findings provide support for the anxiolytic benefits of single episodes of both aerobic and resistance exercise.

Meta-analytic findings (Petruzzello et al., 1991) also demonstrate that exercise training programs consistently result in significant reductions in trait anxiety (effect size = −.33). Individuals exhibiting the highest levels of anxiety prior to exercise have reported the greatest postexercise reductions in trait anxiety. Additionally, although there is limited number of studies that directly compare the effects of exercise with other common treatments for anxiety disorders, preliminary evidence demonstrated that exercise and medication resulted in comparable anxioltyic benefits (Broocks et al., 1998).

It should be recognized that much of the existing exercise-anxiety research has been conducted in samples of nonanxious individuals reporting anxiety levels that are lower than age-related normative values. However, the magnitude of improvement in anxiety has been consistently greater among individuals exhibiting higher levels of anxiety prior to initiating exercise training (Focht, 2002; Petruzzello et al., 1991; Raglin, 1997). Thus, while there have been relatively few investigations examining the benefits of exercise for reducing anxiety symptoms in samples of individuals with diagnosed anxiety disorders, the limited available evidence (Broocks et al., 1998; Martinsen, Hoffart, & Solberg, 1989; Petruzzello et al., 1991) provides support for exercise as an efficacious adjuvant therapeutic strategy for those with elevated levels of anxiety. Clearly, the alarming prevalence of anxiety disorders in the United States indicates further research addressing the benefits of exercise for reductions in trait anxiety and clinical anxiety symptoms is necessary to determine the scope and magnitude of benefit that exercise may have.

Affective Responses to Exercise

Investigation of the effects of acute exercise on the valence and activation dimensions of basic affect has recently emerged as a focal area of interest in the contemporary exercise psychology literature (Ekkekakis, 2003; Ekkekakis & Acevedo, 2007). Prior to 2000, much of the research investigating the relationship between exercise and psychological well-being focused upon categorical psychological responses such as state anxiety or select mood and feeling states. However, a recent trend in recent research has been to conceptualize and measure affective responses from a dimensional perspective utilizing the circumplex model of affect (Russell, 1980). Studies conducted within the context of the circumplex model of affect have examined changes in the bipolar dimensions of pleasure and activation (Ekkekakis, 2008) during and following single episodes of exercise.

Consistent with prior research addressing changes in categorical psychological states, findings from this line of inquiry generally demonstrate that moderate intensity bouts of aerobic exercise result in improvements in ratings of pleasure following exercise (Ekkekakis, 2003; Ekkekakis & Petruzzello, 1999). However, important individual differences have been observed. For example, whereas changes in affective responses from pre- to postexercise are generally homogeneous and positive in nature, responses observed during exercise have been found to be heterogeneous with some participants experiencing improvements, some reporting declines, and others demonstrating no change (Van Landuyt, Ekkekakis, Hall, & Petruzzello, 2000). Furthermore, acute exercise that is sufficiently demanding to cause participants to exceed their ventilatory threshold (i.e., essentially the marker for the lactate threshold and the point of transition to greater use of anaerobic metabolism to meet the exercise demands) results in negative affective responses (Ekkekakis & Lind, 2006). Collectively, these findings suggest there may be considerable individual variability in the affective responses to acute exercise, particularly during activity. Based on these findings, Ekkekakis (2003) proposed the Dual Mode Model in an attempt to explain the individual variability and negative shifts in affect observed when exercise exceeds the ventilatory threshold. The model suggests that there may be systematic shifts in the influence of cognitive and physiological cues upon the affective responses as exercise intensity increases. According to the Dual Mode Model, cognitive factors play a central role in shaping affective responses during exercise performed at a steady state. Conversely, interoceptive, physiological cues are proposed to have primacy in influencing affective responses once exercise demand surpasses the ventilatory threshold.

Exercise performed at intensities that are proximal to, yet below, the ventilatory threshold appears to result in considerable variability in affective responses (Ekkekakis, 2003; Van Landyut et al., 2000). At this intensity, some people report positive affective responses whereas others report declines in pleasure. The divergent responses have been proposed to be related to key cognitive and/or evaluative judgments such as self-efficacy (Ekkekakis, 2003). That is, those that have higher self-efficacy for exercise appear to be better able to tolerate the exertional demands of exercise performed at or near the lactate threshold and, consequently, report more favorable affective responses. However, when exercise intensity exceeds the ventilatory threshold, affective variability decreases with shifts towards less favorable affective responses becoming more common. Findings from this line of inquiry may have important implications for individualized exercise prescription and the development of exercise guidelines. However, while these findings are of considerable interest, evidence supporting the tenets of the Dual Mode Model remains relatively limited. Accordingly, the veracity of this model for explaining affective responses to acute exercise warrants further investigation.

In summary, there is now a considerable body of evidence demonstrating that exercise is consistently associated with psychological benefits including significant improvements in affect, depression, and anxiety. Although it is now well-established that exercise can yield clinically relevant improvements in an array of psychological outcomes, the mechanisms underlying the beneficial effect of exercise upon psychological well-being has yet to be adequately delineated. Numerous hypotheses have been proposed in an attempt to explain the beneficial effect of exercise on psychological well-being. The majority of proposed explanations can be categorized as addressing either primarily psychological or biological mechanisms. A brief overview of the most viable and frequently cited mechanisms proposed to be responsible for the psychological beneficence of exercise is provided in the following section.

PROPOSED PSYCHOLOGICAL MECHANISMS

The *mastery hypothesis* suggests that the psychological benefits of exercise are derived from a sense of accomplishment or increase in one's perceived capabilities that can accompany exercise participation. This perspective proposes that self-efficacy beliefs may play an important role in the psychological benefits of exercise. Self-efficacy, one's belief in his or her ability to successfully satisfy specific situational demands (Bandura, 1997), has been consistently demonstrated to be a relevant antecedent, outcome, and mediator of exercise behavior (McAuley & Blissmer, 2000). It is well-established that self-efficacy is consistently correlated with exercise participation (Dishman & Buckworth, 2002; Trost, Owen, Bauman, Sallis, & Brown, 2002). However, there is also mounting evidence that affective benefits of exercise are related to self-efficacy beliefs (Focht, Knapp, Gavin, Raedeke, & Hickner, 2007; Jerome et al., 2002; McAuley, Talbot, & Martinez,1999; Raedeke, Focht, & Scales, 2007). Notably, individuals reporting the highest self-efficacy demonstrate the most favorable psychological responses to exercise and changes in self-efficacy are strongly related to changes in affect (Focht et al., 2007). Furthermore, findings from a limited number of studies demonstrated that experimental manipulations that successfully enhanced self-efficacy beliefs resulted in significantly improved affective responses to acute exercise (Jerome et al., 2002; McAuley et al., 1999).

The *distraction hypothesis* proposes that exercise improves psychological well-being by distracting individuals from daily worries or stressors (Raglin & Morgan, 1987). Initial support for the distraction hypothesis emanated from studies demonstrating comparable, significant reductions in state anxiety following exercise, relaxation, meditation, and quiet rest sessions (Garvin, Koltyn, & Morgan, 1997; Raglin & Morgan, 1987). However, more recent evidence addressing the viability of the distraction hypothesis has been equivocal, with some studies demonstrating that exercise results in superior improvements in select psychological responses when compared to quiet rest (Focht & Hausenblas, 2001; McAuley, Mihalko, & Bane, 1996). For example, whereas exercise and quiet rest yielded comparable reductions in state anxiety, exercise resulted in significantly greater improvements in positive affective states such as energy, engagement, and enjoyment (Focht & Hausenblas, 2001).

The *enjoyment* and *social interaction* hypotheses propose that exercise elicits psychological benefits because it is perceived as being a pleasurable activity or it promotes interpersonal interaction, respectively (Lox et al., 2006). These explanations have considerable intuitive appeal and may, in part, account for the psychological benefits of exercise. Nonetheless, there is little empirical evidence supporting either hypothesis and it is unlikely that either accounts entirely for improvements in psychological well-being given that: (a) exercise performed alone has been linked with improvements in psychological outcomes and (b) favorable affective responses have been observed following exercise not rated as being particularly enjoyable (Focht, 2009; Lox et al., 2006).

PROPOSED BIOLOGICAL MECHANISMS

The *monoamine hypothesis* suggests that exercise-induced changes in the monoamingeric systems in the brain, similar to those observed with many contemporary psychotherapeutic medications, are responsible for the psychological benefits accompanying exercise (Dishman & Buckworth, 2002; Landers & Arent, 2007). For example, selective serotonin reuptake inhibitors and monoamine oxidase inhibitors work by altering the amounts of neurotransmitters such as serotonin, norepinephrine, and dopamine available in the synapses in the brain. Consistent with this therapeutic mechanism of action, exercise has been shown to result in similar effects on central monoaminergic systems (Chaouloff, 1997; Dishman, 1997). At the present time, however, direct evidence that exercise consistently produces increases in brain levels of monoamines remains sparse. The limited empirical evidence is due, in part, to the challenges associated with obtaining accurate measures of brain levels of monoamine concentrations.

The *endorphin hypothesis* is frequently cited in the popular fitness media as the primary mechanism underlying exercise-induced improvements in psychological states. However, empirical evidence supporting the endorphin hypothesis remains inconsistent. Additionally, the plausibility of endorphins having direct effects on the central nervous system is limited due to the restricted permeability of the blood-brain barrier to endorphins (Dishman & Buckworth, 2002; Landers & Arent, 2007). Thus, whereas endorphins are frequently implicated in the psychological responses to exercise, given the lack of direct effects of plasma endorphins on the brain, it is unlikely they play a primary role in the affective benefits of exercise.

There are numerous additional psychologically and biologically oriented explanations for the exercise-psychological well-being relationship, including social support, hypothalamic-pituitary-adrenal axis, brain-derived neurotrophic factor, and thermogenic hypotheses. Whereas all of these proposed mechanisms remain viable, they have either received insufficient study to confirm their plausibility or have received mixed empirical support at the present time. Each potential explanation warrants further inquiry to determine the extent to which it may contribute to the psychological benefits of exercise.

Although there are equivocal findings for each of the aforementioned explanations, unitary support for any single underlying mechanism is presently absent. Furthermore, the complexity of the relationship between exercise and psychological well-being makes it unlikely that any single mechanism is entirely responsible for these beneficial outcomes. Since each mechanism has unique features that can plausibly influence the psychological responses to exercise, it is reasonable to contend that the psychological beneficence of exercise is due to multiple, redundant mechanisms encompassing both biological and psychological factors. Thus, it is possible that some, or all, of the proposed mechanisms are viable and may operate, at least partially, in conjunction with each other to explain the influence of exercise upon psychological well-being.

THE CHALLENGE OF PROMOTING PHYSICAL ACTIVITY PARTICIPATION: A ROLE FOR PSYCHOLOGICAL OUTCOMES?

Despite considerable evidence of the physical and psychological benefits of an active lifestyle, physical activity participation rates remain disturbingly low in the United States (Blair et al., 2004; Dishman et al., 2004). Physical activity is unquestionably a complex health behavior and numerous factors have been linked with physical activity participation. Correlates of physical activity represent a complex constellation of factors including, but not limited to, demographic and personal, psychological, behavioral, social and cultural, environmental, and activity characteristic factors (Blair et al., 2004; Dishman & Buckworth, 2002; Dishman et al., 2004).

Psychological constructs are proposed to be integral determinants of behavior in several well established theories of health behavior that are frequently applied to explain physical activity participation. The theory of planned behavior is one of the most commonly employed theoretical frameworks used to explain the adoption and maintenance of health behaviors (Ajzen, 1991). This conceptual framework posits that the positive and/or negative evaluation of a behavior (attitude), perceived social pressure to engage in a behavior (subjective norm), and perceived control over participation (perceived behavioral control) determine an individual's intention to engage in health behaviors. There is considerable evidence supporting the relationship between theory of planned behavior constructs and exercise behavior and strong associations between the intention-exercise, perceived behavioral control-intention, and attitude-intention constructs that have been reported in recent meta-analyses addressing the application of the theory of planned behavior in the exercise domain (Symons-Downs & Hausenblas, 2005).

Social cognitive theory proposes there are bidirectional, reciprocally deterministic relationships among the person, environment, and behavior that shape behavioral tendencies and the motivation to take action (Bandura, 1997). Self-efficacy, the primary motivational construct in social cognitive theory, is one of the strongest, most consistent correlates of physical activity behavior (McAuley & Blissmer, 2000; Trost et al., 2002). Consequently, there is considerable support for the position that one's self-efficacy beliefs serve as an integral determinant of physical activity participation.

Hedonic theories of motivation suggest that people generally engage in activities perceived as being pleasurable and avoid participating in activities that elicit feelings of displeasure (Emmons & Diener, 1986; Loewenstein & Lerner, 2003; Watson, 2002). Hence, within this perspective on motivation, affective responses play an integral role in behavioral decision making. Thus, the amount of pleasure or displeasure that one experiences during exercise may influence the likelihood that he or she subsequently adopts or maintains regular participation.

Affective responses observed early in structured exercise programs have been shown to be associated with exercise adherence (Carels, Berger, & Darby, 2006; Kwan & Bryan, in press; Williams et al., Marcus, 2008). Emerging empirical evidence also demonstrates relationships between affective responses to acute exercise and the central motivational constructs identified in social cognitive theories of health behavior. For example, Focht (2009) recently observed that affective responses to a 10-minute walk were significantly related to intention to walk for exercise. Additionally, affective responses to acute exercise are significantly correlated with self-efficacy beliefs in recent findings (Focht, Knapp, Raedeke, Gavin, & Hickner, 2007; Raedeke et al., 2007). Affective responses are also proposed to shape the formation of attitude (Azjen, 1991) and self-efficacy beliefs (Bandura, 1997) providing a conceptual link between how one feels and his or her motivation for behavior as proposed in established theories of health behavior. Thus, the psychological responses to exercise may play an important role in determining the adoption and maintenance of regular physical activity participation. The relationship observed between affective states, adherence, and established theory-based correlates of physical activity in recent research suggests that affective responses to acute exercise merit consideration in physical activity promotion efforts.

Summary

Recognition of the psychological benefits of exercise continues to grow. There is now a considerable body of empirical evidence supporting the beneficial effect of physical activity and exercise on a wide range of psychological responses including anxiety, depression, mood, and affect. These responses represent important aspects of psychological well-being and warrant further inquiry as efforts to attenuate the personal, social, and economic costs of mental health disorders in the United States continue. An important caveat must be acknowledged when considering the exercise-psychological well-being relationship. Although exercise is linked with clinically meaningful improvements in a wide array of psychological responses, it would be imprudent for exercise to be advocated as a substitute for other well-established, efficacious treatment strategies. However, exercise clearly has benefits for improving psychological well-being, and focused efforts to determine how exercise and physical activity can be most effectively integrated into comprehensive approaches to the prevention and treatment of mental health disorders would be particularly informative.

Exercise-related improvements in these outcomes may also favorably influence motivation to adopt and maintain regular physical activity participation. Accordingly, further investigation of the extent to which improvements in psychological well-being may aid in physical activity promotion and obesity prevention efforts is also of great public health importance. Taken collectively, findings from the extant research provide compelling support for the psychological beneficence of exercise and reinforce the notion that a healthy mind does indeed reside within a healthy body.

References

Arent, S. M., Landers, D. M., Matt, K. S., & Etnier, J. L. (2005). Dose-response and mechanistic issues in the resistance training and affect relationship. *Journal of Sport and Exercise Psychology, 27,* 92–110.

Ajzen, I. (1991). The theory of planned behavior. *Organizational Behavior and Human Decision Processes, 50,* 179–211.

Babyak, M., Blumenthal, J. A., Herman, P., Khatri, M., Doraiswamy, P. M., Moore, K., et al. (2000). Exercise treatment for major depression: Maintenance of therapeutic benefit at 10 months. *Psychosomatic Medicine, 62,* 633–638.

Bandura, A. (1997). *Self-efficacy: The exercise of control.* New York: Freeman.

Bartholomew, J. B. & Linder, D. E. (1998). State anxiety following resistance exercise: The role of gender and exercise intensity. *Journal of Behavioral Medicine, 21,* 205–219.

Berger, B. G., & Motl, R. W. (2000). Exercise and mood: A selective review and synthesis of research employing the Profile of Mood States. *Journal of Applied Sport Psychology, 12,* 69–92.

Berger, B. G., & Tobar, D. A. (2007). Physical activity and quality of life: Key considerations. In G. Tennenbaum & R. C. Eklund (Eds.), *Handbook of sport psychology* (pp. 598–620). Hoboken, NJ: John Wiley.

Blair, S. N., LaMonte, M. J., & Nichaman, M. Z. (2004). The evolution of physical activity recommendations: How much is enough? *American Journal of Clinical Nutrition, 79,* 913S–920S.

Blumenthal, J. A., Babyak, M. A., Moore, W. E., Craighead, W. E., Herman, S., Khatri, P., et al. (1999). Effects of exercise training on older patients with major depression. *Archives of Internal Medicine, 159,* 2349–2356.

Bouchard, C. (2001). *Physical activity and obesity.* Champaign, IL: Human Kinetics.

Brenes, G. A., Williamson, J. D., Messier, S. P., Rejeski, W. J., Pahor, M., Ip, E., & Penninx, B. (2007). Treatment of minor depression in older adults: A pilot study comparing sertraline and exercise. *Aging and Mental Health, 11,* 61–68.

Broocks, A., Bandelow, B., Pekrun, G., George, A., Meyer, T., Bartmann, U., et al. (1998). Comparison of aerobic exercise, clomipramine, and placebo in the treatment of panic disorder. *American Journal of Psychiatry, 155,* 603–609.

Carels, R. A., Berger, B. G., & Darby, L. (2006). The association between mood states and physical activity in post-menopausal, obese, sedentary women. *Journal of Aging and Physical Activity, 14,* 12–28.

Caspersen, C. J. (1989). Physical activity epidemiology: Concepts, methods, and applications to exercise science. *Exercise and Sport Sciences Reviews, 17,* 423–473.

Chaouloff, F. (1997). The serotonin hypothesis. In W. P. Morgan (Ed.), *Physical activity and mental health* (pp. 179–198). Washington, DC: Taylor and Francis.

Craft. L. L., & Landers, D. M. (1998). The effect of exercise on clinical depression and depression resulting from mental illness: A meta-analysis. *Journal of Sport and Exercise Psychology, 20,* 339–357.

Dishman, R. K. (1997). The norepinephrine hypothesis. In W. P. Morgan (Ed.), *Physical activity and mental health* (pp. 199–212). Washington, DC: Taylor and Francis.

Dishman, R. K., & Buckworth, J. (2002). *Exercise psychology.* Champaign, IL: Human Kinetics.

Dishman, R. K., Washburn, R. A., & Heath, G. W. (2004). *Physical activity epidemiology.* Champaign, IL: Human Kinetics.

Dunn, A. L., Trivedi, M. H., Kampert, J. B., Clark, C. G., & Chambliss, H. O. (2005). Exercise treatment for depression: Efficacy and dose response. *American Journal of Preventive Medicine, 28,* 1–8.

Ekkekakis, P. (2003). Pleasure and displeasure from the body: Perspectives from exercise. *Cognition and Emotion, 17,* 213–239.

Ekkekakis, P. (2008). Affective circumplex redux: The discussion on its utility as measurement framework in exercise psychology continues. *International Review of Sport and Exercise Psychology, 1,* 139–159.

Ekkekakis, P., & Acevedo, E. (2007). *The psychobiology of exercise.* Champaign, IL: Human Kinetics.

Ekkekakis, P., & Lind, E. (2006). Exercise does not feel the same when you are overweight: The impact of self-selected and imposed intensity on affect and exertion. *International Journal of Obesity, 30,* 652–660.

Ekkekakis, P., & Petruzzello, S. J. (1999). Acute aerobic exercise and affect: Current status, problems, and prospects regarding dose-response. *Sports Medicine, 28,* 337–374.

Ekkekakis, P., & Petruzzello, S. J. (2001). Analysis of the affect measurement conundrum in exercise psychology: II. A conceptual and methodological critique of the Exercise-Induced Feeling Inventory. *Psychology of Sport and Exercise, 2,* 1–26.

Emmons, R. A., & Diener, E. (1986). A goal-affect analysis of everyday situational choices. *Journal of Research in Personality, 20,* 309–326.

Focht, B. C. (2002). Pre-exercise anxiety and the anxiolytic responses to acute bouts of self-selected and prescribed intensity resistance exercise. *Journal of Sports Medicine and Physical Fitness, 42,* 217–223.

Focht, B. C. (2009). Brief walks in outdoor and laboratory environments: Effects on affective responses, enjoyment, and intentions to walk for exercise. *Research Quarterly in Exercise and Sport, 80,* 611–620.

Focht, B. C., & Arent, S. M. (2008). Psychological responses to acute resistance exercise: Current status, contemporary considerations, and future research directions. In J. Giebling & M. Frohlich (Eds.), *Current results of strength training research* (pp. 89–103). Cuvillier Verlag: Gottingen.

Focht, B. C., & Hausenblas, H. A. (2001). Influence of quiet rest and acute aerobic exercise performed in a naturalistic environment on selected psychological responses. *Journal of Sport and Exercise Psychology, 23,* 108–121.

Focht, B. C., Knapp, D. J., Raedeke, T. D., Gavin, T. P., & Hickner, R. C. (2007). Affective and self-efficacy responses to acute aerobic exercise in sedentary older and younger adults. *Journal of Aging and Physical Activity, 15,* 123–138.

Focht, B.C., & Koltyn, K.F. (1999). Influence of resistance exercise of different intensities on state anxiety, mood, and blood pressure. *Medicine and Science in Sports and Exercise*, 31, 456–463.

Focht, B. C., Rejeski, W. J., & Rejeski, A. F. (2005). Treating obesity in patients with knee osteoarthritis. *Journal of Musculoskeletal Medicine*, 22, 491–502.

Focht, B.C., Koltyn, K., Bouchard, L.J. (2000). State anxiety and blood pressure responses following different resistance exercise sessions. *International Journal of Sport Psychology*, 31, 376–390.

Freemont, J., & Craighead, L. W. (1987). Aerobic exercise and cognitive therapy in the treatment of dysphoric moods. *Cognitive Therapy and Research, 112,* 241–251.

Garvin, A. W., Koltyn, K. F., & Morgan, W. P. (1997). Influence of acute physical activity and relaxation on state anxiety and blood lactate in untrained college males. *International Journal of Sports Medicine, 18,* 470–476.

Gauvin, L., & Rejeski, W. J. (2001). Disentangling substance from rhetoric: A rebuttal to Ekkekakis & Petruzzello. *Psychology of Sport and Exercise, 2,* 73–88.

Griest, J. H., Klein, M. H., Eishens, R. R., Faris, J., Gurman, J. S., & Morgan, W. P. (1979). Running as treatment for depression. *Comprehensive Psychiatry, 20,* 41–54.

James, W. (1899). *Talks to teachers on psychology: And to students on some of life's ideals.* New York: H. Holt.

Jerome, G. J., Marquez, D. X., McAuley, E., Canaklisova, S., Snook, E., & Vickers, M. (2002). Self-efficacy effects on feeling states in women. *International Journal of Behavioral Medicine, 9,* 139–154.

Kessler, R. C., McGonagle, K. A., Zhao, S., Nelson, C. B., Hughes, M., Eshlemen, S., et al. (1994). Lifetime and 12-month prevalence of DSM-III-R psychiatric disorders in the United States: Results from the National Comorbidity Survey. *Archives of General Psychiatry, 51,* 8–19.

Kwan, B. M., & Bryan, A. D. (in press). Affective response to exercise as a component of exercise motivation: Attitudes, norms, self-efficacy, and temporal stability of intentions. *Psychology of Sport and Exercise.*

Landers, D. M., & Arent, S. M. (2007). Physical activity and mental health. In G. Tennenbaum & R. C. Eklund (Eds.), *Handbook of sport psychology* (pp. 469–491). Hoboken, NJ: John Wiley.

Lawlor, D. A., & Hopker, S. W. (2001). The effectiveness of exercise as an intervention in the management of depression: A systematic review and meta-regression analysis of randomized controlled trials. *British Medical Journal, 322,* 1–8.

Loewenstein, G., & Lerner, J. S. (2003). The role of affect in decision-making. In R. J. Davidson, K. R. Scherer, & H. H. Goldsmith (Eds.), *Handbook of affective science* (pp. 619–642). New York: Oxford University Press.

Lox, C. L., Martin Ginis, K. A., & Petruzzello, S. J. (2006). *Psychology of exercise: Integrating theory and practice.* Scottsdale, AZ: Holcomb Hathaway.

Martinsen, E. W., Hoffart, A., & Solberg, O. (1989). Comparing aerobic with nonaerobic forms of exercise in the treatment of clinical depression: A randomized trial. *Comprehensive Psychiatry, 30,* 324–331.

McAuley, E., & Blissmer, B. (2000). Self-efficacy determinants and consequences of physical activity. *Exercise and Sport Sciences Reviews, 28,* 85–88.

McAuley, E., Mihalko, S. L., & Bane, S. (1996). Acute exercise and anxiety reduction: Does the environment matter? *Journal of Sport and Exercise Psychology, 18,* 408–419.

McAuley, E., Talbot, H. M., & Martinez, S. (1999). Manipulating self-efficacy in the exercise environment in women: Influence on affective responses. *Health Psychology, 18,* 288–294.

Mutrie, N. (2000). The relationship between physical activity and clinically-defined depression. In S. J. H. Biddle, K. R. Fox, & S. H. Boutcher (Eds.), *Physical activity and psychological well-being* (pp. 46–62). London: Routledge.

Netz, Y. (2007). Physical activity and three dimensions of psychological functioning in advanced age: Cognition, affect, and self-perception. In G. Tennenbaum & R. C. Eklund (Eds.), *Handbook of sport psychology* (pp. 492–508). Hoboken, NJ: John Wiley.

North, T. C., McCullagh, P., & Tran, Z. V. (1990). Effect of exercise on depression. *Exercise and Sport Science Reviews, 18,* 379–415.

O'Connor, P. J. (1997). Overtraining and staleness. In W.P. Morgan (Ed.), *Physical activity and mental health* (pp. 145–160). Washington, DC: Taylor and Francis.

O'Connor, P. J., Raglin, J. S., & Martinsen, E. W. (2000). Physical activity, anxiety, and anxiety disorders. *International Journal of Sport Psychology, 31,* 136–155.

O'Connor, P. J., Smith, J. C., & Morgan, W. P. (2000). Physical activity does not provoke panic attacks in patients with panic disorder: A review of the evidence. *Anxiety, Stress, and Coping, 13,* 333–353.

Paffenbarger, R. S., Lee, I. M., & Leung, R. (1994). Physical activity and personal characteristics associated with depression and suicide in American college men. *Acta Psychiatrica Scandinavia, 257,* 16–22.

Petruzzello, S. J., Landers, D. M., Hatfield, B. D., Kubitz, K. A., & Salazar, W. (1991). A meta-analysis of the anxiety-reducing effects of acute and chronic exercise: Outcomes and mechanisms. *Sports Medicine, 11,* 143–182.

Pitts, F. J., & McClure, J. J. (1969). Lactate metabolism in anxiety neurosis. *New England Journal of Medicine, 277,* 1329–1336.

Raedeke, T., Focht, B. C., & Scales, D. (2007). Social environmental factors and psychological responses to acute exercise for socially physique anxious females. *Psychology of Sport and Exercise, 8,* 463–476.

Raglin, J. S. (1997). The anxiolytic effects of physical activity. In W.P. Morgan (Ed.), *Physical activity and mental health* (pp. 107–126). Washington, DC: Taylor and Francis.

Raglin, J. S., & Morgan, W. P. (1987). Influence of exercise and quiet rest on state anxiety and blood pressure. *Medicine and Science in Sports and Exercise, 19,* 456–463.

Rejeski, W. J., & Mihalko, S. L. (2001). Physical activity and quality of life in older adults. *Journals of Gerontology, 56A,* 23–35.

Russell, J.A. (1980). A circumplex model of affect. *Journal of Personality and Social Psychology*, 39, 1161–1178

Symons Downs, D., & Hausenblas, H. A. (2005). The theories of reasoned action and planned behavior applied to exercise: A meta-analytic update. *Journal of Physical Activity and Health, 2,* 76–97.

Trost, S. G., Owen, N., Bauman, A. E., Sallis, J. F., & Brown, W. (2002). Correlated of adults participation in physical activity: Review and update. *Medicine and Science in Sports and Exercise, 34,* 1996–2001.

Van Landuyt, L. M., Ekkekakis, P., Hall, E. E., & Petruzzello, S. J. (2000). Throwing the mountains into the lakes: On the perils of nomothetic conceptions of the exercise-affect relationship. *Journal of Sport and Exercise Psychology, 22,* 208–234.

Watson, D. (2002). Positive affectivity. In C.R. Snyder and S.J. Lopez (Eds.), *Handbook of positive psychology* (pp. 106–119). New York: Oxford University Press.

Williams, D. M., Dunsiger, S., Ciccoli, J. T., Lewis, B. A., Albrecht, A. E., & Marcus, B. H. (2008). Acute affective response to a moderate-intensity exercise stimulus predicts physical activity participation 6 and 12 months later. *Psychology of Sport and Exercise, 9,* 231–245.

Wing, R. R. (1999). Physical activity in the treatment of adulthood overweight and obesity: Current evidence and research issues. *Medicine and Science in Sports and Exercise, 31,* 542–547.

10 NUTRITION FOR WELLNESS: FUELING THE MIND/BODY

Heather L. Smith

Don't dig your grave with your own knife and fork.

English Proverb

Wellness Connection

We are what we eat. In the United States we are a culture obsessed with eating. I did not say we were a culture obsessed with food because often we have no idea just exactly what is in what we are putting into our mouths. Eating without thinking about nutrition has become a very easy thing to do. The United States has created the most successful food industry in world history and it just might be killing many of us. Wellness counselors need to educate themselves about nutrition so that they can help clients to eat healthily, and also so that they can communicate intelligently with professional nutritionists and dieticians.

An expert in nutrition and a counselor educator, Dr. Diane Smith, shares her insights on how and what we eat can impact not just our physical health but our overall well-being.

The purpose of this chapter is to provide mental health professionals with the information necessary to think critically about their role in supporting increasing levels of client wellness, specifically related to nutrition. The relationship among human emotional, mental, physical, social, and spiritual functioning is tremendously complex. However, it is not necessary to know everything to integrate wellness into counseling practice. Rather, ethical professionals know the limits of their own expertise, engage in continuous inquiry, and use critical thinking to select among the best resources available. An overview of the professional field of nutrition can provide counselors with the tools necessary to (1) advocate for improved nutritional status among individuals, (2) help in bridging the gap between those who use a medical model of patient care and those who use a humanistic model of client interaction, and (3) support the view that although the dominant practice of Western medicine is organized by the body's systems, people function as holistic beings and often need help integrating information into something personally meaningful.

To construct an understanding of nutrition information for the counselor, first, it is necessary to understand the historical language of medical professionals versus the historical language of counselors. This includes a shift from a humanistic and developmental understanding of a person to another way of conceptualizing the human body. Throughout history we have acquired so much information about human existence that it has been organized into many fields of study, forming research and practice specialties. In Western cultures most people access services based upon these information specialties. Helping professions, for example, divide the human body into separate entities. People go to various specialists for help based upon the affected entity or problem. In medical practice, for example, one patient might visit an orthopedist for concerns about the skeletal system, related ligaments or tendons, a urologist for concerns of the genitourinary tract, a dermatologist for the skin, and a podiatrist for the feet. With this approach researchers and practitioners become very well-versed in their own areas of specialty, uncovering more and more details of what ails specific systems of the human body.

This general approach to scientific discovery has been effective in eradicating or controlling many infectious diseases (spread by a pathogen) such as bubonic plague, smallpox, typhus, and influenza. Infectious diseases have afflicted humans since the beginning of time. Such an approach to scientific inquiry has resulted in the exponential compilation of vast amounts of information that now only artificial intelligence can store, categorize, and retrieve in a way that is efficient and helpful to researchers and practitioners. This information is largely responsible for the tremendous increase in the human lifespan that many people enjoy today.

Unfortunately, during the past 100 years, the incidence of chronic diseases has increased while mortality rates from infectious diseases have decreased. Chronic diseases (e.g., cardiovascular disease, cancer, diabetes) are predominantly caused by what people *do or do not do*. Thus, they are often referred to as *lifestyle diseases*. Now, more than ever, the choices we make over the lifespan, along with the environment we live in and our access to preventive services and medical care, can significantly affect the trajectories of our lives. The most influential behavioral risk factors for chronic illness in the United States are poor nutrition and lack of physical activity.

> Factoid: The cost of preventable dietary and physical activity related diseases to the economy exceeds $117 billion annually and is predicted to rise to $1.7 trillion in the next 10 years. Nevertheless, funding for food and nutrition research at USDA has not increased in real dollars since 1983 (American Society for Nutrition, 2007, p. 2).

Nutrition and physical activity are so elemental to human existence that counselors cannot afford to remove themselves from their discussion. Additionally, nutrition and physical activity are so interrelated, a discussion of one inevitably requires mention of the other. Counselors need to know, specifically, how and when they should enter such discussions and how to work alongside medical professionals (for a more complete discussion of this issue, see Wampold, 2001). The goal of this chapter is to provide professional counselors with reliable resources for further study and an integrated model for understanding the dynamic connections that exist between the professions of nutrition and counseling toward a more holistic approach to client care.

HUMAN NUTRITION

The most important individual contributor to a person's wellness is nutrition. Nutrition is responsible for fueling all of life's processes. The atoms, molecules, and cells of your body continually move and change, even though the arrangement of your tissues and organs seems to remain constant. All of the energy you need and all of the pieces of your body come from the nutrients you derive from foods (Whitney & Rolfes, 1993). Every other human system relies first on energy.

Compared to other areas of science, such as astronomy or physics, the science of nutrition is relatively young, dating back to the early 1900s. The first vitamin was identified in 1897 and the first protein structure was fully articulated in 1945 (Sizer & Whitney, 1994). Perhaps due to the importance of nutrition to human life, research has expanded to a great extent since the early 1900s. Although scientists have a good understanding of how nutrition supports human growth and development, our environment continues to change rapidly. Nutrition information needs to remain dynamic and changing as well.

You have probably heard others exclaim with frustration over what seems to be conflicting and confusing nutritional information in the popular press as well as the meanings derived from various professionals. It is true that information is changing as more is revealed about the dynamic interaction between biology and the environment. However, close attention to the foundational science of nutrition largely reveals unchanging principles. One of the most important contributions from use of the scientific method is constant challenge and replication that validates findings. Such findings have lead to the important publication of the Dietary Reference Intakes (DRIs), for example. Since 1998, the Institute of Medicine has issued eight exhaustive volumes of DRIs that offer quantitative estimates of nutrient intakes to be used for planning and assessing diets applicable to healthy individuals in the United States and Canada. In just over 100 years, information about the function of each nutrient in the human body, food sources, usual dietary intakes, and the effects of deficiencies and excesses is readily available to the public.

Unfortunately, such information is sometimes extorted, particularly when public demand is high. The functional foods and nutrition supplement industry is an example. The Dietary Supplement Health and Education Act (DSHEA), established in 1994, stated that dietary supplements were to be regulated like foods instead of medications, meaning that they are considered safe unless proven otherwise and are not required to be clinically tested before they reach the market. It is also up to the U.S. Food and Drug Administration (FDA) to determine whether a particular substance in the market is harmful based upon the information available in the public domain (National Research Council, 2004). For all of the reasons stated above, functional foods and supplements have become an unprecedented lucrative industry in the United States. In a report from the National Institutes of Health Office of Dietary Supplements, Americans spent $20.3 billion on dietary supplements in 2004 (Picciano, 2004).

Reflection Questions:

1. Where do you get most of your nutrition information?
2. Where do you suspect the American public gets nutrition information?
3. How do you communicate nutrition-related information?

NUTRIENTS: THE BUILDING BLOCKS OF NUTRITION

The science of nutrition refers to the study of nutrients in foods, the body's handling of them, and how such processes are affected by genes, the environment, and human behavior. A complete chemical analysis of the human body reveals that it is made up of matter similar to that found in foods. We are, literally, what we eat. Although it may seem that your physical body remains fairly constant with subtle changes over time, in reality, the components continually move and change. Your skin, which seems to have covered you since birth, is almost entirely replaced by new skin over the course of seven years. The lining of the digestive tract is renewed every three days and your oldest red blood cell is only 120 days old. Your human "self" is constantly changing.

The change process requires energy. Three of the six classes of nutrients are broken down to provide this energy. These are carbohydrates, fats, and proteins. When the body metabolizes the energy-yielding nutrients, the bonds between their atoms break. As the bonds break, they release energy. Even though you have never seen these bonds breaking, you are familiar with the energy they are releasing. When wood burns, it releases heat (energy), steam (water), and some carbon (as carbon dioxide); some carbon and minerals remain as ash. The body's metabolism of nutrients is a controlled version of the same process. In the body, some of the energy from food is released as heat just as in the burning of wood, but some is used to send electrical impulses through the brain and nerves and to move muscles.

Carbohydrates are the major source of energy for the body, especially the brain. They are composed mostly of the elements carbon (C), hydrogen (H), and oxygen (O). Through the bonding of these elements, carbohydrates provide energy for the body in the form of kilocalories (kcal), with an average of 4 kcal per gram (kcal/g) of carbohydrates (a kcal is equivalent to a calorie on a nutritional label). Carbohydrates come in a variety of sizes. The smallest carbohydrates are the simple sugars, also known as monosaccharides (meaning constructed of one sugar molecule), and disaccharides (constructed of two sugar molecules). The most well-known simple sugar is a disaccharide known as sucrose, or table sugar. Other simple sugars include the monosaccharides glucose and fructose (fruit sugar), and other disaccharides including lactose (milk sugar), and maltose (in beer and malt liquors). The larger carbohydrates are constructed of smaller simple sugars and are known as complex carbohydrates or polysaccharides (meaning many sugar molecules). One way to distinguish the difference is by taste. Simple sugars (e.g., fructose or sucrose) taste sweet but complex carbohydrates (e.g., dietary fiber) do not. Dietary fiber is especially unique because the body cannot break apart the sugar linkages and thus it passes through the body with minimal changes. Fiber exists as insoluble and soluble. Insoluble fiber provides bulk in the intestines, which helps keep them healthy. Soluble fiber works like a sponge to absorb toxic substances and remove them from the body. The typical American individual consumes more than adequate amounts of carbohydrates, but inadequate amounts of fiber.

The next nutrient, protein, is a vital structural and working material of all cells. Their building blocks, amino acids, form structures such as human insulin (a necessary hormone for energy metabolism), hormones, hemoglobin (the oxygen-carrying protein of the red blood cells), antibodies (protein that attacks foreign substances), opsin (conveys the sense of sight to higher brain centers), and the precursors for neurotransmitters. Proteins are used to make cells. The protein collagen, for example, forms a matrix, which is later filled with calcium, phosphorus, fluoride, and other materials to form hardened bone and teeth. Collagen forms ligaments and tendons and serves as the strengthening glue to withstand the pressure of the blood as it surges through artery walls with each heartbeat.

Fat is actually a subset of the class of nutrients known as lipids, but the term *fat* is often used to refer to all the lipids. The lipids include triglycerides (fats and oils), phospholipids, and sterols; all important to optimal health. The triglycerides provide the body with a continuous fuel supply, keep it warm, protect it from harm, and carry some vitamins to various places in the body. The phospholipids and sterols contribute to the cells' structures, and cholesterol serves as the raw material for hormones, vitamin D, and bile. When most people talk about fats, they are referring to triglycerides since they are the predominant lipids in foods and in the body. Two types of fats are often discussed for their harmful effects on the body when intake is too high. The first is saturated fats. These are naturally occurring fats that are solid at room temperature. It is the fat seen on raw cuts of meat. Hydrogenated fats are lipids that have been mechanically altered to provide specific characteristics for processed foods. Lipids provide desirable flavors and textures and thus, are enticing to overconsume.

Vitamins and minerals are essential for normal growth and development. They trigger thousands of chemical reactions within the human body. Using the genetic blueprint inherited from parents, for example, a fetus develops from the nutrients it absorbs. It requires certain vitamins and minerals to be present at certain times to facilitate the chemical reactions that create such things as skin, bone, and muscle. Vitamins and minerals are critical in the formation of red blood cells, hormones, and neurotransmitters. Some vitamins protect against harmful chemicals known as free radicals. Minerals assist in muscle contraction, nerve reaction, and blood clotting.

Did You Know? When given many food choices since the introduction of first foods, most preschool children naturally choose foods that result in an optimal intake of nutrients and calories. Child-feeding strategies that encourage children to consume a particular food increase children's *dislike* for that food (Birch & Fisher, 1998, p. 543). Rather, children's food preferences are learned through repeated exposure. With a minimum of 8 to 10 exposures to a food, children will develop an increased preference for that food. Thus, parents and other child caregivers can provide opportunities for children to learn to like a variety of nutritious foods by regularly exposing them to these foods (American Dietetic Association [ADA], 2004, p. 666–667).

MISINFORMATION

The proliferation of functional foods and dietary supplements, natural/organic foods, and natural personal care products has led to an explosion of misinformation because the number of such products has outpaced federal regulations (ADA, 2006). Monitoring the claims made by marketers of these products creates an overwhelming task for the FDA, further delaying the time when information can be retracted or products removed from the marketplace. With the burden of proof on the federal government, there are fewer roadblocks to entrepreneurs developing costly but useless products, allowing nutrition-related fads, myths, quackery, and health fraud to flourish. Additionally, many people who exploit fads are themselves consumers of misinformation, sincerely believing that they are providing accurate information (ADA, 2006).

Factoid: In a study to determine nutrition trends among the American public, the American Dietetic Association (ADA) reported that for 72% of those randomly sampled, television was the primary source of information on diet and nutrition, over half (58%) obtained diet and nutrition information from magazines, and about one-third (33%) referred to newspapers as a source of nutrition information (ADA, 2002).

Food and nutrition misinformation can have harmful effects on the health and economic status of consumers (ADA, 2006). The health consequences of food quackery, faddism, misinformation, or the misuse or misinterpretation of emerging science may include delay or failure to seek legitimate medical care or continue essential treatment, undesirable drug-nutrient interactions, effects of nutrient toxicities or toxic components of products, and interference with sound nutrition education and practices. Economic harm occurs when purported remedies, treatments, and "cures" fail to work and when products are purchased needlessly. Indirect impact on health and economic status can occur when the media report conflicting stories or stories that contain information that may be accurate but incomplete.

The Food and Nutrition Science Alliance (FANSA) is a partnership of professional scientific societies whose members have joined forces to speak as one on food and nutrition issues. Its membership includes more than 100,000 food, nutrition, and medical practitioners and scientists. According to FANSA (ADA, 2006), the *10 Red Flags of Junk Science* include:

> (1) recommendations that promise a quick fix; (2) dire warnings of danger from a single product or regimen; (3) claims that sound too good to be true; (4) simplistic conclusions drawn from a complex study; (5) recommendations based on a single study; (6) statements refuted by reputable scientific organizations; (7) lists of "good" and "bad" foods; (8) recommendations made to help sell a product; (9) recommendations based on studies not peer reviewed; and (10) recommendations from studies that ignore differences among individuals or groups. (p. 605)

NUTRITION PROFESSIONALS

Registered dietitians (RDs) are the only nutrition professionals who have completed academic and experience requirements established by the Commission on Dietetic Registration (CDR), the profession's credentialing agency. These include a minimum of a bachelor's degree from an accredited college or university and an accredited preprofessional experience program. RDs must successfully complete a rigorous professional level exam and must maintain ongoing continuing education to maintain their national credential and state licensure. Some RDs hold advanced degrees and additional certifications in specialized areas of practice. Other professionals who may have specialized training in nutrition include nurses (e.g., Certified Diabetes Educators [CDEs]), public health professionals, and physicians (e.g., endocrinologists and gastroenterologists). The title *nutritionist* currently carries no professional standard of training or practice other than those practicing in government-supported public health clinics carrying the titles *Public Health Nutritionist* or Supplemental Food Program for *Women, Infants, and Children (WIC) Nutritionist*. Members of the public should be warned of following the recommendations of any other practicing nutritionist.

Members of the ADA and registered dietitians consistently convey the following:

> (1) healthful eating messages to the public emphasize the total diet or overall pattern of food eaten, rather than any one food or meal; (2) there are no "good" foods or "bad" foods; (3) if foods are consumed in moderation, in appropriate portion sizes and combined with regular physical activity, all foods can fit into a healthful diet; (4) there is no "magic bullet" for safe and healthful weight management; (5) successful weight management is a lifelong process which means adopting a lifestyle that includes a healthful eating plan, coupled with regular physical activity; (6) people are not all alike and one size does not fit all when it comes to planning and achieving a healthful diet; (7) a dietetics professional is best qualified to help devise an eating plan that is right for each individual; (8) the base of most healthy people's

eating plans should be fruits, vegetables, whole grains and low-fat protein; (9) obesity is a complex disease and presents a number of challenging issues; (10) nutrition profoundly affects children's ability to learn, develop and stay healthy. There is no better time than the early years to make an impact on the lifelong eating and exercise habits that contribute to health maintenance and disease prevention. Parental involvement is a key component of children's nutrition. Parents can teach their children about healthy foods, practice what they teach and make sure that physical activity is incorporated into each day; (11) Medical nutrition therapy (MNT), provided by registered dietitians as part of a person's health-care team, has been proven effective in treatment and prevention of nutrition-related diseases and conditions. Patients receiving MNT, have been shown to have fewer complications, fewer hospitalizations, and lower health-care costs. (ADA, 2005, p. 54)

Source: American Dietetic Association and Food and Nutrition Science Alliance (FANSA).

Formal training includes coursework in the sciences (e.g., multiple chemistry, biology, food science courses), statistics, calculus, medical terminology, psychology, counseling, political science, and public speaking. Upon completion of the state licensure requirements, RDs are responsible for providing nutrition education and nutrition counseling using the Nutrition Care Process (NCP).

NUTRITION CARE PROCESS

The NCP is a systematic process describing how dietetics practitioners provide care (Lacey & Pritchett, 2003). It was designed to improve the consistency and quality of individualized patient/client care and the predictability of the patient/client outcomes. The NCP does not standardize nutrition care for each person; rather it standardizes a *process* for providing care. The four steps in the process include nutrition assessment, diagnosis, intervention, and monitoring and evaluation (ADA, 2008). Of greatest interest to counselors, perhaps, is the center of the NCP model: the relationship between patient/client/group and the dietetics professional (see Figure 10.1). However, although Lacey and Pritchett (2003) provided a detailed description of the NCP model in their seminal article, only one short paragraph addressed the center. The fact that registered dietitians view the relationship as "central to providing nutrition care" (p. 1069), combined with the nutrition counseling they are responsible for, would suggest a strong need for collaboration with professional counselors.

NUTRITION COUNSELING

In conjunction with learning about the science of nutrition, dietetics students learn basic relationship-building communication skills in preparation for conducting nutrition counseling. Although nutrition education remains an important component of the work of RDs, findings supported the need for entry-level counseling skills (Isselmann, Deubner, & Hartman, 1993). Four main theories and models are emphasized as they "have proven valuable in providing a theoretical framework for evidence-based individual and interpersonal level nutrition interventions" (ADA, 2008, p. C-1). These include Cognitive-Behavioral Theory, the Health Belief Model, Social Learning Theory, and the Stages of Change Model. Given that overweight and obesity are connected to many chronic conditions, the counseling approaches are described as they apply to the treatment of overweight and obesity.

The cornerstone of obesity treatment continues to be behavior intervention (Berkel, Poston, Reeves, & Foreyt, 2005). Key components of typical behavior modification programs

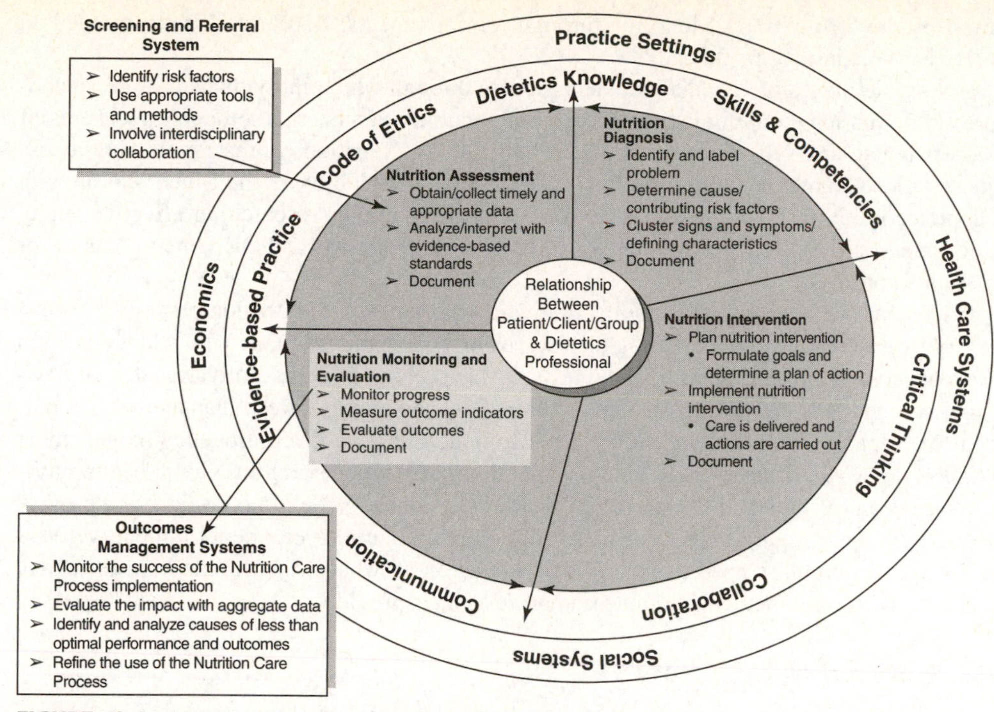

FIGURE 10.1 ADA Nutrition Care Process and Model
Source: © 2010 American Dietetic Association. Reprinted with permission.

include self-monitoring, goal setting, nutrition, exercise, stimulus control, problem solving, cognitive restructuring, and relapse prevention (p. S35). Clients engage in self-monitoring by keeping detailed food and activity records. This helps clients to become more aware of the behaviors surrounding what and when they eat. Goal setting typically involves specific intake and physical activity instructions. A client structures his or her environment for stimulus control, for example, by conducting a "kitchen sweep." This involves allowing only those foods in the home that will assist the client in achieving goals. Problem-solving and cognitive restructuring techniques help clients to recognize and modify their thoughts and beliefs to support their goals. Relapse prevention involves normalizing behavioral "slips" to prevent catastrophizing and subsequent more extreme behaviors and relapse. For a more complete review of specific nutrition behavioral treatments, readers are directed to Wadden and Foster (2000) and Berkel and colleagues (2005).

Next, the Health Belief Model states that clients will behave according to what they believe to be true about (1) their susceptibility to comorbid illness (e.g., overweight and type II diabetes mellitus), (2) the severity of the consequences to their behavior, (3) the benefits to changing behaviors, and (4) the barriers (e.g., "Will I be able to maintain balanced insulin-glucose levels if I start losing weight?). Kirscht (1983) provided more foundational research of the Health Belief Model while Conner and McMillan (2004) provided a comprehensive overview. Social cognitive theory, also known as social learning theory, is based upon the premise that individuals will enact the behaviors, attitudes, and emotional reactions of those they observe and with whom they interact. An example of goals and strategies for the overweight individual would include increasing exposure to the behaviors of those who engage in healthy exercise and intake monitoring, followed by the affirmation of learning through reinforcements. Bandura (1986) provided an extensive explanation of this theory.

Lastly, the Stages of Change include a process through which individuals change, including precontemplation, contemplation, preparation, action, maintenance, outcome measures of decision balance, and self-efficacy (ADA, 2008, p. C-1). Nutrition professionals may assess readiness to lose weight according to this model, intentionally tailoring their intervention with the client accordingly. This model has been used in many studies researching effective health behavior interventions. Readers are directed to Prochaska, Norcross, and DiClemente (1994) for more on this approach.

Counselors who wish to build collaborative relationships with nutrition professionals can gain entry by articulating and marketing themselves first using the language with which nutrition professionals are familiar. Specific strategies RDs learn about include motivational interviewing, goal setting, self-monitoring, problem solving, social support, stress management, stimulus control, cognitive restructuring, relapse prevention, and rewards/contingency management (ADA, 2008, p. C-2). Counselors should become familiar with overarching public health nutrition messages and understand the history of wellness counseling. Next, counselors can provide convincing evidence regarding how collaboration with a counselor can benefit client wellness goals. Overall, counselors need to be able to articulate how what they provide is necessary *in combination* with what medical and nutrition professionals provide.

PROFESSIONAL COUNSELING

The profession of counseling originated from a theoretically different perspective of human functioning than those guiding medical professions or other mental health professions (Gladding, 2000; Lambie & Williamson, 2004; Remley & Herlihy, 2001; Young, 2009). Rather than focusing professional training on the identification and treatment of pathology, counselor education emphasizes the promotion of optimal functioning through the identification of strengths, context, and developmental processes (McAuliffe & Eriksen, 1999; Ryff & Keyes, 1995; Witmer & Sweeney, 1992). Trained to work through the power of the relationship, counselors can be ideal professionals for infusing reliable public nutrition information into their interaction with clients. Counselors can work with nutrition professionals to serve clients in their movement toward wellness. To do so, an understanding of client care from the individual level to the systemic level is crucial.

Leaders in counseling are increasingly articulating the importance of conceptualizing and addressing human experiences within systems and settings (Pope-Davis, Coleman, Liu, & Toporek, 2003; Sue & Sue, 2003). Additionally, taking a contextual perspective maximizes opportunities for prevention and increased well-being (Conye, 2004). Urie Bronfenbrenner offered a bioecological model of human development that emphasized the contextual nature of human functioning (Bronfenbrenner, 1995, 2001, and 2005). It is with this model that the remainder of this chapter is organized in order for the reader to understand the dynamic nature of nutrition and counseling issues—particularly how the two can influence and affect the other within a cultural context.

SYSTEMIC FRAMEWORK: BRONFENBRENNER'S BIOECOLOGY

Counselors hold incredible potential for affecting the positive development of those they serve. Bronfenbrenner (2005) stated, ". . . to a greater extent than any other species, human beings create the environments that shape the course of human development . . . this agency makes humans—for better or worse—active producers of their own development" (p. xxvii).

Bronfenbrenner's *chronosystem, macrosystem, exosystem, mesosystem,* and *microsystem* refer to a complex web of interconnecting systems in which the individual participates throughout the lifespan (Bronfenbrenner, 1995). His theory defines complex layers of environment, each having an effect on our development as individuals. The interaction between factors in our maturing biology, our immediate family/community environment, the society in which we live, and the effect of time and specific moments in history fuels and steers our development. Changes or conflict in any one layer will ripple throughout other layers. Thus, they concurrently and continuously affect each other. He postulates that in order to study a person's development, we must look not only at the person and his or her immediate environment but also at the interaction of the larger environment as well. We are each affected by our environments while our presence concurrently shapes and changes our surroundings. The following are descriptions of each system as well as examples of events and resources that exist within each system.

Chronosystem

The chronosystem refers to the dimension of time as it relates to the person's environments and maturing biology. This system might include sociohistorical influences, such as the fact that women today are much more likely to be encouraged to pursue a career outside the home than they were 30 or 40 years ago (Santrock, 2002). Within the chronosystem, examples of environmental events, transitions, and their impact on society might include changes in the earth's ozone layer (i.e., affecting thc growing season of crops), cultural reliance on energy to fuel the everyday use of technology (i.e., increasing costs of transporting foods), and increasing human interaction with technology (i.e., new food preservation techniques such as irradiation). Elements within this system can be either external, such as the timing of new discoveries in the science of nutrition, or internal, such as the extension of the average human lifespan.

Reflection Questions: Where do you obtain your food compared to how your great-grandparents obtained their food at your age? How many processing plants, transportation vehicles, and preservation techniques were used to allow you the myriad choices you have for lunch in comparison to your grandparents at your age? What international or national historic events have influenced mental health policies? How has time been a factor in each of these?

Macrosystem

Bronfenbrenner's macrosystem refers to the cultural values, customs, laws, belief systems, resources, hazards, lifestyles, life course options, social expectations, and economic, social, and political policies embedded in each of the systems. The macrosystem consists of the overarching pattern of microsystem, macrosystem, and exosystems characteristic of a given culture (Sontag, 1996). The effects of this system have a cascading influence throughout the other layers. For example, a culture may emphasize the goals of the individual more than emphasizing group goals. This, in turn, affects the structures in which people function. People living in a culture that rewards self-reliance and personal independence may view overweight differently, for example, than people living in a culture that places more emphasis on community and interdependence. People living in a culture of individualism may place responsibility for overweight on the overweight individual (or parents in the case of children), whereas those living in a more collectivist culture may view overweight as a problem with the environment or context within which the person lives. The macrosystem can be thought of as a societal blueprint (Sontag, 1996).

Reflection Questions: Congress directed the Centers for Disease Control and Prevention (CDC) to undertake a study with the Institute of Medicine (IOM) to review and make recommendations about appropriate nutrition standards for the availability, sale, content, and consumption of foods at school, with attention to competitive foods. The ensuing report, *Nutrition Standards for Foods in Schools: Leading the Way toward Healthier Youth* (Committee on Nutrition Standards for Foods in Schools, 2007), concluded that: federally reimbursable school nutrition programs should be the main source of nutrition at school; opportunities for competitive foods should be limited; and, if competitive foods are available, they should consist of nutritious fruits, vegetables, whole grains, and nonfat or low-fat milk and dairy products, as consistent with the 2005 Dietary Guidelines for Americans. To what extent do your local school districts allow competitive foods to be available in school? What is the incentive for the school (what are the competing values)? What could you do as a counselor?

Exosystem

The exosystem describes the connection to the larger society of government, religious organizations, educational systems, social welfare systems, healthcare systems, and the media. This system considers the influence that larger societal systems have on an individual's immediate setting. An example would be a television station's limiting of advertisements for low-nutrient foods during scheduled children's programming. A second example would be a person's ability or inability to access nutrition services covered by Medicare or private insurance while in an assisted-living community.

Children in public schools are assured breakfast and lunch because of the government's *National School Breakfast and Lunch Program* based upon the *Dietary Guidelines for Americans*. The Dietary Reference Intakes (DRIs) are quantitative reference values for recommended intakes and safe upper levels of intake of nutrients. The DRI reports implement an approach that (a) reviews nutrients for their role in elimination of nutritional deficiencies and reduction of risk of chronic diseases and (b) uses a risk assessment model to evaluate the extent to which excess consumption may lead to health problems. Food package labeling laws allow the public to easily access grocery item nutrition content. Each is an example of what links larger systems to those in which individuals regularly function.

Counseling practitioners can increase their involvement within the exosystem of the client by increasing their understanding of public health nutrition, specifically. The focus of a public health intervention is to prevent rather than treat a disease through surveillance of cases and the promotion of healthy behaviors. Reliable public health nutrition information sources are extensive. Counselors can begin by visiting the United States Department of Agriculture's (USDA, 2008) *Nutrition.gov* Web site or the American Dietetic Association's (ADA, 2008) Web site (http://www.eatright.org) for the *Good Nutrition Reading List.* Scientists and professionals will find randomized controlled trials and other research reports within the *Evidence Analysis Library* of the American Dietetic Association's Web site. An understanding of key public health nutrition concepts equips the professional counselor with the knowledge to infuse accurate and reliable nutrition information into his or her practice, while preventing the propagation of inaccurate nutrition information. Furthermore, counselors using sound nutrition information will build better collaborations with nutrition professionals.

Factoid: Public health nutrition campaigns attempt to offset many of the profit-motivated commercial nutrition messages. In 2001, Lin, Guthrie, and Frazao reported the food industry advertising and marketing expenditures directed at children and their parents in the United States totaled $12.7 billion. By contrast, the advertising budget for the U.S. National Cancer Institute's *5-A-Day* campaign to promote consumption of fruits and vegetables was $1.1 million in 1999 (Ebbeling, Pawlak, & Ludwig, 2002, p. 478). Advertising, policy, increasing food options of low nutrient quality, sedentary lifestyle, the power of special interest groups, portion distortion, and a treatment versus prevention mentality has created what is now termed as a *toxic environment* for overweight and obesity in the United States (Bray & Champagne, 2005; Ebbeling et al., 2002; Snyder et al., 2004).

Mesosystem

The mesosystem consists of the connection and processes taking place between two or more settings (e.g., the connection between work and home, or school and neighborhood). In other words, a mesosystem is a system of microsystems (Green & Keys, 2001). For example, some individuals choose to ride their bicycle from home to work each day. For that process to take place, the individual needs to have the resources to purchase a bicycle, the capacity to build into his or her schedule the time that it takes to ride to work, and an environment conducive to storing the bike while working. If the route between home and work becomes unsafe, the individual's mesosystem is disrupted. Caregivers play a key role in the mesosystem of the child. For example, parents who learn about the food options available to their children, while away from their care, might provide alternative foods to increase the likelihood that their children will choose a more balanced intake overall. Conversely, when time or financial resources are scarce, many children eat cheaper foods that are calorically dense and nutrient-poor (Fabricatore & Wadden, 2003).

Microsystem

A microsystem is the setting in which most of the individual's direct social interactions occur. It can be thought of as the person's immediate surroundings. For a child these might include family, peers, school, child care environments, and neighborhood; for adults these might include work setting, family, peers, and neighborhood. The microsystem includes the pattern of activities, roles, and interpersonal relations a person experiences. It includes the direct interaction with persons of differing temperament, personality, and systems of belief (Sontag, 1996).

In their work with clients, counselors often concentrate at the microsystem level. This is because interpersonal relationships can be powerful agents of change. Much of the focus of counselor education focuses on specific training to optimize potential for the formation of positive relationships, which then becomes the modus operandi for assisting clients. Research has shown that the therapeutic relationship accounts for about twice as much as technique (Lambert, 1986), and appears to be more predictive of success than the helper's theoretical approach (Nuttall, 2002; Young, 2009). Counseling is predominantly thought of as "the contractual and professional relationship between a trained helper and a client" and historically counselors believed in "seeing each individual as a unique person, rather than a diagnostic label" (Young, 2009, p. 32). Counselors are trained to identify, and consider, the subjective nature of human experience.

Yet human development is driven by both subjective and objective elements, with both forces interdependent and affecting each other (Bronfenbrenner, 2001). The bioecological model assists in conceptualizing the interaction of the subjective and objective elements of human development. Both the profession of counseling and the profession of dietetics view the relationship as central to client care and thus have good reason to function collaboratively. Each can learn from the other. While counselors often work with the complex web of human experience and interaction (subjective processes), most nutrition professionals focus on the objective/scientific details of biological processes. Bronfenbrenner's bioecological model integrates both the subjective and objective into a more complete conceptual whole.

In the bioecological model, the body is part of the microsystem. It is the life support system, the mobility system, and that with which we perceive and interact with the environment. A person's health is determined by how effectively the various subsystems in the body function and the influences of environmental factors. During the course of development from infant to adult, for example, our bodies are assaulted by countless external threats. We are attacked by almost everything we come into contact with. Airborne pathogens are drawn into our lungs and can cause pneumonia, sunlight breaks down our skin cells and can cause melanoma, and the thorn of a rose can pierce our skin causing a bacterial infection. Some of us have genetic disorders that cause malfunctions in our internal systems, such as phenylketonuria, a genetic disorder characterized by deficiency of an important enzyme that breaks down phenylalanine. Others of us develop conditions such as alcoholism or obesity as a result of lifestyle and environmental factors. Since the body is our life support system with its own pathogen-fighting tools, it makes sense that we keep it in good working order to work against the innumerable threats. Modern medical science continues to seek better ways to help us in the battle, but there are some basic things we need to take responsibility for to keep our bodies well maintained.

Reflection Question: Do you drive a car without ever changing the oil? Do you let your car sit for years and then in a moment decide to start it up and drive 1,000 miles? When your vehicle needs repairs, do you keep driving it?

Without intentionally eating well to optimize internal processes, and exercising to prevent muscle atrophy and bone loss, how can the body fight illness or heal injury as effectively? Without enough sleep for the body to naturally finish all of its repairs, how can it keep driving? Although the mental strain of modern society often feels tiring, stress is different than physical exercise. Mental and emotional stress alone does not burn many calories nor does it strengthen bones and muscles.

The basic components necessary to increase wellness include intentional nutrition planning, exercise, and health prevention.

NEW FRONTIERS: NUTRIGENOMICS AND METABOLOMICS

One of the most important advances using the scientific approach in understanding human development at the microsystem level was the sequencing of the human genome. The international scientific community sequenced the human genome in 2001, completing a difficult task of identifying all genes in the nucleus of a human cell, including their locations on human chromosomes. Such an advance has the potential to provide insights into the core biochemical processes that underlie the formation of diseases. Unlike genetics (the study of the functions and effects of single genes), genomics is the study of the entire human genome, exploring not only the actions of single genes, but also the interactions of multiple genes with each other and with the environment. To date, most of the benefits of advances in genomics have been directed as it applies to the individual, focusing primarily on clinical decision-making, healthcare policy, and bioethics. Nutrigenomics, then, is the study of how nutrition changes how our genes work and how genes change our nutrient requirements. Metabolomics is the study of the small molecules that are produced by metabolism. Nutrition scientists are working to measure these chemicals in blood and urine to more completely describe our metabolism (Zeisel, 2007). Analysis techniques are improving and will likely start with detection of group differences followed by recommendations for specific groups. Eventually, nutrition professionals may be able to provide personalized nutrition recommendations based upon each person's unique genetic and metabolic makeup (Zeisel, 2007).

Factoid: In our bodies there are more bacterial cells than there are human cells. Metabolomics is a new tool that can study what it is that these bacteria do with the food that we eat.

Activity: Case Studies

Use Bronfenbrenner's Bioecological Model to consider the nutrition and mental health forces and factors for each of the case studies below:

(1) identify the threats that exist to the individual's well-being,
(2) identify the preventive resources that exist to support the individual's well-being, and
(3) identify the level in which the threat or preventive resource exists.

Activity: Dietary Monitoring

Keep a food record for three days (two week days and one weekend day). Record date, day of week, food item, serving size, brand or restaurant (if applicable), and preparation method (if applicable). Use public health nutrition information available on the Internet to perform a basic assessment of your intake based upon the U.S. Dietary Guidelines and the USDA My Pyramid. Then, set two to three dietary goals that you will attempt to implement over the following week. Once you have written your goals, keep another three-day food record implementing new dietary

CASE STUDY #1

An Eight-Year-Old Child

Mari is an eight-year-old Latina child who lives in Florida with her 30-year-old mother and 50-year-old maternal grandmother. Her father was killed in a motorcycle accident one year ago. Mari once heard her grandmother talk about being worried about her father "because of his epilepsy and he drives a motorcycle to work." Mari's grandmother has type II diabetes mellitus, somewhat controlled by medication. She walks Mari to school in the neighborhood five days a week. Mari's mother was able to arrange to begin work at 6:00 AM three days per week so that she can pick up Mari from school by 3:15 PM. The other two days per week Mari attends an after-school program until her mother picks her up at 5:30 PM.

Mari's mother and grandmother are concerned because their community is considering a rezoning plan that would force Mari to go to a school farther away from home. Also, during Mari's last health checkup, the public health department physician told Mari's mother that her BMI was between the 85th and 95th percentile, meaning that Mari was considered *overweight* for children her age. Although the physician told her that she needed to control the amount of low-nutrient-value foods in the house, Mari's mother prides herself in being able to provide the snacks and foods that Mari wants and "those that (her) friends get." Mari's grandmother states that she believes children need "a little extra" and that "Americans are overly worried about looks."

Mari likes to play with her friends in the neighborhood, but can only play if her grandmother watches them. Her friends like to bring magazines and talk about the things that their older sisters look at. Mari tells her friends that she's "going to get married, live in a big house, have babies, watch TV all day, and eat whatever she wants" when she grows up. ■

CASE STUDY #2

A 42-Year-Old Woman

Brycelyn is a 42-year-old Caucasian woman who lives in Nashville, Tennessee. She is a singer/songwriter who just signed a contract with a major recording company. Her agent's pressure to make decisions is creating increased stress for Brycelyn along with the excitement of possibilities. Several members of her extended family on her father's side have been diagnosed with General Anxiety Disorder. Brycelyn is experiencing increased levels of anxiety when talking with her agent on a daily basis. Her recording contract includes a stipulation that she must follow the producer's directions including "those designed to be physically appealing" during the filming of a music video.

The day after signing, Brycelyn's agent tells her about tabloid articles discussing her experience with celiac disease. As a child, Brycelyn quickly learned that she had to avoid foods with gluten. Gluten is the protein part of wheat, rye, barley, and other related grains. People with celiac disease (sometimes called non-tropical sprue or gluten-sensitive enteropathy) cannot tolerate gluten when it comes in contact with the small intestine. ■

CASE STUDY #3

A 74-Year-Old Man

John is a 74-year-old Caucasian man who lives in Charleston, South Carolina. He is a retired university professor who lives with his partner of 20 years, Preston. John and Preston live in an upscale neighborhood with areas they like to walk. Both use the local gym regularly and believe they are blessed with the ability to schedule routine physical checkups, dine out occasionally, and travel. John has been married twice and has two grown daughters with their own children who are almost grown. Although John keeps in touch with them, he does not see any of them very often. One of his daughters lives in another area of the country. The other daughter chooses not to interact much with John because of his relationship with Preston.

Although John wishes his relationships with his daughters were different, he has integrated his life choices and experiences into his identity in such a way that he has found peace with life. Among their favorite things to discuss, John and Preston discuss the strengths and shortcomings of organized religion, political events and candidates, and the changes in society and culture they have observed over time. They obtain their information from television, newspapers, the Internet, guests they invite to dinner, and life experiences. Preston, 12 years younger than John, has begun feeling depressed by some of the physical deterioration, including some jaw pain he has observed in John. Preston's anxiety has increased and he has begun thinking about possible living situations in the event of John's death. Preston has no living relatives except for a half-sister who lives in Texas. ■

changes. At the end of this activity, submit a total of six days of intake records, a narrative of how you conducted your assessment, and a two to three page typed narrative that addresses the following questions:

1. What obstacles or challenges did you encounter implementing your dietary goals?
2. How might you modify your food environment, behavior, or dietary goals to improve your ability to make these dietary changes?
3. Do you feel these changes are ones that you will incorporate in your lifestyle on a more consistent and long-term basis? Why or why not?
4. In view of your personal dietary and/or fitness goals, list at least three lifestyle habits that would promote your health and longevity.

References

American Dietetic Association. (2002, October). *Nutrition and you: Trends 2002 final report of findings*. Retrieved July 1, 2008, from http://www.eatright.org/cps/rde/xchg/ada/hs.xsl/media_1578_ENU_HTML.htm

American Dietetic Association. (2004). Position of the American Dietetic Association: Dietary guidance for healthy children ages 2 to 11 years. *Journal of the American Dietetic Association, 104*, 660–677.

American Dietetic Association. (2005). *Working with the media: A handbook for members of the American Dietetic Association*. Chicago: Author.

American Dietetic Association. (2006). Position of the American Dietetic Association: Food and nutrition misinformation. *Journal of the American Dietetic Association, 106*, 601–607.

American Dietetic Association. (2008). *International dietetics & nutrition terminology (IDNT) reference manual: Standardized language for the Nutrition Care Process*. Chicago: Author.

American Society for Nutrition. (2007). *Principles and recommendations for the 2007 Farm Bill reauthorization*. Bethesda, MD: Author.

Bandura, A. (1986). *Social foundations of thought and action: A social cognitive theory*. Upper Saddle River, NJ: Prentice Hall.

Berkel, L. A., Poston, W. S., Reeves, R. S., & Foreyt, J. P. (2005). Behavioral interventions for obesity. *Journal of the American Dietetic Association, 105*, S35–S43.

Birch, L. L., & Fisher, J. O. (1998). Development of eating behaviors among children and adolescents. *Pediatrics, 101*, 539–549.

Bray, G. A., & Champagne, C. M. (2005). Beyond energy balance: There is more to obesity than kilocalories. *Journal of the American Dietetic Association, 105*, S17–23.

Bronfenbrenner, U. (1995). Developmental ecology through space and time: A future perspective. In P. Moen, G. H. Elder, Jr., & K. Luscher (Eds.), *Examining lives in context: Perspectives on the ecology of human development* (pp. 619–647). Washington, DC: APA Books.

Bronfenbrenner, U. (2001). The bioecological theory of human development. In N. J. Smelser & P. B. Baltes (Eds.), *International encyclopedia of the social and behavioral sciences* (Vol. 10, pp. 6963–6970). New York: Elsevier.

Bronfenbrenner, U. (2005). *Making human beings human: Bioecological perspectives on human development*. Thousand Oaks, CA: Sage.

Committee on Nutrition Standards for Foods in Schools. (2007). *Nutrition standards for foods in schools: Leading the way toward healthier youth*. Washington, DC: National Academy of Sciences.

Conner, M., & McMillan, B. (2004). Health belief model. In A. J. Christensen, R. Martin, & J. M. Smith (Eds.), *Encyclopedia of health psychology* (pp. 126–128). New York: Kluwer.

Conyne, R. K. (2004). *Preventive counseling: Helping people to become empowered in systems and settings* (2nd ed.). New York: Brunner-Routledge.

Ebbeling, C. B., Pawlak, D. B., & Ludwig, D. S. (2002). Childhood obesity: Public health crisis, common sense cure. *The Lancet, 360*, 473–482.

Fabricatore, A. N., & Wadden, T. A. (2003). Treatment of obesity: An overview. *Clinical Diabetes, 21*, 67–72.

Gladding, S. T. (2000). *Counseling: A comprehensive profession* (4th ed.). Upper Saddle River, NJ: Merrill/Prentice Hall.

Green, A., & Keys, S. (2001). Expanding the developmental school counseling paradigm: Meeting the needs of the 21st century student. *Professional School Counseling, 5*, 84–95.

Isselmann, M. C., Deubner, L. S., & Hartman, M. (1993). A nutrition counseling workshop: Integrating counseling psychology into nutrition practice. *Journal of the American Dietetic Association, 93*, 324–326.

Kirscht, J. P. (1983). Preventive health behavior: A review of research and issues. *Health Psychology, 2*, 277–301.

Lacey, K., & Pritchett, E. (2003). Nutrition care process and model: ADA adopts road map to quality care and outcomes management. *Journal of the American Dietetic Association, 103*, 1061–1072.

Lambert, M. J. (1986). Implications of psychotherapy outcome research for eclectic psychotherapy. In J. C. Norcross (Ed.), *Handbook of eclectic psychotherapy* (pp. 436–462). New York: Brunner/Mazel.

Lambie, G. W. & Williamson, L. L. (2004). The Challenge to Change from Guidance Counseling to Professional School Counseling: A Historical Proposition. *Professional School Counseling, 8*:2, 124–131.

McAuliffe, G.J., & Eriksen, K (1999). Toward a constructivist and developmental identity for the counseling profession: The Context-Phase-Stage-Style model. *Journal of Counseling and Development, 77*, 267–280.

National Research Council, Committee on the Framework for Evaluating the Safety of the Dietary Supplements.

(2004). *Dietary supplements: A framework for evaluating safety*. Washington, DC: Institute of Medicine.

Nuttall, J. (2002). Modes of therapeutic relationship in brief psychodynamic psychotherapy. *Journal of Psychodynamic Process, 89*, 505–523.

Picciano, M. F. (2004). *Who is using dietary supplements and what are they using?* Bethesda, MD: National Institutes of Health Office of Dietary Supplements.

Pope-Davis, D. B., Coleman, H. L., Liu, W. M., & Toporek, R. L. (2003). *Handbook of multicultural competencies in counseling & psychology*. Thousand Oaks, CA: Sage.

Prochaska, J. O., Norcross, J. C., & DiClemente, V. (1994). *Changing for good: A revolutionary six-stage program for overcoming bad habits and moving your life positively forward*. New York: Avon Books.

Remley, T. P., Jr., & Herlihy, B. (2001). *Ethical, legal and professional issues in counseling*. Upper Saddle River, NJ: Prentice Hall.

Ryff, C., & Keyes, C. (1995). The structure of psychological well-being revisited. *Journal of Personality and Social Psychology, 69*, 719–727.

Santrock, J. W. (2002). *Lifespan development* (8th ed.). New York: McGraw-Hill.

Sizer, F., & Whitney, E. (1994). *Nutrition: Concepts and controversies* (6th ed.). St. Paul, MN: West.

Snyder, E. E., Walts, B., Perusse, L., Chagnon, Y. C., Weisnagel, S. J., Rankinen, T., et al. (2004). The human obesity gene map: The 2003 update. *Obesity Research, 12*, 369–439.

Sontag, J. C. (1996). Toward a comprehensive theoretical framework for disability research: Bronfenbrenner revisited. *Journal of Special Education, 30*, 319–344.

Sue, D. W., & Sue, D. (2003). *Counseling the culturally diverse: Theory and practice* (4th ed.). New York: John Wiley.

Wadden, T. A., & Foster, G. D. (2000). Behavioral treatment of obesity. *Medical Clinics of North America, 84*, 441–461.

Wampold, B. E. (2001).*The great psychotherapy debate: Models, methods, and findings*. Mahwah, NJ: Lawrence Erlbaum.

Whitney, E. N., & Rolfes, S. R. (1993). *Understanding nutrition* (6th ed.). St. Paul, MN: West.

Witmer, J. M., & Sweeney, T. J. (1992). A holistic model for wellness and prevention over the life span. *Journal of Counseling & Development, 71*, 140–148.

Young, M. E. (2009). *Learning the art of helping: Building blocks and techniques* (4th ed.). Upper Saddle River, NJ: Pearson.

Zeisel, S. H. (2007). Nutrigenomics and metabolomics will change clinical nutrition and public health practice: Insights from studies on dietary requirements for choline. *American Journal of Clinical Nutrition, 86*, 542–548.

11 PREVENTIVE SELF-CARE: BENEFITS OF MODERN MEDICINE

Maria Elliot

Eating a vegetarian diet, walking (exercising) every day, and meditating is considered radical. Allowing someone to slice your chest open and graft your leg veins in your heart is considered normal and conservative.

DEAN ORNISH (CARDIOLOGIST)

Wellness Connection

Self-care is a vast area, including, for example, such topics as preventive screenings, hygiene, public health, health prevention, and behavioral change. Maria Elliot, clinical counselor, provides us with a brief history of the development of healthcare and overviews some of the critical health issues of which counselors should encourage their clients to be aware.

SELF-CARE: DEFINED

Quality of life is a concept hard to measure, but one which counselors work to help their clients achieve. Quality of life reflects a general sense of happiness and satisfaction with one's life and environment. It encompasses all aspects of life, including health, recreation, culture, rights, values, beliefs, aspirations, and the conditions that support a life containing these elements (Office of Disease Prevention and Health Promotion, 2008). Health-related quality of life reflects a personal sense of physical and mental health and the ability to react to factors in the physical and social environments. A basic concept in both the mental health and medical fields is that the individual has control over this aspect. Self-care is the individual's ability to take responsibility for his or her own wellness through self-care and safety habits that are preventive in nature (Myers, Witmer, & Sweeney, 1997). There are three elements of self-care that will be discussed: (1) habits we learn in order to protect ourselves from injury, disease, or death; (2) healthcare that includes periodic medical checkups that may prevent a disease or enable one to get early treatment; and

(3) avoidance of harmful substances, both those that we might ingest and toxic substances in the environment (Witmer, 1996). Counselors' understanding of preventive self-care related to wellness and their participation in the empowerment of clients to engage in such behaviors and services are crucial elements in wellness counseling.

SELF-CARE: THEN AND NOW

It seems obvious to understand and believe in the value of quality of life and self-care. Especially in one of the wealthiest nations in the world, individuals in the United States must be able to obtain this health-related quality of life due to our advanced medical care system, knowledge, and access to services. You can pick up any magazine or turn on any television station and feel overwhelmed by the amount of resources related to wellness, health, and disease management that are available to individuals within the United States. Yet why is it that the leading causes of death in the United States are all preventable based on lifestyle and early detection? How can individuals in the wealthiest and most medically fortunate nation in the world be killing themselves? Why can we not live longer, higher quality lives and why are counselors doing nothing about it?

It seems appropriate to start by briefly examining what has been done throughout history to stop the occurrence and spread of disease. Societies from history share many similarities with societies today and we can learn from their wisdom and implementation of knowledge. At the beginning of the 1900s, infectious diseases ran rampant in the United States and worldwide and topped the leading causes of death. Societies responded with certain practices and behaviors to prevent the spread of such diseases. Yet the implementation of public health standards, policies, and practices began much earlier than the 20th century. Table 11.1 briefly outlines the development of prevention and treatment through history. Individuals understood the causes of diseases and made changes to their own behaviors, as well as population-wide policies to aid in prevention.

In the United States currently, it appears that recognition of the causes of disease and preventive self-care is needed more than ever. Recent sources attribute two-thirds of all deaths to lifestyle choices (e.g., heart disease, cancer, stroke, injuries, HIV infection, low birth weight, alcohol and drug problems, and inadequate immunization) (Witmer, 1996). These preventable causes of death have been estimated to be responsible for 900,000 deaths annually—nearly 40% of the total yearly mortality in the country (Cohen, Neumann, & Weinstein, 2008). A high prevalence of people with unhealthy lifestyles and behaviors exists in America, such as insufficient exercise, overweight, and tobacco use, which are risk factors for many of these fatal chronic diseases and disabilities (Centers for Disease Control and Prevention [CDC], 2007). Yet these unhealthy behaviors seem to continue and increase despite our knowledge of their damaging effects, demanding attention in the medical and counseling fields. Our nation's changing demographic will also lead to an increasing occurrence of such conditions, especially if the unhealthy behaviors continue through the lifespan. With an aging population and longer life expectancy comes increasing total prevalence of chronic diseases and conditions associated with aging, such as disability and limitation of activity (CDC, 2007).

Both professionals and clients have begun to better understand the necessity of including preventive self-care into their routines to prevent many diseases. With the control of many infectious agents as described earlier and the increasing occurrence of unhealthy behaviors and the rising age of the population, chronic diseases top the list of leading causes of death. Heart disease accounts for 31.4%, cancer accounts for 23.3%, stroke counts for 6.9%, and chronic obstructive pulmonary disease accounts for 4.7% (CDC, 2007; Office of Disease Prevention and

TABLE 11.1 Development of Prevention and Treatment Through History

Dawn of History	Shamans used to diagnose, treat, and in some cases prevent the spread of disease, believed to be malevolent forces to be healed spiritually and physically.
Ancient Rome	Establishment of cities and need for municipal water supplies and sewage systems.
Dark Ages and Medieval Period 500–1000 CE	Public health activities, such as overseeing the water supply and sewerage, street cleaning, and supervision of the markets, fell under the jurisdiction of the Church and councils. Isolation of cases of leprosy represents the earliest application of public health practice still in use.
Renaissance and the Plague Period 1300s and 1400s	Due to the plague and many other epidemics that devastated the population of the world, the organization of boards of health, the promulgation of a theory of contagion, and the introduction of health statistics came about.
Enlightenment and Sanitary Reform 1750–Mid-19th Century	Much study done on the prevalence and causation of preventable diseases. As a result, sewerage, potable and plentiful water supplies, refuse disposal, proper ventilation of residences and places of work, supervision of public works by qualified professionals, and legislative authorization of measures to obtain these results were put forward.
Bacteriology 1870s and 1880s	Louis Pasteur and Robert Koch discovered pathogenic bacteria. Sanitation became science-based and the development of vaccines promised the prevention of many infectious diseases.

Source: Breslow & Cengage, 2002.

Health Promotion, 2008). Figure 11.1 and Figure 11.2 show how these figures have changed over the last century.

STRATEGIES FOR PROMOTING SELF-CARE

Medical research and the expertise of professionals in the field can offer much understanding of the prevalence and causes of these detrimental diseases. Because of the high cost of human life, as well as financial cost, the Office of Disease Prevention and Health Promotion, the U.S. Department of Health and Human Services, and the Centers for Disease Control and Prevention have sought out this knowledge and compiled many reviews of the literature and propose current recommendations to begin to decrease such diseases and deaths, specifically those causing 55% of the deaths—heart disease and cancer. This information helps mental health professionals to better understand these conditions and the clients whom they affect.

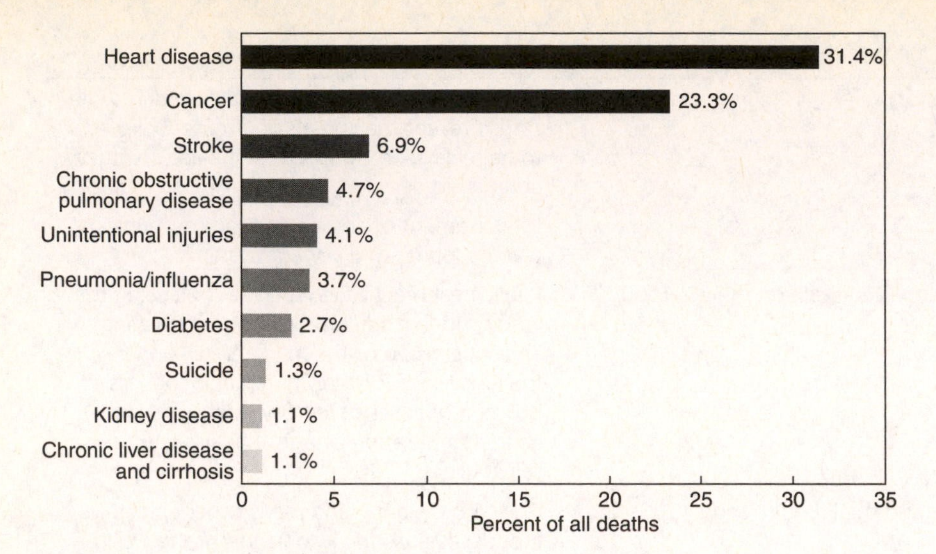

FIGURE 11.1 Leading Causes of Death, 1997
Source: Centers for Disease Control and Prevention, National Center for Health Statistics, National Vital Statistics System, and unpublished data, 1997.

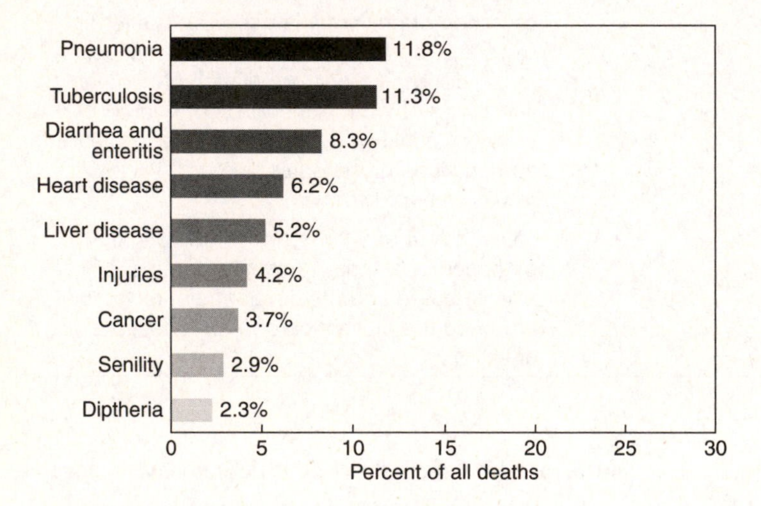

FIGURE 11.2 Leading Causes of Death, 1900
Source: Centers for Disease Control and Prevention, National Center for Health Statistics, National Vital Statistics System, and unpublished data, 1997.

Heart disease is the leading cause of death in the United States and is a major cause of disability. Almost 700,000 people die of heart disease in the United States each year. Heart disease is the leading cause of death for American Indians and Alaska Natives, blacks, Hispanics, and whites. For Asians and Pacific Islanders, cancer is the leading cause of death (26.1%); heart disease is a close second (26.0%). Prevention of heart disease takes the form of screening and healthy lifestyle choices. Lifestyle actions such as healthy diet, regular physical activity, not smoking, and healthy weight will help keep normal blood pressure levels. Professionals recommend having blood pressure checked regularly, and if it is high, to control and bring down the level with lifestyle changes and medicines. Individuals should also prevent and control high blood cholesterol, a major risk factor for heart disease. Preventing and treating high blood cholesterol includes eating a diet low in saturated fat and cholesterol and high in fiber, keeping a healthy weight, and getting regular exercise. Professionals recommend having cholesterol levels checked once every five years and if found to be high, doctors may prescribe medication as well as healthy lifestyle changes. Individuals with diabetes also have an increased risk of heart disease, but can reduce their risk through weight loss and regular physical activity. To prevent heart disease, individuals are also encouraged not to use tobacco as such use increases the risk of high blood pressure, heart disease, and stroke. Excessive alcohol use increases the risk of high blood pressure, heart attack, and stroke, and individuals who drink should do so in moderation. Finally, maintaining a healthy weight, engaging in regular physical activity, and having an overall healthy diet will aid in the prevention of heart disease (CDC, 2007).

Cancer is the second leading cause of death in the United States, claiming approximately 1,500 lives each day (American Cancer Society [ACS], 2008). Many cancers may be prevented by early detection and lifestyle choices. All cancers caused by cigarette smoking and heavy use of alcohol could be prevented completely. The American Cancer Society estimates that in 2008, about 170,000 cancer deaths are expected to be caused by tobacco use (ACS, 2008). Approximately one-third of the 565,650 cancer deaths expected to occur in 2008 will be related to overweight or obesity, physical inactivity, and nutrition and thus could also be prevented. Many of the more than 1 million skin cancers that are expected to be diagnosed in 2008 could have been prevented by protection from the sun's rays and avoiding indoor tanning. Certain cancers are related to infectious agents, such as hepatitis B virus, human papillomavirus (HPV), human immunodeficiency virus (HIV), *Helicobacter pylori (H. pylori),* and others, and could be prevented through behavioral changes, vaccines, or antibiotics. Regular screening examinations by healthcare professionals can result in the detection and removal of precancerous growths, as well as the diagnosis of cancers at an early stage when they are most treatable. Screening can prevent cancers of the cervix, color, and rectum by allowing removal of precancerous tissue, and screening can detect cancers of the breast, colon, rectum, cervix, prostate, oral cavity, and skin at early stages. For most of these cancers, early detection has been proven to reduce mortality (ACS, 2008). Professionals can help encourage the decreased rate of cancer and death from cancer by encouraging some of these healthy lifestyles and preventive screenings.

The Partnership for Prevention (2007) has ranked the preventive services recommended by medical professionals that are most likely to prevent these top diseases and be cost-effective. Their recommendations highlight the need for medical professionals to:

- Discuss daily aspirin use with high-risk adults (prevent heart disease, heart attack, and stroke); immunize children (prevent many diseases); provide tobacco use screening and brief intervention (prevent heart disease, cancer, stroke, and other pulmonary conditions).
- Encourage adult vaccines of influenza and pneumococcal; cervical and colorectal screenings; vision screenings among adults 65+ years; hypertension screenings; cholesterol screenings; problem drinking screenings.
- Screening young women for chlamydia; screening young children for visual impairments.

The U.S. Preventive Services Task Force also recommends that clinicians discuss and offer certain preventive services for the well-being of patients. These are listed in Table 11.2.

Along with preventive screenings, it appears that healthy lifestyle changes have a major effect on the occurrence of these preventable diseases and causes of death. Several recommendations have been made by the medical community and the Centers for Disease Control and Prevention, *Healthy People 2010.*

TABLE 11.2 Preventive Services for the Well-Being of Patients

Recommendation	Adults		Special Populations		Notes
	Men	Women	Pregnant Women	Children	
Abdominal Aortic Aneurysm, Screening	X				One-time screening by ultrasonography in men aged 65 to 75 who have ever smoked.
Alcohol Misuse Screening and Behavioral Counseling Interventions	X	X	X		
Aspirin for the Primary Prevention of Cardiovascular Events	X	X			Adults at increased risk for coronary heart disease.
Bacteriuria, Screening for Asymptomatic			X		
Breast Cancer, Chemoprevention		X			Discuss with women at high risk for breast cancer and at low risk for adverse effects of chemoprevention.
Breast Cancer, Screening		X			Mammography every 1–2 years for women 40 and older.
Breast and Ovarian Cancer Susceptibility, Genetic Risk Assessment and BRCA Mutation Testing		X			Refer women whose family history is associated with an increased risk for deleterious mutations in BRCA1 or BRCA2 genes for genetic counseling and evaluation for BRCA testing.
Breastfeeding, Behavioral Interventions to Promote		X	X		Structured education and behavioral counseling programs.
Cervical Cancer, Screening		X			Women who have been sexually active.
Chlamydial Infection, Screening		X	X		Sexually active women 25 and younger and other asymptomatic women at increased risk for infection. Asymptomatic pregnant women 25 and younger and others at increased risk.
Colorectal Cancer, Screening	X	X			Men and women 50 and older.

	Adults		Special Populations		
Recommendation	**Men**	**Women**	**Pregnant Women**	**Children**	**Notes**
Dental Caries in Preschool Children, Prevention				X	Prescribe oral fluoride supplementation at currently recommended doses to preschool children older than 6 months whose primary water source is deficient in fluoride.
Depression, Screening	X	X			In clinical practices with systems to assure accurate diagnoses, effective treatment, and follow-up.
Diabetes Mellitus in Adults, Screening for Type 2	X	X			Adults with hypertension or hyperlipidemia.
Diet, Behavioral Counseling in Primary Care to Promote a Healthy	X	X			Adults with hyperlipidemia and other known risk factors for cardiovascular and diet-related chronic disease.
Gonorrhea, Screening		X	X		All sexually active women, including those who are pregnant, at increased risk for infection (that is, if they are young or have other individual or population risk factors).
Gonorrhea, Prophylactic Medication				X	Prophylactic ocular topical medication for all newborns against gonococcal ophthalmia neonatorum.
Hepatitis B Virus Infection, Screening			X		Pregnant women at first prenatal visit.
High Blood Pressure, Screening	X	X			
HIV, Screening	X	X	X	X	All adolescents and adults at increased risk for HIV infection and all pregnant women.
Iron Deficiency Anemia, Prevention				X	Routine iron supplementation for asymptomatic children aged 6 to 12 months who are at increased risk for iron deficiency anemia.
Iron Deficiency Anemia, Screening			X		Routine screening in asymptomatic pregnant women.

(continued)

TABLE 11.2 Preventive Services for the Well-Being of Patients *(continued)*

Recommendation	Adults		Special Populations		Notes
	Men	Women	Pregnant Women	Children	
Lipid Disorders, Screening	X	X			Men 35 and older and women 45 and older. Younger adults with other risk factors for coronary disease. Screening for lipid disorders to include measurement of total cholesterol and high-density lipoprotein cholesterol.
Obesity in Adults, Screening	X	X			Intensive counseling and behavioral interventions to promote sustained weight loss for obese adults.
Osteoporosis in Postmenopausal Women, Screening		X			Women 65 and older and women 60 and older at increased risk for osteoporotic fractures.
Rh (D) Incompatibility, Screening			X		Blood typing and antibody testing at first pregnancy-related visit. Repeated antibody testing for unsensitized Rh (D)-negative women at 24–28 weeks gestation unless biological father is known to be Rh (D) negative.
Syphilis Infection, Screening	X	X	X		Persons at increased risk and all pregnant women.
Tobacco Use and Tobacco-Caused Disease, Counseling to Prevent	X	X	X		Tobacco cessation interventions for those who use tobacco. Augmented pregnancy-tailored counseling to pregnant women who smoke.
Visual Impairment in Children Younger than Age 5 Years, Screening				X	To detect amblyopia, strabismus, and defects in visual acuity.

Source: Agency for Healthcare Research and Quality, U.S. Department of Health and Human Services.

INCREASING PHYSICAL ACTIVITY In 1997, only 15% of adults performed the recommended amount of physical activity, and 40% of adults engaged in no leisure-time physical activity (CDC, 2007). Women generally are less active than men at all ages and persons with lower incomes and less education are typically not as physically active as those with higher incomes and education. African Americans and Hispanics are less physically active than white people. People with disabilities are less physically active than people without disabilities. Regular physical activity throughout life is important for maintaining a healthy body, enhancing psychological well-being, and preventing premature death. Regular physical activity decreases the risk of death from heart disease, lowers the risk of developing diabetes, helps prevent high blood pressure, and is associated with decreasing the risk of colon cancer. Muscle and bone strength and lean muscle increase, while body fat decreases with physical activity. The current recommendations for preventive purposes encourage individuals to engage in vigorous physical activity that promotes cardio-respiratory fitness three or more days per week for 20 or more minutes per occasion, and/or to engage in daily moderate physical activity for at least 30 minutes/day. Engaging in physical activity also has psychological effects as it appears to enhance psychological well-being and reduce symptoms of depression and anxiety while improving mood (CDC, 2007).

DECREASING OBESITY AND INDIVIDUALS WHO ARE OVERWEIGHT The number of overweight children, adolescents, and adults has risen over the past four decades, with more than half of adults in the United States estimated to be overweight or obese (CDC, 2007). In 1995, the estimated cost to manage the population effects of overweight individuals was $99 billion (CDC, 2007). Obesity is especially prevalent among women with lower incomes and is more common among African American and Mexican American women than white women. Overweight and obesity are major contributors to many preventable causes of death. Higher body weights are associated with higher death rates as being overweight raises the risk of high blood pressure, high cholesterol, type 2 diabetes, heart disease and stroke, gallbladder disease, arthritis, sleep disturbances and problems breathing, and certain types of cancers. The current recommendations for preventive purposes include choosing a healthful assortment of foods that include vegetables, fruits, whole grains, fat free or low fat dairy products, fish, lean meat, poultry, and beans. Individuals should choose food low in saturated fats and low in added sugars, while limiting portion size. Along with the healthy diet, individuals are encouraged to have at least 30 minutes of moderate physical activity most or all days of the week. Psychologically, obesity affects the individual, as well. Obese individuals may suffer from social stigmatization, discrimination, and lowered self-esteem (CDC, 2007).

END TOBACCO USE Cigarette smoking is the single most preventable cause of disease and death in the United States. Tobacco-related deaths number more than 430,000 per year, representing more than 5 million years of potential life lost. Smoking itself results in more deaths each year in the United States than AIDS, alcohol, cocaine, heroin, homicide, suicide, motor vehicle crashes, and fires combined! It is estimated that tobacco-related diseases cost approximately $50 billion per year. Tobacco use is a major risk factor for heart disease, stroke, lung cancer, and chronic lung diseases—all leading causes of death and environmental tobacco smoking, or secondhand smoking, increase the risk of heart disease and significant lung conditions such as asthma and bronchitis. Due to these risks, the current recommendation for individuals is to cease use. There is no safe level or amount of use.

DECREASE SUBSTANCE USE Excessive alcohol and drug use are associated with various negative outcomes, including child and spousal abuse, sexually transmitted diseases, teen pregnancy, school failure, vehicle crashes, escalation of healthcare costs, low worker productivity, and homelessness. Long-term heavy drinking can lead to heart disease, cancer, alcohol-related liver disease, and pancreatitis. Alcohol use during pregnancy causes fetal alcohol effects, the leading cause of preventable mental retardation. Current recommendations for alcohol use are one drink per day for women and two drinks per day for men. There are not currently recommendations for drug use for individuals (CDC, 2007).

OBTAIN IMMUNIZATION Vaccines are among the greatest public health achievements of the 20th century. Yet in 1998, only 73% of children received all of the vaccines recommended for universal administration. In the United States, immunization rates are significantly lower for African American and Hispanic adults than for Caucasian adults. Immunizations prevent disability and death from infectious diseases for individuals and can help control the spread of infections. Immunizations against influenza and pneumococcal disease, the sixth leading cause of death, can prevent serious illness and mortality. The current recommendations for preventive purposes are that all children born in the United States should be receiving 12–16 doses of vaccine by age two to be protected against 10 vaccine-preventable childhood diseases. For adults aged 65 and older, recommended immunizations include a yearly influenza vaccine and a one-time immunization against pneumococcal disease (CDC, 2007).

BARRIERS TO SELF-CARE

Yet there exists a discrepancy. Residents of the United States have the information and evidence on these leading causes of death. Individuals are provided explanations and proof that these discussed preventive self-care strategies lower the risk of developing these debilitating and deadly diseases. Yet the number of individuals participating in unhealthy lifestyles and ignoring recommended screenings continues to increase. Some researchers have attempted to understand why people are not pursuing these self-care preventive measures. One study points to the effect of mental health on unhealthy behaviors. One study found that people reporting 14 or more "mentally unhealthy" days in the past 30 days had a higher prevalence of adverse behavior-related risk factors for disease than people who did not report being "mentally unhealthy" (Strine et al., 2004). Another study reported similar findings in that persons who had worse self-rated mental health also frequently had unhealthy lifestyles (Rohrer, Pierce, & Blackburn, 2005). Several studies point to systems barriers that prohibit or discourage individuals from pursuing preventive services (CDC, 2007; Cherrington, Corbie-Smith, & Pathman, 2007; Ross, Bernheim, Bradley, Ten, & Gallo, 2007; Strine et al., 2004). Costs such as out-of-pocket expenditures and time lost on the job, limited access to care, lack of healthcare coverage, and low income are all associated with the likelihood that individuals do not use preventive services and more likely to delay seeking medical care, behaviors that increase the risk of developing chronic diseases. Other factors that may affect individuals pursuing services are transportation problems, lack of knowledge of where to obtain care, communication difficulties with the provider, and covert or overt discrimination (Cherrington et al., 2007). Income may be a factor, as one study showed that lower income adults are less likely than higher income adults to receive recommended preventive care, such as cervical, breast, and colorectal cancer screening, blood pressure screening, and cholesterol screening (Ross et al., 2007). Demographics play a role, as well. Men appear less likely to endorse periodic examinations and health services than women, and younger individuals less often value periodic examinations and thus receive less preventive services (Cherrington et al., 2007).

Current health status is a significant predictor of screening and preventive behavior. Results show that individuals who are in poorer health (self-rated) are more likely to get flu shots and cholesterol checks, but less likely to have mammograms, pap smears, breast examinations, and prostate checks (Wu, 2003). Wu asserted that this finding may be explained by behavioral effects where individuals who are generally anxious or pessimistic about the future (characteristics that are related to health status) have a high degree of anxiety, or psychic pain, about finding out results of certain medical tests. Finally, personal beliefs play a role in obtaining preventive services and choosing healthy behaviors. Individuals that believe in the value of periodic health examinations are associated with the receipt of clinical preventive services and individuals who do not value or are ambivalent about periodic examinations less often get the recommended services (Cherrington et al., 2007; Wu, 2003). This finding regarding the importance of personal beliefs may also help us to understand why individuals continue to engage in unhealthy behaviors such as tobacco use, overeating, and lack of exercise.

Researchers have also identified factors that may encourage healthy lifestyle and preventive self-care. Social support may encourage prevention, as one study found a positive association between mammography and being married. Widowed, separated, or divorced women were more likely to have had their last mammogram three or more years ago (Achat, Close, & Taylor, 2005). One study found that counseling strategies from medical professionals that are designed to emphasize a preventive focus while including family members in the discussion are appropriate to populations with different cultural values and beliefs (Sussman et al., 2007). This understanding may be specifically important with African American and Latino populations that value the family unit. Knowledge also plays a role—understanding the individual's beliefs about health, disease prevention, risk factors, and family history of disease could lead to improved targeted interventions aimed at increasing uptake of preventive services (Cherrington et al., 2007; Wu, 2003).

ROLE OF WELLNESS COUNSELORS IN PROMOTING SELF-CARE

The role of counselors in prevention of disease has not often been acknowledged. Yet their duty to encourage the holistic well-being of individuals demands such work. First, the psychological effects of illness and disease cannot be ignored. Counselors working in settings from schools to hospitals to inpatient treatment encounter the anxiety, depression, and existential issues that accompany such diseases. Second, the current leading causes of death in the United States are often preventable through early detection, screening, and lifestyle. Individuals come to counselors for behavior change and to challenge beliefs, so why are lifestyles and beliefs that may lead to disease and death outside of the realm of counselors? They are not, but are a crucial aspect of wellness counseling and counselors must work for wellness in relation to preventive self-care.

First, counselors can help promote life expectancy and quality of life by helping individuals gain the knowledge, motivation, and opportunities they need to make informed decisions about their health (Office of Disease Prevention and Health Promotion, 2008). Counselors can empower individuals to engage in healthy behaviors, create healthy environments for themselves and others, and increase access to high-quality healthcare. Often this involves changing habits, behaviors, and attitudes.

Counselors must also advocate for promoting community-wide safety, education, and access to healthcare (Office of Disease Prevention and Health Promotion, 2008). Many system barriers block clients, and counselors can help advocate for their removal or aid clients in overcoming these barriers and problem-solving.

Counselors may aid in wellness counseling towards preventive self-care by responding to the reasons people engage in unhealthy behaviors and do not seek preventive services, as discussed earlier. Poor self-rated mental health was associated with unhealthy lifestyles and as counselors work towards positive client mental health and perceived positive mental health, healthy lifestyles may increase (Rohrer, Pierce, & Blackburn, 2005). Psychic pains, or high levels of anxiety, have also been associated with lower levels of compliance with self-examination and preventive screening guidelines (Wu, 2003). Counselors can help individuals develop stress-lowering and anxiety-relieving strategies that may help to encourage these self-exams and screening practices, leading to prevention of disease and death. Counselors can also help clients develop or increase coping strategies if screening results highlight possible disease (Wu, 2003). Personal beliefs have been shown to play a role. Counselors can help inform clients of the importance of physical health to overall well-being and the value of preventive self-care. Clients must know that engaging in preventive self-care leads to positive outcomes and not engaging in preventive self-care leads to negative outcomes. Increasing their understanding and belief in the value of healthy lifestyle choices and preventive medical methods may empower clients to take control of their own health and well-being. Social support encourages obtaining preventive services, and counselors can aid clients in the development of a social support network that will enhance their positive environment and choices.

Counselors must be well read in many different areas when working with clients on wellness issues, including self-care health habits (Granello, 2000). Counselors can empower clients to understand that people can be active participants in their own well-being and care. By taking steps to manage their own psychological states, lifestyle, and obtainment of preventive services, they may be able to prevent disease or shorten its course (Witmer, 1996). Choosing to develop healthy habits, practice good medical care, and avoid contact with harmful substances will improve clients' quality of life and extend longevity (Witmer, 1996). The Surgeon General and the U.S. Preventive Services Task Force have suggested that mental health screening as well as physical health screening are important in clinical practice, as they are interconnected, which is highlighted by the research reported above (Strine et al., 2004).

In addition, clinicians need to consider factors external to the client-clinician encounter, such as the diverse cultural and religious beliefs across communities, the impact of mass media advertising campaigns, and competing client demands (Sussman et al., 2007). More study must be done to understand the responses from various social, religious, and political factions, as it is unclear how some prevention services and counseling will affect disparate cultural groups. Presenting information in ways that are sensitive to a range of cultural norms and social values associated with risk factors will likely play a role in enhancing lifestyle recommendations and prevention services acceptance (Sussman et al., 2007). Counselors play a major role in this field of preventive self-care and wellness, though. Their unique interaction with clients and other professionals put them at a point to empower clients to make changes in their lives that will positive effect their well-being and longevity. Counselors must engage in this work, first of understanding the aspects of physical wellness, and next, of implementing this knowledge into their practice. Without doing so, wellness counseling misses a primary element and clients do not receive adequate care.

References

Achat, H., Close, G., & Taylor, R. (2005). Who has regular mammograms? Effects of knowledge, beliefs, socioeconomic status, and health-related factors. *Preventive Medicine, 41*: 312–320.

American Cancer Society. (2008). *Facts and statistics*. Retrieved from http://www.cancer.org/docroot/home/index.asp

Breslow, L., & Cengage, G. (2002). *History of public health*. Encyclopedia of Public Health. Retrieved from http://www.enotes.com/public-health-encyclopedia/history-public-health

Centers for Disease Control and Prevention. (2007). *Health, United States, 2007*. Retrieved from http://www.cdc.gov/nchs/hus.htm

Cherrington, A., Corbie-Smith, G., & Pathman, D. (2007). Do adults who believe in periodic health examinations receive more clinical preventive services? *Preventive Medicine, 45*, 282–289.

Cohen, J., Neumann, P., & Weinstein, M. (2008). Does preventive care save money? Health economics and the presidential candidates. *The New England Journal of Medicine, 358*(7), 661–663.

Granello, P. (2000). Integrating wellness work into mental health private practice. *Journal of Psychotherapy in Independent Practice, 1*(1), 3–16.

Myers, J. E., Witmer, M. J., & Sweeney, T. J. (1997). *The WEL workbook: A guide to assessing personal resources for wellness and developing a plan for living life more fully.* Unpublished monograph.

Office of Disease Prevention and Health Promotion. (2008). *Healthy People 2010.* Retrieved from http://www.healthypeople.gov/

Partnership for Prevention. (2007). *Priorities for America's health: Capitalizing on life-saving, cost-effective preventive services.* Retrieved March 21, 2008, from http://www.prevent.org/images/stories/clinicalprevention/executive%20summary.pdf

Rohrer, J., Pierce, J. R., & Blackburn, C. (2005). Lifestyle and mental health. *Preventive Medicine, 40,* 438–443.

Ross, J., Bernheim, S., Bradley, E., Ten, H. M., & Gallo, W. (2007). Use of preventive care by the working poor in the United States. *Preventive Medicine, 44,* 254–259.

Strine, T., Balluz, L., Chapman, D., Moriarty, D., Owens, M., & Mokdad, A. (2004). Risk behaviors and healthcare coverage among adults by frequent mental distress status, 2001. *American Journal of Preventive Medicine, 26*(3), 213–216.

Sussman, A., Helitzer, D., Sanders, M., Urqueta, B., Salvador, M., & Ndiaye, K. (2007). HPV and cervical cancer prevention counseling with younger adolescents: Implications for primary care. *Annals of Family Medicine, 5*(4), 298–304.

Witmer, J. M. (1996). *Reaching towards wellness: A holistic model for personal growth and counseling*. Unpublished monograph.

Wu, S. (2003). Sickness and preventive medical behavior. *Journal of Health Economics, 22,* 675–689.

12 MEANING AND WELLNESS: PURPOSE FOR LIVING

Mark Young

The meaning of life is to give life meaning.

Ken Hudgins (Actor)

Wellness Connection

Dr. Mark Young illustrates the central importance of "meaning in life" for individual wellness. He reviews key research and provides insight in how a counselor can use assessment and therapy interventions to help a client develop a clearer sense of meaning.

Victor Frankl, in his book *Man's Search for Meaning,* asserted that victims of the Nazi holocaust who fought despair and found meaning and purpose in their lives despite atrocities were more likely to survive (Frankl, 1963). This book and Frankl's later work provided evidence of the interaction between health and the ability to cope with catastrophic stressors. In the 1970s and 1980s the search was for psychological mediators of the stress response that might buffer the deleterious effects of an unrecognized source of disease: failure to cope. Among the areas of research were cognitive variables such as realistic thoughts as well as exercise, nutrition, and social support (Korotkov, 1998). Thus, it could be argued that Frankl's discovery of the will to meaning was the beginning of a trend to discover what psychological variables can protect our health and propel us towards wellness. Yet research into the effect of meaning on health and wellness has shown mixed results (cf. Baumeister & Vohs, 2005).

MEANING IN THE WELLNESS LITERATURE

Nearly all of the writers who have written about spirituality and wellness incorporate a sense of meaning and purpose in life as part of what they mean by spirituality (Chandler, Holden, & Kolander, 1992; Hettler, 1980; Myers, Sweeney, & Witmer, 2000; Sweeney & Witmer, 1991; Zimpfer, 1992). Yet meaning and purpose can be thought of as a separate area of study in wellness. Writers such as Savolaine and

Granello (2002) have indicated that a strong sense of meaning and purpose in life affects health and wellness for several reasons. First, a sense of meaning and purpose in life can help one establish a personal identity and bolster one's self-esteem if one is living a life in accordance with his or her principles. An individual might, for example, gain a sense of meaning and purpose by working to help others at a homeless shelter. Such a person approves of himself or herself. Second, having meaning and purpose is potentially a lead to good interpersonal functioning and social connection as one interacts with others. Third, meaning helps overcome the existential vacuum and despair with which so many cope. Theoretically, this vacuum leads to diminished capacity to respond to stressors and takes a toll on health. Finally, a meaning and purpose in life can give one a sense of coherence—the ability to make sense of life experiences and stressful events. In short, this sense of coherence and control, as well as a courageous attitude towards life, seem to be common denominators in the impact of meaning on wellness. Following are contemporary conceptualizations of the sense of meaning that have dominated the literature and which serve as vehicles for inquiry into meaning and wellness. They also help us understand the scope of the definitions of meaning as it is used in research and counseling.

Richard Lazarus, Coping and Meaning

Richard Lazarus is regarded as one of the most important figures in stress and coping research (Lazarus & Folkman, 1984). Lazarus (1995, p. 5) identified coping as the "cognitive and behavioral efforts a person makes to manage demands that tax or exceed his or her personal resources." Inability to cope has been linked with increased susceptibility to various physical disorders. Lazarus saw coping as a transaction between the person and the environment—each affecting the other. He felt that too much emphasis has been placed on stress when all stress is not the same. An individual's reaction to stress can vary depending on whether it is seen as threat, harm, or challenge. Later in his career, Lazarus began to emphasize the importance of meaning as it relates to how people react to stressful situations (Lazarus, 1995). These meanings for events are derived from the psychological set that an individual possesses. Lazarus's work is foundational or at least supportive to other notions of meaning, including sense of coherence and hardiness.

Folkman and Moskowitz (2000) assert that a sense of meaning does not only aid reducing stress through the appraisal process but is also a coping technique in itself. Through the processes of assigning positive meaning to events, positive emotions are evoked. Positive affect in long-term stressful situations (strains) has a number of physiological benefits. In Fredrickson's (2001) theory, "Broaden and Build Model of Positive Emotions," she asserts that negative emotions make people narrower and more constricted in their plans of action while positive emotions embolden people to widen their search for solutions. Frederickson believes that positive emotions also counteract the physical effect of negative emotions. Thus finding personal meaning leads to positive emotions which can be used as a treatment for anger, anxiety, and depression and can buffer the effects of stress (Schwarzer & Knoll, 2003).

Sense of Coherence

By 1979, Antonovsky had proposed that researchers examine the sources or causes of health (salutogenesis), not just search for the cause of disease (pathogenesis). One of the salutogens he identified is related to the sense of meaning and purpose in life. Antonovsky called this construct "sense of coherence" (SOC), which has three components: comprehensibility, manageability, and meaningfulness (the last is the central tenet). *Comprehensibility* occurs when an individual can make sense of the world. It appears orderly and predictable. When people grow up in highly predictable circumstances, they have the sense that the world is not random. *Manageability,* by contrast, refers to the knowledge or sense that one has the resources to adapt, cope, and survive. According to Richard Lazarus (1995), secondary appraisal in the coping process involves assessing whether one has these resources. If one recognizes that help is on the way, stress is reduced. Yet sense of coherence does not seem to be synonymous with *sense of control* which has consistently been found to moderate stress and stress-related disorders (cf. Taylor, Helgeson, Reed, & Skokan, 1991). Amirkhan & Greaves (2003) contend that SOC is a general disposition or trait that involves tackling problems as they arise rather than reacting. Reacting has been associated with poor coping and stress-related disorders while facing and dealing with problems seems to have the opposite effect.

Finally, SOC involves *meaningfulness*. Meaningfulness is the emotion or feeling that life makes sense. Meaningfulness seems to be related to whether a person thinks that they have freedom in making choices that lead to outcomes. People with a sense of helplessness do not have a feeling of meaningfulness. Antonovsky believed that sense of coherence was related to immune functioning. A person who has a high sense of coherence interacts with stressors in a different way. He or she is more likely to view stressors as understandable and to be able to marshal resources. Individuals with a strong SOC are likely to see stressors as challenges rather than threat. Thus, there is less physiological response.

Generally, attempts to find a link between stress coping and sense of coherence have yielded mixed results (Korotkov, 1998). Yet a recent study by Agardh et al. (2004) of more than 4,800 Swedish women found that stress factors such as low decision-making ability at work and low SOC were associated with type 2 diabetes. SOC has also been found to be related to higher quality of life in lupus patients (Abu-Shakra et al., 2006).

Hardiness

The concept of hardiness fits nicely with the above discussion of Lazarus, although it arises from existential psychology. *Hardiness* is another word for "existential courage" (Maddi, 1998, p. 9). Existential thought asserts that an individual's own sense of meaning is the central cause of thinking and action (Maddi, 1998). Thus, an effective and courageous sense of meaning influences how one views the world and how one responds to it. Hardiness was identified in individuals who seemed to be especially resistant to stress based on their worldview (Kobasa, 1979). Hardiness was one of the first personality variables to be associated with resistance to cardiovascular disease.

Hardiness as described by Maddi & Kobasa (1984) involves three beliefs about the world —the three C's; *Commitment, Control, and Challenge*. People who have *commitment* believe in active involvement in the world as opposed to those who are alienated. Those who have the quality of *control* believe that one must work hard and struggle and that they have to power to affect outcomes in life. Alternately, those low in control feel powerless. Finally, the state of *challenge* is present in individuals who see stress and discomfort as opportunities to cope. Those low in this trait wish comfort and security. They are more likely to view stressors as discomfort and hardship. Together, these three traits form a disposition that helps individuals tolerate both the stresses and strains of life (Maddi, 1998). Hardiness has been shown to moderate the effects of stress and its tendency to produce depression (cf. Pengilly & Dowd, 2000).

MEASURING MEANING AND PURPOSE IN LIFE

The Purpose in Life test (Crumbaugh & Maholick, 1964) has been used most often to assess meaning in research, but it has been criticized for its mixture of existential constructs such as "freedom" in the questions. Certainly logotherapy concepts helped to form the basis of this and other instruments (Melton & Schulenberg, 2008). Other instruments with acceptable reliability and validity data are described briefly in Table 12.1. Their definitions of meaning vary, and therefore an appropriate instrument should be selected based on the needs of the client. Most measures of personal meaning have been negatively correlated with depression (Debats, 1998). On the other hand, many researchers in the area of health and coping favor a qualitative approach to assessment of meaning (see Schwarzer & Knoll, 2003) because different medical diagnoses have such varied experiences associated with them. Among the most often utilized qualitative methods are the analysis of personal narratives and interviews (see Schwarzer & Knoll, 2003). Table 12.1 shows paper and pencil tests that have been commonly used in the assessment of meaning in life.

TABLE 12.1 Selected Instruments for the Measurement of Meaning in Life

Instrument	Construct Measured	Brief Description of the Instrument	Citation
Personal Views Survey (PVS)	Hardiness	50-item revised with three subscales: Challenge, Commitment, Control.	Hardiness Institute (1985)
Sources of Meaning Profile (SMP)	Sources and strength of personal meaning in one's life	16-item scale that has been used with older adults.	Reker & Wong (1988)
Pargament's Meaning Scale (PMS)	Meaning that spirituality provides in one's life	20-item scale that does not measure spirituality but the degree that religion and spiritual practice add meaning.	Pargament (1999)
Sense of Coherence Scale (SOC)	Sense of coherence	13 items on three subscales: Comprehensibility, Manageability, and Meaningfulness.	Antonovsky & Sagy (1986)
Purpose in Life (PIL)	Overall meaning and purpose in life	20 items. It is an attitude scale that measures the degree to which a person feels meaning and purpose in life; includes existential elements.	Crumbaugh, & Maholick (1964)
Life Regard Index (LRI)	Positive life regard, a synonym for personal meaning in life	28 items. Two subscales: Framework (the person has a meaningful perspective), and Fulfillment (Am I fulfilling my life goals?).	Battista & Almond (1973) Debats (1998)
Personal Meaning Profile (PMP)	Measures specific domains of meaning as well as magnitude, breadth, and balance	57 items measuring seven factors: achievement striving, relationship, intimacy, religion, self-transcendence, self-acceptance, fair treatment.	Wong (1998)

(continued)

TABLE 12.1 Selected Instruments for the Measurement of Meaning in Life *(continued)*

Instrument	Construct Measured	Brief Description of the Instrument	Citation
Life Purpose Questionnaire (LPQ)	Overall meaning and purpose in life similar to the PIL	A 20-item test. Agree/disagree format allowing geriatric and brain injured to respond.	Hablas & Hutzell (1982)
Seeking of Noetic Goals (SONG)	Overall meaning and purpose in life	20 Likert items.	Crumbaugh (1977)
Meaning in Suffering Test (MIST)	Multidimensional	A 29-item scale with three subscales and one overall score.	Starck (1985)
Life Attitude Profile-Revised (LAP-R)	Multidimensional	48 items, six subscales, and two composite scores.	Reker (1992)

HOW CAN A COUNSELOR HELP CLIENTS DEVELOP A SENSE OF MEANING?

The list of meaning-finding interventions is long. Certainly seeking spiritual and religious goals is one such way that people have traditionally found meaning. Besides encouraging spiritual development, we have chosen to make four general suggestions in the following sections for counselors who wish to use meaning-finding to enhance wellness: Use Logotherapy, Reflect Meaning and Ask Meaning Questions, Help Clients Find a Vocation, and, finally, Benefit Finding and Reminding.

Use Logotherapy

Logotherapy, Viktor Frankl's (1969) meaning-oriented theory, is based on three basic ideas: (1) life always has meaning even when things are hopeless; (2) the "will to meaning" is the most potent factor in motivating a person to live; and (3) people can find meaning through experience and action. When action is impossible, meaning can be found through attitudes which imbue situations with meaning.

Logotherapists help clients develop the view that even when we cannot change the outcomes, we can decide how we take it (Lukas, 2000). Frankl believed that it was through challenge that a person finds the motivation to make meaning in life. Hence a large literature has arisen in the area of finding meaning during serious illness and imminent death (cf. Hannan, 2007).

Logotherapy utilizes a variety of techniques including the intriguingly named paradoxical intention, tragic optimism, and self-distancing. Yet in helping clients develop meaning, perhaps the most basic tool is Socratic dialogue. Socratic dialogue has always been aimed at helping clients find their own wisdom through a one-on-one interview. In the dialogue, the logotherapist helps clients find optimism and meaning in their stories by changing themselves to accommodate the worst experiences in life, even those that cause posttraumatic stress disorder. Through continual probing, the interviewer encourages the client to focus on what can be done and how optimism can be developed. As one veteran, treated with logotherapy, said, "War is about destroying lives and everything beautiful. I was a kid then, but now that I am older, it just makes me want to create and build things and appreciate the beauty all around me" (Southwick, Gilmartin, McDonough, & Morrisey, 2006, p. 168).

Reflect Meaning and Ask Meaning Questions

By identifying the meaning issues in client statements, both counselor and client gain insight into motivation and worldview which is deemed critical to change (Young, 2009). In basic counseling skills courses, we teach counselors to find meaning and reflect it in clients' statements. For example, the client tells a story about a disagreement with a parent. While the facts and feelings are one aspect, at a deeper level, the client has come away with a deeper meaning, "I cannot trust my parent to take my side in life." This conclusion and feeling can be reflected by the counselor as, "You felt deeply sad because you sensed that you could not trust your father to support you when you are in trouble." Unfortunately, we cannot always discern and then reflect meanings in client statements because they are embedded and subtle. Similar to Frankl's Socratic method, the counselor can also rely on some stock questions to elicit meanings when they elude detection:

Why does this problem bother you so much?

What is the purpose of telling me this story?

How would you feel about your whole life, if you looked back and…?

Why did you come to this conclusion?

What do you intend to accomplish by this action?

A closely allied method is called the "ultimate meanings technique" (Leontiev, 2007). The method consists of asking the client a series of questions with the stem, "Why do people . . .?" For example, the counselor asks, "Why do people work?" Below is an example:

Counselor: Why do people play?

Client: To reduce stress.

Counselor: Why reduce stress?

Client: So you can be more effective at work.

Counselor: Why be more effective at work?

Client: To get an edge on your competitors.

Counselor: Why get an edge on your competitors?

Client: So people will respect you.

While this is a short example, it reveals a number of the ways that a client currently makes meaning in life. He or she is looking for respect and self-esteem. The answers to one question may not be enough. But the technique can be repeated with additional questions such as, "Why do people watch TV, smoke cigarettes, get married, buy a house, and so forth?"

Help Clients Find a Vocation

The word *vocation* implies a calling, an idea that implies a sense of meaning and purpose. For many, work can provide meaning or can be a source of frustration if work does not provide this sense. In general, people find work meaningful if they believe that they are making a contribution. It is not that the work itself is meaningful but what the person finds meaningful in it. Thus, it is not the counselor's job to steer individuals to work that is humanitarian but rather to help clients find work and a career that they can invest in (Super, 1984).

Meaning and wellness are connected to one's life work (de Klerk, 2005). Mark Savickas (1991) describes the process of helping a client develop meaningful work as first using nondirective counseling to understand the client and then helping the client to recognize the dysfunctional ideas that he or she has about work. For example, sometimes work is not seen as meaningful by the client if he or she is not the top performer or is not meeting some arbitrary standard of success. To help clients find meaning at work, they must reevaluate the reasons they work. Savickas prescribes writing tasks such as completing the following sentence stem, "When I work, I. . . ." The client is to put in an evaluation such as "am happy," "get anxious," "feel useful," and so on rather than merely describing the work. This approach could be called "attributional probing" because it involves finding out why clients see the world the way they do based on the causes they assign to events. Understanding why a person engages in neurotic or maladaptive behavior helps the counselor understand his or her meaning making system. In the client's world, there are good reasons and good causes for his or her behavior.

Benefit Finding and Benefit Reminding

Glenn Affleck and Howard Tennen (Affleck & Tennen, 1996; Tennen & Affleck, 2002) have studied individuals facing severe adversity since the 1980s. Such individuals frequently reported positive experiences in the midst of their trials. Frequently, this ability to find benefits occurs later in the coping process. The ability to find benefits in times of physical pain, heart attack, having an acutely ill newborn, and experiencing a natural disaster is predictive of emotional symptom reduction, fewer mental health diagnoses, decreased death rate, and reduced complications. Yet this area of research is in its infancy. Interviews are the current method for assessing this ability (Tennen & Affleck, 2002).

The implications for counselors are that we can carefully help clients find benefits in a way that does not diminish the impact and significance of their loss. Apparently the maximum benefit occurs after two or more years after the event occurs because the process of finding benefits itself may be upsetting (Folkman, 2008). At the same time, clients can also utilize *benefit reminding* as a "meaning focused" coping strategy. By keeping a daily diary in which the client reminds himself or herself of benefits, positive emotions are evoked that seem to counteract the negative emotions associated with the loss (Folkman, 2008).

Summary

The assessment of meaning in research has been both qualitative and quantitative, and this research is extensive. This has led to the conclusion that finding a sense of meaning and purpose in daily events, work, and catastrophes is linked to improvements in ability to cope with stress and improve health. Therefore, helping clients find meaning through techniques of logotherapy, basic counseling skills, benefit finding and reminding, and vocational counseling should be part of every counselor's basic methods for wellness counseling.

References

Abu-Shakra, M., Keren, A., Livshitz, I., Delbar, V., Bolotin, A., Sukenik, S., et al. (2006). Sense of coherence and its impact on quality of life of patients with systemic lupus erythematosus. *Lupus, 15*, 32–37.

Affleck, G., & Tennen, H. (1996). Construing benefits from adversity: Adaptational significance and dispositional underpinnings. *Journal of Personality, 64*(4), 899–922.

Agardh, E. E., Ahlbom, A., Andersson, T., Efendic, S., Grill, V., Hallqvist, J., et al. (2003). Work stress and low sense of coherence is associated with type 2 diabetes in middle-aged Swedish women. *Diabetes Care, 26*, 719–724.

Amirkhan, J. H., & Greaves, H. (2003). Sense of coherence and stress: The mechanisms of a healthy disposition. *Psychology & Health, 18*, 31–62.

Antonovsky, A. (1979). *Health, stress and coping: New perspectives on mental and physical well-being*. San Francisco: Jossey-Bass.

Antonovsky, A., & Sagy S. (1986). The development of a sense of coherence and its impact on responses to stress situations. *Journal of Social Psychology, 126*, 213–225.

Battista, J., & Almond, R. (1973). The development of meaning in life. *Psychiatry, 36*, 409–427.

Baumeister, R. F., & Vohs, K. D. (2005). The pursuit of meaningfulness in life. In C. R. Snyder & S. J. Lopez, *Handbook of positive psychology* (pp. 608–618). New York: Oxford University Press.

Chandler, C. K., Holden, J. M., & Kolander, C. A. (1992). Counseling for spiritual wellness: Theory and practice. *Journal of Counseling & Development, 71*, 168–175.

Crumbaugh, J., & Maholick, L. T. (1964). An experimental study in existentialism: The psychometric approach to Frankl's concept of noogenic neurosis. *Journal of Clinical Psychology, 20*, 200–201.

Crumbaugh, J. C. (1977). *Manual of instructions: The Seeking of Noetic Goals test (SONG)*. Abilene, TX: Viktor Frankl Institute of Logotherapy.

Debats, D. L. (1998). Measurement of personal meaning: The psychometric properties of the Life Regard Index. In P. T. P. Wong & P. S. Fry (Eds.), *The human quest for meaning: A handbook of psychological research and clinical application* (pp. 237–260). Mahwah, NJ: Lawrence Erlbaum.

de Klerk, J. J. (2005). Spirituality, meaning in life and work wellness: A research agenda. *International Journal of Organizational Analysis, 13*, 64–88.

Folkman, S. (2008). The case for positive emotions in the stress process. *Anxiety, Stress & Coping, 21*, 3–14.

Folkman, S., & Moskowitz, T. J. (2000). Positive affect and the other side of coping. *American Psychologist, 55*, 647–654.

Frankl, V. (1963). *Man's search for meaning*. Boston: Beacon Press.

Frankl, V. (1969). *The will to meaning: Foundations and applications of logotherapy*. New York: New American Library.

Fredrickson, B. L. (2001). The role of positive emotions in positive psychology: The broaden-and-build theory of positive emotions. *American Psychologist, 56*, 218–226.

Hablas, R., & Hutzell, R. (1982). The Life Purpose Questionnaire: An alternative to the Purpose in Life test for geriatric, neuropsychiatric patients. In S. A. Wawrytko (Ed.), *Analectica Frankliana: The proceedings of the First World Congress of Logotherapy: 1980* (pp. 211–215). Berkeley, CA: Strawberry Hill.

Hannan, T. J. (2007) End of life stories that give meaning to the individual's existence. *International Journal of Environmental Studies, 64*, 291–300.

Hardiness Institute. (1985). Personal Views Survey. Arlington Heights, IL: Author.

Hettler, B. (1980). Wellness promotion on a university campus. *Family and Community Health, 3*, 77–95.

Kobasa, S. C. (1979). Stressful life events, personality, and health: An inquiry into hardiness. *Journal of Social Psychology, 37*, 1–11.

Korotkov, D. (1998). The sense of coherence: Making sense out of chaos. In P. T. P. Wong & P. S. Fry (Eds.), *The human quest for meaning: A handbook of psychological research and clinical applications* (pp. 51–78). Mahwah, NJ: Lawrence Erlbaum.

Lazarus, R. S. (1995). Psychological stress in the workplace. In R. Crandall & P. F. Perrewe (Eds.), *Occupational stress: A handbook* (pp. 3–14). Philadelphia: Taylor & Francis.

Lazarus, R. S., & Folkman, S. (1984). *Stress, appraisal, and coping*. New York: Springer.

Leontiev, D. A. (2007). Approaching worldview structure with ultimate meanings technique. *Journal of Humanistic Psychology, 47*, 243–266.

Lukas, E. (2000). *Logotherapy textbook: Meaning-centered psychotherapy*. Saratoga, CA: Institute of Logotherapy Press.

Maddi, S. R. (1998). Creating meaning through making decisions. In P. T. P. Wong & P. S. Fry (Eds.), *The human quest for meaning: A handbook of psychological research and clinical applications* (pp. 1–26).

Maddi, S. R., & Kobasa, S. C. (1984). *The hardy executive: Health under stress*. Homewood, IL: Irwin Professional Publishing.

Melton, A. M., & Schulenberg, S. E. (2008). On the measurement of meaning: Logotherapy's empirical contributions to humanistic psychology. *The Humanistic Psychologist, 36,* 31–44.

Myers, J. E., Sweeney, T. J., & Witmer, J. M. (2000). *Journal of Counseling & Development, 78,* 251–266.

Pargament, K. I. (1999). *Multidimensional measurements of religiousness/spirituality: Use in health research.* Kalamazoo, MI: Fetzer Institute.

Pengilly, J. W., & Dowd, E. T. (2000). Hardiness and social support as moderators of stress. *Journal of Clinical Psychology, 56,* 813–820.

Reker, G. T. (1992). *Manual of the Life Attitude Profile-Revised.* Peterborough, Ont.: Student Psychologists Press.

Reker, G. T., & Wong, P. T. P. (1988). Aging as an individual process: Toward a theory of personal meaning. In J. E. Birren & V. L. Bengston (Eds.), *Emergent theories of aging* (pp. 214–286). New York: Springer.

Savickas, M. (1991, January 1). The meaning of work and love: Career issues and interventions. *Career Development Quarterly*, 39(4), 315.

Savolaine, J., & Granello, P. F. (2002). The function of meaning in individual well-being. *Journal of Humanistic Counseling, Education, and Development.*

Schwarzer, R., & Knoll, N. (2003). Positive coping: Mastering demands and searching for meaning. In J. Lopez & C. R. Snyder (Eds.), *Positive psychological assessment: A handbook of models and measures* (pp. 393–410). Washington, DC: American Psychological Association.

Southwick, S. M., Gilmartin, R., McDonough, P., & Morrissey, P. (2006). Logotherapy as an adjunctive treatment for chronic combat-related PTSD: A meaning-based intervention. *American Journal of Psychotherapy, 60,* 161–174.

Starck, P. L. (1985). *Guidelines–Meaning in Suffering Test.* Abilene, TX: Viktor Frankl Institute of Logotherapy.

Super, D. (1984, January 1). Quality of life and the meanings and values of work. *Educational and Vocational Guidance Bulletin.* (ERIC Document Reproduction Service No. EJ300994) Retrieved July 17, 2008, from ERIC database.

Sweeney, T. J., & Witmer, M. J. (1991). Beyond social interest: Striving toward optimum health and wellness. *Individual Psychology, 47*(40), 527–540.

Taylor, S. E., Helgeson, V. S., Reed, G. M., & Skokan, L. A. (1991). Self-generated feelings of control and adjustment to physical illness. *Journal of Social Issues, 47,* 91–109.

Tennen, H., & Affleck, G. (2002). Benefit-finding and benefit-reminding. In *Handbook of positive psychology* (pp. 584–597). New York: Oxford University Press, 2002.

Wong, P. T. P. (1998). Implicit theories of meaningful life and the development of the Personal Meaning Profile. In P. T. P. Wong & P. S. Fry (Eds.), *The human quest for meaning: A handbook of psychological research and clinical application* (pp. 111–140). Mahwah, NJ: Lawrence Erlbaum.

Young, M. E. (2009). *Learning the art of helping*. Upper Saddle River, NJ: Prentice Hall.

Zimpfer, D. G. (1992). Psychosocial treatment of life-threatening disease: A wellness model. *Journal of Counseling & Development, 71,* 203–209.

13 SPIRITUALITY: BENEFITS OF BELIEF

Leila Roach and Mark Young

A sad soul can kill you quicker than a germ.

JOHN STEINBECK (AUTHOR)

Wellness Connection

Spirituality is a much talked about topic in the field of counseling today. Drs. Leah Roach and Mark Young illustrate the relationship of spirituality and religious practice to individual wellness. They provide examples of how a counselor can directly help or provide an appropriate referral for a client with spiritual issues.

In this chapter, we look at the relationship between spirituality, religion, and wellness, detailing the history of the topic and examining models of wellness that include spirituality as a component. Due to recent findings that religious and spiritual activities and beliefs are related to health (Hill & Pargament, 2003; Koenig, 2004; Larson & Larson, 2003), many are coming to recognize the potential of spiritual and religious factors to change people's lives. Research in positive psychology in quasi-religious areas such as hope, gratitude, and forgiveness has reminded us that spiritual and religious techniques have been used since time immemorial. In this chapter, we will try to give an overview of the present status of research and also try to include practical suggestions for counselors to encourage a client's religious and spiritual practices or refer them for help from their own tradition.

SPIRITUALITY AND RELIGION IN WELLNESS

Definitions

Religion, as we define it here, could also be labeled *extrinsic religion.* It is the outer forms of worship that includes the rites, rituals, pilgrimages, recitation of scriptures, singing, chanting, and the assembly of individuals in an organized way. Religion is a characteristic of a group of people. On the other hand, one's spirituality is conceived of as a direct inner experience and search for the sacred or a higher power that is a characteristic of an individual rather than a group. Spiritual individuals have transcendent experiences such as inner light and sound, peace, inner visions, bliss and joy, and awe and wonder which are spontaneous or achieved through practice. These are also the experiences of the saints, sages, and mystics that have come in the past. In the literature, spiritual people are said to practice *intrinsic religion.* Using these definitions, it is easy to see that one may be spiritual without being religious and religious without being spiritual. Finally, one may be both religious and spiritual. The importance of the distinction for us as counselors is that the major benefits to health and wellness seem to derive mainly from *intrinsic religion* or what we will call a personal spirituality (G. Miller, 2003).

A Brief History of Spirituality and Religion in Psychotherapy and Counseling

Inherent in psychotherapy's beginnings was a suspiciousness of religion and spirituality due to a new scientific *zeitgeist*. In *The Future of an Illusion* (1927/1964), Freud identifies religious beliefs as "fulfillments of the oldest, strongest, and most urgent wishes of mankind" (p. 30). He saw religion as patently unscientific and fundamentally unhealthy because it was based on dreams rather than reality (Freud, 1913/1950). Human beings wish for a godlike father and find one in the illusion of religion.

Both Skinner (1953) and Ellis (1980, 1981) claimed that religious ideas were harmful to psychological health. They saw little support for the benefits of the spiritual aspects of life. This belief was pervasive through the era of "scientism" beginning in the 1950s until the last decade. For example, as late as the 1970s when one of the authors (Young) worked in an inpatient unit of a psychiatric hospital, patients were not allowed to bring Bibles with them as they might feed their delusions (even if they were not delusional). This statement that spirituality and religion is unhealthy has now been challenged on its scientific merits (I. S. Richards & Bergin, 2005).

While Freud, Ellis, and Skinner seemed to see science and faith as antithetical, it must be remembered that a number of important theoreticians in counseling such as Jung (1938, 1970), Allport (1950), Rogers (1980), and Maslow (1971) saw spirituality and religion as a powerful treatment tool and also as essential to understanding human functioning. Carl Jung viewed spirituality and the religious traditions, embedded in Eastern and Western cultures, as essential to the development of self because spiritual issues were a fundamental part of the human psyche (1938, 1970). The humanistic movement in psychology brought forth a positive, growth-enhancing view of human beings that incorporated spiritual needs and values. Gordon Allport, one of the leaders in this movement, studied religious orientation and identified six traits (well-differentiated, dynamic, directive, comprehensive, integral, and heuristic) characteristic of a person's spiritual or religious maturity (1950). Carl Rogers's person-centered theory conceptualized an authentic, empathic, and safe counseling relationship where true self-understanding could occur on a level that exemplified transcendence (1980). In addition, Abraham Maslow's theory of human motivation conceptualized a hierarchy of needs that culminated in the quest for self-actualization and transcendence. Because of the work of these and other theorists, subsequent research in the area of wellness included spirituality as a central component.

MODELS OF WELLNESS THAT INCORPORATE SPIRITUALITY

Spirituality is an integral construct in several holistic wellness models (Baldwin & Baldwin, as cited in Lundy & Janes, 2003); Chandler, Holden, & Kolander, 1992; Crose, Nicolas, Gobble, & Frank, 1992; Dorn, 1992; Eberst, 1984; Hettler, 1984; McDonald, as cited in Lundy & Janes, 2003; Myers, Sweeney, & Witmer, 2000; Purdy & Dupey, 2005; Witmer & Sweeney, 1992;

Zimpfer, 1992). In the mid 1970s, Donald B. Ardell at the University of Central Florida wrote *High Level Wellness: An Alternative to Doctors, Drugs and Disease* published by Rodale in 1977, Bantam in 1979, and Ten Speed Press in 1986. This book, the first of its kind, has been credited with starting the wellness movement. Later, Dr. Bill Hettler, cofounder and president of the board of directors of the National Wellness Institute, developed the Six Dimensional Wellness Model that included the following domains: spiritual values and ethics; occupational/vocational; physical fitness/nutrition; emotional; social/family/community/environmental; and intellectual (1984). In his model, the spiritual domain meant the search for meaning and purpose in life that ultimately led to consistency in action with values and beliefs. About the same time, Richard Eberst developed a new conceptual model that could be utilized with students in school health classes. He described the Health Cube Model of holistic wellness based on the six-dimensional Rubik's Cube (Eberst, 1984). The six dimensions of health included physical, emotional, mental, spiritual, social, and vocational. Spirituality, considered more than just one of the elements of wellness, was defined as a deeper dimension, an axis of the cube, on which the synergistic relationships of the others pivoted.

Following these models, David Zimpfer expounded on an approach to counseling and healing disease. He developed a wellness model for cancer treatment focused on mobilizing all resources of the self to maximize wellness (Zimpfer, 1992). His model included several lines of treatment: medical treatment, immune function, lifestyle management, a spiritual dimension, beliefs and attitudes, psychodynamics, energy forces, and interpersonal relations, all focused on marshalling the body's instinctive healing forces. He pointed out that the spiritual dimension, which encompassed the existential issues related to understanding the meaning and purpose of one's illness, the ability to reach a state of mental calm, and the use of prayer for comfort and healing facilitated renewal and potentially healing forces.

Crose et al., (1992) discussed a systems model of wellness developed by Nicolas & Gobble (1990) that looked at the various aspects (physical, emotional, social, vocational, spiritual, and intellectual) of health as multidimensional, variable, and self-regulating. The model proposed that a normal range existed within each dimension of wellness, as well as a self-regulating, cybernetic feedback process between the dimensions. That is, changes in one dimension affected other aspects of wellness. Specifically in the area of spiritual health and wellness, this model looked at religious and spiritual history, life satisfaction, purpose and meaning in life, beliefs about death, and attitudes toward the transpersonal aspects of living (Crose et al., 1992).

Chandler et al. (1992) developed the Model of Spiritual Wellness, a holistic wellness model similar to a lifespan model that consisted of five dimensions (intellectual, physical, emotional, social, and occupational) with spirituality as an integral component of each. They considered "spiritual wellness to be a balanced openness to or pursuit of spiritual development" (p. 170). "Optimum wellness exists when each of these five dimensions has a balanced and developed potential in both the spiritual and personal realm. Working to achieve high-level wellness necessitates the development of the spiritual component in each of the five dimensions of wellness. Without attention to spiritual health in each dimension, the individual remains incomplete" (p. 171). The concept of occupational wellness in relation to developing a healthy, integrated career and personal identity was discussed by Dorn (1992). He believed that when people were faced with negative career-related situations, they experienced a ripple effect into other areas of life that could have detrimental effects, including spiritual functioning.

Sweeney & Witmer (1991) and Witmer & Sweeney (1992), with revisions by Myers et al., (2000), developed the Wheel of Wellness, a lifespan model, based on the theoretical foundation of Adler (social interest and striving for mastery), Maslow (striving toward self-actualization, growth, and excellence), and cross-disciplinary research on characteristics of healthy people. The model included the five life tasks: spirituality, self-direction, work and leisure, friendship, and love. Self-direction was further divided into 12 subtasks. This model has recently been revised to the Indivisible Self: An Evidence-Based Model of Wellness, IS-WEL, a five-factor contextual model (Myers, Luecht, & Sweeney, 2004). The IS-WEL conceptualizes wellness as a higher order, indivisible self factor and as a factor composed of identifiable subcomponents that represent the original hypothesized areas of wellness. These subcomponents group within the five second order factors and 17 third order factors that include the Creative Self (thinking, emotions, control, work, positive humor); the Coping Self (leisure, stress management, self-worth, realistic beliefs); the Social Self (friendship, love); the Essential Self (spirituality, gender identity, cultural identity, self-care); and the Physical Self (nutrition, exercise). Spirituality within this model refers to one's personal beliefs and behaviors involving a higher power; hope and optimism; worship, prayer or meditation; purpose in life; moral values; and transcendence (Myers et al., 2004).

Another model developed by McDonald (cited in Lundy & Janes, 2003) is based on the Medicine Wheel grounded in a Native American understanding of health and wellness. In this model, the sacred dimensions of the medicine wheel represent physical, vocational, psychological, social, emotional, environmental, spiritual, and intellectual wellness. Spiritual wellness in this model is defined as a state of balance and harmony with self and others and includes trust, integrity, principle, ethics, purpose in life, feelings of selflessness, and commitment to a higher power or being.

Baldwin and Baldwin (cited in Lundy & Janes, 2003) developed the 4+ Model of Wellness to assist in critical thinking regarding characteristics and settings that might either negatively deplete or positively nurture wellness. Within the spiritual domain, they identified several sources of nurture, including giving love and connecting with others; being of service and loving animals; beauty, music, and art; quiet, peace, meditation, and prayer; physical exercise; being loved; and intellectual stimulus and creativity.

Finally, Purdy & Dupey (2005) built a Holistic Flow Model of Spiritual Wellness that conceptualizes the spirit at the center of life. Their model of flow posited that, when an individual was healthy in spirit, he or she has incorporated activities in everyday life that strengthen and reinforce the dimensions of spirit. The themes described in the model include "a belief in an organizing force in the universe, connectedness, faith, movement toward compassion, the ability to make meaning in life, and the ability to make meaning in death" (Purdey & Dupey, 2005, p. 99).

To summarize, holistic models of wellness have continually recognized spirituality as vital to a definition of wellness. Several envision spirituality as a central concept including the Wheel of Wellness (Witmer & Sweeney, 1992). Thus, spirituality, which has long been relegated to the realm of pseudoscience by psychotherapy's founders, is now the focus of a great deal of research interest. In the next section, we will look at specific spiritual practices that have been found to be effective in enhancing wellness.

THE EFFECTS OF SPIRITUAL PRACTICE ON WELLNESS

There are many spiritual practices that merit attention as potentially healing but none has received as much attention in the scientific literature as meditation and prayer. In addition, they could be seen as generic spiritual tools that can be used by those who are not attracted or attached to religious organizations and might then have more acceptance by clients who are nonreligious. Prayer and meditation have similarities in that both involve concentrating on the higher power. Meditation is sometimes called "prayer with attention." It has also been said that prayer is talking to God and meditation is listening to God.

Meditation

Meditation has been a spiritual practice for more than 5,000 years and has been associated with all the major religions, including Christianity, Hinduism, Sikhism, Buddhism, Jainism, Islam, Taoism, Shintoism, and Judaism. While there are several hundred varieties of meditation, there are two basic types of meditation that are currently practiced—mantra based and mindfulness. Mantra based meditation uses a phrase or word that is repeated mentally, with the tongue of thought, slowly and perhaps at intervals. This technique gives the mind a focus during meditation and prevents it from wandering (Singh, 1999). Mindfulness, on the other hand, does not use a mantra and normally the practitioner focuses on the breath.

There are also two types of mantra meditation—unfocused and focused meditation. Unfocused meditation is best exemplified by Transcendental Meditation, promulgated by Maharishi Mahesh Yogi. The technique involves the use of a unique mantra or repeated phrase, given to you at the time of initiation. The TM meditator sits for 20 minutes twice daily with eyes closed but not concentrating on any thought or focusing the sight on any internal object. One repeats the mantra and brushes away all other thoughts. Focused meditation encompasses many forms but a simple method in wide use is the Jyoti meditation technique (Singh, 1999), which involves repeating the mantra and staring directly into the darkness, focusing on the third or single eye. The aim of this focused meditation is to hear inner light and to experience inner sound. Unlike the TM 20 minutes twice daily, this form of meditation can be practiced for several hours per day.

The original research on meditation was conducted with TM and Herbert Benson developed a generic form which he released in his 1975 book, *The Relaxation Response*. Benson claimed that the basics were a quiet environment, a passive attitude, repetition of a mantra, and a comfortable position. Benson originally thought that the healing property was mostly relaxation; but later, in his book *Timeless Healing* (1996), he quoted research indicating that faith potentiates the healing power of meditation and other practices.

Mindfulness meditation is a very popular meditation form at the moment. It is derived from the Theravadin Buddhist practice and was popularized and westernized by Jon Kabat-Zinn (Kabat-Zinn, 1993). It involves being in the present and focusing on the breath. The mindfulness practitioner tries to avoid thoughts of the future and thoughts of the past and stay in the living present. A crucial aspect of the meditation is to stay away from judgment of the self. Kabat-Zinn's modification of mindfulness has been applied to stress reduction at the University of Massachusetts Medical Center. Mindfulness Based Stress Reduction (MBSR) is an eclectic eight week program involving various forms of physical activity including Hatha Yoga. The program has received strong research support and has been adopted for a variety of physical illnesses including patients with heart disease and those who are HIV positive. In addition to MBSR, Kabat-Zinn and his colleagues have combined mindfulness and cognitive therapy in a format called Mindfulness Based Cognitive Therapy (MBCT), aimed mainly at alleviating Major Depression. In MBCT as opposed to other cognitive therapies, the individual does not try to push thoughts out of consciousness but learns to accept them. The eight week program does not attempt to increase feelings of relaxation but rather to increase the client's ability to not react automatically to thoughts that cause depression (Segal, Teasdale, & Williams, 2002).

Prayer

PRAYER AND RELIGION Prayer is an essential practice in religious traditions as a way to promote well-being. In Judaism, one of the world's oldest religions, prayer is considered communication between the individual and God. In addition, communal prayer is practiced in synagogues three times a day (morning, afternoon, and evening), with additional services on Sabbath days (Saturday), festival days, and the Day of Atonement (Yom Kippur). Prayer, in the Jewish faith, facilitates a virtuous attitude and a concern for the well-being of others (G. Miller, 2003).

Prayer has long been a part of Native American healing traditions (Portman & Garrett, 2006). The connection between healing practices and spirituality across native peoples acknowledges that the gentle guidance provided by the celestial world can be experienced through prayer. Prayer is an integral part of many healing rituals, including the Sweat Lodge Ceremony (purification), the Vision Quest (self-reflection with a spiritual focus), Smudging (the burning of herbs to create a cleansing smoke), the Pipe Ceremony (translating the prayers of a person into smoke), the Sun Dance, and other tribal ceremonies. The Blessing Way uses prayer and song on a daily basis to promote and restore harmony and balance (Portman & Garrett, 2006).

Prayer is a major practice of both Hinduism and Buddhism. In Hinduism, adherents pray to God for worldly and spiritual blessings. Prayer also takes the form of asking God for blessings and may include mantras (unique repeated phrases) that are believed to take one to higher levels of consciousness and to cure diseases (Bhaskarananda, 2002). In various forms of Buddhism prayer is different. Theravadin Buddhists generally do not pray to the Buddha. However, they may in other forms of Buddhism. Or they may utilize mantras. For example, in Tibetan Buddhism, the repetition of the phrase, Om Mane Padme Hum (The Jewel is in the Lotus) may be repeated several hundred times per day. Other forms of Buddhism may use chanting of the sutras (sacred writings) (Gethin, 1998).

Islam, often defined as the religion of submission to God (Allah), is practiced by Muslims. The fundamental practices of Muslims are outlined in the Five Pillars and include the repetition of the Islamic Creed, Shahada (a declaration of belief in the oneness of God and acceptance of Muhammad as his prophet), and daily prayer. The Salat is formal ritualized prayer practiced five times per day (dawn, midday, midafternoon, sunset, and bedtime) that can be accompanied by voluntary prayers as a way to draw closer to God and create an inner sense of harmony and peace. Friday is a special day of prayer for Muslims and includes a reading from the Qur´an, a sermon, and the ritual of prayer (salat) in the mosque (Gulevich, 2004).

Prayer that promotes well-being is often embedded within a religious tradition that connects an individual with a supreme being. The various types of prayer indicate that prayer provides a structure to understand and cope with life events, as well as to achieve a sense of meaning and purpose, enhance feelings of self-efficacy, and promote connection with others.

PRAYER AND HEALTH Prayer is a religious or spiritual practice associated with health and well-being (Fry, 2000; George, Larson, Koenig, & McCullough, 2000; Hill & Pargament, 2003; Larson & Larson, 2003). Prayer is frequently cited as a coping strategy and need for people dealing with a wide range of physical, mental, and emotional illnesses, including advanced cancer, HIV/AIDS, chronic or serious illness, depression, and anxiety. Reliance on religious practices such as prayer is also associated with increased chances of living longer; improved surgical outcomes; faster recovery from depression and anxiety; lower suicide rates; lowered risk of substance abuse; greater well-being, hope, and optimism; improved protective health-related behaviors; more meaning and purpose in life; greater social support; and increased marital satisfaction and stability (Close, 2001; Hampton, Hollis, Lloyd, Taylor, & McMillan, 2007; Harvey & Silverman, 2007; Koenig, 2004; Larson & Larson, 2003; Maltby, Lewis, & Day, 1999).

Christian prayer, the most frequently researched form of prayer, seems to be relevant to all ages—however, a deeply active prayer life seems to help the elderly and those suffering from a terminal illness stay connected to others and the world (Close, 2001). In addition, the type of prayer an individual engages in has been shown to be relevant to one's spiritual and physical health and well-being. For example, Close (2001) found a link between personality style and prayer, noting that the elderly engaged in the Augustinian tradition of personalizing prayer (seeking a comforting, personal relationship with God); intercessory prayer (praying for someone else) as a way to have meaning and purpose in life as well as to stay connected to loved ones, the community, and the world by being an active agent in God's ongoing plan; and utilizing prayer as an avenue for letting go of long-held negative, troublesome thoughts and beliefs. Francis and Robbins (2008) found a significant correlation between psychological types and prayer preferences, lending support to the notion that the benefits of prayer may be related to the way a person prays and the perceived significance of prayer within the religious context. It must be said that studies of intercessory prayer have not yielded encouraging results for its effect on health. A recent and significant study by Benson et al. (2006) examined over 1,000 heart bypass patients and found no benefit associated with intercessory prayer. In fact, researchers found that patients who were certain that they were being prayed for actually had more complications.

Direction, intentionality, and motivation for prayer are also important aspects of the prayer experience as it relates to health and well-being. Neyrinck, Vansteenkiste, Lens, Duriez, and Hutsebaut (2006) noted that symbolic interpretations and more personally significant, internalized motivations for religious behaviors, including prayer, were associated with increased cognitive flexibility and open-mindedness toward Christian beliefs, resulting in a stronger adherence to goals, values and ideals, higher well-being, and increased engagement in specific religious behaviors. Prayer can also be viewed as a direct connection or communication with the sacred or divine involving both direction and intentionality. Ladd and Spilka (2006) offer a theoretical basis for understanding prayer as a means of forming cognitive connections that include inward (focusing on self-examination), outward (strengthening human to human connections), and upward (centering on the human-divine relationship) dimensions. In addition, they identify factors that represent the intentionality of prayers, including intercession (outward prayer on behalf of someone's difficulties); suffering (outward prayer to share another's pain); examination (inward prayer to evaluate one's spiritual status); rest (upward prayer searching for stillness); sacrament (upward prayer encountering tradition); tears (inward prayer experiencing personal turmoil); radical (outward prayer using assertiveness); and petitionary prayer (outward prayer seeking material requests). The connectivity sought through the various forms of prayer may address a "felt need for cognitive and spiritual structure. Prayer may help to clarify the state of one's internal affairs, reveal the fundamental issues associated with paradoxical situations, and define the character of desire" (p. 2).

ISSUES FOR PRACTITIONERS

Assessing Spirituality and Religion

Whether someone is considered to be a religious/spiritual person does not, in and of itself, predict health and well-being. Studies of religious orientation (Allport & Ross, 1967; Batson & Ventis, 1982) seem to indicate that *intrinsic religion* (personal spirituality) is more predictive of health indicators than *extrinsic religion* (religiosity). Thus, assessment is needed if one wants to determine the potential health benefits of religious or spiritual practices.

Religion and spirituality are complex constructs involving cognitive, emotional, behavioral, interpersonal, and physiological dimensions and, for the most part, have been assessed using only global measures. Recently, researchers have defined concepts and measures that are more related to health and well-being. Some of these include perceived closeness to God; spirituality and religion as orienting and motivating forces in one's life; religious support systems; and religious and spiritual struggles (Hill & Pargament, 2003). However, as George and colleagues (2000) point out, most assessments measure religion rather than spirituality, thus neglecting those who view themselves as spiritual but not religious, and these measures do not directly inquire about one's beliefs in relation to and experiences with the sacred.

In some cases, spiritual and religious practices may be used by clients to avoid, or bypass, psychological wounds and other personal emotional unfinished business. Spiritual bypass can result in a number of problems including "compulsive goodness, repression of undesirable or painful emotions, spiritual narcissism, extreme external locus of control, spiritual obsession or addiction, blind faith in charismatic leaders, abdication of personal responsibility, and social isolation" (Cashwell, Bentley, & Yarborough, 2007, pp. 140–141), highlighting the need for careful assessment of the complex role of spirituality in the life of the client. Some of the current methods for assessing the complex dimensions of spirituality are addressed here.

First and foremost, questions regarding the role of spirituality in a client's life can be asked as part of a psychosocial assessment interview. Types of relevant questions include the following: Are spiritual or religious issues important to you? Do you wish to discuss them in counseling, when relevant? Clients can also be asked to rate their current and past experiences with religion and spirituality. For example, "How would you rate your involvement in spiritual on religious activities?" or "Growing up, how would you describe your spiritual or religious experiences?" and "What would you say about your current spiritual or religious experiences?"

Table 13.1 and Table 13.2 illustrate a selection of qualitative and quantitative instruments, respectively.

Other qualitative measures include: spiritual histories that utilize a series of questions to explore spiritual and religious themes that may highlight issues related to spiritual and religious struggles; spiritual genograms (Frame, 2000; Hodge, 2001) that can be utilized to organize data that chart a spiritual family tree, noting themes, patterns, and generational messages; and spiritual autobiographies that identify significant events in a client's life that contribute to current spiritual perspective.

Counselors are encouraged to include assessment of spiritual and religious issues as part of a comprehensive treatment plan. Understanding these issues could help both counselors and their clients recognize salient spiritual dimensions that play a role in fully appreciating strengths and comprehending psychological needs.

Qualifying With the Client

An important issue for counseling practitioners working with spiritual and religious issues in counseling involves qualifying with the client. *Qualifying* is a term used by Yalom (1995) to describe the ability of the therapist to gain the confidence of their clients. In deaf culture, for example, deaf clients want to know what qualifies a counselor to work with them. Is the counselor deaf? What does the counselor know about deaf culture? What connections does he or she have with the deaf community? How fluent is the counselor in American Sign Language (ASL)? What knowledge does the counselor have of culturally syntonic therapeutic interventions?

Accordingly, what qualifies the counselor to work with a client from a particular spiritual tradition? Regarding any significant aspect of a client's life—ethnicity, culture, gender, sexual orientation, age, or spiritual affiliation—it is important that the counselor has an awareness of his/her own values and biases, an awareness of the client's worldview, and an understanding of appropriate intervention strategies (Arredondo et al., 1996). First, counselors must understand

TABLE 13.1 Selected Instruments for the Qualitative Measure of Spirituality and Religion

Instrument	Construct Measured	Brief Description of the Instrument	Citation
Spiritual Narrative	Awareness of the Holy, providence, faith, grace or gratefulness, repentance, communion, and sense of vocation.	Provides an understanding of the client's spiritual narrative in relation to 7 Christian themes	Pruyser (1976)
Spiritual Dimensions	Beliefs and meaning; vocation and consequences; experiences and emotions; courage and growth; ritual and practice; community; and authority and guidance.	Offers guidelines for assessing 7 spiritual dimensions in two subdivisions; holistically and explicitly spiritual; and can be utilized with a wide variety of faith traditions	Fitchett (1993)
Spiritual Quest Form (SQF)	Seeks to understand the client's process toward spiritual growth and development.	10-item sentence completion task followed by an in-depth dialog that produces a narrative	Nino (1997)
Experience Based Spiritual Development Scale (EBSDS)	Scourge, Emerge, Purge, Diverge, Resurge, Converge, and Merge.	Identifies seven stages of spiritual realization	Sandhu & Asrabadi (2003) Sandhu (2007)
Faith Development	Intuitive-Projective Faith, Mythical-Literal Faith, Synthetic-Conventional Faith, Individuative-Reflective Faith, Conjunctive Faith, and Universalizing Faith.	Assesses stages of faith development through the use of Faith Interviews	James Fowler (1981)

their own values and beliefs regarding existential and spiritual issues and what biases might surface in their work with clients. A second important consideration is the counselor's knowledge of spiritual principles and practices as well as specific religious traditions. How willing is the counselor to be open and accepting of diverse spiritual beliefs and practices? When a client embraces specific religious doctrines, how knowledgeable and aware is the counselor of utilizing specific traditions? When would a referral be appropriate? And finally, what interventions might be appropriate when incorporating spiritual practices into a comprehensive treatment program? Favier & Ingersoll (2005) emphasize the importance of counselors knowing their limits in order to practice ethically by engaging in self-assessment, seeking consultation, and making referrals.

Counselors can become more aware of their ability to counsel clients on issues related to spirituality and religion by becoming familiar with the Association for Spiritual Ethical and Religious Values in Counseling (ASERVIC) competencies. ASERVIC is the division of the American Counseling Association that focuses on writing, research, and practice in the religious and spiritual aspects of counseling. In 1995, the association held a Summit on Spirituality in North Carolina (G. Miller, 1999). Experts initially developed a set of 10 competencies associated

TABLE 13.2 Selective Instruments for the Quantitative Measure of Spirituality and Religion

Instrument	Construct Measured	Brief Description of the Instrument	Citation
Human Spirituality Scale (HSS)	Global measure of spirituality.	20-item scale rated from 1 (never, almost never) to 5 (constantly, almost constantly)	Wheat (1991)
Spiritual Assessment Inventory (SAI)	Spiritual maturity from a Judeo-Christian perspective.	43-item inventory scored on a 5-point scale of 1(not true of me) through 5 (true of me)	Hall & Edwards (1996)
Index of Core Spiritual Experiences (INSPIRIT)	Two core elements of spirituality; experiences that convince an individual God exists, and a perception that God dwells in the individual.	Online, 7-item instrument (item 7 has 13 parts)	Kass, Friedman, Leserman, Zuttermeister, & Benson (1991)
Spiritual Well-Being Scale (SWBS)	Religious Well-Being (RWB) as it relates to concepts of God, and Existential Well-Being (EWB) as it relates to a sense of purpose and satisfaction in life.	20-item scale with 6 responses ranging from strongly disagree to strongly agree	Ellison (1983)
Systems of Belief Inventory (SBI-15R)	Quality of life, stress, and coping with life-threatening illness by examining 2 factors: beliefs and practices; and social support.	15-item measure scored on a 4-point Likert scale ranging from 0 (strongly disagree) to 3 (strongly agree)	Holland et al. (1998)
The Functional Assessment of Chronic Illness Therapy-Spiritual Well-Being Scale (FACIT-Sp)	Two subscales: sense of meaning and peace; and role of faith in illness. Produces a total score for spiritual well-being.	12-item measure scored on a 5-point Likert scale ranging from 0 (not at all) to 4 (very much)	Peterman, Fitchett, Brady, Pharm, & Cella (2002)
Spiritual Health Inventory (SHI)	Personal Spiritual Experience, Spiritual Well-Being, Sense of Harmony, and Personal Helplessness.	18-item scale with 6 responses ranging from strongly disagree to strongly agree	Veach & Chappel (1992)
Spirituality Assessment Scale (SAS)	Unifying Interconnectedness, Purpose and Meaning in Life, Innerness or Inner Resources, and Transcendence.	28 statements rated from 1 (strongly disagree) to 6 (strongly agree)	Howden (1992)
Spiritual Support Scale	Emotional, intimacy, and faith aspects of spiritual support.	3-items rated on a 5-point scale	Maton (1989)
Religious Orientation Inventory (ROI)	Orientation toward religion on both an intrinsic and extrinsic dimension.	20-item measure	Allport & Ross (1967)
Age Universal I-E	Adapted from Allport and Ross's Religious Orientation Scale that can be used with children and adolescents.		Gorsuch and Venable (1983)

Instrument	Construct Measured	Brief Description of the Instrument	Citation
Quest (Interactional) Scale	Adds 3rd dimension to religious orientation: quest (degree to which one's religion involves open-ended, responsive dialogue to existential questions raised by contradictions and tragedies in life).	9-item scale version 6-item scale version 12-item scale version Each rated on a 9-point scale from 1 (strongly disagree) to 9 (strongly agree)	Batson (1976) Batson & Ventis (1982) Batson & Schoenrade (1991)
Christian Religious Internalization Scale (CRIS)	Degree of self-determination for Christian beliefs and practices (could be adapted for other religions).	12-item measure rated on a 4-point scale from not at all true to very true	Ryan, Rigby, & King (1993)
Religious Coping Scale (RCOPE)	Methods of coping with life situations based on a Judeo-Christian perspective.	105-item scale consists of 21 subscales with 5 items each, that asks respondents to rate the degree to which various types of religious coping were involved in dealing with a negative life event on a 4-point Likert scale from not at all to a great deal	Pargament, Koenig, & Perez (2000)
Religious Support Measure	Relationships between perceived religious support and life satisfaction and religious attendance.	Assesses three factors: God support, congregational support, and church leader support	Fiala, Bjorck, & Gorsuch (2002)
Spiritual History Scale (SHS-4)	Spiritual and religious practices and attributions over the lifespan.	23-item, 4-dimensional retrospective summary	Hays, Meador, Branch, & George (2001)
Spirituality Scale (SS)	Spirituality from an Afro-cultural perspective.	20-item measure rated on a 6-point scale ranging from 1 (completely false) to 6 (completely true)	Jagers & Smith (1996)
Daily Spiritual Experience Scale	Ordinary experiences of spirituality; awe, joy that lifts one up, deep inner peace, gratitude, and love.	16-item measure with 6 responses ranging from never or almost never to many times a day	Underwood & Teresi (2002)
Brown-Peterson Recovery Index (B-PRPI)	Spirituality in members of Alcoholics Anonymous (AA).	53-item instrument rated on a 5-point scale from 0 (no or never) to 4 (yes, daily, or always)	Brown & Peterson (1991)
Spiritual Competency Scale (SCS)	Competency to counsel on spiritual and religious issues.	28-item, 6-factor instrument with seven response format	Robertson (2008)

with the eight core areas of training established by CACREP (G. Miller, 1999). The competencies that came out of this meeting were later reduced to nine which are called "Competencies for Integrating Spirituality into Counseling." They are:

Competency 1 The professional counselor can explain the differences between religion and spirituality, including similarities and differences.

Competency 2 The professional counselor can describe religious and spiritual beliefs and practices in a cultural context.

Competency 3 The professional counselor engages in self-exploration of religious and spiritual beliefs in order to increase sensitivity, understanding, and acceptance of diverse belief systems.

Competency 4 The professional counselor can describe her/his religious and/or spiritual belief system and explain various models of religious or spiritual development across the lifespan.

Competency 5 The professional counselor can demonstrate sensitivity and acceptance of a variety of religious and/or spiritual expressions in client communication.

Competency 6 The professional counselor can identify limits of her/his understanding of a client's religious or spiritual expression, and demonstrate appropriate referral skills and generate possible referral sources.

Competency 7 The professional counselor can assess the relevance of the religious and/or spiritual domains in the client's therapeutic issues.

Competency 8 The professional counselor is sensitive to and receptive of religious and/or spiritual themes in the counseling process as befits the expressed preference of each client.

Competency 9 The professional counselor uses a client's religious and/or spiritual beliefs in the pursuit of the clients' therapeutic goals as befits the clients' expressed preference (ASERVIC, 2008).

Source: ASERVIC competencies for integrating spirituality into counseling.

Is It a Spiritual Problem?

The process of searching and questioning spiritual and religious beliefs is a necessary component of growth and development. Additionally, spiritual and religious struggles can be instrumental in leading an individual on or off the path toward growth. Research suggests that spiritual struggles represent a critical "fork in the road" for many individuals that can lead in the direction of health and well-being or significant health problems. Hill & Pargement summed up the need to resolve spiritual struggles stating: "How well the individual is able to resolve these struggles may hold the key to which road is taken" (Hill & Pargament, 2003, p. 70).

Spiritual and religious issues are often infused in Twelve Step programs designed to treat various forms of addiction, in the treatment of eating disorders (P. S. Richards, Hardman, & Berrett, 2007), childhood sexual abuse (Parker, 1997), and a variety of other mental disorders (Mijares & Khalsa, 2005). Spiritual problems may also surface when childhood experiences with religious or spiritual teachings result in feelings of shame and fear. Many excellent resources exist for addressing both growth-enhancing and problem-focused spiritual issues. In this section three issues that tend to emerge in a clinical setting will be discussed: questioning spiritual or religious traditions, such as a crisis of faith, often involving a tragic life experience (illness, death, or serious accident) or other developmental issues that cause a person to question his or her belief system; a betrayal by a spiritual teacher or religious authority within an institution; or a difference in religious or spiritual beliefs and traditions within a couple or family system.

QUESTIONING SPIRITUAL OR RELIGIOUS TRADITIONS Normal developmental transitions, life stages, or traumatic events may trigger uncertainty regarding spiritual or religious traditions. For example, in the Christian faith, one hears statements such as, "If God really existed, he would never let this happen," or "I did everything I was supposed to do and God let me down." In the midst of suffering, it is difficult to make sense out of painful life experiences and one is tempted to look for someone or something to blame. Often anger is directed toward God for allowing difficult life experiences. Frankl (1969) reminds us that the attitude one takes toward suffering and how meaning is constructed out of difficult experiences is central to well-being. Finding meaning in challenging life circumstances and reconnecting with the sacred can be central to restoring faith and resolving spiritual and religious struggles.

Counselors can facilitate healing by being authentically present and connecting with the client in a nonjudgmental way that conveys unconditional positive regard and empathic understanding (Rogers, 1980). The use of person-centered counseling when a client is questioning spiritual or religious traditions allows the counselor to meet the client in the depths of their pain and confusion. Rogers conceptualized this sacred space as a touching of inner spirits that allows two people to connect on the deepest level (1980). Within the safety of the relationship, clients are able to experience true acceptance, explore the deeper meaning of events in their lives, and facilitate growth and change (Stanard, 2007).

Experiential techniques, such a souldrama (C. Miller, 2000), allow counselors to facilitate movement in a client who may be stuck as a result of a spiritual or religious struggle. Souldrama, an adjunct to psychodrama (Moreno, 1965), is an action-oriented process that integrates both psychodramatic and narrative techniques that help clients access a deeper wisdom within themselves to better understand the purpose and meaning of a situation by aligning the ego and the soul. Souldrama can help clients to better understand an experience and the spiritual component of the situation.

BETRAYAL BY A SPIRITUAL TEACHER OR RELIGIOUS AUTHORITY Spiritual and religious beliefs and practices that form the foundation for one's faith are often used a vehicles for developing a coherent sense of values and identity. James Fowler (1981) describes faith as "the most fundamental category in the human quest for relation to transcendence." In his stages of faith development, Fowler describes the Synthetic-Conventional stage (beginning in adolescence and extending into adulthood) as a period when one synthesizes valued images, aligns with a certain perspective, internalizes a sense of goodness and badness, is deeply concerned about the evaluations and feedback from significant people in one's spiritual or religious community, and defers to spiritual and religious authorities. Consequently, when spiritual leaders appear to betray one's trust by engaging in activities such as improper sexual behavior (affairs or child sexual abuse) or adopting polices or practices once seen as sacred or unbreachable (ordaining a gay or lesbian priest), these events can give rise to personal despair about principles related to one's higher power or interfere with one's relationship with a higher power.

In these cases, the counselor has an opportunity to engage the client in a critical reflection of how beliefs and values have formed and changed, and to assist in the acceptance of personal responsibility for these beliefs, attitudes, and lifestyle choices. Accepting personal responsibility for oneself versus abdicating responsibility to an authority figure can facilitate forgiveness and acceptance of one's own humanness and the humanness of others, thus facilitating movement toward a more intrinsic spiritual and religious orientation.

COUPLES AND FAMILY COUNSELING INTERVENTIONS Conflict can arise in a family system when couples reach an impasse over differences in religious or spiritual beliefs and traditions. Over time, each member of the couple feels increasingly criticized and unaccepted by his or her partner for holding different beliefs and values. The more one partner becomes entrenched in the *rightness* of his or her position, the more the other partner is vilified, resulting in emotional disengagement and isolation in the relationship. In addition, disagreements may escalate regarding how to raise children, attending religious and spiritual activities, and achieving life goals.

A useful framework for addressing this issue in couple relationships is John Gottman's (1999) Dreams-within-Conflict intervention that focuses on the regulation of perpetual conflict. When couples become deadlocked in their differences over spiritual and religious beliefs, they tend to feel intense pain, criticism, and alienation from their partner. The central tenants of this intervention involve revealing the metaphors, stories, hopes, and dreams that underlie each partner's position, and then changing the influence patterns in the relationship ". . . so that both people can proceed to honor one another's dreams" (p. 234).

Couples begin by talking about their conflicts while the counselor listens carefully for *loaded* words and phrases that hold symbolic meaning beyond the conflict and may go back to spiritual and religious beliefs and values held by the primary family of origin. Counselors can convey genuine interest in each partner by asking questions that uncover the meaning and metaphors underlying each position. Couples can also practice recognizing the stories and meaning underlying the inflexible position in someone else's conflict, before engaging in the often difficult task of discovering the unacknowledged dreams that underlie their own fixed position. Here, Gottman (1999) stresses the importance of couples taking responsibility for these positions and moving on, rather than becoming stuck in feelings of hurt, anger, and disappointment with their partner and themselves. The goal is to discover the hidden meaning or dream behind the conflict and ". . . try to understand and support your partner's dream" (p. 250). The intervention then moves to helping couples find ways to honor each other's dream by identifying both core nonnegotiable areas and areas of greater flexibility, and then developing a temporary compromise and plan, so that ultimately couples can dialogue about important issues such as spirituality and religion, rather than becoming gridlocked.

Addressing spiritual and religious conflicts within the couple's subsystem can affect overall family functioning. In addition, parents can be counseled on how to handle a child or adolescent's spiritual beliefs that may differ from the beliefs and traditions valued in the family. Utilizing a similar process, counselors can encourage mutual respect between parents and youth by helping them develop a dialogue that includes listening to (not agreeing with) each other, identifying the parent's core nonnegotiable areas, as well as areas of flexibility, and then developing a compromise and plan.

Because a high level of compassion and support are needed in assisting couples and families, the counselor's own spirituality can serve as a resource in couple and family counseling. According to Anderson & Worthen (1997), spirituality is considered the fourth dimension of the human experience and, in reflecting a spiritual orientation to counseling, the therapist is guided by three basic assumptions: an awareness of God or a Divine Being; the yearning of the human spirit to connect with this Divine Being; and a belief that this Being is interested in humans and acts upon their relationship to promote constructive change. These assumptions influence how the counselor listens and responds, therefore utilizing "spirituality as a positive resource in the relational process" (p. 10). In addition, counselors can use specific religious traditions shared by the family, and can incorporate spirituality and religion into existing family counseling perspectives (Wolf & Stevens, 2001).

Summary

Spirituality and religion are an integral part of the human condition and preceded psychology in the treatment of intrapsychic and interpersonal concerns. In fact, many cultures still consult spiritual leaders for mental health problems and wellness promotion. While spirituality and religion were once considered as unhealthy, an overwhelming number of theorists and researchers now consider spirituality and religion fundamental to human development, healing, and overall well-being. Spirituality is an integral construct in several holistic wellness models.

The assessment of spiritual and religious beliefs and the impact on health and well-being has been both qualitative and quantitative and the research is extensive. This has led to the conclusion that spiritual beliefs and religious activities can be linked to improvements in the ability to cope with stress and improved health. Therefore, utilizing clients' spiritual and religious belief systems can be a significant resource in facilitating growth and development, as well as in helping them cope with uncertainty regarding spiritual or religious traditions, resolving feelings of betrayal from a spiritual teacher or religious leader, and helping them handle couple and family differences in religious or spiritual beliefs and traditions. Counseling interventions that include religious and spiritual beliefs should be part of every counselor's basic methods for assessment and wellness counseling.

References

Allport, G. W. (1950). *The individual and his religion: A psychological interpretation.* New York: Macmillan.

Allport, G. W., & Ross, J. M. (1967). Personal religious orientation and prejudice. *Journal of Personality and Social Psychology, 5,* 432–443.

Anderson, D. A., & Worthen, D. (1997). Exploring a fourth dimension: Spirituality as a resource for the couple therapist. *Journal of Marital and Family Therapy, 23,* 3–12.

Ardell, D. B. (1986). *High level wellness: An alternative to doctors, drugs, and disease.* Berkeley, CA: Ten Speed Press.

Arredondo, P., Toporek, M. S., Brown, S., Jones, J., Locke, D. C., Sanchez, J., et al. (1996). *Operationalization of the Multicultural Counseling Competencies.* AMCD: Alexandria, VA.

Batson, C. D. (1976). Religion as prosocial: Agent or double-agent? *Journal for the Scientific Study of Religion, 15*(1), 29–45.

Batson, C. D., & Schoenrade, P. A. (1991). Measuring religion as quest: 2) Reliability concerns. *Journal for the Scientific Study of Religion, 30*(4), 430–447.

Batson, C. D., & Ventis, W. L. (1982). *The religious experience: A social-psychological perspective.* New York: Oxford University Press.

Benson, H. (1975). *The relaxation response.* New York: Avon.

Benson, H., Dusek, J. A., Sherwood, J. B., Lam, Pl, Bethea, C. F., Carpenter, W., et al. (2006). Study of the therapeutic effects of intercessory prayer (STEP) in cardiac bypass patients: A multicenter randomized trial of uncertainty and certainty of receiving intercessory prayer. *American Heart Journal, 15,* 934–942.

Benson, H., & Stark, M. (1996). *Timeless healing: The power and biology of belief.* London: Simon and Schuster.

Bhaskarananda, S. (2002). *The essentials of Hinduism: A comprehensive overview of the world's oldest religion* (2nd ed.). Seattle, WA: Viveka Press.

Brown, H. P., & Peterson, J. H. (1991). Assessing spirituality in addiction treatment and follow-up: Development of the Brown-Peterson Recovery Progress Inventory. *Alcoholism Treatment Quarterly, 8*(2), 21–50.

Cashwell, C. S., Bentley, P. B., & Yarborough, J. P. (2007). The only way out is through: The peril of spiritual bypass. *Counseling and Values, 51*(1), 139–148.

Chandler, C. K., Holden, J. M., & Kolander, C. A. (1992). Counseling for spiritual wellness: Theory and practice. *Journal of Counseling & Development, 71,* 168–175.

Close, R. E. (2001). The role of prayer in the health concerns of elderly Christians. *Journal of Religious Gerontology, 13*(2), 35–44.

Crose, R., Nicolas, D. R., Gobble, D. C., & Frank, B. (1992). Gender and wellness: A multidimensional systems model for counseling. *Journal of Counseling & Development, 71*(2), 149–156.

Dorn, F. J. (1992). Occupational wellness: The integration of career identity and personal identity. *Journal of Counseling & Development, 71*(2), 176–178.

Eberst, R. (1984). Defining health: A multidimensional model. *Journal of Social Health, 54*(3), 99–104.

Ellis, A. (1980). Psychotherapy and atheistic values: A response to A. E. Bergin's "Psychotherapy and Religious Values." *Journal of Consulting and Clinical Psychology, 48*, 635–639.

Ellis, A. (1981). Science, religiosity, and rational emotive psychology. *Psychotherapy: Theory, Research, and Practice, 18*, 155–158.

Ellison, C. W. (1983). Spiritual well-being: Conceptualization and measurement. *Journal of Psychology and Theology, 11*, 330–340.

Favier, C., & Ingersoll, R. E. (2005). Knowing one's limits. In C. S. Cashwell & J. S. Young (Eds.), *Integrating spirituality and religion into counseling: A guide to competent practice* (pp. 169–183). Alexandria, VA: American Counseling Association.

Fiala, W. E., Bjork, J. P., & Gorsuch, R. (2002). The Religious Support Scale: Construction, validation, and cross-validation. *American Journal of Community Psychology, 30*(6), 761–786.

Fitchett, G. (1993a). *Assessing spiritual needs: A guide for caregivers.* Minneapolis, MN: Augsburg/Fortress.

Fitchett, G. (1993b). *Spiritual assessment in pastoral care: A guide to selected resources.* Decatur, GA: Journal of Pastoral Care Publications.

Fowler, J. W. (1981). *Stages of faith: The psychology of human development and the quest for meaning.* San Francisco: Harper & Row.

Frame, M. W. (2000). Spiritual genogram in family therapy. *Journal of Marital and Family Therapy, 26*, 211–240.

Francis, L. J., & Robbins, M. (2008). Psychological type and prayer preferences: A study among Anglican clergy in the United Kingdom. *Mental Health, Religion, & Culture, 11*(1), 67–84.

Frankl, V. (1969). *The will to meaning: Foundations and applications of logotherapy.* New York: New American Library.

Freud, S. (1950). *Totem and taboo: Some points of agreement between the mental lives of savages and neurotics* (J. Strachey, Trans.). New York: Norton. (Original work published 1913)

Freud, S. (1964). *The future of an illusion* (J. Strachey, Ed.; W. D. Robson-Scott, Trans.). Garden City, NY: Doubleday. (Original work published 1927)

Fry, P. S. (2000). Religious involvement, spirituality, and personal meaning for life: Existential predictors of psychological wellbeing in community residing and institutional care elders. *Aging & Mental Health 4*(4), 375–387.

George, L. K., Larson, D. B., Koenig, H. G., & McCullough, M. E. (2000). Spirituality and health: What we know, what we need to know. *Journal of Social and Clinical Psychology, 19*(1), 102–116.

Gethin, R. (1998). *The foundations of Buddhism.* New York: Oxford University Press.

Gorsuch, R. L., & Venable, G. D. (1983). Development of an "Age Universal" I-E Scale. *Journal for the Scientific Study of Religion, 22*(2), 181–187.

Gottman, J. M. (1999). *The marriage clinic.* New York: W. W. Norton.

Gulevich, T. (2004). *Understanding Islam and Muslim traditions: An introduction to the religious practices, celebrations, festivals, observances, beliefs, folklore, customs, and calendar system of the world's Muslim communities, including an overview of Islamic history and geography.* Detroit, MI: Omnigraphics.

Hall, T. W., & Edwards, K. J. (1996). The initial development and factor analysis of the Spiritual Assessment Inventory. *Journal of Psychology and Theology, 24*, 233–246.

Hampton, D. M., Hollis, D. E., Lloyd, D. A., Taylor, J., & McMillian, S. C. (2007). Spiritual needs of persons with advanced cancer. *American Journal of Hospice & Palliative Care, 24*(1), 42–48.

Harvey, I. S., & Silverman, M. (2007). The role of spirituality in the self-management of chronic illness among older African and whites. *Journal of Cross-Cultural Gerontology, 22*(2), 205–220.

Hays, J. C., Meador, K. G., Branch, P. S., & George, L. K. (2001). The spiritual history scale in four dimensions (SHS-4): Validity and reliability. *The Gerontologist, 41*(2), 239–249.

Hettler, B. (1984). Wellness: Encouraging a lifetime pursuit of excellence. *Health Values: Achieving Higher Level Wellness, 8*(4), 13–17.

Hill, P. C., & Pargament, K. I. (2003). Advances in the conceptualization and measurement of religion and spirituality: Implications for physical and mental health research. *American Psychologist, 58*(1), 64–74.

Hodge, D. R. (2001). Spiritual genograms: A generational approach to assessing spirituality. *Families in Society: The Journal of Contemporary Human Services, 82*, 35–48.

Holland, J. C., Kash, K. M., Passik, S., Gronert, M. K., Sison, A., Lederberg, M., et al. (1998). A brief spiritual beliefs inventory for use in quality of life research in life-threatening illness. *Psycho-Oncology, 7*(6), 460–469.

Howden, J. W. (1992). Development and psychometric characteristics of the Spirituality Assessment Scale. *Dissertation Abstracts International, 54*(01), 166B.

Jagers, R. J., & Smith, P. (1996). Further examination of the Spirituality Scale. *Journal of Black Psychology, 23,* 429–442.

Jung, C. G. (1938). *Psychology and religion.* London: Yale University Press.

Jung, C. G. (1970). *Modern man in search of a soul.* New York: Harcourt, Brace. (Original work published 1933)

Kabat-Zinn, J. (1993). Mindfulness Meditation: Health benefits of an ancient Buddhist practice. In D. Goleman & J. Gurin (Eds.), *Mind/Body medicine* (pp. 259–275). New York: Consumer Reports Books.

Kass, J. D., Friedman, R., Leserman, J., Zuttermeister, P. C., & Benson, H. (1991). Health outcomes and a new index of spiritual experience. *Journal for the Scientific Study of Religion, 30,* 203–211.

Koenig, H. G. (2004). Religion, spirituality, and medicine: Research findings and implications for clinical practice. *Southern Medical Association, 97*(12), 1194–1200.

Ladd, K., & Spilka, B. (2006). Inward, outward, upward prayer: Scale reliability and validation. *Journal for the Scientific Study of Religion, 45*(2), 233–251.

Larson, D. B., & Larson, S. S. (2003). Spirituality's potential relevance to physical and emotional health: A brief review of quantitative research. *Journal of Psychology and Theology, 31*(1), 37–51.

Lundy, K. S., & Janes, S. (2003). *Essentials of community-based nursing.* Boston: Jones and Bartlett.

Maltby, J., Lewis, C. A., & Day, L. (1999). Religious orientation and psychological well-being: The role of the frequency of personal prayer. *British Journal of Health Psychology, 4*(4), 363–378.

Maslow, A. (1971). *Religions, values, and peak-experiences.* New York: Viking.

Maton, K. I. (1989). The stress-buffering role of spiritual support: Cross-sectional and prospective investigations. *Journal of the Scientific Study of Religion, 28*(3), 310–323.

Mijares, S. G., & Khalsa, G. S. (Eds.). (2005). *The psychospiritual clinician's handbook: Alternative methods for understanding and treating mental disorders.* New York: Haworth Press.

Miller, C. (2000). The technique of souldrama and its applications. *International Journal of Action Methods: Psychodrama, Skill Training, and Role Playing, 52*(4), 173–186.

Miller, G. (1999). The development of the spiritual focus in counseling and counselor education. *Journal of Counseling & Development, 77*(4), 498–501.

Miller, G. (2003). *Incorporating spirituality in counseling and psychotherapy: Theory and technique.* New York: John Wiley.

Moreno, Z. T. (1965). Psychodramatic rules, techniques and adjunctive methods. *Group Psychotherapy, 18*(1–2), 73–86.

Myers, J. E., Luecht, R. M., & Sweeney, T. J. (2004). The factor structure of wellness: Reexamining theoretical and empirical models underlying the Wellness Evaluation of Lifestyle (WEL) and the Five-Factor WEL. *Measurement and Evaluation in Counseling and Development, 36,* 194–208.

Myers, J. E., Sweeney, T. J., & Witmer, J. M. (2000). The Wheel of Wellness counseling for wellness: A holistic model for treatment planning. *Journal of Counseling & Development, 78*(3), 251–266.

Neyrinck, B., Vansteenkiste, M., Lens, W., Duriez, B., & Hustebaut D. (2006). Cognitive, affective, and behavioral correlates of internalization of regulations for religious activities. *Motivation & Emotion, 30,* 323–334.

Nicholas, D. R., & Gobble, D. C. (1990). On the importance of disregulatory processes in models of health. *American Psychologist, 45*(8), 981–982.

Nino, A. G. (1997). Assessment of spiritual quests in clinical practice. *International Journal of Psychotherapy, 2*(2), 193–212.

Pargament, K. I., Koenig, H. G., & Perez, L. M. (2000). The many methods of religious coping: Development and initial validation of the RCOPE. *Journal of Clinical Psychology, 56*(4), 519–543.

Parker, R. J. (1997). Sarah's story: Using ritual therapy to address psychospiritual issues in treating survivors of childhood sexual abuse. *Counseling and Values, 42*(1), 41–54.

Peterman, A. H., Fitchett, G., Brady, M. J., Pharm, L. H., & Cella, D. (2002). Measuring spiritual well-being in people with cancer: The Functional Assessment of Chronic Illness Therapy—Spiritual Well-Being Scale (FACIT-Sp). *Annals of Behavioral Medicine, 24*(1), 49–58.

Portman, T. A. A., & Garrett, M. T. (2006). Native American healing traditions. *International Journal of Disability, Development and Education, 53*(4), 453–469.

Pruyser, P. W. (1976). *The minister as diagnostician: Personal problems in pastoral perspective.* Oxford, England: Westminster.

Purdy, M., & Dupey, P. (2005). Holistic flow model of spiritual wellness. *Counseling and Values, 49,* 95–106.

Richards, I. S., & Bergin, A. E. (2005). *A spiritual strategy for counseling and psychotherapy* (2nd ed.). Washington, DC: American Psychological Association.

Richards, P. S., Hardman, R. K., & Berrett, M. E. (2007). *Spiritual approaches in the treatment of women with eating disorders.* Washington, DC: American Psychological Association.

Robertson, L. (2008). *The Spiritual Competency Scale: A comparison with the ASERVIC competencies.* Unpublished doctoral dissertation, University of Central Florida, Orlando, FL.

Rogers, C. R. (1980). *A way of being.* Boston: Houghton Mifflin.

Ryan, R. M., Rigby, S., & King, K. (1993). Two types of religious internalization and their relations to religious orientations and mental health. *Journal of Personality and Social Psychology, 65*(3), 586–596.

Sandhu, D. S. (2007). Seven stages of spiritual development: A framework to solve psycho-spiritual problems. In O. J. Morgan (Ed.), *Counseling and spirituality: Views from the profession* (pp. 64–85). Boston: Lahaska Press/Houghton Mifflin.

Sandhu, D. S., & Asrabadi, B. R. (2003). *Development of Experienced Based Spiritual Development Scale (EBSDS): Some preliminary findings.* Unpublished manuscript. University of Louisville, Louisville, KY.

Segal, Z., Teasdale, J., & Williams, M. (2002). *Mindfulness-Based Cognitive Therapy for Depression.* New York: Guilford Press.

Singh, R. (1999). Inner and outer peace through meditation. Boston: Element.

Skinner, B. F. (1953). *Science and human behavior.* New York: Macmillan.

Stanard, R. P. (2007). Remembering the lessons of the angel. In O. J. Morgan (Ed.), *Counseling and spirituality: Views from the profession* (pp. 64–85). Boston: Lahaska Press/Houghton Mifflin.

Sweeney, T. J., & Witmer, M. J. (1991). Beyond social interest: Striving toward optimum health and wellness. *Individual Psychology, 47*(40), 527–540.

Underwood, L. G., & Teresi, J. (2002). The Daily Spiritual Experience Scale: Development, theoretical description, reliability, exploratory factor analysis, and preliminary construct validity using health related data. *Annals of Behavioral Medicine, 24*(1), 22–33.

Veach, T. L., & Chappel, J. N. (1992). Measuring spiritual health: A preliminary study. *Substance Abuse, 13,* 139–147.

Wheat, L.W. (1991). Development of a scale for the measurement of human spirituality (measurement scale). *Dissertation Abstracts International, 52*(09), 3230A.

Witmer, M. J., & Sweeney, T. J. (1992). A holistic model for wellness and prevention over the life span. *Journal of Counseling & Development, 71*(2), 140–148.

Wolf, C. T., & Stevens, P. (2001). Integrating religion and spirituality in marriage and family counseling. *Counseling and Values, 46*(1), 66–75.

Yalom, I. D. (1995). *Theory and practice of group psychotherapy* (4th ed.). New York: Basic Books.

Zimpfer, D. G. (1992). Psychosocial treatment of life-threatening disease: A wellness model. *Journal of Counseling & Development, 71,* 203–209.

14 OUR COLLECTIVE WISDOM ON SOCIAL RELATIONSHIPS AND WELLNESS

Anne M. Ober

No road is long with good company.

TURKISH PROVERB

Wellness Connection

In his book *Love and Survival* Dean Ornish eloquently makes a salient point concerning the importance of relationships and our well-being. He writes: "Love and intimacy are at the root of what makes us sick and what makes us well, what causes sadness and what brings happiness, what makes us suffer, and what leads to healing" (p. 3). In this chapter Dr. Ober illustrates some of the knowledge that we have acquired concerning the importance of our social relationships and our wellness.

We seem to live a paradoxical existence with respect to our relationships. While we have numerous technologies connecting us to people across the country and the world, we find ourselves more and more alone and lonely. Authors analyzed this phenomenon in such recent books as *The Lonely American: Drifting Apart in the Twenty-first Century, Bowling Alone,* and *Pursuit of Loneliness* (Olds & Schwartz, 2009; Putnam, 2000; Slater, 1990). On college and high school campuses, students prefer to text rather than directly speak to others, sometimes while they are sitting in same room. Take a moment to observe people in coffee shops or restaurants. Many times conversations are happening over cell phones, between one person who is present and another at the other end of the phone, rather than among the people sitting together. Our behaviors suggest using the technology is primary and having the conversation is secondary.

These observations are not intended to criticize technology, but rather to suggest a more mindful use of this tool. Important connections happen electronically and technology can be very beneficial. I was recently traveling out of the country and texting was my only method of communication with loved ones. It is remarkable the power of a few characters to make you feel connected. Additionally, technology is not the only force contributing to a disconnection among people. Our Western culture encourages individualism and distraction from the present moment, materialism, and results rather than progress. If you observe the images of our popular culture, we seem to be focused on the relatively insignificant aspects of our lives (i.e., the length of our eyelashes, the freshness of our produce, and the smell of our carpets to name a few) rather than our happiness, relationships, and well-being.

In our profession of counseling, we work with individuals and families on a daily basis who are struggling to connect with others and have meaningful relationships. Relationships are crucial to well-being, both in the counseling session and beyond. Our training in helping others echoes the wisdom of previous generations. We have heard from many sources in various ways that "everybody needs somebody" and research findings support this wisdom, from Bowlby's studies of attachment (1988) to recent studies on forgiveness (Bono, McCullough, & Root, 2008). This chapter provides a broad overview of the research that supports the traditional wisdom on the complex interaction between the intra- and interpersonal worlds. Primary focus is given to the benefits of relationships on the individual. However, the stressors of relationships on well-being are also presented. The chapter concludes with some thoughts on the implications of this collective wisdom for counselors, both personally and professionally.

EVOLUTION OF RESEARCH ON SOCIAL RELATIONSHIPS AND WELLNESS

In the 1970s, the concept of "social support" was defined and researchers explored the role of relationships in helping people manage crises, transitions, and difficult environments (Caplan, 1974; Cassel, 1974). Initial research found a positive association between social support and physical well-being (Cobb, 1976) and later findings suggested social relationships improved coping skills and directly increased immunological and psychological defenses (Pilisuk & Minkler, 1985). Current research is exploring the specific mechanism(s) by which social support impacts physical and mental health and vice versa to better understand the strong association between these concepts (Cohen, 2004; Ell, 1984).

Social support is thought to impact physical and mental well-being in several different ways. Social support provides an individual with a route to receiving psychological and material resources. These resources exist in three categories: instrumental (money or services), informational (advice or important information), and emotional (empathy, caring, trust, and reassurance) (Cohen, 2004). Being a part of a community offers various social relationships that provide many different emotional benefits. Relationships provide a sense of belonging for the individual and identification with social roles (Brissette, Cohen, & Seeman, 2000). Additionally, the person who has a sense of belonging in a community can experience the benefits of stress-buffering and the main psychological effects of social relationships. Our interactions with others help to reduce the effects of stressful experiences through providing a more objective and less threatening interpretation of the event as well as coping strategies (Cohen, 1988; Cohen & Willis, 1985; Uchino, Cacioppo, & Kiecolt-Glaser, 1996). Relationships also promote positive psychological conditions such as purpose, meaning, a sense of identity and self-worth. Finally, relationships provide sources for information to prevent illness and injury and motivation and social pressure to care for one's physical and emotional self (Cohen, 2004).

As research developed and expanded on social relationships and well-being, criticism emerged regarding the lack of a consistent definition of "social support" and questions remained about the manner by which relationships produce main and/or buffering effects on well-being.

House, Landis, and Umberson (1988) reviewed the literature, specifically the association between social relationships and mortality. Many of the earlier studies demonstrated higher mortality and morbidity rates for those individuals who were socially isolated (unmarried) in comparison to the social integrated (married) (Berkman & Syme, 1979; Carter & Glick, 1970; Kitigawa & Hauser, 1973), but it was unclear if a "causal direction" existed for these associations, nor was the process by which relationships may influence well-being or vice versa understood (House et al., 1988). The specifics of how and why social relationships influence well-being continue to be the focus of various studies.

VARIETY OF RESEARCH ON SOCIAL RELATIONSHIPS AND WELLNESS

Over the past 20 years, relationship and well-being research has become more specialized in terms of the types of social relationships, different aspects of wellness, and the importance of social connections throughout the lifespan. From the vulnerability of infancy to the selectivity demonstrated in older adults and from relationships to spouses and siblings to relationships with our furry, four-legged friends, researchers are exploring the importance of connections to our well-being.

"It Takes a Village to Raise a Child"

—George Washington Carver

Maternal and infant well-being are the subjects of many research studies. Several studies have investigated the role of social relationships on aspects of maternal well-being, including mitigation of postpartum depression (Dennis & Ross, 2006), reduction of stress related to parenting (Raikes & Thompson, 2005), improvement of overall well-being of mother (Hall, Schaefer, & Greenberg, 1987), and positive influence on mother-child relationship (Burchinal, Follmer, & Bryant, 1996; Marshall, Noonan, McCartney, Marx, & Keefe, 2001; Melson, Ladd, & Hsu, 1993).

Balahi et al. (2007) reviewed several studies of social support and maternal well-being and suggested the quantity of relationships was less significant than the quality and nature of the relationships. The researchers identified the benefits of parenting (sense of purpose, responsibility, and meaning) in addition to the stressors, specifically the demand of resources including: physical, emotional, and mental and potential conflict with other social roles. The mother's perception of the stressors and coping style was found to impact her mental health, wherein self-efficacy was found to be linked with well-being (Evenson & Simon, 2005; Nomaguchi & Milkie, 2003; Peterson, 1999; Umberson & Gove, 1989). The key relationships in the mother's life provided resources to learn coping skills, emotional and financial support, and increased mother's knowledge of child development (Cunningham & Zayas, 2002).

Several studies demonstrated the positive benefits for the mother who had a spouse/partner, including lower levels of stress and depression in comparison to single mothers (Hall, Gurley, Sachs, & Kryscio, 1991; Levitt, Weber, & Clark, 1986; McLanahan, Wedemeyer, & Adelberg, 1981). Interestingly, the positive impact of social relationships was not limited to the role of an intimate partner. A few studies demonstrated the positive impact of maternal grandmothers living with single mothers and grandchildren on mother's parenting skills and general well-being (McLoyd, 1995; Wilson & Tolson, 1990). Social support is essential for parents and especially mothers to help with the physical, emotional, and mental changes that come with pregnancy and raising a child. The resources, knowledge, and support provided to the mother help to increase her well-being and in turn, the well-being of the child.

Childhood and Adolescence: "Even as kids reach adolescence, they need more than ever for us to watch over them. Adolescence is not about letting go. It's about hanging on during a very bumpy ride."

—Ron Taffel

The importance of social relationships, specifically affection and nurturing of young children by a primary caregiver, has been studied extensively and findings support the importance of human connection for healthy psychological and physical development (Bowlby, 1988; Diener, & McGavran, 2008). As the child grows, the parent remains a significant person. But adolescence is thought to bring change in terms of the teen's primary social support, shifting attention and reliance towards peers rather than family. Huebner and Diener (2008) studied the life satisfaction of children ages 10–13 years old, specifically the influence of different relationships and demographic factors. Interestingly, the researcher found that the teens' family life, specifically their relationship with parents, was found to be more strongly associated with global satisfaction than either their relationships with friends or their recent academic performance. Other factors that were thought to have some impact on life satisfaction (i.e., parents' occupational status, race, and gender) were not significantly associated with life satisfaction. Although adolescence is a time for developing one's identity and thus perhaps rebelling against the authority and association with parents, it is important to remember the significance of the parent-child relationship. Parents can promote the well-being of their teens by providing support and structure within their relationships.

Siblings: "Both within the family and without, our sisters [and brothers] hold up our mirrors: our images of who we are and of who we can dare to be."

—Elizabeth Fishel

The relationship between siblings is unique. Our brothers and sisters are (potentially) present for the majority of our lives, from early childhood, adolescence, adulthood and into later life. They are witnesses to our changes and continuity and many times share with us the experience of growing up within our families. The positive influence of siblings, specifically in older adulthood, has been studied. Circirelli (1989) explored the association between relationships with siblings and depression in older adults (sample with a mean age of 72 years). The study found men and women who had close relationships with their sisters reported lower levels of depression than those who did not have close relationships with their sisters. Close relationships with a brother were found to be associated with lower levels of depression in men, but not in women. Additionally, Circirelli found that women who perceived conflict in their relationships with their sisters were related to higher levels of depression in the sample.

Subsequent studies have maintained the importance of sibling relationships to promote well-being in older and younger adulthood. O'Bryant (1988) studied widows' relationships with their married sisters and found interactions were related to an increase in positive affect. Shortt & Gottman (1997) completed a study on sibling relationships in early adulthood and found those participants with close ties to brothers and sisters enjoyed many benefits in comparison to those with strained sibling relationships, including: greater positive affect and greater emotional regulation in conflict situations. Some studies suggest sibling relationships may provide a buffer to stress and negative affect (Circirelli, 1991; Diener & McGavran, 2008). These one of a kind connections provide a resource to support our well-being and maintain connection to our past.

Spouses/Partners: "Marriage is like a violin. After the music is over, you still have the strings."

—Simone de Beauvoir

The research findings on the impact of intimate relationships on physical well-being are varied. Furthermore, the findings differ between the genders. Many studies support the belief that healthy intimate relationships benefit individuals in many ways, such as positive physical health, improved coping mechanisms, increased life satisfaction, and reduced levels of depression, anxiety, and stress levels (Kawachi & Berkman, 2001; Myers, 2000). However, the impact of negative relationships has also been studied. A longitudinal study on marital quality and physical health suggested marital strain accelerates the decline of physical health and has stronger adverse effects on health as participants aged. The authors concluded, ". . . having a bad marriage is worse for your health than having a good marriage is good for your health" (Umberson, Williams, Powers, Lui, & Needham, 2006). These findings underscore the importance of putting effort towards improving marital relationships, both for the immediate and long-term benefits for both parties.

The connection between cardiovascular disease and social relationships is an important research question due to the prevalence of various illnesses. A longitudinal study completed with over 9,000 British men and women resulted in some interesting findings. The researchers followed the participants for over 12 years and adjusted for variables such as age, gender, obesity, hypertension, diabetes, cholesterol level, depression, alcohol and tobacco use, and exercise and found that those participants who experienced negative close relationships (marriages) had a 1.3 greater risk of coronary disease. This study found no significant difference between men and women (De Vogli, Chandola, & Marmot, 2007).

Other studies suggested married women's physical health was negatively impacted in comparison to married men's health (Coyne et al., 2001; Johnson, Backlund, Sorlie, & Loveless, 2000; Kiecolt-Glaser & Newton, 2001; Lett et al., 2005; Orth-Gomer et al., 2000; Troxel, Matthews, Gallo, & Huller, 2005). Some researchers proposed this difference between women and men results from the importance relationships play in the lives of women. Women are more likely than men to focus their resources on relationships and therefore may be more affected when problems and conflicts arise (Notarius, Benson, Sloane, Vanzetti, & Hornyak, 1989). Although women report having more close relationships and giving/receiving more support than men, they also reported higher levels of psychological distress and negative interactions in their relationships (Fuhrer, Stansfeld, Chemali, & Shipley, 1999, and Pagel, Erdly, & Becker, 1987). It would seem that women may receive great benefits from their marital relationships, but also bear the greater risks. Further, research on the impact of intimate partnerships on the well-being of men and women needs to be completed to find conclusive results.

Older Adults: "The older the fiddler, the sweeter the tune."

Ageism is pervasive in our culture resulting in stereotypes about life as an older adult. When I recently asked students in a lifespan and development class which words they associated with "older adults," the majority of terms were negative (*grumpy, lonely, sad, helpless,* and *sickly*) and few were positive (*wise, experienced,* and *nurturing*). With the aging of the Baby Boomer generation, it is expected that these assumptions will be further challenged.

Current research presents a different understanding of life beyond the age of 55. The Socioemotional Selectivity Theory was articulated to explain the behavior of older adults in which they became more selective in their social relationships. Older adults tend to focus their resources on close relationships with family and friends, rather than acquaintances, as these connections provide meaning and positive emotional experiences (Carstensen, Isaacowitz, & Charles, 1999). Although the amount of social interaction may decline with older age, social relationships become more satisfying to older adults, as evidenced by participants of a study who reported being less lonely than their younger cohorts (Lang & Carstensen, 1994).

Older adults benefit in many important ways from strong social supports. In studies of non-institutionalized older adults, those participants with greater amounts of social involvement were found to have better cognitive functioning than their less socially involved peers (Bassuk, Glass, & Berkman, 1999; Seeman, Lusignolo, Albert, & Berkman, 2001). Programs to promote healthy lifestyles in older adults were found to be more successful, even at long-term follow up, when social support was incorporated into the program (Lalonde & FallCreek, 1985; Lalonde, Hooyman, & Blumhagen, 1988).

However, older adults are also vulnerable to the effects of negative aspects of relationships. A longitudinal study of middle and early older adults found that lack of reciprocity in a variety of close relationships (partner, parent-child, sibling and or close friend) was associated with poorer physical and mental health in both men and women. Reciprocity was defined as a "match between efforts spent and rewards received in turn" (Chandola, Marmot, & Siegrist, 2007, p. 408). Even when the researchers adjusted for negative support in close relationships, the findings remained consistent. The lack of reciprocity is thought to result in increased negative emotions and stress reactions, either acute or chronic (Chandola et al., 2007).

Man's/Woman's Best Friend: "Dogs are not our whole life, but they make our lives whole."

—Roger Caras

The bond between a dog and his or her owner is unique. The unconditional love and positive response we receive from our pets provides a sense of comfort and joy. Additionally, research has found these interactions between human and four-legged family members result in physical health benefits. Relating to dogs has been found to produce serotonin and reduce high blood pressure, decrease coronary heart disease, improve immune functioning, and facilitate recovery from illness and injury (Allen, 2003; Anderson, Reid, & Jennings, 1992; Friedmann, Katcher, Thomas, Lynch, & Messent, 1983; Friedmann, Katcher, Lynch, & Thomas, 1980; Patronek & Glickman, 1993; Rowan & Beck, 1994; Serpell, 1991; Siegel, 1990; Wells, 2007).

A recent study of 62 residents of the United Kingdom, average age of 60 years, explored the impact of dog ownership on motivating health lifestyle choices. The study found that most participants walked their dogs at least once a day, promoting exercise and social relationships with other dog owners. In addition to the benefits of daily exercise, the participants reported owning a dog provided them with a better quality of life, companionship, and a sense of security and protection (Knight & Edwards, 2008). Although we typically discuss the importance of social relationships between people as impacting wellness, these studies remind us to encourage and appreciate the power of connections among all beings.

CURRENT TOPICS OF INTEREST IN SOCIAL RELATIONSHIPS AND WELLNESS

The association between positive social interactions and individuals' well-being has been established in a variety of studies with samples from across the lifespan. However, this interaction is not believed to be one-directional. Individuals who are well in body, mind, and soul are likely to be more able and willing to engage in social relationships and provide support for their family, friends, and community. Researchers are attempting to better understand the interaction and influence of the interpersonal relationships on intrapersonal well-being and vice versa.

Brain and Social Relations

With the advancement of technology, scientists are investigating the impact of social relationships on the brain and specifically cognition. Ybarra et al. (2008) studied the effects of social interaction on the cognitive functioning of individuals over 3,500 individuals, ranging in age from 24 to 96 years old. The results suggested social contact had a positive relationship with cognitive functioning. Interestingly, the study demonstrated that a relatively small amount of social interaction (10 minutes speaking with another person) can improve cognitive performance comparable to engagement in other intellectual exercises (i.e., puzzles and reading comprehension tasks).

Effectively, the study suggests social interaction is a workout for our brains, helping to increase our abilities to remember, process information, and appropriately inhibit behaviors. This increase in cognitive performance also impacts our social cognition skills (i.e., empathizing, remembering details of others' stories, and taking different perspectives). The researchers suggested that social interaction provides an increase in cognitive abilities, which in turn promotes better social cognition and interactions, and thus creates a positive cycle of increasing intra- and interpersonal well-being. However, the type of social interaction is crucial to increasing cognitive abilities. Those interactions that were identified to have a low to moderate level of difficulty, such as interactions with acquaintances and family or friends which included some periods of rest, were found to improve cognitive abilities. Those interactions categorized as having a high level of difficulty, defined as interactions with strangers who are not part of the individuals' group or interactions including high levels of conflict, did not have the same positive relationship with increased cognitive abilities (Ybarra et al., 2008).

This study, along with other recent research, provided some better understanding of the link between social cognition and interactions and other brain function. Social cognition and interaction is believed to be a complex process, requiring multiple, concurrent processes such as: paying attention to verbal and nonverbal cues, maintaining memory of content and contributions to conversation, adaption to different perspectives, inferences about the other person's beliefs and needs, assessing potential problems or conflicts, and inhibiting irrelevant and/or inappropriate responses (Ybarra et al., 2008). Research has shown that the prefrontal cortex, the area of the brain responsible for executive functioning such as working memory, attention, and inhibition, is the same area responsible for helping us understand others' beliefs and perspectives (Amodio & Frith, 2006; Baron-Cohen & Ring, 1994; Brunet, Safati, Hardy-Bayle, & Docety, 2000; Royall et al., 2002). Therefore, stimulation of this region, either through social interaction or other mental tasks, results in improved abilities both for general cognitive abilities and social cognition.

Negative Impact of Social Relationships

Although much of the research on social relationships and well-being demonstrates the positive interaction between these two concepts, the impact of negative social relationships is also of interest. Our relationships can produce a significant amount of stress, either from conflict, demands on resources, or losses. To cope with these stressors, individuals may turn to unhealthy behaviors as ways to reduce or remove the immediate effects of the stressors, such as overeating, alcohol/drug use, tobacco use, and various other addictions. Our social relationships also include a certain level of risk in that they expose us to disease, conflict, exploitation, and feelings of loss and loneliness. These environmental stressors may result in cognitive, affective, and physiological responses, which may result in poor physical and mental health (Cohen, 2004).

The quality of the relationship has been found to impact well-being, especially those relationships defined as having poor quality, such as consistent conflict and higher levels of stress and anxiety for those persons involved. These relationships result in lower levels of subjective well-being as do those relationships characterized by mostly negative interactions (Antonucci, Akiyama, & Lansford, 1998; Finch, Okun, Barrera, Zautra, & Reich, 1989; Pagel et al., 1987; Rook, 1992). Again, gender seems to have a role to play in perceptions of negative relationships and well-being. Whereas lower levels of well-being in men were associated with social relationships in which the other person was perceived to be too demanding, lower levels of subjective well-being in women were found to be related to social interactions with persons who were viewed as irritating (Antonucci et al., 1998).

Even in the best relationships, there is disagreement, disappointment, and loss. A relationship that may provide many positive benefits for well-being may also present significant difficulty and stressors. This is evident in relationships where one person becomes ill or disabled and the other becomes the primary caregiver. Although this role may provide the caregiver with a sense of purpose and meaning, it can also be a tremendous stressor on his or her physical and emotional well-being (Adams, McClendon, & Smyth, 2008; Blyth, Gumming, Brnabic, & Cousins, 2008; Shippy, 2005; Spillers, Wellisch, Kim, Matthews, & Baker, 2008). It is important

Important Components of Relationships and Well-Being

1. Love vs. Success: "Money Can't Buy It"

   Perkins (1991) found that those persons who expressed a preference for high incomes and occupational success at the expense of marriage/partnership and close friendships were more likely to describe themselves as unhappy.

2. Forgiveness: "Forgive and Forget" or "Holding onto Your Pain Hurts You"

   Forgiveness has been found to be positively associated with well-being. Although it is uncertain if the benefits result from maintaining an important relationship or reducing psychological stress, a study of college students found those who forgave others had increased levels of satisfaction with life, positive mood increase, negative mood decrease, and fewer physical problems than their peers who refused to forgive. This association was stronger for those participants who reported stronger relationships before the transgression and for those who reported their partner apologized. Additionally, those persons with higher levels of well-being before the transgression were more likely to offer forgiveness to their partner (Bono et al., 2008).

3. Comparing Self to Others: "Never compare yourself with others—there is always someone who is better or worse"

   Frequent comparison with others can result in an increase in negative feelings. A study of college students found that social comparison frequency predicts negative emotions in general, but specifically shame. Those people who engage in social comparison more frequently tend to experience more negative emotions and are more likely to participate in social comparisons on days when they are experiencing increased levels of negative feelings (Fujita, 2008).

4. Healthy Eating Behaviors: "Tell me who you run with and I'll tell you who you are"

   Our eating habits can influence those loved ones around us. Several studies suggest romantic partners have power to encourage or discourage healthy eating behaviors, such as increasing consumption of fruits and vegetables, reducing fat and high calorie foods, and cutting down on snack food (Markey, Markey, & Birch, 2001; Schafer, Keith, & Schafer, 2000). Markey, Gomel, & Markey, (2008) found women were more likely than men to attempt to regulate their partners' eating behaviors, and women's efforts to modify their partners' diets was positively associated with healthy behaviors. Regardless of gender, participants' efforts made to monitor or restrict their partners' diets was positively correlated with the partners' increased concern about their health and diet.

5. Grief and Loss: "Do something for someone else—you'll feel better"

When a person loses a loved one, support is invaluable. Although having the support of others is vital, recent studies of widows and widowers found it may be more important for the bereaved to reach out and help others. Researchers analyzed data from the Changing Lives of Older Couples (CLOC) study, specifically grief responses to the loss of a spouse and providing instrumental support to others. They found that widows and widowers who provided support to others had accelerated decline in their depressive symptoms 6–18 months after the death of their spouse. Additionally, helping behavior was found to increase longevity in older adults in the same sample (Brown, Brown, House, & Smith, 2008). It is thought that helping may result in lower levels of depression because of its related benefits to the helper, including self-efficacy, self-esteem, sense of meaning and purpose, and belonging (Baumeister, 1991; Taylor & Turner, 2001).

to remember that our social relationships have a remarkable amount of influence on our well-being, in terms of both stressors and benefits.

APPLYING OUR COLLECTIVE WISDOM

With all of the data we have gained from research and the wisdom of previous generations, we are presented with the challenge of making this knowledge useful. How do we as counselors improve social relationships and in turn well-being for our clients and ourselves? Here are some suggestions for steps we can take, both personally and professionally, to promote positive connections and well-being.

1. Model Healthy Relationships: Relationships take work and this rule applies to our partnerships, friendships, clients, and our coworkers. Being honest and genuine is not always easy, but these characteristics can be contagious and powerful. "Be the change that you want to see in the world." —Mohandas Gandhi.
2. Make an Effort to Care for Each Other: With the stressors and problems of life, it is easy to become focused on the self and assume our concerns are not only at the top of the list—but are the only ones that exist. Be willing to listen to your partner's or coworkers' concerns and give them your full attention, even if only for a few minutes. You will both benefit from this time and connection.
3. Encourage Clients to Take a Risk and Connect With Others: We are likely doing this work already, but it is important enough to state clearly and again. Acknowledge the work clients have done already to attempt connecting with others and give them feedback when they connect with you in session.
4. Practicing What We Preach—Making Our Relationships a Priority: Perhaps the most difficult thing for many of us is to find a balance between our work and our lives outside the 9–5. Schedule time with those you love and care about, and even pencil some time in for yourself. Although our work is very important, we must be able to replenish our energy and resources to be able to continue to give to others.
5. Combat the Loneliness: Although we spend our days with people, we can feel lonely because these interactions are not reciprocal. Set up some time during the workday to talk with peers/friends and allow yourself to relax, distance yourself from your work, and laugh. You may want to set up regular meetings among the counseling staff to discuss cases and provide each other scheduled consultation and support.

There are many other ways to improve our relationships and well-being. Start a conversation within your social network and make some plans for improving your individual and collective well-being.

References

Adams, K. B., McClendon, M. J., & Smyth, K. A. (2008). Personal losses and relationship quality in dementia caregiving. *Dementia: The International Journal of Social Research and Practice, 7*(3), 301–319.

Allen, K. (2003). Are pets a healthy pleasure? The influence of pets on blood pressure. *Current Directions in Psychological Science, 12*, 236–239.

Amodio, D. M., & Frith, C. D. (2006). Meeting of minds: The medial frontal cortex and social cognition. *Nature Reviews Neuroscience, 7*, 268–277.

Anderson, W. P., Reid, C. M., & Jennings, G. L. (1992). Pet ownership and risk factors for cardiovascular disease. *Medical Journal of Australia, 157*, 298–301.

Antonucci, T. C., Akiyama, H., & Lansford, J. E. (1998). Negative effects of close social relationships. *Family Relations, 47*, 379–384.

Balahi, A. B., Claussen, A. H., Smith, D. C., Visser, S. N., Morales, M. J., & Perou, R. (2007). Social support networks and maternal mental health and well-being. *Journal of Women's Health, 16*(10), 1386–1396.

Baron-Cohen, S., & Ring, H. (1994). The relationship between EDD and ToM: Neuropsychological and neurobiological perspectives. In P. Mitchell & C. Lewis (Eds.), *Origins of an understanding of mind* (pp. 183–207). Hillsdale, NJ: Lawrence Erlbaum.

Bassuk, S. S., Glass, T. A., & Berkman, L. F. (1999). Social disengagement and incident cognitive decline in community-dwelling elderly persons. *Annals of Internal Medicine, 131*, 165–173.

Baumeister, R. F. (1991). *Meanings of life*. New York: Guilford.

Berkman, L. F., & Syme, L. (1979). Social networks, host resistance, and mortality: A nine-year follow-up study of Alameda county residents. *American Journal of Epidemiology, 109*, 186–203.

Blyth, F. M., Gumming, R. G., Brnabic, A. J. M., & Cousins, M. J. (2008). Caregiving in the presence of chronic pain. *Journals of Gerontology: Series A: Biological Sciences and Medical Sciences, 63A*(4), 399–407.

Bono, G., McCullough, M. E., & Root, L. M. (2008). Forgiveness, feeling connected to others, and well-being: Two longitudinal studies. *Personality and Social Psychology Bulletin, 34*(2), 182–195.

Bowlby, J. (1988). *A secure base: Parent-child attachment and healthy human development*. New York: Basic Books.

Brissette, I., Cohen, S., & Seeman, T. E., (2000). Measuring social integration and social networks. In S. Cohen, L. Underwood, & B. Gottlieb (Eds.), *Measuring and intervening in social support* (pp. 53–85). New York: Oxford University Press.

Brown, S. L., Brown, R. M., House, J. S., & Smith, D. M. (2008). Coping with spousal loss: Potential buffering effects of self-reported helping behavior. *Personality and Social Psychology Bulletin, 34*(6), 849–861.

Brunet, E., Sarfati, Y., Hardy-Bayle, M. C., & Decety, J. (2000). A PET investigation of the attribution of intentions with a nonverbal task. *Neuroimage, 11*, 157–166.

Burchinal, M. R., Follmer, A., & Bryant, D. M. (1996). The relations of maternal social support and family structure with maternal responsiveness and child outcomes among African American families. *Developmental Psychology, 32*(6), 1073–1083.

Caplan, G. (1974). *Support systems and community mental health*. New York: Human Sciences Press.

Carstensen, L. L., Isaacowitz, D. M., & Charles, S. T. (1999). Taking time seriously: A theory of socio-emotional selectivity. *American Psychologist, 54*, 165–181.

Carter, H., & Glick, P. C. (1970). *Marriage and divorce: A social and economic study*. Cambridge, MA: Harvard University Press.

Cassel, J. (1974). An epidemiological perspective of psychosocial factors in disease etiology. *American Journal of Public Health, 64*, 1040–1043.

Chandola, T., Marmot, M., & Siegrist, J. (2007). Failed reciprocity in close social relationships and health: Findings from the Whitehall II study. *Journal of Psychosomatic Research, 63*, 403–411.

Circirelli, V. G. (1989). Feelings of attachment to siblings and well-being in later life. *Psychology and Aging, 4*, 211–216.

Circirelli, V. G. (1991). Sibling relationships in adulthood. *Marriage and Family Review, 16*, 291–310.

Cobb, S. (1976). Social support as a moderator of life stress. *Psychosomatic Medicine, 38*, 300–314.

Cohen, S. (1988). Psychosocial models of social support in the etiology of physical disease. *Health Psychology, 7*, 269–297.

Cohen, S. (2004). Social relationships and health. *American Psychologist, 59*(8), 676–684.

Cohen, S., & Willis, T. A. (1985). Stress, social support, and the buffering hypothesis. *Psychological Bulletin, 98*, 310–357.

Coyne, J. C., Rohrbaugh, M. J., Shoham, V., Sonnega, J. S., Nicklas, J. M., & Cranford, J. A. (2001). Prognostic importance of marital quality for survival of congestive heart failure. *American Journal of Cardiology, 88*(5), 526–529.

Cunningham, M., & Zayas, L. H. (2002). Reducing depression in pregnancy: Designing multimodal interventions. *Social Work, 47*(2), 114–123.

Dennis, C. L., & Ross, L. (2006). Women's perceptions of partner support and conflict in the development of postpartum depressive symptoms. *Journal of Advanced Nursing, 56*(6), 588–599.

De Vogli, R., Chandola, T., Marmot, M. G. (2007). Negative aspects of close relationships and heart disease. *Archives of Internal Medicine, 167*(18), 1951–1957.

Diener, M. L., & McGavran, M.B.D. (2008). What makes people happy? A developmental approach to the literature on family relationships and well-being. In M. Eid & R. J. Larsen (Eds.), *The science of subjective well-being* (pp. 347–375). New York: Guilford.

Ell, K. (1984). Social networks, social support, and health status: A review. *Social Service Review, 56,* 133–149.

Evenson, R. J., & Simon, R. W. (2005). Clarifying the relationship between parenthood and depression. *Journal of Health and Social Behavior, 46*(4), 341–358.

Finch, J. F., Okun, M. A., Barrera, M., Zautra, A. J., & Reich, J. W. (1989). Positive and negative social ties among older adults: Measurement models and the prediction of psychological distress and well-being. *American Journal of Community Psychology, 17,* 585–605.

Friedmann, E., Katcher, A. H., Lynch, J. J., & Thomas, S. A. (1980). Animal companions and one year survival of patients after discharge from a coronary care unit. *Public Health Reports, 95,* 307–312.

Friedmann, E., Katcher, A. H., Thomas, S. A., Lynch, J. J., & Messent, P. R. (1983). Social interaction and blood pressure: Influence of companion animals. *Journal of Nervous & Mental Disease, 171,* 461–465.

Fuhrer, R., Stansfeld, S. A., Chemali, J., & Shipley, M. J. (1999). Gender, social relationships and mental health: Prospective findings from an occupational cohort (Whithall II study). *Social Science and Medicine, 48*(1), 77–87.

Fujita, F. (2008). The frequency of social comparison and its relation to subjective well-being. In M. Eid & R. J. Larsen (Eds.), *The science of subjective well-being* (pp. 239–257). New York: Guilford.

Hall, L. A., Gurley, D. N., Sachs, B., & Kryscio, R. J. (1991). Psychosocial predictors of maternal depressive symptoms, parenting attitudes, and child behavior in single-parent families. *Nursing Research, 40*(4), 214–220.

Hall, L. A., Schaefer, E. S., & Greenberg, R. S. (1987). Quality and quantity of social support as correlates of psychosomatic symptoms in mothers with young children. *Research in Nursing Health, 10,* 287–298.

House, J. S., Landis, K. R., & Umberson, D. (1988). Social relationships and health. *Science, 241,* 540–545.

House, J. S., Umberson, D., & Landis, K. R. (1988). Structures and processes of social support. *Annual Review of Sociology, 14,* 293–318.

Huebner, E. S., & Diener, C. (2008). Research on life satisfaction of children and youth: Implications for the delivery of school-related services. In M. Eid & R. J. Larsen (Eds.), *The science of subjective well-being* (pp. 376–388). New York: Guilford.

Johnson, N. J., Backlund, E., Sorlie, P. D., & Loveless, C. A. (2000). Marital status and mortality: The national longitudinal mortality study. *Annals of Epidemiology, 10*(4), 224–238.

Kawachi, I., & Berkman, L. F. (2001). Social ties and mental health. *Journal of Urban Health, 78*(3), 458–467.

Kiecolt-Glaser, J. K. & Newton, T. L. (2001). Marriage and health: His and hers. *Psychology Bulletin, 127*(4), 472–503.

Kitigawa, E. M., & Hauser, P. M. (1973). *Differential mortality in the United States: A study in socio-economic epidemiology.* Cambridge, MA: Harvard University Press.

Knight, S., & Edwards, V. (2008). In the company of wolves: The physical, social, and psychological benefits of dog ownership. *Journal of Aging and Health, 20*(4), 437–455.

Lalonde, B. I., & FallCreek, S. J. (1985). Outcome effectiveness of the Wallingford wellness project: A model health promotion program for the elderly. *Journal of Gerontological Social Work, 9,* 49–64.

Lalonde, B. I., Hooyman, N., & Blumhagen, J. (1988). Long-term outcome effectiveness of a health promotion program for the elderly: The Wallingford wellness project. *Journal of Gerontological Social Work, 13*(1/2), 95–112.

Lang, F. R., & Carstensen, L. L. (1994). Close emotional relationships in later life: Further support for proactive aging in the social domain. *Psychology and Aging, 9,* 315–324.

Lett, H. S., Blumenthal, J. A., Babyak, M. A., Strauman, T. J., Robins, C., & Sherwood, A. (2005). Social support and coronary heart disease. Epidemiologic evidence and implications for treatment. *Psychosomatic Medicine, 67*(6), 869–878.

Levitt, M. J., Weber, R. A., & Clark, M. C. (1986). Social network relationships as sources of maternal support and well-being. *Developmental Psychology, 22*(3), 310–316.

Markey, C. N., Gomel, J. N., & Markey, P. M. (2008). Romantic relationships and eating regulation: An investigation of partners' attempts to control each others' eating behaviors. *Journal of Health Psychology, 13*(3), 422–432.

Markey, C. N., Markey, P. M., & Birch, L. L. (2001). Interpersonal predictors of dieting practices among married couples. *Journal of Family Psychology, 15*, 464–475.

Marshall, N. L., Noonan, A. E., McCartney, K., Marx, F., & Keefe, N. (2001). It takes an urban village: Parenting networks of urban families. *Journal of Family Issues, 22*(2), 163–182.

McLanahan, S. S., Wedemeyer, N. V., & Adelberg, T. (1981). Network structure, social support, and psychological well-being in the single-parent family. *Journal of Marriage and Family, 43*(3), 601–612.

McLoyd, V. C. (1995). Poverty, parenting and policy: Meeting the support needs of poor parents. In H. Fitzgerald, B. Lester, & B. Zuckerman (Eds.), *Children of poverty: Research, health, and policy issues* (pp. 269–281). New York: Garland Press.

Melson, G. F., Ladd, G. W., & Hsu, H. C. (1993). Maternal support networks, maternal cognitions, and young children's social and cognitive development. *Child Development, 64*(5), 1401–1417.

Myers, D. G. (2000). The funds, friends, and faith of happy people. *American Psychologist, 55*, 56–67.

Nomaguchi, K. M., & Milkie, M. A. (2003). Cost and rewards of children: The effects of becoming a parent on adults' lives. *Journal of Marriage and Family, 65*(2), 356–374.

Notarius, C. I., Benson, P. R., Sloane, D., Vanzetti, N., & Hornyak, L. (1989). Exploring the interface between perception and behavior: An analysis of marital interaction in distressed and nondistressed couples. *Behavioral Assessment, 11*, 39–64.

O'Bryant, S. L. (1988). Sibling support and older widows' well-being. *Journal of Marriage and Family, 50*, 173–183.

Olds, J., & Schwartz, R. S. (2009). *The lonely American: Drifting apart in the twenty-first century*. Boston: Beacon Press.

Orth-Gomer, K., Wamala, S. P., Horsten, M., Schench-Gustafsson, K., Schneierman, N., & Mittleman, M. A. (2000). Marital stress worsens prognosis in women with coronary heart disease: The Stockholm Female Coronary Risk Study. *Journal of the American Medical Association, 284*(23), 3008–3014.

Pagel, M. D., Erdly, W. W., & Becker, J. (1987). Social networks: We get by with (and in spite of) a little help from our friends. *Journal of Personality and Social Psychology, 53*(4), 793–804.

Patronek, G. J., & Glickman, L. T. (1993). Pet ownership protects the risks and consequences of coronary heart disease. *Medical Hypothesis, 40*, 245–249.

Perkins, H.W.: 1991. Religious commitment, yuppie values and well-being in post-collegiate life, Review of *Religious Research, 32*. 224–251.

Peterson, C. (1999). Personal control and well-being. In D. Kahneman & E. Diener (Eds.), *Well-being: The foundations of hedonic psychology* (pp. 288–305). New York: Russell Sage Foundation.

Pilisuk, M., & Minkler, M. (1985). Supportive ties: A political economy perspective. *Health Education Quarterly, 12*, 93–106.

Putnam, R. D. (2000). *Bowling alone: The collapse and revival of American community*. New York: Simon & Schuster.

Raikes, H. A., & Thompson, R. A. (2005). Efficacy and social support as predictors of parenting stress among families in poverty. *Infant Mental Health Journal, 26*(3), 177–190.

Rook, K. S. (1992). Detrimental aspects of social relationships: Taking stock of an emerging literature. In H. O. F. Viel & U. Baumann (Eds.), *The meaning and measurement of social support* (pp. 157–169). New York: Hemisphere.

Rowan, A. N., & Beck, A. M. (1994). The health benefits of human-animal interactions. *Anthrozoos, 5*, 85–98.

Royall, D. R., Lauterbach, E. C., Cummings, J. L., Reeve, A., Rummans, T. A., & Kaufer, D. I. (2002). Executive control function: A review of its promise and challenges for clinical research. *Journal of Neuropsychiatry and Clinical Neuroscience, 14*, 377–405.

Schafer, R. B., Keith, P. M., & Schafer, E. (2000). Marital stress, psychological distress, and healthful dietary behavior: A longitudinal analysis. *Journal of Applied Social Psychology, 20*(8), 1639–1656.

Seeman, T. E., Lusignolo, T. M., Albert, M., & Berkman, L. (2001). Social relationships, social support, and patterns of cognitive aging in healthy, high-functioning older adults: MacArthur studies of successful aging. *Health Psychology, 20*, 243–255.

Serpell, J. (1991). Beneficial effects of pet ownership on some aspects of human health and behavior. *Journal of Royal Society of Medicine, 84*, 717–720.

Shippy, R. A. (2005). We cannot go it alone: The impact of informal support and stressors in older gay, lesbian and bisexual caregivers. *Journal of Gay & Lesbian Social Services: Issues in Practice, Policy & Research, 18*(3–4), 39–51.

Shortt, J. W., & Gottman, J. M. (1997). Closeness in young adult sibling relationships: Affective and physiological processes. *Social Development, 6*, 142–164.

Siegel, N. (1990). An article that addresses health and senior citizens that have pets. *Journal of Pavlovian Biological Science, 14*, 104–107.

Slater, P. (1990). *The pursuit of loneliness* (3rd ed.). Boston: Beacon Press.

Spillers, R. L., Wellisch, D. K., Kim, Y., Matthews, B. A., & Baker, F. (2008). Family caregivers and guilt in the context of cancer care. *Psychosomatics: Journal of Consultation Liaison Psychiatry, 49*(6), 511–519.

Taylor, J., & Turner, J. (2001). A longitudinal study of the role and significance of mattering to others for depressive symptoms. *Journal of Health and Social Behavior, 42*, 310–325.

Troxel, W. M., Matthews, K. A., Gallo, L. C., & Huller, L. H. (2005). Marital quality and occurrence of the metabolic syndrome in women. *Archives of Internal Medicine, 165*(9), 1022–1027.

Uchino, B. N., Cacioppo, J. T., & Kiecolt-Glaser, J. K. (1996). The relationship between social support and physiological processes: A review with emphasis on underlying mechanisms and implications for health. *Psychological Bulletin, 119*, 488–531.

Umberson, D., & Gove, W. R. (1989). Parenthood and psychological well-being: Theory, measurement, and stage in the family life course. *Journal of Family Issues, 10*(4), 440–462.

Umberson, D., Williams, K., Powers, D. A., Lui, H., & Needham, B. (2006). You make me sick: Marital quality and health over the life course. *Journal of Health & Social Behavior, 47*(1), 1–16.

Wells, D. L. (2007). Domestic dogs and human health: An overview. *British Journal of Health Psychology, 12*, 145–156.

Wilson, M. N., & Tolson, T. F. J. (1990). Familial support in the black community. *Journal of Clinical Child Psychology, 19*(4), 347–355.

Ybarra, O., Burnstein, E., Winkielman, P., Keller, M. C., Manis, M., Chan, E., & Rodriguez, J. (2008). Mental exercising through simple socialization: Social interaction promotes general cognitive functioning. *Personality and Social Psychology Bulletin, 34*(2), 248–252.

15 SOCIAL RELATIONSHIPS: BURDENS AND BENEFITS

Andrew P. Daire

Call it a clan, call it a network, call it a tribe, and call it a family. Whatever you call it, whoever you are, you need one.

JANE HOWARD (ENGLISH NOVELIST)

Wellness Connection

Our relationships with others have a profound effect on all domains of our health and wellness. In this chapter, Dr. Daire illustrates the importance of social relationships and the impact on several domains of wellness.

Researchers in human development, psychology, anthropology, and history can all agree on one thing: *humans are social beings that need to belong*! From infancy to late adulthood, we have a biological and psychological drive to bond and connect with others and to become part of a group. Social relationships serve as our primary source for a sense of belonging, so much so that from infancy to late adulthood, those who lack social relationships are at greater risk for emotional, psychological, and health problems. So it is no surprise that social relationships hold an important role in wellness.

SOCIAL RELATIONSHIPS AND WELLNESS: AN OVERVIEW

Social relationships provide an essential role in developing effective attachments, meeting emotional and psychological needs, maintaining physical health, and contributing to one's overall well-being across the lifespan. The term *social relationships*, which appears simple at first, is more complex when incorporated with related concepts such as social integration, social networks, and relational content (House, Landis, & Umberson, 1988):

- Social integration is the quality and frequency of social relationships and interaction.

- Relational content defines the functional qualities of those relationships.
- Social networking composes the structural qualities within a set of relationships.

Across the lifespan, these three components of social relationships provide a foundation for overall wellness.

Social relationships begin through early attachments. Parental attachments and bonding, particularly maternal, create the foundational environment for the development of social relationships (Bowlby, 1969; Hofer, 1987). Attachment behavior, which is phylogenetically rooted, possesses strong biological influences in humans and various animals both with higher and lower levels of emotional and cognitive development (Hofer, 1987). So strong biological needs exist from infancy for us to attach, and the success of the resulting attachments can impact social relationships in the future. During infancy, caregiving and nurturing behaviors impact the development of attachments and future social relationships. For example, children who were abused by early attached objects (i.e., parents and caregivers) had more strained peer relationships during adolescence, were rated as more disturbed by teachers, and possessed lower peer status (Salzinger, Feldman, Hammer, & Rosario, 1993). During childhood and adolescence, social integration impacts peer development (Salzinger et al., 1993), motivation towards educational aspirations, and prosocial goal-oriented behaviors (Wentzel, 1998), and overall self-esteem. It can also influence engagement in negative or maladaptive behavior (Johnson, Myers, Webber, & Boris, 2004). In early adulthood, social relationships influence the development and maintenance of effective interpersonal and intimate relationships, contribute to increased productivity and success in the workplace, and impact psychological and emotional health. In later adulthood, social relationships contribute to better physical health and longevity. So we can see that the systemic impact exists because poorer attachment and social relationship skills can impact the level and quality of parental-child caregiving behaviors, subsequently impacting that child's ability to develop effective social attachments during adolescence, adulthood, and late adulthood.

Cohen (2004) examined social relationships from the variables of social support, social integration, and negative integration. Cohen (2004) proposes that social support "eliminates or reduces effects of stressful experiences by promoting less threatening interpretations of adverse events and effective coping strategies" (p. 617). Social support, being fairly complex, consists of instrumental support (direct support), informational support (new knowledge and relevant information), and emotional support (behaviors that express caring) (House, Kahn, McLeod, & Williams, 1985). "Social integration promotes positive psychological states that include: health-promoting physiological responses, provides information, and is a source of motivation and social pressure to care for oneself" (Cohen, 2004, p. 617). One way to view social integration is through the quantity and quality, also known as relational content, of social interactions (House et al., 1988). The third component of social relationships, negative interactions, "elicits psychological stress and in turn behavior and physiologically concomitants that increase risk for disease" (Cohen, 2004, p. 617). Positive social interactions can promote psychological well-being, but negative interactions, along with poor relationships, contribute to higher levels of emotional distress (Umberson, Chen, House, Hopkins, & Slaten, 1996; Yurkovich & Smyer, 1998). Additionally, those who are less confident about their social skills and abilities, which can result from persistent negative interactions, correlate with higher levels of loneliness and depression (Caplan, 2003; Segrin & Flora, 2000). However, the relationship between social relationships and psychological or emotional well-being is more complex with the involvement of numerous variables (Lakey & Cohen, 2000). For example, when other variables were controlled, sociability correlated highly with more positive health outcomes (Cohen, Doyle, Turner, Alper, & Skoner, 2003). However, this conclusion has been challenged in studies examining increased social interactions for individuals with acute or chronic illnesses (Cohen, 2004). This chapter will provide additional clarity to the complexity of social relationships and well-being by presenting benefits and burdens of social relationships as they relate to the various wellness tasks.

Although research suggests that happiness and overall life satisfaction have more importance than money as life goals (Diener & Oishi, 2005; Diener & Seligman, 2004), economic benefits do result from positive social relationships on an individual and community-wide level. Imagine this: economists and others are interested in the financial and economic impact of social relationships. Putnam (2001), for example, found that the well-being of individuals and the community positively influence social capital. Putnam also reported that social capital is on the decline in the United States. Trust proved to be a key factor. An increase in social relationships contributed to a greater sense of trust for people in general, organizations, the government and other institutions (Diener & Seligman, 2004; Helliwell, 2003). Additionally, social relationships increase in value as individuals and societies become wealthier. So the impact of social relationships goes beyond individual emotional and psychological health and well-being into a broader societal impact.

When considering the influence and impact social relationships have on our physical, emotional, psychological, and societal well-being and overall wellness, it would be easy to conceptualize social relationships as the fundamental component of wellness. This would be a fairly large statement that would significantly impact the reader's expectations of this chapter. However, closer consideration illuminates the dynamic and interactive impact social relationships have on the different components of wellness. The Wheel of Wellness (Myers, Sweeney, & Witmer, 2000; Witmer & Sweeney, 1992) proposes five life tasks: spirituality, self-direction, work and leisure, friendship, and love. Social relationships impact and are impacted by these five life tasks. For example, social relationships contribute to the development of greater spiritual supports and spiritual awareness. Social relationships and the ability to develop effective social relationships influence one's self-direction, sense of worth, exercise, stress management, and cultural identity, which are all subtasks in the self-direction life task. Social relationships have a positive influence on work productivity and worker satisfaction. The life task of friendship "incorporates all of one's social relationships" (Myers et al., 2000, p. 78) and the effectiveness in the development of social relationships will impact the development of intimate relationships. Take a moment and reread this paragraph on how social relationships impact the various life tasks within the Wheel of Wellness. Now, consider how these various life tasks also impact the development and maintenance of effective social relationships.

OUR "CROSS-DEVELOPMENTAL" RELATIONSHIP TASK

As biological beings, we have a strong drive to develop attachments and to be part of a group. In many ways, it proves to be our task in life to develop and maintain healthy social relationships. It is understood that attachment and bonding is a drive and a need. In other words, we are biologically programmed (i.e., programmed, or driven), to form attachments and to bond. These attachments and bonds initially serve a physical survival purpose with respect to being cared for, fed, and protected from harm. However, attachment and bonding appear to transition from a biological drive to an emotional and psychological need. Social relationships develop from the interaction and communication with attached objects over time (hopefully) meeting the emotional and psychological need for attachment and bonding. In both family relationships and nonfamily relationships, social rules and roles develop along with expectations, boundaries, and verbal and nonverbal behaviors that shape those relationships. Communication, problem-solving, conflict resolution, and self-esteem will also influence the maintenance and continued development of these social relationships. Social learning and family systems theorists both point to the importance of these early relationships in shaping and influencing how we approach and form long-term social relationships. But why should we consider social relationships a task? In many ways, we can consider tasks to be things we have to do or are expected to do that will lead toward some type of desired outcome. The relationship task then is to develop and maintain healthy social relationships. Individuals with healthy social relationship suffer from less emotional distress, fewer psychological problems, and live longer (Antonucci, Birditt, & Webster, 2010). The "cross-developmental" component proves important because regardless of one's developmental stage in life, social relationships will play an integral role in enhancing the quality and success within the stages. Whether in infancy, adolescence, young adulthood, or late adulthood, social relationships play a key role in almost everything we do. Although the days of needing our tribal members for help with food gathering or for physical protection have past, we do suffer emotionally and physically when social relationships are not a part of our lives.

FIVE LIFE TASKS FOR WELLNESS AND SOCIAL RELATIONSHIPS

The field of wellness grew from a need to find and provide an alternative to traditional medical models of physical and emotional health (Myers et al., 2000). The Wheel of Wellness (Myers et al., 2000; Sweeney & Witmer, 1991; Witmer & Sweeney, 1992), born from theoretical and research inquiry, reigns as the most widely accepted holistic model of wellness and prevention. As mentioned earlier the model purports five interrelated and interconnected life tasks (spirituality, self-direction, work and leisure, friendship, and love) which have subtasks. According to Myers and colleagues (2000), "these life tasks interact dynamically with various life forces, including but not limited to family, community, religion, education, government, media, and business/industry" (p. 242).

As we go deeper in our inquiry on social relationships and wellness, let us now take a look at the role social relationships play in our five wellness life tasks.

Spirituality: Burdens and Benefits

When considering spirituality, especially with respect to social relationships, it proves beneficial to begin by differentiating or clarifying spirituality from religion. Spirituality is our need to relate to something greater while religion is the implementation of specific and shared beliefs, approaches, or rituals. In their revision and modification of the Wheel of Wellness model, Myers and colleagues (2000) define spirituality as "an awareness of a being or force that transcends the material aspects of life and gives a deep sense of wholeness or connectedness to the universe" (p. 252). Spirituality transcends race, gender, socioeconomic status, and nationality in that most cultures have some form of spirituality. In other words, there is a need to relate to something greater. Spirituality brings people together with common and shared beliefs and values. Additionally, it can contribute to a sense of community. This sense of community is one of the places where spirituality, wellness, and social relationships intersect.

When considering social relationships and spirituality, attendance to religious services and the resulting sense of community appear as an obvious example. Those that attend religious services consistently have greater social relationships than those who do not (Strawbridge,

Shema, Cohen, & Kaplan, 2001). Many religious organizations facilitate social relationships, recognizing the impact social connections have on recruitment and retention of members. These social relationships also provide a key foundation for social support, which serves as a buffer to stress. Thus, spirituality and religion provides a common goal to draw people together.

A common spiritual belief plays a unification or relationship strengthening role. A religious saint once said, "Love is not looking into each other's eyes. Love is looking in the same direction." This sentiment explains the power of a shared spiritual belief in focusing two people in one direction towards a common goal, thus bringing them together. Imagine the top of a triangle being the shared spiritual belief with the couple on each side of the bottom working their way closer towards the shared belief. Not only does the shared spiritual belief give them a focus as they move towards this shared belief, but they also move closer together as a couple. Additionally, this occurs in groups as well as individuals. Groups working toward a shared spiritual belief, or any shared belief, eventually become closer together.

On the other side though, spirituality can be divisive and burdensome in and on social relationships. For a couple, not having a shared spiritual belief can move them further apart, an opposite effect of the aforementioned shared spiritual belief triangle. Different spiritual views, traditions, and expectations create additional challenges in intimate relationships. Although a couple's love may be strong, the relationship can succumb to constant struggles of different spiritual beliefs and resulting behaviors and expectations. Just as spirituality can bring people together, it can drive groups of people apart. Collectivist views prove to be divisive to those that do not espouse to the commonly accepted view. The division created leads to conflict, persecution and, for those history buffs, wars. These disagreements and conflicts can occur between countries, groups of people, and within intimate relationships.

Self-Direction: Burdens and Benefits

The self-direction wellness task proves to be the broadest task, containing 12 subtasks. It is the "sense of mindfulness and intentionality in meeting the major tasks of life" (Myers, et al., 2000, p. 253). The subtasks include sense of worth, sense of control, realistic belief, emotional awareness and coping, problem solving and creativity, sense of humor, nutrition, exercise, self-care, stress management, gender identity, and cultural identity. The literature overwhelmingly purports the benefits of social relationships. Men and women with positive social relationships were found to have lower levels of psychological distress along with higher levels of distress when social relationships were strained (Umberson et al., 1996; Yurkovich & Smyer, 1998). So when we consider how social relationships can impact wellness tasks and subtasks, it begs attention. For example, personality characteristics such as introversion and extraversion, sociability, and shyness all impact the quantity and quality of social relationships (Asendorpf & Wilpers, 1998). Also, sense of humor and spirituality play a role in the development of social relationships. It might be interesting to conceptualize into subtasks those that impact social relationships, those that are impacted by social relationships, and those that do both. In some ways, this could be considered an oversimplification of the complexities involved in these subtasks. However, in the spirit of intellectual and clinical examination of social relationships' role in the self-direction task, this categorization should have some benefits for student and clinician. See Table 15.1.

As you can see from Table 15.1, there appears to be an even distribution in the number of subtasks that impact social relationships, are impacted by social relationships, and do both. Sense of worth, or self-esteem, gender identity, and cultural identity impact and are impacted by social relationships. For example, individuals with greater levels of self-esteem will more comfortably

TABLE 15.1 Self-Direction Subtasks and Social Relationships

Self-Direction Subtasks	Impact Social Relationships	Impacted by Social Relationships
Sense of Worth	√	√
Sense of Control	√	
Realistic Belief	√	
Emotional Awareness & Coping	√	
Problem Solving & Creativity	√	
Sense of Humor	√	
Nutrition		√
Exercise		√
Self-Care		√
Stress Management		√
Gender Identity	√	√
Cultural Identity	√	√

initiate and sustain social relationships. However, success or failure in social relationships can positively or negatively impact sense of worth. Gender and cultural identities reflect one's identification with the behaviors, stereotypes, and appreciations of a particular gender or culture, respectively. Comfort level and acceptance, within oneself and from the community, also impact self-esteem, personal development, and social relationship-seeking behavior. In other words, those more comfortable with their gender and cultural identity will also be more comfortable in engaging and relating with others. Conversely, opportunities to develop and sustain social relationships within one's cultural or gender group along with the quality of those experiences can support or challenge these identities. Additionally, acceptance of one's gender or cultural identity from peer groups also impacts self-acceptance of one's own cultural identity.

Sense of control, realistic belief, emotional awareness and coping, problem solving and creativity, and sense of humor all impact social relationships. Those that see themselves as having control over their experiences and emotions have more confidence and see themselves as more socially competent (Taylor & Brown, 1988). Similarly, those who are more realistic in their perceptions of reality, more accurate in their self-perceptions, and more accurate in their perceptions of their environment tend to have more success in their intimate and social relationships. For those who are challenged in their emotional awareness and coping, Myers and colleagues (2000) stated, "The quality and quantity of relationship events within their lives are limited" (p. 254). Emotional awareness and coping also impacts and is impacted by problem solving and creativity. Problem solving ability affords one the skills to navigate the interpersonal challenges that periodically occur in all social relationships and the intrapersonal challenges that contribute to anxiety and depression (Hughes, Waite, Hawkley, & Cacioppo, 2004). Sense of humor, particularly laughter, contributes positively to psychological and physiological well-being (Myers et al., 2000). It aids in decreasing conflict and serves a reparative function in interpersonal and romantic relationships (Gottman, 1994) and is important in problem solving and decision-making. Basically, individuals with a good sense of humor are more pleasant to be around. In many ways, these four self-direction subtasks that impact social relationships could collectively be viewed as general skills needed for interpersonal effectiveness.

Nutrition, exercise, self-care, and stress-management, which are all impacted by social relationships, could be collectively viewed as general skills needed for intrapersonal care and overall health. The benefits of these subtasks on overall wellness have been well established (Cohen et al., 2003; Lakey & Cohen, 2000; Myers et al., 2000; Witmer & Sweeney, 1992). However, social relationships also contribute to overall health (Cohen, 2001; Cohen et al., 2003; Lacham, 2004). Substantial research exists in the role social relationships play in physical health (Bergstrom & Holmes, 2000; Cohen, 2004). Social support plays an integral role in health behaviors such as nutrition and exercise (Gruber, 2008; Sergin & Passalacqua, 2010).

Social support and social relationships also impact pro-social behaviors (Wentzel, 1998), including self-care behaviors. Finally, positive social relationships are associated with lower levels of emotional distress, improved coping, and improved stress management (Cohen, 2004; Umberson et al., 1996; Yurkovich & Smyer, 1998), which is arguably the most important intrapersonal skill to master.

In this section, I took the unique approach of categorizing self-direction into subtasks impacted by social relationships, those that impact social relationships, and those that do both. Additionally, these subtasks relate to people's perceptions of themselves along with interpersonal and intrapersonal effectiveness. However, what is most unique about the self-direction life task is that "It refers to a sense of mindfulness and intentionality in meeting the major tasks of life" (Myers et al., 2000, p. 253). In other words, success (or failure) in this life task will impact success and failure in the other life tasks.

Work and Leisure: Burdens and Benefits

The role that social relationships play in leisure is a bit more obvious than with work. Although leisure does not assume or imply time with others, we know that quality and frequency of social relationships, along with ample social networks, prove beneficial in enhancing leisure opportunities (House et at., 1988). Possessing a broad array of social activities also contributes greatly to the quantity and quality of social relationships and the resulting positive impact on wellness (Brissette et al., 2000). Physically active leisure activities, such as team sports, also have a natural emotional healing effect due to release of endorphins. The self-direction life task will play an important role in this life task. The previous section discussed how some self-direction subtasks impact social relationships. These can also impact engagement in leisure (and work) activities. When considering successes or challenges along with quantity and quality of leisure activities, examination of these self-direction subtasks will prove valuable.

The same skills to develop and maintain healthy social relationships also impact workplace relationships. Most Westerners spend more time at work, on the job, or pursuing their career aspirations (i.e., college or university) than they do with family members, friends, or engaged in leisure activities. Additionally, work itself proves to be an important psychological and developmental need (Myers et al., 2000; Witmer & Sweeney, 1992). Work provides us with a purpose and with opportunities to make a difference in our community or in the lives of others, and it affords us the financial needs to take care of our families. Work is an important wellness task, and the quality of the workplace experiences and relationships will shape one's success in achieving this task. Social scientists and business management researchers continue to tout the importance of quality workplace relationships as a key factor in employee job satisfaction. Employees with high levels of job satisfaction are more productive, less depressed, less stressed, and have lower turnover. Effective social relationships at work prove to be a more important factor in job satisfaction and employee well-being than salary (Diener & Seligman, 2004). For example, refer to the business management book *12: The Elements of Great Managing* (Wagner, Harter, & Books, 2006), which is grounded in the results as the Gallup Organization's 10 million interviews with employees and managers spanning 114 countries, identified 12 elements in harnessing employee engagement, improving employee retention, and increasing productivity. Four of the 12 elements were related to social relationships with managers or between employees: recognition and praise, someone at work cares about me as a person, someone at work encourages my development, and having a best friend at work. It punctuates the importance of workplace social relationships to know that 4 of the 12 elements identified from such a broad cross cultural research initiative were relational! However, balance between work and leisure is the key. Greenhaus, Collins, and Shaw (2003) defined balance as quality of time, involvement, and satisfaction. In their study on work and family balance, they found that individuals balanced in their family and work roles have greater life satisfaction along with those who might be imbalanced in favor of family roles (2003). Csikszentmihalyi and LeFevre (1989) had an interesting finding in their research study on work and leisure. They reported a paradoxical finding in people reporting, ". . . more positive feelings at work than in leisure, yet saying that they 'wish to be doing something else' when they are at work, not when they are in leisure" (p. 821). These authors suggested that we might be too fatigued at the end of a hard day's work to engage in more active and enjoyable leisure activities or that an overreliance on media stifled our creative abilities in identifying and engaging in more stimulating and positive leisure activities. This brings an interesting point to light: we might not know how to be good and active "leisurites."

"Back in the day," when we did not have iPods, Game Boy, and over 400 cable or satellite television channels, we got a stick and a rock and had a great time with friends and neighbors. We spent more time in the backyard or garage with our children or parents. We went somewhere and played tennis, bowling, or baseball opposed to playing them on Nintendo Wii®. If we as human beings are drawn to what is more pleasurable and to what makes us feel more successful, which is supported by research (Csikszentmihalyi & LeFevre, 1989), it might explain a subtle move towards being a workaholic creating a damaging imbalance between our work and leisure. Instead of asking our clients what leisure activities they engage in, we might need to inquire about their ability to create, identify, or find creative and positive leisure activities.

Based on clinical experiences with counseling individuals and couples, I have identified four clinical considerations with respect to the work and leisure balance and to social relationships. First, we must consider socioeconomic level. Individuals with fewer resources will have fewer opportunities for leisure activities. There might be safety issues in their neighborhood, less money to fund leisure activities, or less time because they are working multiple jobs. Second, we must consider the job types and job quality of the clients. Their ability to engage in consistent leisure activities, particularly group activities, will be impeded if they work the night shift and sleep during the day or have a work schedule that frequently changes. Additionally, job quality and satisfactory workplace relationships will impact satisfaction with work. Third, we must consider family, peer relationships, and support. An ample and supportive social and family network affords opportunities for greater leisure activities with a variety of people to engage in them, and also grants opportunities for child care. I am sure readers with children will connect with this last aspect. The fourth consideration, organizational skills, might initially appear out of place. However, time management, budgeting, problem solving, boundaries, and creativity will be critical in creating, managing, and sustaining healthy social relationships along with more consistent involvement in leisure activities.

Friendship: Burdens and Benefits

The friendship life task plays a vital role in wellness since it is nearly synonymous with the definition and concept of social relationships. Friendship is at the very core of one's social relationships, and an individual's quality and quantity of friendships often determines the level of satisfaction with social relationships and contributes to wellness in the other life tasks. In fact, research suggests that friendships could potentially be more beneficial than romantic or familial relationships for long-term health (Vaillant, Meyer, Mukamal, & Soldz, 1998). Friendship is also vital for maintaining emotional health (Hintikka et al., 2000). Men and women with multiple friendships they classify as close relationships suffer from mental distress less frequently, whereas those men and women with only one close friendship or with none at all more frequently experienced mental distress (Hintikka et al., 2000).

All of us have an inborn desire to establish connections with one another. The "belongingness hypothesis," a concept devised by Baumeister and Leary (1995), states "human beings possess a pervasive drive to form and maintain at least a minimum quantity of lasting, positive, and significant interpersonal relationships" (p. 497). The idea of belongingness is discussed in terms of its ability to increase the social connections of an individual and its assistance in helping to avoid stressors like loneliness and isolation (Baumeister & Leary, 1995). So once again we come across the notion that friendships can provide a solid base for personal well-being, since social relationships can hypothetically all fall under the umbrella of friendship. However, lack of friendship can have severely damaging effects for both mental and physical health, especially since we all have an innate desire and need to connect to one another. Research indicates that as a culture, individuals born in the United States allow self-esteem to impact their overall well-being more so than in other cultures (Uchida, Norasakkunkit, & Kitayama, 2004). This suggests that it is of particular importance for the wellness of Americans since well-being can be enhanced by forming, maintaining, and strengthening social relationships, and friendships factor in significantly to this equation.

When looking at the friendship task, it is essential to recognize the symbiotic relationship that exists between friendship and love. The foundations of friendship can act as a jumping-off point for love, just as love can oftentimes regress or transform into friendship without intimacy. However, friendship exists on a unique level separate from relationships involving intimate love, sexual relations, or family members (Myers et al., 2000). Although friendship and love frequently overlap and impact one another, people often have separate needs that must be fulfilled in each area. For instance, one's system of social support can be divided into various subparts that are accessed separately depending on the current needs of the person. So if a person is struggling with his or her intimate or familial relationships, the person would turn to the friendship arm of his or her social support system as a means of coping and as a source for empathy, comfort, and mutual reflection. Similarly, since friendship networks can be so diverse, a person can turn to one friendship to discuss or solve dilemmas with another friendship. This interconnectedness can be both a benefit and a burden for friendship in terms of wellness. If, as is being suggested, friendship plays the role of the mediator or the thing one calls on in any time of need, then it is serving to protect and nurture personal well-being. However, if friendship comes into competition with another of the wellness tasks, like love, it can become burdensome and potentially harmful to a person's well-being.

In terms of wellness, research has shown that those people who have limited or no means of social support tend to be more susceptible to health risks such as sickness and disease (Hafen, Franksen, Karren, & Hooker, 1992). On the other hand, those who maintain strong, healthy friendships have a greater chance to lead full and satisfying lives. More often than not it is the quality of these friendships that has a positive impact on a person's well-being, not the quantity of contact that occurs. Even as we enter the later stages in our lives, our quality of relationships and communication with friends acts as a better indicator of mental and physical health than the actual number of friends or amount of time spent communicating with them (Ishii-Kuntz, 1990). In this way, friendship serves as a benefit since it enhances overall quality of life. According to Maslow's hierarchy of needs, the ultimate goal for any being is self-actualization, the process of discovering oneself in the context of the larger world, particularly what role one is supposed to play and what comprises that person's individual identity (Funder, 2007). However, Adler also explained that we as human beings have an inborn ability and desire to connect with one another on a deeper level. So there appears to be a strong relationship between forming one's identity and sharing oneself with others in a mutually beneficial manner. People often characterize and define themselves to a certain degree through the strength and quality of their relationships with others. So friendship often acts as an essential stepping-stone for self-actualization, so much so that without it, Maslow's hierarchy would appear as a triangle with no solid base.

While friendship generally contributes to the overall recipe for wellness, there are times when it can become burdensome and infringe upon one's well-being. Where do friendships cross the line from acting as aids and lifelines to increasing stress and creating additional hardship? In general, when considering unhealthy social relationships, most probably think of either love or family relationships. However, friendships can also act as a burden when a person's whole self is invested in the maintenance and quality of friendships to the point that personal stability and health are at risk when this investment does not pay off. Those that define themselves through their friendships with others are in danger of losing or sacrificing personal identity, resulting in detriment to the self. Just as counselors must learn to disassociate from the issues of their clients to maintain individual sanity and well-being, we as people must also learn to recognize when our social relationships hinder rather than help.

Love: Burdens and Benefits

When examining love as a life task, it is impossible not to differentiate between the various types of social relationships that exist within the realm of love. For instance, love between a mother and a child must certainly be distinguished from that mother's love for her spouse. While both contain shared elements, the relationships carry different foundations and are shaped different qualities. Therefore, it warrants examination of love in the realms of both family and intimacy and to pay attention to the interaction between the two. In general, love consists of "relationships that are formed on the basis of a sustained, long-term, mutual commitment and involve intimacy" (Myers et al., 2000, p. 257). So while distinctive types of love exist, universal qualities like commitment and intimacy also define love.

Let us examine love from the perspective of family. In many ways, your social relationships with your family members are almost forced upon you as a social necessity and obligation to your blood relatives. The family unit is the cornerstone of human life, for it provides us with our first examples of person-to-person connection and interaction. When friendships and intimate relationships fail, the enduring bond of the family can act as an infinite source of

Special Focus: Online Social Relationships

When viewing social relationships and their impact on personal wellness through the lens of modern society, one must look at the surging presence and influence of online dating and networking Web sites such as MySpace® and Facebook®. Although these sites existed throughout the last decade of the twentieth century, they did not begin to receive the overwhelming attention and business that they do now until the early 2000s. After the infamous Internet boom that took place in the late 1990s, online networking went beyond being a resourceful perk for speedy communication to being a tool of necessity in both the professional and social world. Today, we live in an age of instant connectivity where unlimited access to information is taken for granted and personal information in the public domain is commonplace. So with the rising tide of online networking and dating shaping our social relationships with one another, what are the positive and negative impacts on our personal well-being?

One of the main areas of interest when examining impacts of online communication on personal wellness and social relationships involves the differences between face-to-face and online interaction and factors that define both. Xie (2007) looked at the potential communication benefits of the Internet by bridging the gap between online interaction and offline social relationships. In his study, Xie approached the Internet from the perspective of people from older generations. He concluded that the Internet actually increased healthy interpersonal relationships when it was discussed and learned about in group settings where members could openly and freely interact with each other in person. Xie found that his participants viewed the Internet as a tool for exchange of information and access to personal information, not as a means of forming, sustaining, or maintaining relationships with others. Therefore, the Internet did not directly impact social relationships, but rather it acted as a gateway or connecting point for people to initiate discussion. In other words, "the process of learning to use the Internet . . . can be a social process that allows the formation and development of meaningful social relationships" (Xie, 2007, p. 402). So while the Internet was not shown to have a direct effect on increased social stimulation, it did play a roundabout role in bringing individuals together in a healthy and stimulating group setting.

Let us take a look at the benefits of online social relationships. First of all, networking Web sites provide people opportunities to reconnect with friends, loved ones, and other acquaintances from the past. Many sites create a venue for long-distance or same-city friends to communicate in groups, organize social and professional functions, discuss classes, debate about politics and world affairs, and connect to different generations. With online dating Web sites, people have the chance to evaluate potential partners based upon specific qualifications and to make use of sorting and categorizing mechanisms that match people together based upon desired traits and shared interests. This stress-free and open environment gives individuals a chance at finding a partner who may have trouble meeting people in social settings due to overbearing social pressures, confidence problems, or perceived personal weaknesses. In a recent study, Stevens and Morris (2007) looked at college students with social and/or dating anxiety to see if they were more likely to form and maintain romantic relationships online rather than meet people in person. While they hypothesized that those students experiencing stress and anxiety in social and dating situations would seek out online relationships more often to avoid face-to-face encounters, their study produced results that were incongruent with this hypothesis. The authors did however discuss findings that those participants experiencing high dating or social anxiety were more likely to use webcams in an attempt to replicate face-to-face interaction over the Internet. Although this attempt at fabricating a pseudosocial environment may appear contradictory to the nature of these individuals, the researchers point out that "although communicating partners can see each other, there is a buffer of cyberspace between them and certain physiological characteristics (such as trembling or blushing) may not be easily noted" (Stevens & Morris, 2007, p. 686).

There are certainly many burdens that either coexist or overrule these benefits. In fact, one might make the argument that the very same benefits can be turned into burdens. For instance, is the quality of communication over the Internet comparable to face-to-face interaction or even talking on the phone? As time goes by, do people rely too heavily on these immediate methods of communication for sheer ease and consequently sacrifice the irreplaceable experience of being with someone, speaking to them directly, and seeing them in person? Also, how are people monitoring what information they are putting into the public domain of the Internet? Do adequate standards exist to help preserve good judgment for what should and should not be made accessible to online browsers? Looking within the work and leisure task on the wellness wheel, it is easy to point to the inevitable and oftentimes awkward interface between one's professional and social life. For young professionals, there is often an unfortunate relationship between maturity, measured strictly by age, and lack of judgment. Oftentimes, young people do not consider the long-term professional and personal consequences of posting inappropriate information on the Internet. In other words, some aspects of social relationships, when publicized online, can negatively impact other social relationships due to lack of discretion. As practitioners, it would not be up to us to determine what was universally appropriate to post on the Internet, but rather it would fall on us to help our clients determine what would constitute exercising good judgment.

Looking further at potentially positive impacts of the Internet for personal well-being, one must take into account the variability of Internet users. In their research, Kraut et al. (2002) reported that extraverts who used the Internet frequently maintained a better balance between the Internet and their involvement in the community as opposed to introverted Internet users who struggled with this balance. These findings expand upon previous research by exploring groups within heavy Internet users that manage to strike a healthy balance between their computer world and their social world.

While the Internet can have vicarious, positive effects on interpersonal communication and social relationships, it can also detract from them. Caplan (2003) discussed the connection between psychosocial stress and preference for Internet-based communication, which he refers to as "computer-mediated communication" (CMC) (Caplan, 2003, p. 625). Looking at the risk factors that influence overuse of online communication methods and the potential problems that arise from such behavior, Caplan creates the label "problematic Internet use" (PIU) (Caplan, 2003, p. 626) to describe Internet usage that becomes personally or professionally detrimental. In general, Caplan refers to the correlation between psychosocial stress and use of the Internet for the purposes of social interaction. Previous research has shown that negative life stressors like depression and loneliness increase with escalating Internet use (Kraut et al., 2002). Conversely, Caplan's study suggests an opposite relationship in which loneliness and depression act as predictors for individuals who prefer online social interaction to face-to-face interaction. Overall, however, loneliness was found to contribute more significantly to PIU than depression (Caplan, 2003). These findings suggest that lonely individuals seek to fulfill their social relationship needs through Internet-based communication rather than interacting on a personal basis. Essentially, psychosocial distress and online social interaction can feed off of one another and initiate a cyclical process in which each impact and influences the other. In many of these cases, individuals begin to live within and be defined by online personalities they create for themselves that stem from a desire to be accepted by others and to be seen as they want others to see them. These individuals create a new identity and choose to let it dictate their interaction with others (Cornwell & Lundgren, 2001; Noonan, 1998). Rather than engaging in a chicken-and-egg argument about whether psychosocial stressors like loneliness and depression cause or contribute to increased online social interaction or vice versa, it is important simply to acknowledge the potential relationship that exists between Internet use and a decreased sense of well-being as related to social relationships.

strength and comfort. However, familial fortitude and depth cannot be taken for granted and still require just as much effort to maintain as other social relationships. For example, resentment can spread quickly among family members when a sense of obligation overcomes the natural desire to preserve healthy bonds; in other words, when social relationships in a family cease to be mutually beneficial, they can become a strain, and rifts can begin to grow. Looking at follow-ups to

John Bowlby's work on attachment theory (1977), current research supports the fact that people who have strong relationships with their parents are more likely to have strong peer relationships; conversely, those with estranged parental relationships tend to be more isolated from peers (Love et al., 2009).

Quality time can act as a powerful means to safeguard social relationships within the family. Whether looking at a family with young children or one with all adult members, quality time can serve as a positive distraction from day-to-day stress by encouraging emotional support and fulfilling needs. Research on older adult's states family members can be important resources by helping them with instrumental needs and by providing ongoing emotional support. Personal relationships are a source of pleasure and companionship and can buffer stress and "help elderly adults accomplish the activities of daily living, do household chores, and sometimes even meet financial obligations" (Adams & Blieszner, 1995, p. 216). Overall, these authors state, "Directly, in the case of emotional support, and indirectly, in the case of instrumental support . . . family members enhance older adults' psychological well-being" (Adams & Blieszner, 1995, p. 216). These findings remind us of the importance of maintaining familial relationships well into adulthood.

What is equally important for social relationships within a family are respect for an acknowledgement of personality and lifestyle differences. When families embrace their own diversity and learn to incorporate it into their positive interactions, members are free to grow as individuals within the overarching umbrella of the family system. In contrast, when individual traits are ridiculed or repressed, members can begin to develop bitterness and distrust for others in the family, removing individuals from the family umbrella.

When comparing love between family members and love between romantic partners, one must acknowledge the connecting points that tie them together. Qualities such as cohesion, loyalty, acceptance, and support are qualities that define all loving relationships. However, romantic love contains unique qualities of intimacy and closeness that cannot be replicated in the family unit. Romantic, committed relationships help individuals respond better to stress (Winefield, Winefield, & Tiggemann, 1992), so we again see the positive physical and emotional benefits that can result from healthy maintenance and careful attention to the different components of wellness. When examining social relationships in the context of romantic love, focus can remain on the unique relationship between two people rather than on a number of relationships within a larger social system or network. In terms of distinctions, the most obvious entails what one seeks from a romantic relationship. The combination of physical intimacy, emotional intimacy, devotion, and deep connection places romantic love in an entirely different realm with distinctive benefits and burdens. Mongeau, Carey, and Williams et al. (1998) compare romantic relationships to something of a dance where "the dyad must coordinate their movements to have a mutually enjoyable time. If partners are doing different dances altogether, they will likely end up stepping on each other's toes" (p. 424). This quote speaks to the crucial role that communication and collaboration play in a romantic relationship. In this way, love can act as both a benefit and a burden depending on the level of cohesion or distance between the couple. When there is mutual understanding and the couple works together as an alliance, the personal well-being of each person increases. On the other hand, if communication in the relationship is damaged or ineffective, the teamwork element is removed and couples act more as two individuals sharing time and space against their will.

It is commonly known that an individual who experience divorce, death of a spouse, separation, or anything else that isolates them from romantic love have higher mortality rates (Antonucci et al., 2010; House et al., 1988) and are at greater risks for disease and premature death (Ornish & Scherwitz, 1998). Social isolation, especially when it entails a lack of romantic love, causes significant harm to one's personal wellness. Therefore, lack of love can act as a serious burden. However, burdens can exist within romantic love as well, particularly when two people allow their relationship to stray away from the fundamental connections that brought them together. For instance, when a couple allows themselves to become entrenched in spite, jealousy, and contempt, the relationship loses the positive elements that once defined it. Similarly, when two people become enmeshed with one another to the point that they abandon their individual identities for the sake of one common identity in the relationship, they risk investing too much into each other; in other words, they come to define themselves solely through the relationship. The detrimental effect this can have on wellness is significant. These are the couples in counseling we see who claim to be "empty" on the inside after separation or divorce, for they have lost their essence and their sense of themselves.

References

Adams, R. G., & Blieszner, R. (1995). Aging well with friends and family. *American Behavioural Scientist, 39*, 209–224.

Antonucci, T. C., Birditt, K. S., & Webster, N. J. (2010). Social relations and mortality. *Journal of Health Psychology, 15*(5), 649–659.

Asendorpf, J.B., & Wilpers, S. (1998). Personality effects on social relationships. *Journal of Personality and Social Psychology, 74*(6), 1531–1544.

Baumeister, R. F., & Leary, M. R. (1995). The need to belong: Desire for interpersonal attachments as a fundamental human motivation. *Psychological Bulletin, 117*(3), 497–529.

Bergstrom, M. J., Holmes, M. E., & Pecchioni, L. (2000). Lay theories of successful aging after the death of a spouse: A network text analysis of bereavement advice. *Health Communication, 12*(4), 377–406.

Bowlby, J. (1969). *Attachment and loss: Vol. 1. Attachment* London: Hogarth.

Bowlby, J. (1977). The making and breaking of affectional bonds: I. Etiology and psychopathology in the light of attachment theory. *British Journal of Psychiatry, 130*, 201–210.

Brissette, I., Cohen, S., & Seeman, T. E. (2000). Measuring social integration and social networks. In *Social support measurement and intervention: A guide for health and social scientists*. (pp. 53–85) Oxford University Press, New York, NY, US.

Caplan, S. E. (2003). Preference for online social interaction. *Communication Research, 30*(6), 625.

Cohen, S. (2001). Social relationships and susceptibility to the common cold. In C. D. Ryff & B. H. Singer (Eds.), *Emotion, social relationships, and health* (pp. 221–233). New York: Oxford University Press.

Cohen, S. (2004). Social relationship and health. *American Psychologist, 59*(8), 676–684.

Cohen, S., Doyle, W. J., Turner, R. B., Alper, C. M., & Skoner, D. P. (2003). Emotional style and susceptibility to the common cold. *Psychosomatic Medicine, 65*(4), 652.

Cornwell, B., & Lundgren, D. C. (2001). Love on the Internet: Involvement and misrepresentation in romantic relationships in cyberspace vs. realspace. *Computers in Human Behavior, 17*(2), 197–211.

Csikszentmihalyi, M., & LeFevre, J. (1989). Optimal experience in work and leisure. *Journal of Personality and Social Psychology, 56*(5), 815–822.

Diener, E., & Oishi, S. (2005). Target Article: The nonobvious social psychology of happiness. *Psychological Inquiry, 16*(4), 162–167.

Diener, E., & Seligman, M. E. P. (2004). Beyond money. *Psychological Science in the Public Interest (Wiley-Blackwell), 5*(1), 1–31.

Funder, D. C. (2007). Beyond just-so stories towards a psychology of situations: Evolutionary accounts of individual differences require independent assessment of personality and situational variables. *European Journal of Personality, 21*(5), 599–601.

Gottman, J. (1994). *What predicts divorce? The relationship between marital processes and marital outcomes.* Hillsdale, NJ: Lawrence Erlbaum.

Greenhaus, J. H., Collins, K. M., & Shaw, J. D. (2003). The relation between work–family balance and quality of life. *Journal of Vocational Behavior, 63*(3), 510–531.

Gruber, K. J. (2008). Social support for exercise and dietary habits among college students. *Adolescence, 43*(171), 557–575.

Hafen, B. Q., Franksen, K. J., Karren, K. J. & Hooker, K. R. (1992). *The health effects of attitudes, emotional relationships*. Provo, UT: EMS Associates.

Helliwell, John F. 2003. 'Well-Being, Social Capital and Public Policy: What's New? *Economic Modelling 20*(2): 331–360.

Hintikka, J., Koskela, T. T., Kontula, O. O., Koskela, K. K., & Viinamäki, H. H. (2000). Men, women and friends: Are there differences in relation to mental well-being? *Quality of Life Research: An International Journal of Quality of Life Aspects of Treatment, Care & Rehabilitation, 9*(7), 841–845.

Hofer, M. A. (1987). Early social relationships: A psychobiologist's view. *Child Development, 58*(3), 633–647.

House, J. S., Kahn, R. L., McLeod, J. D., & Williams, D. (1985). Measures and concepts of social support. In S. Cohen, S. Syme, S. Cohen & S. Syme (Eds.), *Social support and health* (pp. 83–108). San Diego, CA: Academic Press.

House, J. S., Landis, K. R., & Umberson, D. (1988). Social relationships and health. *Science, 241*(4865), 540–545.

Hughes, M. E., Waite, L. J., Hawkley, L. C., & Cacioppo, J. T. (2004). A short scale for measuring loneliness in large surveys. *Research on Aging, 26*(6), 655.

Ishii-Kuntz, M. (1990). Social interaction and psychological well-being: Comparison across stages of adulthood. *International Journal of Aging & Human Development, 30*(1), 15–36.

Johnson, C. C., Myers, L., Webber, L. S., & Boris, N. W. (2004). Profiles of the adolescent smoker: Models of tobacco use among 9th grade high school students: Acadiana coalition of teens against tobacco (ACTT). *Preventive Medicine, 39*(3), 551–558.

Kraut, R., Kiesler, S., Boneva, B., Cummings, J. N., Helgeson, V., & Crawford, A. M. (2002). Internet paradox revisited. *Journal of Social Issues, 58*(1), 49–74.

Lachman, M. E. (2004). Development in midlife. *Annual Review of Psychology, 55*(1), 305–331.

Lakey, B., & Cohen, S. (2000). Social support theory and measurement. *Social Support Measurement and Intervention: A Guide for Health and Social Scientists*, 29–52.

Love, K., Tyler, K., Thomas, D., Garriott, P., Brown, C., & Roan-Belle, C. (2009). Influence of multiple attachments on well-being: A model for African Americans attending historically black colleges and universities. *Journal of Diversity in Higher Education, 2*(1), 35–45.

Mongeau, P. A., Carey, C. M., & Williams, M. L. M. (1998). First date initiation and enactment: An expectancy violation approach. *Sex Differences and Similarities in Communication: Critical Essays and Empirical Investigations of Sex and Gender in Interaction* (pp. 413–426). Mahwah, NJ: Lawrence Erlbaum.

Myers, J. E., Sweeney, T. J., & Witmer, J. M. (2000). The Wheel of Wellness counseling for wellness: A holistic model for treatment planning. *Journal of Counseling & Development, 78*(3), 251–266.

Noonan, R. J. (1998). *The psychology of sex: A mirror from the Internet*. In J. Gackenbach, *Psychology and the Internet: Intrapersonal, interpersonal, and transpersonal implications* (pp. 143–168). San Diego, CA: Academic Press.

Ornish, D., & Scherwitz, L. W. (1998). Intensive lifestyle changes for reversal of coronary heart disease. *Journal of the American Medical Association, 280*(23), 2001–2007.

Putnam, R. D. (2001). Civic disengagement in contemporary America. *Government & Opposition, 36*(2), 135.

Salzinger, S., & Feldman, R. S., Hammer, M. & Rosario, M. (1993). The effects of physical abuse on children's social relationships. *Child Development, 64*(1), 169–187.

Segrin C., & Flora, J. (2000). Poor social skills are a vulnerability factor in the development of psychosocial problems. *Human Communication Research, 26*(3), 489–514.

Sergin, C., & Passalacqua, S.A. (2010). Functions of loneliness, social support, health behaviors, and stress in association with poor health. *Health Communication, 25*(4), 312–322.

Stevens, S. B., & Morris, T. L. (2007). College dating and social anxiety: Using the Internet as a means of connecting to others. *CyberPsychology & Behavior, 10*(5), 680–688.

Strawbridge, W. J., Shema, S. J., Cohen, R. D., & Kaplan, G. A. (2001). Religious attendance increases survival by improving and maintaining good health behaviors, mental health, and social relationships. *Annals of Behavioral Medicine, 23*(1), 68–74.

Sweeney, T. J., & Witmer, J. M. (1991). Beyond social interest: Striving toward optimum health and wellness. *Individual Psychology: Journal of Adlerian Theory, Research & Practice, 47*(4), 527.

Taylor, S. E., & Brown, J. D. (1988). Illusion and well-being: A social psychological perspective on mental health. *Psychological Bulletin, 103*(2), 193–210.

Uchida, Y., Norasakkunkit, V., & Kitayama, S. (2004). Cultural constructions of happiness: Theory and empirical evidence. *Journal of Happiness Studies, 5*(3), 223–239.

Umberson, D., Chen, M. D., House, J. S., Hopkins, K., & Slaten, E. (1996). The effect of social relationships on psychological well-being: Are men and women really so different? *American Sociological Review, 61*(5), 837–857.

Vaillant, G. E., Meyer, S. E., Mukamal, K., & Soldz, S. (1998). Are social supports in late midlife a cause or a result of successful physical ageing? *Psychological Medicine, 28*(05), 1159.

Wagner, R., Harter, J. K., & Books, I. (2006). *12: The elements of great managing.* New York: Gallup Press.

Wentzel, K. R. (1998). Social relationships and motivation in middle school: The role of parents, teachers, and peers. *Journal of Educational Psychology, 90*(2), 202–209.

Winefield, H. R., Winefield, A. H., & Tiggemann, M. (1992). Social support and psychological well-being in young adults: The multi-dimensional support scale. *Journal of Personality Assessment, 58*(1), 198.

Witmer, J. M., & Sweeney, T. J. (1992). A holistic model for wellness and prevention over the life span. *Journal of Counseling & Development, 71*(2), 140–148.

Xie, B. (2007). Using the Internet for offline relationship formation. *Social Science Computer Review, 25*(3), 396.

Yurkovich, E., & Smyer, T. (1998). Strategies for maintaining optimal wellness in the chronic mentally ill. *Perspectives in Psychiatric Care, 34*(3), 17–24.

16 CREATIVITY: SPARK OF WELLNESS

Samuel T. Gladding

Creativity requires the courage to let go of certainties.

ERICH FROMM (SOCIAL PSYCHOLOGIST)

Wellness Connection

Dr. Samuel Gladding discusses the relationship of creativity to wellness. Creativity is shown to be a characteristic that can enhance an individual's wellness through several modalities. Dr. Gladding provides examples of specific techniques a counselor may use to encourage clients to creatively work to improve their wellness.

Creativity is "the ability to produce work that is both novel (i.e., original or unexpected) and appropriate (i.e., useful or meets task constraints)" (Sternberg & Lubart, 1999, p. 3). It is a worldwide phenomenon that knows no bounds in regard to ethnicity, culture, gender, age, or other real or imagined barriers (Lubart, 1999; Maslow, 1971). Sometimes creativity is associated with disorders and what Plato called "divine madness" (Kottler, 2006). However, most creative people are well adjusted and motivated. Through creativity individuals are able to express their originality, inventiveness, and problem solving ability. As a phenomenon, "creativity is universally recognized as a basic human attribute" (Cohen, 2000, p. 13).

The importance of creativity in life can be found in Mihaly Csikszentmihalyi's (1996) statement: "Creativity is a central source of meaning in our lives . . . most of the things that are interesting, important, and human are the results of creativity" (p. 1). He goes on to say that creativity is "so fascinating that when we are involved in it, we feel that we are living more fully than during the rest of our lives" (p. 2).

Creativity correlates highly with a person's overall sense of well-being and wellness (Goff, 1993; Myers & Sweeney, 2005; Myers, Sweeney, & Witmer, 2000). Through creativity individuals are able to navigate through the shoals of life and find direction, significance, and intentionality in their existence. At its best creativity empowers and enables its users to explore new courses and vistas they might not otherwise have considered. Creative people as a group have: "autonomy, acceptance of self, others, and nature; a democratic character structure; confidence; intrinsic motivation; a wide range of interests; and a tolerance for ambiguity" (Carson, 1999, p. 328).

To be creative, people need to have intelligence, knowledge, a thinking style that utilizes their abilities, a risk taking and strong personality, motivation, and a supportive environment (Sternberg & Lubart, 1995). No one of these factors by itself guarantees creativity. However, in combination these ingredients are powerful in the creative process. For example, Jonas Salk, the developer of the polio vaccine, spent eight years creating the final product that eradicated one of the most deadly and dreaded diseases on the planet. He characterized himself as a risk taker who learned from his triumphs and failures. However, his motivation, intelligence, knowledge, thinking style, and supportive environment all played strong roles in his ultimate success (Kluger, 2006).

Some professions are good fits for people who value creativity. Counseling is one of them. According to Frey (1975), "In the broadest sense, counseling is actually a creative enterprise within which client and counselor combine their resources to generate a new plan, develop a different outlook, formulate alternative behaviors, [and] begin a new life" (p. 23). Through creativity new, exciting, and productive ways of working, living, and healing are formulated and implemented. The process involves both choice and change. Through counseling, clients and counselors work together to create: fresh thoughts, novel plans, new outlooks, innovative behaviors, and productive lives (Carson, 1999). In addition, counseling at its best provides clients with hope that their lives can be better (Gladding, 1995).

THE BENEFITS OF CREATIVITY IN WELLNESS

Individuals in many walks of life outside of counseling can and do use creativity to help themselves become healthy and stay well. It is an everyday occurrence. In daily life creativity plays a vital part in people's well-being and outlook on humanity. The reasons are multiple but seven stand out as follows.

1. **Creativity opens up new worldviews.** People become limited in their outlooks and behaviors because they have narrow perspectives. They observe from only a few vantage points and act accordingly. However, creativity helps expand people's horizons. It gives them a new way of experiencing the world. For instance, having seen Picasso's *Guernica*, individuals' views are expanded and they can never envision war in the same way again (Weisberg, 2006). The destructiveness, horror, and pain of human conflict and suffering are captured graphically in the artist's painting. The glory sometimes associated with war is replaced with scenes of gore and carnage.

   Likewise, having heard Michael Jackson's and Lionel Richie's (1985) composition "We Are the World," or songs like it about collectively making a difference in others lives, people often feel that they can play a positive part in what happens internationally. They become aware of what is going on globally on a different level because of the emotions aroused within them. Thus a number begin to strive to make a significant change in human environments.
2. **Creativity allows for innovations both in initiation and continuation of positive human activities.** For example, as an innovator Maud Lewis, a Canadian folk artist, best known as Grandma Moses, started her career simply. She began her initiation into the world of art by painting after the early onset of juvenile rheumatoid arthritis. While she

began modestly by making greeting cards, her talent continued to develop a unique style that many found pleasing. More importantly, her work gave her great joy and satisfaction (Bogart & Lang, 2002).

In contrast, through creativity, the French painter Henri Matisse changed his artistic style because of intestinal cancer at age 70 from oil painting to doing paper cutout murals for the last 13 years of his life (Zausner, 2007). His latter originality added to his reputation and his place in art history but more significantly, Matisse's creativity added to his energy and outlook on life. Most likely Matisse's creativity added to his longevity since he found a new purpose and outlet in life.

3. **Creativity promotes co-creation.** People respond to creative activities from life experiences and in doing so often gain insight into dreams, images, and memories they have harbored. For instance, plays such as those by Sophocles, Shakespeare, Tennessee Williams, and Arthur Miller that parallel painful events in people's lives, such as wasted potential, suffering, or trauma, may spark within members of an audience a catharsis and a resolve in regard to what they can do or should do with the remainder of their lives (Winn, 2005). Take, for example, the character of Walter Lee Younger in *A Raisin in the Sun* (Hansberry, 1959). He foolishly gives his money to a con artist but later shows character and strength by refusing to be intimidated or bought out when offered a bribe if he will get his family, which is African American, to move out of a white neighborhood.

   The co-creation process, in this case and in others, can result in individuals devising ways to become different and rectify situations, such as focusing on what they, as protagonists in their own life dramas, can do to get through difficulties. In this way vision and energy are aroused and abilities are enabled as opposed to the fostering of feeling helpless or hopeless that comes in ruminating over what individuals are incapable of doing.
4. **Creativity strengthens resilience.** Individuals who are mentally and physically healthy and well do not succumb readily to the unfairness or capriciousness of life events. Rather, they strive toward goals and rebound when down (Benard, 2004). The self-portrait of Rembrandt is an example of how creativity impacts resilience. This painting, finished towards the end of Rembrandt's life, is of an older man who, while looking worn with the wear and tear of life events, also appears to be determined and fit. Interesting, towards the end of his life Rembrandt suffered the loss of his wife, the death of three of his four children, and a number of financial setbacks. Yet he continued to paint and found a creative outlet for his expression and solace for his sorrow, which may explain his relatively long lifespan.
5. **Creativity shores up psychological and physical dimensions of people's lives, too.** Research by James Pennebaker (1997) is an excellent example of this benefit. In having individuals write for 20 minutes a day about matters stressful to them, Pennebaker found that not only did their scores on mental health assessments improve but their immune systems became stronger and their visits to physicians decreased. His use of two control groups who either did not write or wrote about other aspects of life confirmed that writing can save people from needless emotional and even physical pain. In short, writing and the creative expression that goes with it can be a path to wellness.
6. **Creativity helps us remember and respect those who have come before us with a sense of reverence not possible otherwise** (Whitfield, 1988). This type of connection links the historical with the contemporary in a way that is healthy as people realize others have had similar thoughts, feelings, and behaviors before them. As such, individuals identify more with past human actions as well as what it means to be a

person in today's world. From paintings of Madonnas and other religious figures to 9/11 drawings and poems by children of their relatives lost in the tragedy of terrorism, creativity promotes understanding and an awe for what has been as well as what is (Morrow, 2006).

7. **Creativity enables people to take control of their lives and keep events in perspective.** While the Ruyard Kipling (1910) poem "If" may not be considered great literature today, it reminds those who read its lines that many situations in life can be dealt with better when they are seen from the angle of persons who take charge of their lives. Such individuals keep their heads when those about them are losing theirs. They make the most of their time, too, and stay focused.

WAYS OF PROMOTING WELLNESS THROUGH CREATIVITY

John Gardner lived an exemplary life as a public figure. His creativity as the founder of Common Cause and other projects that benefited the public has been documented by Mihaly Csikszentmihalyi (1996), who in reference to Gardner and other creative persons has said: "The ability to discover what one can do well, and enjoy doing it, is the hallmark of all creative people" (p. 314). Creative people, whether in science, business, government, or the public domain, flourish and live fully when they engage their strengths and build upon them. In the process they promote human welfare as well as their own well-being.

Positive actions involving creativity that have an impact on wellness can be expressed in many ways. One of the most prevalent ways of promoting wellness through creativity is conveyed through the arts (e.g., performing or expressing abilities visually, verbally, and behaviorally). The arts are action oriented and require concentration and movement (e.g., shaping an event, molding an action, and constructing materials in such a way that the end result is productive). Among the healthiest and most lasting specific ways of promoting wellness through the arts are the following.

1. **Recitation:** Assisting people in their struggle to deal with and resolve negative feelings, such as anger, and move toward healthy emotions can sometimes be handled by helping them voice their sentiments. In such situations verbally expressing what individuals want to say can be therapeutic, healing, and lead to wellness. One form of such speech is called "line savers." In this approach people can recall and recite useful sayings they were given or gave themselves. This process can be used to dissipate troublesome feelings and promote more positive ones (e.g., "Take your time," "Don't go to bed angry," or "When upset, a good rule is to keep your cool").

   In addition to recalling and reciting such line savers, learning words that can be meaningful or useful to people is helpful also. These wise sayings are found in literature from ancient scripts to popular lyrics. Take the emotion of anger again and the use of William Blake's first stanza from "A Poison Tree" (Kazin, 1946). The stanza reads:

   I was angry with my foes

   I told it not, my wrath did grow.

   I was angry with my friend

   I told my wrath, my wrath did end. (p. 114)

In using the poetic stanza, people who want to reconcile a relationship memorize the words. Then they role play going up to their friend and saying: "I want to give you something. The gift is of words. They are not mine but of a poet named William Blake." The person then says the words if his or her adversary is receptive and open to hearing them, followed by the sentence: "I have been angry with you but I do not want to continue to be or be seen as your foe. I want to discuss with you my feelings (maybe in the presence of someone else who can be neutral and helpful). I want to hear your feelings too. In talking and listening, I hope we can be friends again."

If both parties are willing through the catalyst of words, negative or hostile thoughts or actions are replaced with renewed friendship or at least neutrality and a sense of well-being is restored. When such occurs, the people involved are then able to focus on positive aspects of life.

2. **Writing:** Regularly expressing thoughts through writing them down is another way wellness can be courted through creativity. Ann Frank put it this way: "I can shake off everything if I write; my sorrows disappear, my courage is reborn" (Frank, 1958, p. 177).

   As mentioned earlier, keeping a diary or journal focused on stressful difficulties is one way to use writing in a wellness way. James Pennebaker (2002) and other researchers have found that when people of all ages and stages in life write about worrisome events in their lives, they not only score higher on mental health measures but actually become physically healthier. The number of trips they make to a physician decreases and their immune system is strengthened. Interestingly, college students who engage in a systematic writing program about subjects that really matter to them find their efforts paying off in higher grade point averages too.

   An abbreviated version of Pennebaker's technique has been developed by Kay Adams (1998). It is called the Five Minute Writing Sprint. It is a daily event where a timer, two pencils, a pad of paper, and a comfortable place are employed. Writers find a relaxing and familiar spot in which to write and begin by letting their pencils keep moving on the paper before them until the timer signals five minutes are up. Research still needs to be gathered on this approach, but heuristically it holds promise.

3. **Photography:** Taking pictures with a camera as a creative endeavor can also make a difference in promoting wellness. Shooting pictures of an object from different perspectives may give people a multiple perceptions and change their views concerning the entity (Gladding, 2004). For instance, a client who stubbornly refuses to see other points of view may become more open after taking pictures of a familiar object from numerous angles, such as mailbox or a door. In the process, the client may discover that there is more than one view in regard to what something looks like. In the case of the mailbox, the photographer may realize that the mail carrier may see the mailbox in a different way from the neighborhood dog. The photographer may through such insight realize that his or her view of a situation may not be the only one that is valid. Pictures may lead then to words and thoughts so that insight gained in a nonverbal way becomes more useful and a healthier outlook on the world is created.

4. **Movement:** Dance, exercise, and movement can be used as a way to wellness (Goodill, 2004). The power of these types of behavior has been shown to improve individuals' health on many levels. Specific dance and movement steps are employed in some cases. In other situations, 30 minute walks three days a week are used as a way to stay fit and healthy. Even 10 minute exercises three times a day can be beneficial.

However, movement can also be used in a wellness way through moving toward or away from people or places that either nourish or discourage health. For instance, moving towards individuals who have encouraging words or who have cultivated healthy habits may lead to an increase in one's sense of well-being. Likewise, moving away from those individuals who are toxic in words or in deeds may be life enhancing if not life saving.

5. **Humor:** Creativity can promote wellness also through mirth and laughter (Salameh & Fry, 2002). People usually laugh because something surprises them or seems incongruent. Humor nourishes individuals biologically and mentally. One of the most famous cases of humor and wellness combining is found in Norm Cousins's (1981) *Anatomy of an Illness,* where Cousins describes using humor as a way to relieve pain. He was diagnosed with ankylosing spondylitis, a painful spine condition. He found that a diet of comedies ranging from slapstick to contemporary sitcoms helped him feel better. He said that 10 minutes of laughter allowed him two hours of painfree sleep. Overall, humor can ease tensions, distill hostility, promote positive communication, raise infection-fighting antibodies in the body, and boost the levels of immune cells (Salameh & Fry, 2002).

   Humor may be employed in helping people who are dedicated to their depression or misery feel differently, too. If their dysfunctional thought processes are exaggerated, they may smile or laugh, which is incongruent with their negative state of mind. Telling a nonoffensive joke or story that has a universal message also may promote humor and the wellness that goes with it, as the physician Patch Adams found out. An example of such a story is one about Casey Stengel, the New York Yankees manager of the 1950s. He purportedly said about a Yankees pitcher: "The guy is 21 now and in 10 years he has a good chance to be 31."

   Basically, to be creative with humor for wellness' sake takes courage, timing, and good taste.

6. **Story Telling:** Another way to help promote wellness through creativity is through generating stories. Lives can be reshaped or changed through storytelling. Herminia Ibarra (2003) emphasizes that telling good stories is essential to making smooth transitions in life.

   Change is unsettling, in part because major transitions, like job changes, can make people feel that they have lost the narrative thread of their lives. At these times, it is important to tell stories about life that are rooted in identity. A coherent life story is one that suggests what we all want to believe about ourselves and those we help or hire—that our lives are series of unfolding, linked events that make sense. In other words, the past is related to the present, and from that trajectory, we can glimpse our future. The process of constructing a story can help make sense of the past.

   So Ibarra along with narrative-focused counselors, such as Larry Cochran (1997) and Mark Savickas (2005), point out that healthy career change involves creating or modifying stories. When people get off balance, they need to change their stories (and often their careers) to make themselves cohesive and coherent and find new meaning in their lives.

7. **Music:** Finally, creativity can be a servant of wellness by reinventing and re-energizing people through music. Albert Ellis proposed that individuals rid themselves of irrationality through a number of different means, one of which was the creative act of singing rational songs. He created such songs to sing for those who might tend to not optimize their own potential for wellness. For instance, to the tune of the Whiffenpoof song, Ellis (1977) penned these words:

I cannot have all of my wishes filled
Whine, whine, whine!
I cannot have every frustration stilled
Whine, Whine, Whine!
Life really owes me the things that I miss
Fate has to grant me eternal bliss
And if I must settle for less than this:
Whine, Whine, Whine!

While singing Ellis's songs, or other similar compositions such as those by Richard Watts or Jeffrey Guterman, will only get people so far, they can be enlightening in ways that are creative and healthy. Other music, such as popular songs, have some subtle or even blatant messages that can contribute towards wellness too (Gladding, Binkley, Henderson & Newsome, 2008).

Summary

Creativity is associated with wellness in many ways. Becoming and staying well requires individuals to be active and creativity is a dynamic and interactive process.

As this chapter has pointed out, creativity correlates with a number of factors that are found in people who are healthy, well, and living life to the fullest. Creative individuals are adaptive, intelligent, open, playful, determined, motivated, and have a wide range of interests as well as considerable energy. They gravitate toward environments that are supportive of their efforts or they find ways to devise and positively utilize the surroundings in which they live.

In addition, creativity is correlated with wellness in that it enables people to become healthier through:

- perceiving new worldviews,
- being innovative,
- co-creating,
- strengthening their resiliency,
- shoring up psychological and physical dimensions of their lives,
- remembering and respecting the past, and
- taking control of their lives by keeping events in perspective.

Furthermore, individuals may promote wellness through creative efforts such as using those found in the arts. Different art forms that may increase health and wellness include those involving recitation, writing, photography, dance/movement, humor, stories, and music.

Overall, creativity and wellness belong together in the promotion of healthy human beings. They overlap. It is probably impossible to be fully alive and well without being creative. Wellness and a sense of well-being can be enhanced by employing creative methods, such as those found in the arts. Regardless, creativity in everyday life enriches everyone associated with it. Planning to stay well, grow, and live to the fullest includes cultivating creativity. Sometimes the process may be hard, but the rewards associated with this procedure yield rich results and a sterling quality of life.

References

Adams, K. (1998). *The way of the journal: A journal therapy workbook for healing* (2nd ed.). Baltimore: Sidran.

Benard, B. (2004). Resiliency: What we have learned. San Francisco: WestEd.

Bogart, J. E., & Lang, M. (2002). *Capturing joy: The story of Maud Lewis*. Toronto, Canada: Tundra Books.

Carson, D. K. (1999). The importance of creativity in family therapy: A preliminary consideration. *The Family*

Journal: Counseling and Therapy for Couples and Families, 7(4), 326–334.

Cochran, L. (1997). *Career counseling: A narrative approach.* Thousand Oaks, CA: Sage.

Cohen, G. D. (2000). *The creative age: Awakening human potential in the second half of life.* New York: Avon.

Cousins, N. (1981). *Anatomy of an illness.* New York: Bantam.

Csikszentmihalyi, M. (1996). *Creativity.* New York: HarperCollins.

Ellis, A. (1977). *A garland of rational songs.* New York: Albert Ellis Institute.

Frank, A. (1958). *Diary of a young girl.* New York: Globe.

Frey, D. H. (1975). The anatomy of an idea: Creativity in counseling. *Personnel & Guidance Journal, 54*(1), 22–27.

Gladding, S. T. (1995). Creativity in counseling. *Counseling and Human Development, 28*, 1–12.

Gladding, S. T. (2004). *Counseling as an art: The creative arts in counseling* (3rd ed.). Alexandria, VA: American Counseling Association.

Gladding, S. T., Binkley, E., Henderson, D. A., & Newsome, D. W. (2008). *The lyrics of hurting and healing: Finding words that are revealing.* Honolulu: American Counseling Association Convention.

Goff, K. (1993). Creativity and life satisfaction in older adults. *Educational Gerontology, 19*, 241–250.

Goodill, S. W. (2004). *An introduction to medical dance/ movement therapy: Health care in motion.* London: Jessica Kingsley.

Hansberry, L. (1959). *A raisin in the sun.* New York: Vintage.

Ibarra, H. (2003). *Working identity.* Boston: Harvard Business School Press.

Jackson, Michael, & Richie, Lionel. (1985). We are the world (U.S.A. for Africa) [Video recording]. New York: Columbia Records.

Kazin, A. (Ed.). (1946). *The portable Blake.* New York: Viking Press.

Kipling, R. (1910). *If.* New York: Doubleday.

Kluger, J. (2006). *Splendid solution: Jonas Salk and the conquest of polio.* New York: Penguin.

Kottler, J. A. (2006). *Divine madness.* San Francisco: Jossey-Bass.

Lubart, T. I. (1999). Creativity across cultures. In R. J. Sternberg (Ed.), *Handbook of creativity* (pp. 339–350). New York: Cambridge University Press.

Maslow, A. H. (1971). *The farther reaches of human nature.* New York: Viking Press.

Morrow, A. (2006, September 11). Ways of creatively remembering those lost on September 11, 2001. Retrieved March 14, 2008, from http://dying.about.com/b/2006/09/11/ways-ofcreatively-remembering-those-lost-on-september-11-2001.htm

Myers, J. E., & Sweeney, T. J. (Eds.). (2005). Counseling for wellness: Theory, research, practice. Alexandria, VA: American Counseling Association.

Myers, J. E., Sweeney, T. J., & Whitmer, J. M. (2000). The Wheel of Wellness counseling for wellness: A holistic-model for treatment planning. *Journal of Counseling & Development, 78.*

Pennebaker, J. W. (1997). *Opening up: The healing power of expressing emotions.* New York: Guilford.

Pennebaker, J. W. (Ed.). (2002). *Emotion, disclosure, and health.* Washington, DC: American Psychological Association.

Salameh, W. A., & Fry, W. F. (Eds.). (2002). *Humor and wellness in clinical intervention.* New York: Praeger.

Savickas, M. (2005). The theory and practice of career construction. In S. D. Brown & R. W. Lent (Eds.), *Career development and counseling* (pp. 42–70). Hoboken, NJ: John Wiley.

Sternberg, R. J., & Lubart, T. I (1995). *Defying the crowd: Cultivating creativity in a culture of conformity.* New York: Free Press.

Sternberg, R. J., & Lubart, T. I. (1999). The concept of creativity: Prospects and paradigms. In R. J. Sternberg (Ed.), *Handbook of creativity* (pp. 3–15). New York: Cambridge University Press.

Weisberg, R. W. (2006). *Creativity.* Hoboken, NJ: John Wiley.

Whitfield, S. J. (1988). *A death in the delta.* Baltimore: Johns Hopkins University Press.

Winn, S. (2005, January 1). Endings are a catharsis. They give meaning to what comes before, and change us from the way we were. *San Francisco Chronicle*, p. E-1.

Zausner, T. (2007). Artist and audience: Everyday creativity and the visual art. In R. Richards (Ed.), *Everyday creativity* (pp. 75–89). Washington, DC: American Psychological Association.

INDEX

D

E

S

T

FEB 0 8 2013